Women of Their Times

a memoir

Women of Their Times

a memoir

ANNA ROSE GALSTUCK

Rose Jam Press
rosejampress.com

Edited by Doug Cooper and Mike Shur

ISBN 979-8-9879786-0-3
Library of Congress Control Number: 2023904952
Manufactured in the United States of America

First edition, 2023

Cover artwork by Diane Shur
Cover design by Mike Shur with Eva Braiman
Original artwork facing p. 349: "Mirele Poil," by Adrienne Ottenberg. Reproduced by permission.

Rose Jam Press
rosejampress.com

Whereof what's past is prologue;
what to come, in yours
and my discharge.

– Shakespeare, *The Tempest*

There is no private life which
has not been determined by
a wider public life.

– George Eliot, *Felix Holt: The Radical*

Contents

New York City

A note on names

The memoir that follows unfolds in the Russian Empire of the late 19th and early 20th centuries. It begins in an area that is today part of Ukraine. Like other parts of that empire, the active suppression of non-Russian cultures meant many Jews were Russified; they identified as *Russian* Jews, even though they were overwhelmingly excluded from Russian society.

Anna Galstuck's memoir was written in the Russified cultural context of her times and memory. So she speaks of Russian winters, Russian books, and Russian schools. Place-names in the memoir are the Russian names of the time. The maps of the Jewish Pale of Settlement and of Kamenets-Podolski also reflect those Russian names. Current Ukrainian place-names are noted in the foreword.

The editors also researched the Jewish, Russian, and Ukrainian personal names used in the book. Many of them were spelled by Anna phonetically and as remembered decades after the events.

Jewish names of that time and place were of Hebrew origin, of Yiddish origin (reflecting the different dialects of Yiddish used in the Pale), and of the many countries and cultures that Jews were part of and expelled from over several millennia. Jews also have names of Assyrian, Babylonian, Byzantine, Egyptian, Greek, Roman, Spanish, Dutch, English, German, Polish, and other origin. One result of this was that in the Pale, you could find men named Moishe who spelled it numerous different ways.

Until the 18th century in eastern Europe, most Jewish surnames were patronymic or matronymic. Through diktats from the Prussian, Austro-Hungarian and Russian empires, other names developed.

Where incorrect spellings of Hebrew or Yiddish names could be confirmed, they were corrected. A few spellings of Russian and Ukrainian names were also corrected. But on the whole, personal names were left as the author wrote them.

Foreword

A decade ago, I inherited a 400-page, 40-year-old manuscript. It was a memoir written by my maternal grandmother Anna Galstuck. Written on a manual typewriter, it had been edited with cross-outs and handwritten corrections, scribbled notes, and partially retyped. The pages had darkened to yellow and brown and were beginning to crumble at the edges. But what a story lay within those aging pages!

My grandmother combined her life experiences with stories told to her by her mother, grandmother, and older sisters to create a series of vignettes that stretch from a small city in the Jewish Pale of Settlement in the Russian Empire (today in independent Ukraine) in the early 1860s to New York City in the years before World War I.

The harsh conditions of life and oppression of the Jewish people in eastern Europe that Anna records are well documented. Yiddish writers of the time published stories, plays, and novels reflecting Jewish life. Sholem Aleichem (pen name of Solomon Naumovich Rabinovich, 1859–1916), one of the founders of Yiddish literature and one of the most prominent of them, was born in the Jewish Pale. He gave the world a series of stories entitled *Tevye the Milkman*, along with his many other writings. These stories were the basis for the immensely popular musical *Fiddler on the Roof* seen by millions of people. Since its initial performance in 1964, *Fiddler* has been performed every day somewhere in the world. It was made into a movie and is part of a large body of music and film on this topic. Many histories, memoirs, and works of fiction have been published about this time and place.

Anna Galstuck's memoir is a worthy addition to this body of work. She paints a picture of the social conditions of working-class women in

Jewish society at the time in eastern Europe and America. A major part of her story is how those conditions compelled her mother, Mirele, to leave her family in 1908. She travelled by herself, an unaccompanied married woman, by horse and cart, train, and steamship to come to New York City. There she became a garment sewer and labored to raise the money so her children, mother, and husband could join her. Anna tells how Mirele, inspired to fight against the horrible working conditions she and her coworkers faced, helped lead a strike for union recognition in the factory.

The book recounts the jobs the women of her family did in the old country, from running a small store to working as cooks, servants, and garment sewers. This was in the context of a community that emphasized religious study and occupations for many men, usually jobs that did not pay enough to support a family.

Anna also illustrates the illiteracy among Jewish women, which differed based on their social class and changed over the decades she recounts.

The richness of the story and subject matter made it worthwhile to spend a considerable amount of time and effort over several years to convert the battered manuscript into a working digital file and publish it.

The story opens in Kamenets-Podolski (today Kam'ianets'-Podil's'kyi), a small city in today's western Ukraine that is 30 miles east of what was then the Russian border with the Austro-Hungarian Empire. It was a trading center located on the Smotrych River. The Smotrych winds through the city, a little more than 10 miles from its confluence with the Dnister River, which flows to the Black Sea. The original town sits on a high plateau within a loop formed by the river and surrounded by newer neighborhoods.

The region has been populated for millennia. Archaeological finds of stone tools and the remains of mammoths date to the Neolithic period (approximately 10,000 years ago).

The earliest written mention of the city is in an Armenian chronicle from the 11th century that refers to it as a town of the Kievan Rus, the first east Slavic state, which reached its peak in the early-to-mid 11th century.

The settlement of that period was overrun and destroyed by the Mongols' Golden Horde in 1241 at the time they conquered parts of eastern Europe. It was rebuilt and became part of the Grand Duchy of Lithuania.

In the 1430s the town passed from Lithuania to Poland; from 1569 to 1792 it was the center of Podolia province of the Polish–Lithuanian Commonwealth. During this period there were restrictions on Jews living or trading in Kamenets. From 1672 to 1699 the city was part of the Ottoman Empire and the ban on Jewish settlement was lifted and the Jewish community grew substantially.

After the city was once more incorporated into the Polish state in 1699, Christian merchants resumed their opposition to Jewish settlement. Restrictions on Jews residing, and doing business, in Kamenets-Podolski weren't fully abolished until the 1850s. This new freedom led to a rapid increase in the Jewish population from 4,629 Jews in 1847 to 16,211 in 1897 (40 percent of the total population). It had become an important trading and religious center.

The Jewish population of the city in the late 19th and early 20th centuries was made up mainly of emigres from central Europe and Poland, as well as those who emigrated from the Ottoman Empire and from communities that had existed along the coasts of the Black Sea since antiquity.

Kamenets-Podolski has been called the "city of seven cultures" for the number of nationalities who contributed to its development (Ukrainians, Armenians, Poles, Jews, Lithuanians, Turks, and Tatars).

During the 18th century, Russia's rulers, notably Peter I and Catherine II, waged a series of wars with the Polish–Lithuanian Commonwealth and the Swedish, Austro-Hungarian, Prussian, and Ottoman empires. The combination of Russian numerical superiority and internal divisions and crisis within each of those adversaries led to major military victories for the czarist armies despite Russia being more economically and culturally backward. These victories led to a major expansion of the Russian Empire and, in 1793, the Russian Empire took possession of Kamenets-Podolski.

By the early 19th century what is today Finland, Poland, Lithuania, Latvia, Estonia, Belarus, Ukraine, Crimea, and Moldova were incorporated into the Russian Empire. The national rights, languages, and cultures of the conquered nations and peoples were suppressed, as had been those of the Siberian indigenous peoples, central Asians, Georgians and other Caucasian peoples who had also been conquered by czarist Russia. The czarist empire that emerged had a population that was only about 40 percent Russian. The majority of that Russian population were serfs tied to land owned by the nobility. They were regularly conscripted to be cannon fodder in the czars' wars.

Another consequence of these conquests was that the Russian Empire had about a million Jews living within its borders. The overwhelming majority lived in what is today Lithuania, Poland, Ukraine, Belarus, and Moldova. Poland had been partitioned several times in the course of the late 18th-century wars, areas in the north having been taken by the Prussian Empire, Galicia in the south by the Austro-Hungarian Empire, and huge swathes in the east by the czarist empire, with the remaining central area becoming the Russian-dominated Kingdom of Poland.

The existence of this large Jewish population led to the creation of the Jewish Pale of Settlement by the czarist government (see the map following p. 20) in 1791. It was decreed by Catherine II that Jews were permitted to reside and trade in some areas where they had previously lived and in the areas that had been taken from the Ottoman Empire on the Black Sea's northern coast. In many areas of the Pale, Jews could only reside outside of larger towns and cities. The decrees setting up the Pale were primarily intended to prevent Jewish merchants from competing with Russian merchants. At the same time Jewish merchants were prohibited from trading in the provinces of interior Russia.

The same ukase, or czarist decree, which restricted the areas of Jewish residence and trade, included another discrimination: taxation. Jews who wished to be part of the mercantile class in the cities were to pay taxes "doubly in comparison with those imposed on the burghers and merchants of the Christian religion.

"The punitive tax did not relieve the Jews from the special military assessment, which, by the ukases of 1794 and 1796, they had to pay, like the Russian mercantile class in general, in exchange for the personal discharge of military service."*

The Pale did not include the Kingdom of Poland, where a different set

---

* Simon M. Dubnow, *History of the Jews in Russia and Poland*, vol. 1 of 3 (Philadelphia: Jewish Publication Society of America, 1916), p. 318.

of Russian-imposed restrictions governed Jewish life. Jews were allowed to move freely between the kingdom and the Pale but were barred from the Russian interior. Over the next century additional laws and regulations governing Jewish life in the Russian Empire were imposed. The May Laws of 1882 confiscated the rural landholdings of Jews and restricted them to the towns and cities in the Pale. By the opening years of the 20th century there were more than 100 such restrictions. At the time it was created, the majority of Jews in the Pale were engaged in trade or supported those who did.

By the 1897 Russian census, the Jewish population had grown to 4.87 million Jews in the Pale and 5.3 million Jews in the Russian Empire as a whole. As capitalist development advanced in Russia in the course of the 19th century, those Jews became divided into several social classes. The Jewish population encompassed a large layer of workers who labored in the textile, garment, tobacco, and furniture industries; others were artisans, such as cabinetmakers and jewelers, or servants for middle-class and wealthy Jews. Others became pauperized.

There was also a substantial middle layer of small merchants and lawyers, doctors, and engineers; and a small layer of big capitalists: railroad owners, bankers, sugar magnates, and owners of textile, furniture, and tobacco factories.

According to that 1897 census, 37.9 percent of Jews were employed in manufacturing and mechanical jobs, 31.6 percent in commerce, 19.4 percent as servants (mostly women), and 5 percent were professionals. An additional 3.2 percent were involved in transportation and 2.9 percent engaged in agriculture.*

This class stratification was also true in the rest of eastern Europe, where much of the Jewish population had become largely poor and working class. To fully understand the evolution of the Jewish people from the traders and merchants of antiquity, through to becoming moneylenders and bankers during feudalism to becoming the class-divided social groups of capitalism, and the episodic rise of antisemitism through the centuries to today, I suggest reading Abram Leon's

---

* Isaac M. Rubinow, "Economic Conditions of the Jews in Russia," *Bulletin of the Bureau of Labor*, no. 72 (Washington, D.C.: Department of Commerce and Labor, 1907; repr. New York: Arno Press, 1975), p. 500.

The Jewish Question: A Marxist Interpretation.*

As seen in Anna's memoir, the rules of the Pale were applied differently depending on what class you were part of. Wealthy Jews were able to send their children to universities in Kiev and Moscow and carry on business outside the Pale. The toiling majority, however, could not buy their way out of czarist military service.

Anna Galstuck draws a vivid picture of the pogroms that her family lived through and that Jews in the Russian Empire and eastern Europe faced. These became a regular feature of life across the Pale as social and economic crises deepened in Russia in the latter part of the 19th century.

The attackers burned down many neighborhoods and businesses, leaving dozens killed and hundreds wounded. Large-scale pogroms occurred in Odessa, Kishinev, Kiev (today's Odesa, Chișinău in Moldova, and Kyiv). Smaller-scale attacks across towns in the Pale were carried out with government approval and assistance from the Interior Ministry and the police. Ultranationalists and groups of thugs known as the Black Hundreds who carried out the attacks were egged on by the czarist regime.

The notorious Jew-hating tract the *Protocols of the Elders of Zion* was fabricated and produced by the Okhrana, the Russian czarist secret police, and first published in 1903. The *Protocols* scapegoated Jews by accusing them of being behind the various crises and incited much antisemitic, divide-and-rule violence during years of revolutionary unrest. It is still in print and quoted by Jew-haters of all stripes, including neo-Nazis, white supremacists, Holocaust deniers, and others in the United States and worldwide.

The crises and violence of the time led some of Anna's cousins to join socialist groups. Far outstripping their percentage in the population of the empire, many Jews became involved in the growing fight against the czarist autocracy, joining the socialist parties: Bolsheviks, Mensheviks, Socialist Revolutionaries, Poale Zion, and the Jewish Bund. A majority

---

* New York: Pathfinder Press, 4th edition, 2020. www.pathfinderpress.com

of the politically active Jewish workers were part of the Bund. Other Jews supported the Zionist movement.

Anna's family were part of the massive Jewish emigration from eastern Europe to the United States, Canada, South America, western Europe, and Palestine. Between 1880–1924, the combined effects of successive economic crises of capitalism, the increasing pauperization of Jews, oppressive conditions, and increasing number of pogroms in the Pale and other parts of eastern Europe drove several million Jews to emigrate, with 1.75 million coming to the United States. The majority settled in New York City and the surrounding area. This included several thousand from Kamenets-Podolski and environs.

The majority of these immigrants became garment workers. There were more than 100,000 workers in the garment industry in New York City by the early 1900s. Anna's mother Mirele and her older sister Bena were among the 40,000 shirtwaist and dress sewers. Most were young Jewish and Italian female immigrants. Many Jewish men were sewers and also worked in the "skilled" garment trades as cutters and pressers. There were also hundreds of Black workers who labored in the garment stock rooms and transported material from shop to shop.

Conditions in the sweatshops were horrendous. Wages had been slashed after the recession of 1908 from $12 to $9 per week. Most sewers were paid piece rate. Much of the work was seasonal with several months of downtime every year. Real wages were actually closer to $5 per week for a workweek of 54–59 hours. Employers charged for needles, thread, the electricity used by a sewing machine during each worker's shift, and the rental of seats at a machine. The picture of screaming foremen and owners Anna recounts was common to most garment shops.

Between 1908 and 1910 there were strikes for better wages and conditions and for union representation in a number of shops that involved the International Ladies' Garment Workers' Union (ILGWU), founded in 1900. The escalating strikes were also supported by the United Hebrew Trades, a federation of Jewish labor unions that was organized in New

York in 1888. The UHT supported demands for the eight-hour day, regulation of child labor, and the abolition of the sweatshop system.

In 1909 the strikes spread to additional shops. One of them was the Triangle Shirtwaist Company. When its owners heard that the workers had voted to join the union, they locked out the workers and fired them, bringing in replacement workers. Hundreds of the fired workers went to the ILGWU headquarters and demanded to join the union.

Over many weeks, the strikers were beaten by thugs hired by the garment shop owners and many were arrested and sentenced to the workhouse. The New York City Workhouse was established in the early 1800s as a place for petty criminals, vagrants, and the poor. The rulers of the city believed that the only effective way to eradicate poverty was to commit the poor to institutions like the workhouse, where their failings could be "cured."

The conditions in the shops and the ongoing battle in the struck shops led to agitation by the workers for a general strike of shirtwaist workers and dressmakers. A November 23, 1909, mass meeting was called by the ILGWU, the United Hebrew Trades, and other labor organizations at the Cooper Union. Thousands of garment workers filled its great hall and the surrounding streets. Many New York labor union leaders spoke to the crowd condemning the situation in the shops but warning that strikes were difficult and a last resort. The amassed workers, unsatisfied by the speeches, grew angry. One of them was Clara Lemlich, a militant unionist in one of the shops on strike. While on the picket line for 11 weeks she had been beaten by thugs and arrested and thrown in the workhouse several times.

Lemlich became frustrated that the speakers did not offer a way forward and strode to the front of the room demanding to take the floor. Speaking in her native Yiddish, she said, "I am a working girl, one of those who are on strike against intolerable conditions. I am tired of listening to speakers who talk in general terms. What we are here for is to decide whether we shall strike or shall not strike. I offer a resolution that a general strike be declared now."

After a prolonged roar of approval, Lemlich and the thousands in attendance took a Yiddish-language oath to strike the following day, pledging, "If I turn traitor to the cause I now pledge, may this hand wither from the arm I now raise."

Thus began what became known as the Uprising of the Twenty Thousand. This was the most significant battle waged by women workers in the United States up to that time. Over the course of months on picket lines, facing thugs organized by the garment owners' association and arrests by the police, these women stayed the course.

A number of the smaller shops signed contracts raising wages, eliminating the charging for electricity, needles, and seats, and recognizing the union. Most of the larger clothing manufacturers stubbornly refused to settle and the strike continued for months. Eventually most shirtwaist and dress shops agreed to contracts, but many refused to recognize the union and maintained nonunion shops. The strikers went back to work knowing that they had forced the garment bosses to back down on key issues of working conditions, hours, and wages. Five months later, in 1910, a second general strike of 60,000 cloak and suit makers was organized with similar mixed results.

On March 25, 1911, more than 500 garment workers were busy at work in the Triangle Shirtwaist Company factory in Lower Manhattan when a fire erupted and rapidly spread. The ten-story building's exit doors had been locked to prevent workers from taking "unauthorized" breaks from work and to prevent "theft." The lone fire escape collapsed during the fire. Some of the workers, unable to reach an exit, jumped from windows in an attempt to save themselves. Others died as the fire gutted the building in less than 40 minutes. In the ashes were 146 dead. Many more were injured. The victims, mostly recent Jewish and Italian immigrants, were women between 14 and 23 years old.

Ten days later, on April 5, Anna's mother, grandmother, and eldest sister joined more than 120,000 workers filling the streets and marching from the Lower East Side past the burned-out building and into Washington Square Park. Over 400,000 viewed the memorial procession as it then moved up 5th Avenue in the midst of a downpour. Isaac Harris and Max Blanck, the owners, were indicted for manslaughter in the first and second degree. Their trial in December 1911 lasted three weeks. On December 27, after the court heard emotional testimony from more than

100 witnesses, both Harris and Blanck were acquitted of all charges.

The anger and outrage at the mass murder of workers led Anna's mother Mirele, like thousands of other garment workers, to fight to organize her shop. That story unfolds in the pages that follow.

Over the next several years more workers in sections of the garment industry struck, including fur workers, men's tailors, and kimono and wrapper makers, and then once again the shirtwaist makers. In early 1913 over 150,000 needle trades workers were on strike. After weeks of battle, once again there were victories with mixed results. Better pay was won, as was a shorter workweek, and the worst working conditions were pushed back. Many shops became union shops with contracts. Many remained open shops, albeit with better conditions and pay, but filled with union members who remained solid in the fight.

With health problems and advancing age, Anna was unable to take the story of her family further. The unfinished manuscript ends abruptly, soon after telling of her mother Mirele's work in organizing her garment shop coworkers into the union.

This chronicle provides rich texture to what millions of Jews in eastern Europe faced from the late 19th century to the early decades of the 20th century and their experiences after their migration to a new home.

With Jew-hatred once again on the rise, Anna's story and vignettes of pre–World War I Jewish life in the Russian Empire and New York's Lower East Side can inspire us with her heartfelt portrayal of the human desire to break down divisions both on the personal and societal level.

Mike Shur
New York City
July 2023

KAMENETS-PODOLSKI

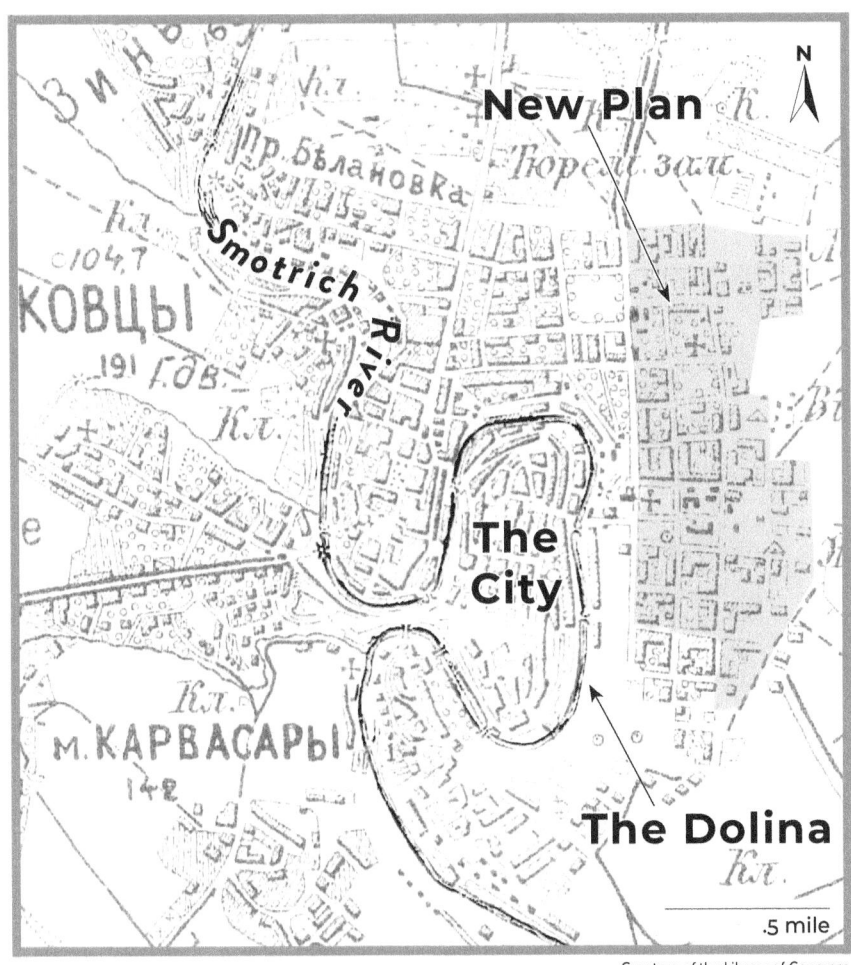

Detail from 1915 Russian map of Podolia Gubernia

Kamenets-Podolski

Lithograph from the 19th century of Kamenets-Podolski Fortress, built in the 14th century, with a settlement on the Smotrich River in the foreground.

Novoplanovsky Bridge over Smotrich River. To the left is an entrance to the Old Town of Kamenets-Podolski, c. 1885.

The people of Kamenets-Podolski

Mirele	the author's mother, Chaya's daughter
Avraham	Mirele's husband, the author's father
Chaya	Mirele's mother
Simon	Chaya's deceased husband
Bena	Mirele's first daughter
Rachel	Mirele's second daughter
Adah	the author, Mirele's third daughter
Isaiah	Mirele's first son
Raphael	Mirele's second son
Hannah	Chaya's other daughter, Mirele's sister
Fishl	Chaya's son-in-law, Mirele's brother-in-law
Moishe	Hannah and Fishl's son
Schmuel	Chaya's son
Yhitta	Schmuel's wife, Chaya's daughter-in-law
Katynka	Mirele's Ukrainian friend and neighbor
Stepan Gorezdykh	Katynka's deceased husband
Evdokiya	Ukrainian farmer, Katynka's cousin
Dr. Popov	family physician and landlord, Katynka's cousin
Kolmin-Dodya	Adah's uncle
Gittel	Kolmin-Dodya's wife
Baba	Avraham's sister
Nahama	Avraham's sister
Dovid	Avraham's friend
Sima	Mirele's kin, Velvl's wife
Buroch	the matchmaker
Mortkhe	the rabbi
Rachel	the midwife
Rayzil	Rachel and Adah's friend
Ginendle	garment workshop manager
Zalman Goldstein	wealthy landlord and lawyer

1

Chaya

I T IS THE END OF A cold Russian winter month, and a full, brilliant
moon freed herself from a heavy cloud, and with all her power
and glory lit up the dark areas of a room through its only window,
which stood witness to the activities of the souls within. Slowly
she moved her beam of light, licking white calcimined walls and
earthen floor, discovering on the way the bare essentials of a poor
man's home. A table and some backless benches came into view and
became lost again in darkness as the light swept on and rested on
the high-built, Russian-style brick stove, ere to spend some time as
if to admire some old, blackened earthenware pots and a banged-up
teakettle on the hearth, when she slowly peered into the long, smoke-
stained oven and tried to reach into its very innards. However,
lacking elasticity she gave up and instead reached to the very top.

Now the brilliance spread herself partly over the ample flat top
of the stove that gave much comfort and warmth to the sick, the
very young, and the very old during the bitter-cold Russian winters.
Here too she tried to measure her length fully but was forced away,
continuing course to a tall bookcase, with its glass doors displaying
many shelves crowded with religious books. In the very corner of the
upper shelf, the moon's ray found a gleaming bauble winking back at
her! And upon extending herself more generously, two golden lions
shimmering on a blue velvet pouch! How she admired and bathed
them in her pure love-light! But she never got to know that they

were guarding Avraham's phylacteries that Mirele, now his wife, had embroidered with gold thread when she became betrothed to him. Again, the ray was pulled away as if by force to a high chest of drawers, but not interested by her ordinary find stayed there but a short time and soon found herself on the bed where Avraham was making love to his wife Mirele. As if understanding their wish for secrecy, she moved on to the floor and suddenly disappeared under a big cloud leaving the room in utter darkness.

With a rapid movement Avraham slid out of the warm bed and tucked the covers around his wife's shoulders and ran swiftly across the ice-cold floor to the other end of the room and in the dark found a small cupboard from which he took a stone crock of tea-rose preserves and a spoon and ran back with his find to the bed. Unable to open the jar he put it between his raised knees and with some difficulty forced the cover from it, letting a delightful aroma escape into the room and fed some of the preserves to Mirele, all the while holding her head in the crook of his free arm.

"No more, had enough of it," she pushed the spoon away from her mouth.

"But you said that you liked this jam, here take a bit more," he insisted, worried with her waning appetite and restless sleeping of late. "Oh, but I do like it, but I do not have much desire for any food now. I guess I am too worried about my mother's decision. What are we to do if for some reason she refuses to come and live with us?" She sounded troubled.

"Don't be so upset, I feel that she will not let us down. If she does, we will find another way to solve our problems. The Lord will not forsake us. Now go to sleep, you need your rest," he cuddled into her warm heavy body and fell asleep before her.

Avraham was a miracle child, so the family told. When his mother gave birth to her first child, a girl, she lamented, "Why a girl, why not a man-child? A man-child grows into a man who studies the Torah and says the Kaddish for his parents when they pass on, but a girl, what more than a woman can she grow into?" It was then that she prayed to her God, reading with Him, that should He deem her worthy of another child, she would gladly give her eyesight for a son; though she would not see him, she would hear him and would be able to touch him, and he would bring the glories that a Jewish son brings his parents. Her petition was granted, the second child born was a son, and she lost her sight in the ninth month of her pregnancy when Cossacks threw a lighted torch on the thatched straw roofs of the crooked little houses in the Jewish community.

And it was indeed a miracle! Avraham grew to manhood handsome and of gentle mien, becoming a fine student of his religion. When he married Mirele, townspeople asked him to be their rabbi, but he refused. Although he had much learning and he was deeply religious, he questioned dogma and was not willing to be a religious leader of his people. Then the very same people asked him to become their *shochet*,* a vocation involving the ritual manner of fowl and cattle slaughter that can be practiced only by pious Jews, and that he agreed to. He prepared himself for weeks, then when he was about to apply the sharpened blade to the neck of the first chicken, he grew faint and slumped to the ground, thus taking this means of their livelihood from him.

It took some time for him to look around for something that he could make a living at and chose to become a teacher of Hebrew to advanced pupils, and the townspeople named him Avraham the Scribe. At the outset of their marriage, the little he earned Mirele made do with, for she was raised by a widowed mother who taught her to be frugal, and when their babies began to come, sicken and die before their first year, and dire poverty poked its head into their lives, Mirele looked around for something to augment his small earnings.

She rented a house of two rooms, of which she made a living quarter in the rear and the front room she turned into a grocery store, separating one from the other with burlap sacks. It was then that she turned to her mother Chaya asking for help, pleading with her to come and live with her. "I carried and gave life to five children since I married Avraham, and not one lived long enough to call me Mother. Now I am with child again and I am afraid to bring it into the world to suffer and die as the others. Mother, perhaps in your care and with

* Hebrew.

the help of the One above, it will have the chance the others did not."
Mirele's eyes filled with tears and Chaya had to turn her head away
to not see her misery.

"You took me unawares my child, let me go home and think about
it. I had expected to give you as much help as was possible for me to
give, but giving up my home I never thought of. But let me go now
and I will be back tomorrow and will see what we can do."

Chaya left somewhat confused and walked slowly home and sat
down at a window as if peering out, but her eyes saw nothing, her
thoughts were turned inward. Dusk had already fallen and overtook
the room that served as her home for the last thirty-odd years. The
window still loaned enough daylight to show up the strong features of
her face that seemed so still while she worked her thoughts. Had her
body not been so deeply pushed into the chair, one could see how spare
it was, as it did not carry one more ounce of flesh than she needed to
give her the appearance of a young woman, despite the slight curva-
ture of her back. Even her supple legs belied her forty-nine years and
the hardships she imposed on them at whatever work came her way.
She kept turning her new problem over and over again in her mind,
without finding a solution to satisfy and bring her a small measure of
peace. All her life she had been independent of help from others. She
worked for her daily bread ever since she was a young girl, except for
the few years she was married to Simon. After his death she continued
to work and never felt subordinate to anyone.

And now was she to give up her freedom and live with Mirele, to
be chained to an infant day and night? But then how could she herself
deny her daughter's plea for help? At no other time did Mirele ask
while she struggled so hard with poverty, illnesses, and deaths of their
children. But now with the work in the store and her tiredness and
apprehension, it is too much to endure. But still, how could she efface
her own way of life? She would be glad to give her all the time she
could spare and whatever little money she would make. But give up
her home and unhampered way of living and stay with her children?
That seemed unthinkable!

Full darkness now moved in and covered every corner of the room, but Chaya remained sitting in the same position, hands folded in her lap and her brown luminous eyes set deep in their sculpted sockets, closed. She looked the relaxed sleeper but in truth she was reliving her past more deeply than was her wont when she was troubled. She was now absorbed. She was betrothed to her dear Simon and dressing for their wedding ceremony in the new clothes that had cost her father a half year's work in the tobacco factory. The features in her face softened while her aquiline nose's nostrils moved tremulously. She smiled broadly as she recalled the grand procession that had formed outside the synagogue where they were married, to walk to her newly acquired in-laws for the wedding feast and how it turned into a grand fiasco!

Chaya threw her head back and laughed until the tears rolled down her face as she vividly pictured what became of that magnificent parade. How Simon's mother placed them at the head, to lead the nearest and dearest of both families to her home with instructions that they do not walk too fast, as it was unbecoming for a bride to show too much anticipation.

Not understanding her, they strutted ahead very much like a couple of peacocks who had just opened their colorful tails to display to the entire world. However, Simon soon tired of the slow, pretentious gait and pulled out a rubber ball from his new trousers and began to bounce it on the road, raising dust in their faces. She tried hard to stop him with pleas and continued, her feeling of importance and dignity reduced to the very dust he was raising. With a strong swing of her arm, she caught the ball and flung it into a field of late fall corn before he had a chance to grasp her intentions.

"You should not have done that," he shouted, his face turning red. "A wife must never interfere with her husband's pleasures." His mother then stepped up to the front from her place midways, but not too hurriedly, not wanting to appear flustered before her guests, and quietly but sharply told them to behave like a Jewish married couple should and not like peasants.

Well it turned out that they did not know how either should behave and as soon as she went back to her former place, he turned to his bride again and said, "Had I known that you would be so contentious,

I would not have let them marry me to you." He did not look into her face.

"And had I known that you would be so lacking in respect despite the years you had spent in the house of learning with the sages, I would not have let them marry me to you either," she answered him.

This hurt him badly and he retaliated with more reasons why he should not have become her husband. "You are ugly, and, and, ah, your dress is too long and you look like my little sister not like a wife. Besides, you are too tall for me and you don't know how a wife should behave," he raved.

"You had better stop being so critical of me and look at yourself, or better that you don't see yourself as others do, especially not as I see you now." Fire sparks seemed to fly from her eyes.

One taunt led to another and to this day Chaya does not know who slapped whose face first. They gave and took from each other until she heard her gentle father say that he was ready to die of shame! Again Chaya laughed out loud as she recalled how her mother-in-law went to her son, covering for his part of the blame with her big "mother apron," and getting her relatives to forgive the bride, that she is an orphan, that in time she will learn better manners, after all she was still young, and no, no, she had no dowry to give, just their family name is so good. Not one word of her son's abusive conduct, but she went on and on in her monotonous tone until Chaya's face burned deeper from her mother-in-law's sly remarks than Simon's hard slaps, while her kindly father looked helplessly at his relatives.

Had they been left to themselves a little longer they would probably have settled their differences in their own way soon enough, but no, his mother decided to walk with them in the front of the procession and courted more trouble than she counted on by speaking harshly first to one, then to the other, and shaming them for the fracas without giving them a chance to say one word in their defense. Their young tempers could hold out no longer as she succeeded in goading them into an anger that flared so high and fierce that they had to be separated and taken to their respective homes.

What did they expect from such young children, miracles? Chaya said to herself. Simon was a sheltered boy, less than fourteen years of age, who had at nine of these years went with old men in the house of learning, never taking his nose from the religious books long enough to see what was going on around him. And myself? A young foolish calf not quite thirteen—and they expected us to behave like a mature couple!

The outcome was that after his parents had knocked some sense into his head and her father had spoken harshly but with sympathetic understanding to her, that Simon came to claim her as his wife eleven days later. She now recalled how he came into the house with downcast eyes and went very close to her to tell her that his parents wanted her to come home with him as a guest, to stay a full year (neither had an alternative, neither one knowing how to earn their daily bread). And his mother said to hurry because she was cooking *kreplekh** for supper. How happy she felt that he came for her! She forgot her anger, anxiety, and even her fear of his mother with whom she was to spend the next year under the same roof. She flew ahead of Simon, her feet barely touching the ground, while he labored with hard breathing to keep up with her.

Still, their marriage was a good one. They began playing house like children, but soon grew into their responsibilities, moving into their own dwelling after the first year when Simon had learned cigar-making. Before she reached her sixteenth year, she presented a son whom they named Schmuel and a daughter named Hannah. Yes, their marriage was a blessed one. And when she knew that she was pregnant again at twenty-three she was so full of joy that she danced the entire length of the room and back while Simon watched in despair, fearing loss of the child. The love she felt for her husband was akin to her heartbeat and never left her until the end of her life. But her happiness was suddenly and cruelly cut from under her when Simon fell victim to the cholera and together with hundreds of other victims of the epidemic was buried while she was in the last month of her pregnancy.

She raved on her bed for weeks, her despair so great she lost meaning

---

* Yiddish for dumplings, filled with either cheese by the working classes or ground meat by the middle classes, usually served in soup.

of time or place as well as her children's welfare until she felt the birth pangs of her newborn seeking life. The birth of the little girl whom she named for Simon's now dead mother, snapped her back to reality knowing that now she had to be both father and mother to her three orphans. As soon as she was able to get on her feet, she set out to find some means of support for her little family and worked at anything that came her way.

When one hesitated to offer some menial work "not becoming the wife and daughter of such learned men" as her father and husband had been, she laughed and told them that her children's empty stomachs knew no pride and set to work. She cooked for wedding feasts, washed clothes, delivered meat and fowl for butchers from one end of town to the other, carrying her infant at the breast with one arm and on the other a heavy reed basket that tore at her shoulder. When the child did not have to depend on her breast any longer, she let the older children care for her while she sat for days and half into the nights plucking down from duck and goose feathers to be made into pillows and comforters for rich, marriageable daughters.

The Czar's Cossacks twice burned her home down to the ground when they attacked the Jewish quarter and both times she worked with good neighbors to rebuild, her workworn hands handling stone and lime as the men did until she was once again able to give her children the comfort of a home. How she managed to raise her children under such dire troubles is a trick the poor knew.

Her body turned solid and muscular while her face took on a bronze hue from the miles of walking in all sorts of weather. But her deep laughter that caused the tears to flow from her eyes belied her hard life. Not only did she like to tell amusing anecdotes but she was also held spellbound by folk maxims that wittily related to Jewish life. When too many problems pressed on her, she exchanged her facetiousness for curses, they being the only relief.

She cursed her fate, her heavy burdens, and the many problems that gave her no peace, but most of all the Russian Czar. "So long should he live as it will take my poor orphans to finish this small loaf of bread, dear God," or "The little Father of Russia should have to be healed by the same doctors that he imposes on the poor people in the clinic." But her classic curse was, "The antisemites should turn on him and his dear ones as they do against our defenseless people."

She improvised as she went along, depending on her stress and mood. Matchmakers buzzed around her with all sorts of marriage propositions but she turned them away, fearing a stepfather who may hurt her children, though her young spirit sorely missed the strong arms of a man about her.

When her son Schmuel reached his fourteenth year, she took him from his learning and apprenticed him to the tobacco factory where her father and her husband had worked and the little earnings he brought home to her helped ease her difficulties a bit. When he began to earn more money, he was a grown man of eighteen, taller than his father had been, broad-shouldered, bearded, and dignified. All who knew his father told the youth that he reminded them of him, except that he also matched his mother's love of laughter and wittiness. It was at that time that Chaya found out that her son was smitten by the aggressive, big-bosomed Yhitta, an orphan raised by an aunt who lived down the road from them. She never got to like the girl even when she was a mere child and came to play with her girls, although she tried—for was she not an orphan like her own children? But Yhitta had even then a fast and sharp tongue and had to have her way in the childish games they played. As she grew older, she seemed to quiet down somewhat, but still assumed leadership in all their games. And now Schmuel, her good-humored, benign son, was letting this girl lead him by the nose while she, Chaya, stood helplessly by.

Later on, she had to accept her as her daughter-in-law, nay, as one of her own children, all the while fearing that Schmuel's manly stature and dignity will be undermined by his wife. But her fears were unfounded, for even though he let his Yhitta "tie him to her apron strings," he shone with an inner light of happiness and pride.

Soon after their marriage, Chaya went to see a *shadkhan*,* a matchmaker, and asked him to find a good and pious man for her Hannah, although she had not one ruble to offer as dowry. But, she told him,

---

* Yiddish.

my daughter is an orphan and I worked very hard to raise her to her present age and she turned out healthy and very beautiful, *kinehora*,* so that even my best friends are envious of me.

Then you must not forget who her grandfathers were. Their names were linked with the Rabbi's and the learned and their knowledge of Torah and reverence to our God were of the foremost! And the esteemed dignity they were accorded by all who knew them that you don't take into account? Nu, I too have been an orphan and though I had such an honorable father, was too poor to put by any money for my dowry but didn't I marry a pious man from a good family? And didn't I have a sweet life with him? God should help you find such a man for my Hannah and later on one for my Mirele too, and I will be thankful to Him for the rest of my life, and don't forget that I was not the beauty that Hannah is, *kinehora*.

While she held the one-sided debate, the *shadkhan* sat back in his chair and his mind sifted his stock-in-trade of bridegrooms to be, knowing that he has on hand a complicated task to perform between her lack of money and her high requirements. The Jews have a rhythmic maxim, *Der Mensch tracht und Gott lacht*, a man plans and God laughs, and so it was with Chaya's attempt to get herself a son-in-law by way of a matchmaker.

It turned out that her pretty daughter Hannah had already met her destined husband, was preparing to tell her mother about it but not knowing how to approach the delicate news went instead to her sister-in-law Yhitta, who in turn told it to Chaya, who became resentful.

"Such things you tell others, not your own mother." Chaya looked baffled.

"But, Mama, I was dying to tell you, but I was afraid to!"

"Afraid of your own mother? Afraid your mother was a monster?"

"No, no, but because I met him myself and I did not want you to think I was too bold." Her words faltered.

"So, who is he and from where, and how did you get to meet him alone and how can you speak of marrying him if I did not see him myself?"

---

* Yiddish for "May no evil eye set on her."

"I met him in my friend Rivka's house when he came to be fitted for the new suit her father was making for him. After seeing me there two more times he asked Rivka's father who I was and then if he would introduce him to me." Her cheeks were stained red. "I like him Mother, he wants to come Saturday night to ask you if he can marry me. You see he does not believe in matchmakers, he thinks them old-fashioned, you will let him come, Mother, won't you?" she spilled quickly what was on her mind.

"Well, I still do not know who he is you are talking of."

"Alright, I will tell you all you want to know. You heard of the family named Schmysers of the City,* they used to manufacture reed furniture and luggage, well Fishl is now the only one left of that family, having lost both his parents. Fishl himself as an only child had not lived in Kamenets-Podolski from when he was thirteen years old. His father paved his way with much money to send him to the Moscow schools and universities from which he recently graduated. His father sent for him six months ago when he knew that he had no chance to recover from his sickness and begged him to take over the business and continue the chain of inheritance and Fishl promised to do so.

"But after his father's death he found himself unhappy and alone and decided to go back to Moscow and make it his home. The governor sent for him and asked him to become the notary for New Plan† as well as the City. It was while he was thinking it over that he met me and he decided to accept the position. We met a few times in the City with Rivka accompanying us, and it is almost two months that we know each other, and a few days ago he asked me to marry him! You will let me Mother, won't you?" Her beautiful eyes danced with eagerness.

And when Fishl did come to Chaya's home to spend an hour, her heart sank for dislike of him. She saw before her a short, stocky pompous man who was no longer young, who spoke through his nose without once looking direct into her eyes, very much like the

---

* The Old Town of Kamenets-Podolski.
† In the Pale of Settlement a notary was a Jewish official, appointed by the local czarist governor, who liaised with the courts and government bureaucracy on issues that involved the Jewish population. New Plan is the neighborhood to the east of the City across the Smotrich River.

cosmopolitan addressing a peasant. Before he left the house he did not ask but told Chaya that he will marry her daughter Hannah and that she should make the preparations. Never asking what she thought of their marriage, if she would accept him as her son-in-law, if she had anything she wanted to discuss about the plans for the wedding!

Well Hannah wanted him and married him, then moved out of her mother's house and moved into the big, richly furnished home that was left by his parents. The seven-room house with the heavy carpets and silken drapes and lamps trimmed with gleaming fringe of cut glass required servants for its upkeep and Fishl hired so much help that Hannah became alarmed! Her husband dressed her in silks and rich furs and they luxuriated with their newly acquired friends in the big salons on all occasions.

Although her child's happiness gave Chaya much joy, it did not add any more liking for her son-in-law, and she managed to see Hannah only on the days when she knew Fishl to be at the governor's office or otherwise away from home. Then she was left only with her twelve-year-old, gentle and graceful Mirele, who sweetened her life with her soft personality and charm. Although she was born small and plain, Mirele slowly developed to her mother's height and grace, and inherited from her father his sparkling black eyes that were set far apart over her high cheek bones.

She freed her mother from all the housework, doing all the cooking and other household chores, and had time left to help Yhitta with her babies who tumbled into the world each year. At seventeen she was so attractive that Chaya had difficulty in keeping the many youths from her door, who came with any excuse to get a glimpse of her daughter. On an afternoon while Mirele was putting one of her brother's children to sleep, there came a knock on the door and Avraham put in an appearance. He looked around and asked for Schmuel, and Yhitta told him he was at the factory, all the while clearing a chair for him, and begged him to sit down.

"No, I can't wait for him, but I would like to borrow his Mishnah*

---

* The Mishnah is the first major collection of the Jewish oral traditions, also known as the Oral Torah.

for a day or two if I may," he told her. But his eyes had seen Mirele, and he caught himself staring at her, when Yhitta pointed to the bookshelf and told him to help himself. He thanked her and walked from the house wondering why Yhitta did not think of introducing him to Mirele. Never had he seen so much beauty and grace rolled into one girlish face and body and he could barely wait until the next evening to return the book and have another glimpse of her.

But when he came he was chagrined not to find her there and he had to wait until the Sabbath to see Schmuel in the synagogue to ask about her. "Oh, you mean Mirele. Yes, she is my youngest sister, she is nice, isn't she though? It is a pleasure to have her in the house," he laughed with pride. Avraham lost no time but sent a matchmaker to Chaya's house asking for her daughter in marriage. Chaya was very happy and proud to have him for a son-in-law, owing that he came from a good family and that he himself was an earnest student of the Torah and was very pious. When she got to know him, her happiness increased when she learned that he was warm and sensitive in his dealings with others.

Suddenly Chaya shifted her position and sat straight up and, agitated, began to untie and retie her head kerchief, feeling that her reverie led her to the present, to the reality of her problems ahead. She felt Mirele's need of her as never before. She knew well that her daughter did not ask for help lightly. Never before had she in her struggles with so much poverty, sickness, and death of her children suggested that she come live with them, and when she was forced to accept any help, she took it as if ashamed and devoured by guilt.

Chaya got up from her chair and felt her way around in the dark room until she found the matches and lit the kerosene lamp that hung from the ceiling in an iron frame and stood a while looking around the room where she spent so much of her time with her Simon and their children, where they took the bitter and the sweet that life held out to them. Slowly she edged herself onto the bed and began to remove her clothes and pulled her nightshirt over her head, absentmindedly pulling along her kerchief and lace-trimmed skullcap that she had forgotten to remove first, disclosing her close-cropped white hair. She tied her bare head with a kerchief peasant-fashion, turned down the wick in the lamp and fell into a deep sleep.

In the morning she remembered dreaming of water, then recalled seeing many heads bobbing like corks in it and began feeling the dream was like some kind of a sign or omen. It seemed to repeat the proverbial answer she gave long ago when asked how she and her children were getting along: "Thank the Lord, we are keeping our heads above the water." Now she knew that she had to help her children keep their heads above water, no matter what the cost to her own freedom and comfort.

The room became flooded with sunshine and she stood looking around its old furniture and not-so-old dining room set Hannah forced on her a few years back. She recalled how she fought against taking it, knowing well that Fishl knew nothing about it and that Hannah felt safe in giving it to her because he would never see it in her mother's house, deeming it below his dignity to visit her. And it was not until Chaya saw Hannah crying bitterly and Mirele pleading gently with her that she told the driver to bring it inside the house. The large round table and the straw-bottomed chairs were so highly polished, they shamed the other furniture in the room, making it look as if it wanted to crawl into the walls. But now, after a good many years of use they look almost alike, the table having lost the high gloss and the chairs their secure straw seats that were now replaced with unvarnished wooden covers. They were all akin as if one happy family now.

Her eyes were roaming over her intimate objects and she began to shake her head and laugh, saying loudly to herself: Oh, Chaya, Chaya, you who always looked into the face of your hard life without fear and worked so tirelessly to bring your three orphans to man and woman-hood now stand and take time out to vacillate on whether you should exchange your struggling children's security for this—the leftovers of yesteryear! You consider if you should let the shadows cut off the light! Thank you, dear Lord, for pointing the way for an old, foolish woman. I must hurry to assure my children that I did not lose all my senses yet, and that I will be happy to share their home with them!

Two weeks later she brought to Mirele's one-room home her own bed and a clothes closet which she put trunk fashion under her bed for things she needed and things she could not part from. The bed she placed at the extreme end wall leading to the store, the full length of the room away from the bed in which Mirele and Avraham slept. She made it up as she had in her own home, the pillows placed pyramid fashion, boasting lace in the four corners exposing the red ticking. The white coverlet she brought along she had preserved for the holidays only, but in Mirele's home she used it every day to brighten the room they all lived in, not as a token.

Mirele and Avraham felt her presence in their home like a good prophecy, her silent assurance, stamina, and good humor filled the house. Mirele's pregnancy was no worse than the others in spite of her hard work and worries in the store. One week after Chaya came to live with them, she gave birth to a girl. Their happiness mingled with fear for the child's life, and fear of an "evil eye" was always with the women, and although Avraham laughed at them, he too secretly feared the worse. Who knows how much longer she would be with them before she would be taken away? However, the Lord was good to them and He let them keep her, and the child grew on, slowly revealing a sensitive and quick mind that was no match for her undersized body and both her parents thanked her grandmother over and over again for giving the child so much care and love, but Chaya hushed them, not wanting to take some of the glory away from Him who giveth and He that taketh away when He saw fit.

Avraham named the child Bena, after his mother, and Bena grew into a very happy child, although a quiet one, who loved Chaya for her gaiety and her warm, strong arms that cuddled her so much. Toward her mother she felt somewhat strange because she saw her only briefly and always in a hurry to go back into the store.

While the child was still on all fours she explored the room from end to end, finding objects of interest to play with and learning how to use her hands and fingers with great dexterity. Mirele's high-buttoned shoes enthralled her for a long period of time, her little fingers manipulating the buttons with little effort. No less entertainment she derived from the empty thread spools that she rolled all over the floor and tried to catch up with. For noise, she relied on two tin pot covers that Chaya left on the floor for her to play with and from those she learned that all she had to do was to bang one against the other and they would give out such noise that her grandmother would screw up her face and lift her shoulders.

Best of all the child enjoyed pulling at the bed-covers. She would sit on the floor and slowly begin to draw at the bottom of a cover then pull harder and soon with all her might until she heard Chaya shout, "Look what you are doing you little imp, stop it!" and she was gathered into the strong arms she loved so. It was during one of her coverlets-pulling that she found her legs. Chaya had tucked the covers on the inside of the bed facing the wall real tight, putting much of the material under the mattress this time and when Bena began to pull and tug and could make no headway, her hands reached higher up on the bed and grabbed two fistfuls of the cover and forced them toward herself and found herself on her feet! There she stood panting and puzzled until Chaya saw her and laughed out loud while she waited to see what she would do next. Then the child's soft legs could hold her no longer and she dropped back to the floor. Later on she not only raised herself to her legs from the floor by holding on to something but also found that she could walk a short distance by putting one foot in front of the other.

Now her eyes lit up with adventure, she forgot her playthings that had taken so much of her growing weeks and months, and made ready to mount the three steps leading into the store. One day she nearly made them but fell back on the second one and she howled so loud with disappointment that she brought both her mother and grandmother in great panic. But her tears like blossoms after a summer rain soon dried and she was at it again. This time she used the burlap curtain for support as she made each step, pulling her wobbly legs with excited effort until she was on top of the landing! The black mop of hair on her head was disheveled and her freckled nose-saddle all wrinkled up, she "stood" laughing triumphantly, and Chaya, who watched her progress, called into the store to her daughter, "Nu, nu, I can see where we are going to have a fine time keeping her in the house now!"

Both stood looking at the excited child and felt choked with emotion, while the child peered into the store with wonder in her eyes looking from her grandmother to her mother. Nothing could keep Bena in the house now for very long, she was broadening her horizons and was done with the little world she had lived in for close to two years.

The store held forth too many attractions for her to ignore. There were the wooden boxes full of raisins, barrels of pickled melons and drums of kerosene oil that made her little delicate nose itch, and she loved the attention she got from the tradespeople who petted her and called her endearing names.

Most of all she wanted to be with her mother now, from whom she received sweets every now and then and in a short time really became her mother's child, running to her grandmother only for her needs. "I am afraid that your daughter does not want me anymore, Mirele," Chaya said laughingly, "she does not rest until she finds herself in the store with you."

"No need for you to worry, Mother, you know how she loves you and depends on you, and don't forget that you are her very first love, like a child, she discovered another corner in her world and she is happier here until she will be able to get outside the store by herself. How can the child know how big a stake you have in her life, and how much Avraham and I need you and want you with us? Yes, she will always be grateful! To you for what you have done for her, and need I tell you what your presence in the house means to us. You can tell Bena that I will give her a little sister or brother soon, if she will be a good little girl." And Bena was a good little girl a long time, waiting until the promise of a sister or brother wore off and she forgot about it.

In the following four years Mirele had conceived and miscarried two times, and was now pregnant again. The constant hard work and worries in the store wore her strength and spirits down and she had no one to turn to for help. Avraham was not good in the store no matter how he tried, and she had to come to his aid too many times, tactfully, not to hurt his feelings but he knew that the people who came into the store saw how things dropped from his hands, how he had to ask Mirele the price of things all the time and how slow he was in his actions. He began to look so perplexed that in silent agreement between the two, he stayed out of the store, nor were his small earnings much help when she had pressing bills to pay, and she lived in hope of a day when she would reconcile her difficulties somehow.

Bena was her ray of sunshine during those hard-pressed days, the little girl helped in the store like a grownup; she swept, cleaned, and delivered orders that she was able to carry. Her pet project was to make the store look prosperous, and with the help of her little friends she brought into the store sawdust from the lumberyard that was in back of the house and filled large burlap sacks half-full and covered each with clean paper, then placed on top such dry items as rice, wheat, groats, peas, and beans, making each sack look as if filled from the bottom up. Seeing how it pleased her mother, Bena did the same with the wooden 5-pound boxes and put into them on top of the white paper, dry figs, prunes, cinnamon sticks, and boxer.* In the smaller boxes she also put strings of rock candy, poppy-seed rattlers, and whatnot. The displays made the store attractive to customers and put some confidence into the creditors.

Chaya spoke to the child as if she was an adult and never turned her away without answering her many questions. To her she told many tales of woe, but not to her older grandchildren, who were yet too puerile to understand. To Bena she talked about the struggles the Jews suffered to survive in czarist Russia, and how worried she is that her son Schmuel has to run away to America to escape the military service. The girl looked confused at her grandmother and asked, "But why does he have to go away to America? Why can't he just stay here and not become a soldier?"

Those boys who want to avoid serving in the army in Russia must damage themselves badly and then perhaps they will be left alone, Chaya told the child, and then added, yes, our uncle froze his toes off for nothing and they would not consider that enough. He did as

---

* Saint John's bread, made from carob flour.

some of the others in that summons, who shot off their trigger fingers, or pierced their eardrums, they all try to avoid the battlefields except perhaps the sons of rich fathers who become officers and live a good life there.

In America your uncle will be a free man, he will not undergo the indignities the Jews in Russia suffer, the golden land will protect him with God's help, she ended on that note as if to reassure herself.

Bena turned many things over in her mind that she could make no head nor tail of, many words got in her way! So what is a golden land? Is a golden land made of gold and how could they grow potatoes and cabbage and other things in it? And what is a trigger finger? It must be a finger perhaps very different than her own ten fingers are! Most painful to her was that her beloved long-legged uncle was going to run away and she will never see him again! She looked at her grandmother deep into her eyes and asked, "Will he take all my cousins and aunt with him when he goes?"

"Little one, you ask so many questions, I don't know which one to answer first. All I can tell you is that your uncle must go away and that he must go away with his children and your Aunt Yhitta, for he is too sick to go into a strange land by himself! I can also tell you that my destiny is such that up to recently the mothers who had but one son were spared the agony of seeing him go into the wilderness, saving his family, his livelihood and his religion behind. But now the Czar takes everyone no matter how badly he may damage himself and puts him to the grind! My only son, scholarly son, who does not know how to boil water, who sat over the Holy books for more than ten years, while I worked so hard to put bread into his mouth, him they would put into the kitchen to wash dirty dishes! No longer should the Czar live, as long as your Uncle Schmuel will remain in Kamenets-Podolski!"

In 1898 Russia was sinking in convulsions, unable to feed her populace and fearing a revolution that would sweep her off the throne, took whatever means available to divert the hungry masses from herself and turned them against each other. The Jews for so many centuries the scapegoat of the world's sins—in Russia particularly—were the victims of bitter starvation and feared for their lives now. The Czar's Cossacks, dressed in grey greatcoats trimmed with red lapels, adorned with token gold braid and buttons, wearing black karakul hats at perilous angles, mounted on strong, black glistening horses that forced fire sparks from the cobblestones with their ferocious speed, would suddenly fall on a Jewish community with bestial shouting and ransack and burn the homes, killing whoever got in their way.

Just as suddenly would they disappear leaving the pillaged, beaten, and dead. It was on one such night that Mirele felt that she was going into labor, though she had not expected the baby so soon. The commotion in the streets and the flames that lit up the room threw her and her mother into great panic as they sat near Bena's bed hoping to shield her from fright should she wake up. Avraham was not at home, having left earlier in the day to make his rounds with the students, and now the two women visualized him in the clutches of the infuriated Cossacks. They tried to hide their fears from each other by keeping their eyes on the floor while listening to the screams and the clip-clop of the galloping horses. The acrid smells of burning straw-thatched roofs forced through the window and door spaces bit their nostrils and irritated their eyes. Afraid to light the lamp, they sat in the dark room lit only by leaping patterns of flame from without making the walls and ceiling grotesque.

Mirele raised herself from the bench with difficulty and walked across the room to sit near the window where she allowed herself to moan when the pains became too strong. Chaya watched as she did so and when she heard her cry out loud, asked in a harsh voice, "Why are you weeping, have you never went through a pogrom before? Is this the first time you face danger for yourself and your family? You should be steeled by now. Now come, you must not wake the child. We are safe here, the little house is of stone and its roof is of tin. Why do you sit and worry so much that it makes you cry? The beasts cannot burn us out of here, and you better come back over here, the smoke near the window will suffocate you." Chaya closed her mouth now, as she felt the tears choking her.

Mirele tried to get back to her seat but could not raise herself. "Oh, Mother, I am in labor, I feel the child coming," she cried out.

Chaya looked at her in panic, and muttered, "Oh dear God, now?" She went quickly across the room to console her with forced calm, "So you decided to bring your child into the world now, just when the blackguards are trying to wipe us off the Earth, good, we will show them that we are not ready to do their bidding. Let me put you into bed and I will go to fetch Rachel the Midwife."

She tried to lift Mirele into the bed, but had a difficult time, and listened while Mirele pleaded with her, crying in pain and terror, "Mother, how can you go out into that inferno, what makes you think you will find Rachel in the house at such time? Mother, what are we to do?"

"I'll tell you what to do, you just stay here as you are and I'll go through the rear of the courtyard and if Rachel is alive yet, I'll bring her back with me." She was already halfway out of the window before she finished and forced the shutters back into place leaving Mirele, with the added guilt for her mother's safety, who screamed, "Oh Mother, don't go, I can wait, please don't go out of the house alone," as she felt the water break in her and run down between her thighs, the infant's head forcing down with determination.

How long she suffered her torment she was unable to gauge, till she became aware that the patterns of flame on the ceiling became almost invisible, leaving the room quite dark, a sign that the perpetrators of disaster were already satisfied with their fiendish executions and on the way out of the plundered community. Her ears however began to pick up noise that sounded like pressure on the door and she froze in terror. "Good God, not now, not when I can't run with my child somewhere for safety," she crouched, fearing to let a groan escape her, her eyes wandering for a place to hide Bena, before the door was broken in.

The pressure increased and with it fears that mingled together with her birth pangs and she found herself on her knees, her head bobbing in anguish on the edge of the bench, and without restraint now gave way to uncontrolled shrieks.

"Mirele let me in, hurry, open the door fast." She recognized Avraham's voice through her screams and felt somewhat pacified but still so muddled in her mind that she was powerless and stayed in the same position, the water wetting her clothes, forming a pool around her. "Mirele, it is me, Avraham, don't be afraid to open the door, I want to come in," she heard him say and something in his voice lent her a bit of rationality and hushed her. She tried to get to her feet but failed and awkwardly dragged her heavy body to the door, pulled the bar that held it fast then shrieked as an agonizing pain shot through her and she fell in the way of the opening. Avraham heard her torment and heavy fall and gently managed to squeeze himself through the narrow space and get inside. He was unable to raise her up but dragged her with difficulty to the bed and helped her get into it, and not knowing what to do for her, pulled her wet clothes off and finally got her into a dry nightshirt. "Tell me what you want me to do for you to help you," he pleaded with her, above her intermittent cries. But she only shook her head and pointed to the door and he understood that she was waiting for help from the midwife, and he stood by the bed feeling very helpless.

Bena awoke and began to whimper that she had a bad dream and wanted to go into Mama's bed, and sat rubbing her sleep-swollen eyes. Mirele sent him to pacify the child, but before he reached her, he had to answer Chaya's knock at the door.

She came in with Rachel, both their faces black with soot, but with a show of triumph. "Light the lamp, Avraham, we cannot welcome a new Jewish life in the dark. Thank God you are home safe and that the sons of mad dogs are gone, may their loves and lives be as wretched as they make ours. Rachel and I will help you Mirele, and with God's help you will not suffer much longer."

Both women washed their blackened hands while Avraham went to calm Bena, but found her fast asleep again. Hunger pains tormented him but he went to the watershed and washed from head to toe, then replaced his torn clothes and went back inside to find that Mirele had already delivered and that a small voice announced her arrival with hesitant infant cries. He stood waiting while Rachel attended to Mirele's needs, then went to her and looked down on her pale, tear-stained face and was shaken by remorse that she had to suffer so much pain for the birth of their children. Mirele was resting on her back, and her eyes beckoned to him to lean close to her, then in a weak voice that was almost a whisper, asked if he had been caught by the Cossacks in the City.

"Yes, but let us forget it now. I feel fine so let's not worry about what might have been. Do you want something, can I get for you an orange or preserves? Are you comfortable?" He smiled down at her and she returned the smile and said slowly and quietly, "Another girl, Avraham." And just as quietly he answered her complaint with, "*Mazel tov*, my wife, may the Lord bless you and our child that you brought forth with so much pain and anxiety! I did not order from you a son or daughter, I just wanted a healthy child. Mirele, you sound like my mother must have sounded when she gave birth to my sister Nahama. My father used to tell us how she carried on and never forgave my sister for having been born a girl and not a boy. Thank God for another child whom we will love as much as we do Bena. Now rest before the baby begins to try out her lung power."

He began to walk away from the bed but noticed her weeping eyes and wondered how silly such a clever woman can be to eat her heart out because she did not give birth to a boy. Halfway across the room he stopped when he heard her sobbing, turned back to her and gently said, "Oh dear Lord, forgive this irreverence and thank Thee for your blessings. You delivered both mother and child without mishap to their beings, and we are thankful to Thee." He pleaded with his eyes turned ceilingwise, then added to his wife, "I think the reason you women want sons is so that you will be able to manipulate their wives when your own children get too wise for you."

This bit of philosophy brought a twinkle to her eyes and a smile to her face and Avraham felt free to leave her. He went to the table where the new baby was being bathed and swaddled by Rachel and his mother-in-law, and looked closely at his child and broke into joyous laughter as he called back to the bed, "I do not know whom this child resembles, but never did I see an infant this beautiful before, she is a delight to behold."

The following few days convinced Chaya and Mirele that Bena was not overly happy with her new sister. She took to fussing with her food and whining a good deal and refused to play with little friends. When asked what troubled her, the girl ran to her mother's bed in tears and buried her head deep into the pillows and cried, "Grandma will drop the baby to the floor, just look how she holds her, her little head will come off."

She sobbed as if her heart would break until Mirele raised her to the side of her bed and put her arms around her. "Why do you say such things and why are you so cranky?" Mirele wanted to know.

"Can't you see little Rachel's hands and feet hanging down like they will drop off? And look how she wiggles her little head!" Bena rubbed her eyes and nose while the two women looked at each other with some understanding and Chaya said to her, "I'll tell you what, while I bathe your sister you can roll her swaddling bands up into neat bundles, and after that you can make a little bed of the long pillow for her, putting it on its side and making a deep trench in it by pounding hard with your arm. Would you like to do that for her?"

Bena looked with some distrust at her grandmother's smiling face, then at her mother's reassuring nod and later did just that and was pleased with herself. Gradually she began to help care for the baby and became so absorbed that she forgot to cry or fuss with her food, and when Chaya encouraged her to help bathe the infant, and she touched the pink soft body of her little sister that stretched and yawned in the soapy water, warmth of love such as she never felt before spread over her.

Rachel's laughing disposition grew with her, filling the house with her constant joy of living, and drawing her sedate sister along her path with her childish prattle.

2

Katynka

IN THE COURTYARD FACING THE BACK room of Avraham's family home, stood a one-room house built of stone and mortar in which Katynka lived. She was left this house by her father, who had beat her mother to death while in a drunken rage, then disappeared from Ukraine. Katynka was his only child, fourteen then, and was already married to thirty-nine-year-old Stepan Gorezdykh, petty officer in the czarist army, stationed at the fort outside New Plan, the second-largest neighborhood in the city of Kamenets-Podolski.

Officer Gorezdykh had been fond of the "bitter drop" in his youth; he drank to be gay among his peers but later on it served him to forget his childless marriage and the hate for his wife Katynka. He drank heavily, bringing home very little of his earnings for their needs. Drinking was a way out. He could not think then how the young, red-cheeked Katynka, whose teeth used to bite into a raw cabbage like into a dainty cookie, her cheeks bright with color and hard as apples, had turned into a colorless, toothless shrunken stranger who hated his very existence.

When he died of typhus, she was only thirty-six years old but looked at least sixty. Her hair was grey, her toothless mouth shrunken, and she walked with a dragging gait. It was during his illness that Stepan had an inkling of what kind of a mother Katynka might have been. He felt her tender compassion when she fed or washed him, handling him as one would a helpless child, singing all the while in a monotone that amused him. A few days before he took a turn toward the end, she told him that she will give him a family of children for whom he must make an effort to get well. He did not know what to think of her promise, whether her mind was straying or perhaps his own. Why had she become so good to him now?

In back of their little house was a lime hill from which the leather tanners of New Plan carried off bucketfuls to use as hair remover from animal hides. From this lime hill, Katynka too carried off a bucketful and took it into the house and turned it over on the table, added water, and began kneading it into a mound, while Stepan looked on. When she felt the dough-like consistency in her hands becoming firmer, she divided it into five separate pieces, dividing them into five shaped balls, and formed faces into them. As she worked, she tried to make them look like Stepan, but no matter how many times she kneaded them and reshaped them they all emerged from her hands looking very much like her Mongolian father. They all had inherited his high cheekbones, deep-set eyes, and round face.

"They all look like little Kalmukies," Stepan laughed with ridicule, but she paid no attention to him and when she finished them to her liking, placed them in a row on the windowsill near his bed. When his fever was not too high, he scrutinized each one separately and fabricated pipedreams, planning their education—a much higher one than he had (he didn't question Katynka whether she had designated them sons). His sons were to go to Kiev universities and become cadets before they became Cossacks in the czarist cavalry!

He even planned their marriages—not to poor ignorant girls from poor backgrounds, no, his sons will marry nobility and live the good life! Nevertheless, for the few days that remained while his mind and body were deteriorating toward death, he felt those "children" bring him closer to Katynka and merge them all into an intimate family.

After his death, Katynka went to church and begged her priest to baptize the "children," and was deeply wounded when he told her to throw those "pieces of mud" on the garbage heap and forget them. She stalked off in great anger, her face sullen and stubborn, owing that now for the first time in her life she will disobey him. When she came home, she picked up each child-head and tenderly petted and kissed it, giving it an endearing name, and moved them from the windowsill to the table in a semi-circle facing her own seat so that she could see them better and converse with them at close range.

Katynka had no friends. Of the two relatives she had, one was a busy doctor and the other a farmer, both living far from her. At the time she had inherited the house, her neighbors were Gentiles, and the few Jewish families that lived nearby knew that they had to keep their distance. But with the years the small houses were left behind either because of death or because they were too small for the growing families, and were taken over one at a time by Jewish families, so that in the last ten years or so Katynka was the only non-Jew left in the all-Jewish community. At no time did she exchange a "good morning," or a "good day" with her neighbors. She carried within her the animosity for Jews she had sucked in with her mother's milk and later strengthened in her church, where the belief was that they, the Jews, killed her Christ.

Now that Stepan was dead these two years, she lived in complete isolation and loneliness. One day on the way home from marketing, she noticed a grocery store had opened cross corner from hers, and a woman seen from the window looked like a bewigged Jewess. Katynka walked very fast to get to her home and in great excitement told her "children" what she had seen, and warned them, "Never should you go in there to spend your good money, take it direct to Stanko Stremilkov's store as you always did!" She did not allow herself as much as another glance into Mirele's store for more than six months.

In midwinter of that year a heavy blizzard broke out covering all the houses, courtyards, and street so high with snow drifts that it was hard to distinguish one from the other. And to such a morning Katynka awoke to find herself without kerosene oil and food in the house, because she had not yet received her pension check, which was delayed for some reason. She stood shivering at the snow-covered window and wondered what to do. She looked at her children and pacified them gently, "You need not whimper, your Mama will dress warm and go to the Post Office for the check, I am sure it is there already. From there I will go to Stanko's store and buy everything for you. Promise that you will not cry, you hear me?" She spoke to them all the while feeling the hunger that tormented her; she will not be able to venture outdoors. That night she went to sleep in a cold, dark house, miserable and depressed but with hope in her heart that in the morning she will find the blizzard cleared, and then she will be able to help herself.

And so it was, the blizzard had cleared, completely died as if for lack of force, but it left a corpse of snow around so that it stood in the way of anyone who tried to pass a doorstep. Katynka came out of her house bundled in a large shawl with the kerosene can in her hand and the intention of forcing her way to the Post Office for her check, but after a few steps knew that her hopes were in vain and came back into the house. "You see my children, I can't go, the snow wants to bury me like the earth did your father. We will have to wait for tomorrow, perhaps then it will not be so badly piled up." She smiled at them to placate their fears and their disappointment. Hunger and cold made her restless and found her either near the door or window, poking out at the small snow-covered homes and the story-high stacks of planks in the lumberyard.

The tall hills of wood planks were completely enveloped in hard-packed mountains of snow that glistened back at the brilliant sun with thousands of tiny crystal jewels. But most of all, Katynka's eyes came back to chimneys that spouted smoke that told her that there in those little homes were warmth, food, and most likely the smells of fresh baked bread. How she envied those chimney owners! She turned to the table, drawer, and her cold stove again and again in desperate hope of finding a crust of bread she may have overlooked, but turned away in despair. In the late afternoon she tied her shawl around herself again and picked up the oil can again, this time with great determination to get to Stanko's store intending to ask him for credit, something she had never done before in all the years of her dire poverty.

As soon as she stepped out of her door, the snow began to dance before her eyes and dizziness overtook her; when she took a few steps she found both shallow and deep trenches to trap her. Slowly and with a fast-beating heart she made some progress in reaching the corner, and then saw her folly. The broad main street was absolutely impassable, not even a wagon's wheel rut broke the undisturbed continuity of the hard, high snow that stood in huge ridges like ghosts in the night. She felt a queer lightness in her head and was forced to turn back; as she did she faced the Jewess's store just across the narrow courtyard and without much thinking made a desperate move and began to cross over the huge snowdrifts, raising her legs high in the air and after much struggle found herself mounting three icy, snow-covered stairs to the door. There she stood a while breathing hard, pulling the cold air through her runny nose, then opened the door and shuffled inside.

A strong aroma of spices, dry cereals, herring, and kerosene oil hit her frozen sense of smell and increased her hunger to wild heights. She stood waiting for someone to ask her what she wanted; the store was silent as a tomb, and when she raised her tearing eyes found it just as gloomy and cold. Her anger began to rise as she muttered, "Just like a Jew, no consideration for others," fearing that she would have to go home empty-handed. She stood a while longer, then turned to the door ready to leave, and heard someone approaching from another direction and waited.

"I am sorry if I kept you waiting, I did not think anyone would brave this weather," Mirele said, as she lit two lamps. "What do you need?" she asked, watching Katynka's frozen sullen face, and added helpfully, "Look around, perhaps you will see what you came for." Seeing that she didn't seem to remember, Mirele took the can out of Katynka's frozen hand and brought it back filled to the top.

"I can't pay for it now, I have to wait until I get my pension check, can't go for it now because of the snow." Katynka looked down at the can as she spoke.

"But you did not come out in such a snow storm just for the oil alone? Have you enough food in the house? In such weather one cannot know when we can leave our home." Mirele watched her customer's hunger-shriveled face with the down-cast eyes running over with tears and waited until she said that she wanted black bread and a herring, and then reminded her that she had no money to pay with. "When you will have it, you will come in and pay for those things," Mirele simply told her as she slipped the things into a sack and helped her down the slippery stairs with the can full of oil.

The way back was even more hazardous for Katynka because of her inability to balance herself with her bundles and the hunger weakness that assailed her and magnified the dizziness she suffered from the white of the snow. At last inside the house, she pulled the bread from the sack and tore at it like an animal, stuffing her mouth full, pushing it down with tears that choked her throat, which gave out strange, crying sounds. She looked around at her silent brood and lit a fire in the stove and lit the lamp even though it was early in the day. Little by little she peeled some of her outdoor clothes off that she lived in since the house became so cold and began to feel better.

"Now my dear children your mother feels good, it's warm and light in our house and we have bread and herring. I will tell you what I have done while I left you alone here, but you won't believe it. I went to the Jewess's store for food and oil. But you know there was no other way for me, don't you? The snow got in my way with every step and your mother felt like she would die out there. And what would become of you? I didn't bring you any cinnamon sticks or brown rock candy because I think that Jews don't know about such things and they sell only what they eat themselves. Oh yes, she gave me what I asked for without money until I will get the pension check, but she will want twice as much for everything." Katynka, like her mother, taught her children how evil the Jews were.

When the snow packed down and wagons began to move in the streets, Katynka made her way to the Post Office and received her check, and went direct to Mirele's store to pay her debt but found Avraham there standing at a counter reading something from a book, and she did not know what to say to him. "Wait, I'll call my wife," he said without raising his eyes from the book, and went through a door from which Mirele soon came, and seeing Katynka, smiled cheerfully and said to her, "See, we overcame our hardship with God's help. Now we can go into the streets again and go on with our lives." Mirele buttoned her cotton padded jacket as she spoke and was prepared to wait on her.

"How much do I owe you," Katynka asked. "Here, I marked it down, it came to 12 kopeks." Mirele held out the little book of accounts to show her, not knowing that the woman did not know one numeral from another, and Katynka counted the money into her palm and left without another word.

When she came home, she sat down at the table and looked at her children very thoughtfully, then clucked her tongue looking a bit bewildered, and spoke up as if in apology for her act. "Who can be smart enough to understand a Jew? I came into her store for the first time and told her that I had no money to pay her and she wanted to know if I had enough food in the house! One would think that she is a sister. And if I had taken more food, she would let me, although I am sure that she does not even know where we live, who I am. She could see that I am not of her people, that I am a Christian, and still when I went to the store to pay her, I counted for her to take the skin off my back for the things she trusted me with. But this I don't understand: why did she ask me for less money than Stanko asks for the same things. A Jew does a good deed only when he makes a profit on it. She did not fool me yet."

Her children listened but made no comment. They were good children, they listened to their mother without countering statements or disobeying her wishes, no matter how hard a task they were given. When she sent one to the well for water, she put the bucket near him and after a short while said quickly to him, "Sit, I'll go for it myself, you will get yourself all wet." When she sent another one for firewood to the lumberyard, she changed her mind shortly and stopped him with, "No, you better don't go, you'll get splinters into your fingers." Stepan, the one she called her oldest son, was always "sent" for kerosene oil, and she stopped him like the others with a motion of her hand that told him to "sit, I'll go myself, you will spill the kerosene all over you and smell from it so bad your brothers wouldn't want to be near you."

The two encounters she had with Mirele threw her into some befuddlement and she was drawn to the store time and again. She began to buy her daily necessities there, one item at a time, so she could find herself more often in the store. From Stanko she bought only meat, and when he asked her where she got the other groceries, she just shrugged her shoulders; when he pressed her for an answer, she left him altogether and went for meat to the public market. She came to the store more often as time went by and sometimes spent two and three hours a day watching while Mirele worked hard and talked to her tradespeople in her pleasant, soft voice. Katynka became acquainted with many customers of the store, Jewish in the main, and she noted that most of them wore worn and faded clothes like herself and shoes that were overturned, as were many of her own people's. And as a drunk coming out of his stupor, she saw for the first time that not all Jews are rich, as she heard many times. When Mirele had to leave the store for a while, she simply left it in her care, saying, "I'll be back soon, please keep an eye on the store."

Saturdays and on Jewish holidays when the store was closed, Katynka talked most of the day to her children, telling them how long those days seemed to be; of course she sent them on more errands, then generally had to tell them, "Sit, sit, I'll go myself for it," by which she ended all her solicitations with them. But to Stepan, her eldest, she would nod her head and say, "Yes, I understand well why you don't want to go to the priest and ask him to baptize you and your brothers. I know that he does not even want to forgive me for loving you and your brothers. You are right in not going to him."

Time slipped by while Katynka fused with the store fixtures and they became as one. Tradespeople stopped and talked to her and she answered in the beginning with a motion of the head, to denote her attention, later on however she began to exchange words with them and soon found herself talking to them about herself. When they did not find her in her accustomed place on the overturned wooden box in the corner of the store, they told Mirele that they missed her and Mirele never failed to tell her that. On two occasions when Katynka became sick, Mirele came to her house to make fire in the stove and light in the room and brought cooked food from her house.

It was then that she became acquainted with the "children" for the first time. Katynka watched from the bed as Mirele stood a long time at the table and examined and admired each head separately, and felt impressed. Mirele not only admired them, but wondered how the backward, crude woman with clumsy hands that had known only rough labor had the ability to produce such skill. Every one of the heads and faces looked different from the others and at the same time carried a resemblance to each other! She looked back at her neighbor and smilingly said, "Katynka, you did not make these children with your hands and fingers but with your heart and soul."

On Friday eve a Jew feels like a king when he ushers in the Sabbath like a bride to the four corners of his home while the entire household is full of joy and pride that sings. Avraham stands at the table waiting for his wife and mother-in-law to be done with the last-minute supper preparations so they can join him before he says the benediction over the little glass of raisin wine. Four candles that the women blessed a few minutes back shed a soft light from the height of their polished brass candlesticks to the leaf-patterned, white tablecloth that was set for five. Bena and Rachel were dressed in their Sabbath best, with hair that glistened from a recent wash and kerosene rinse and was braided with red ribbons. They were impatient for their father to begin the blessing over the wine so they could partake of some food. A restless little hand began in the meantime to touch things, a spoon, fork, and even a knife, then reached for the white napkin that covered the *challah*.* But before she pulled it off, Bena began to tug at her dress and whispered, "Don't do that!" calling her father's attention. Avraham looked at his children with affection and said to the younger one, Rachel, "You can't sit still very long can you? A big three-year-old girl must wait for her father to make the Sabbath blessing over the *challah* before she could uncover it." Rachel lowered her head but looked sideways at Bena and smirked.

At last the two women took their places at the table and Avraham raised the little glass of wine into the palm of his hand and with his eyes closed began to sway back and forth and chant the Kaddish. "And it was evening, and it was morning, the sixth day. And the Heaven and the Earth were finished and all their host. And on the seventh day God had finished his work which He had made. And God blessed the

---

* Hebrew for a loaf of leavened bread, typically plaited in form, traditionally baked to celebrate the Jewish Sabbath.

seventh day, and hallowed it, because he rested thereon from His work which He had created and made." Holding now the little glass a little bit higher, he added, "Blessed are thou, O Lord, King of the Universe, who created the fruit of the wine." Now he drank some of the wine and passed the glass to Mirele, who also drank a bit and passed it on to her mother, who sipped a little and then gave it to Bena.

All this time Rachel's mischievous eyes followed the glass around with much concern, seeing how the contents lowered with each turn, fearing that none would be left for her. Bena who knew what was in her sister's mind, purposely held the glass longer to her mouth and looked teasingly into her face to make her think that she meant to drink it all up. "Mama, Mama, look, she is drinking all the wine from the glass," the youngster cried.

"Bena, give the rest of the wine to your sister, you have had enough," Avraham told Bena, and to Mirele he pleaded to serve supper fast or he would fall asleep at the table.

"Yes, my husband, I know that the little bit of wine already went to your head and has the effect of a cudgel on you, it must be stronger than you are," she jested, and began to serve the soup with thin, long noodles that her mother had made early in the morning.

There was a knock at the door and before anyone had a chance to answer it, Katynka shuffled in, clenching her hands and crying that her middle son Venya got lost, using this strategy to come into the house. "Sure," Chaya thought, "when a poor man sits down to a meal, the devil sends him a guest!" She knew that someday Katynka would find a way into the house. Mirele raised herself from her seat and told her neighbor to sit down to supper with them, and when she saw her hesitate, added, "Sit down between the girls, there is plenty of room on the bench, and by the time we are finished with our meal, your Venya will come back to you."

But Katynka made out not to hear or see, and found a place in a corner, near the stove, and sat down there. Mirele brought her a plate with fish, fish soup, and a big piece of the Sabbath *challah*. The food tasted good, and Katynka enjoyed it, chewing it slowly to make it last longer while she sat warming her bitter soul in the glow of the Jewish

Sabbath. Her eyes followed all the actions of the children at the table, smiling at the pranks they played on each other. Mirele brought her some tea and cornmeal cakes her mother had baked, and Rachel slipped off her seat to bring her a lump of sugar, asking, "Katynka, you want to take some sugar to your children?" although she had never seen them. "No, I have sugar at home, you better sit down and finish your supper," she told her, feeling that Avraham and Chaya did not like to see the children near her.

The meal finished, and Avraham began saying grace, filling the room with melodious singsong, and Chaya told the children to make ready for bed. Chaya helped Mirele to clear the table and she put the dishes in a deep pan of hot water. Katynka stayed on, her eyes were half-closed and she seemed asleep, but she was fully aware of what was going on around her; she liked the warmth of the stove and the good smells of the Sabbath food that Chaya had prepared. It had taken her years of yearning to peer into this house and now she sat there as an uninvited guest, and on their Sabbath night.

The harmony of the room and its inhabitants were strange but enchanting to her and she did not think of moving and undo it. "Come Katynka, the candles are almost burnt out and we will be left in the dark soon, let me take you home." Mirele put her hand on her shoulder to encourage her to get up, and Katynka raised herself from the bench and left without saying good night. "What did she want here? Who needs her around the children?" Chaya muttered under her breath. "Who knows, childless woman and a Gentile at that, she might give the children the evil eye."

Mirele was about to leave Katynka at her door after bidding her good night, but felt her arms caught in an embrace, while Katynka stammered, "I don't know how to make you understand how much better I feel now, I was so heavy-hearted all day."

"Why did you wait so long to come into my house? I told you many times not to isolate yourself. You sit in the store all the time, yet you never come into the house. You know you can, whenever you feel like being with others."

Mirele could not see Katynka in the dark of the night, but she felt her struggling with tears in her throat, and asked her, "What is it Katynka? You have not been yourself lately, you want to tell me what is troubling you?"

"I do not know, but of late I feel my loneliness more than ever. Even my children don't matter to me now. Tell me the truth, my friend, should I be in the way if I came in to your house once in a while in the evenings? I would sit and mend the children's stockings and their clothes if I were sure that no one in the house would mind." Mirele felt hot drops on her wrist, and pulled the lonely woman close to reassure her that she would be welcome, knowing well that her mother would grumble and that Avraham would probably never say a word to her, and both would try to keep the children away from her. She said a cheerful good night, and left her to walk across the courtyard to her door, pity stirring in her for her forlorn neighbor.

Buroch the *shadkhan*, known from one end of New Plan to the other, is a short, emaciated, kindly red-bearded man, past fifty, with a wife who gave him six children, all girls! He was proclaimed as a man of wonders who could produce a bride or bridegroom out of his sleeve if need be, though for his own daughters, who were overdue for the marriage canopy, he was unable to show any miracles. First of all, he did not have money for their dowries—which is a big drawback. But worse still, if he found a prospective bridegroom who was willing to take a wife without a dowry, and he was a son from a good family (and that carried great esteem in the community) then his "profession" had to be considered first, for that would be his livelihood. Buroch knew all the young people around him from the day of their birth, and he kept a watchful eye on them as they blossomed into young men and maidens. When he saw the time draw near for a boy or girl to be considered a likely "candidate," at the age of thirteen or fourteen, he began to weave his web around them, stopping at no handicap. And handicaps there are plenty among the children of the poor Jews with whom he did his business—and he did not have to go out of his way to find them.

Childhood sicknesses left faces with pockmarks, deaf ears, partial blindness, and crippled limbs. To this was added small or no dowries among the girls, and little knowledge of how to make a living among the boys. As if these disadvantages were not enough stones in Buroch's way, he found yet a bigger one, nay the biggest, known as *yichus*,* or family dignity, honor. Each side had to be convinced that the other side comes from a religious, honest, and learned family, that their forbearers were among the Talmudic sages. However, Buroch's motto was, "Every girl needs a husband, and every boy needs a wife, and I, Buroch, must provide food and dowries for my six daughters." And so he tried to meet all the requirements of his clients.

He walked briskly, his red beard high in the air, looking very preoccupied as if with very important business but just the same Buroch saw everybody that passed him by, and he fine-combed them one by one, fearing that he might overlook someone important to him. Now he was on his way on a mission of "mercy."

He came to the back door of Avraham's home and opened it without so much as a warning. Chaya was bent over a bench trying to pick up something from the floor and when she straightened up, came face to face with him. "My, you gave me a fright! I did not hear you come in. Sit down Buroch, and tell me how your wife and children are." She was quite busy, but she could not turn her back on him.

"Thank the Lord, my family is in good health. Chaya, I came to talk to you about something very important. Sit down so that you can listen to me," he motioned her to a bench.

"Buroch, now? Don't you see that I am in the middle of cleaning? If you came to talk to me about our Bena, then you should go to her father or mother, not to me, though I believe that it is a little too early for your services yet. Don't worry, no one will snatch her away from your eager hands; please go home in peace," and she tried to continue with her cleaning.

"I did not come here to talk about Bena, I came to do you the biggest favor one person can do for another. I have a match for you that will make up for all the unhappiness in your widowed life!" His

* Yiddish for lineage.

red beard trembled with eagerness.

Chaya straightened her back and slowly and in a mocking tone asked, "Are you out of your mind? God forbid, Buroch, what do I want with a husband now? I am an old woman bent with the load of troubles I carried all my life. Stop poking fun at me and go. Go with you, don't talk nonsense to me, I am too busy to listen to you."

"But I am not poking fun at you, I mean every word I say, and I will not leave you until you promise to see him. He is a widower, all his children are married off, and he is a cantor with a voice that can melt a heart of stone. He sings in the big synagogue in Zhvanets. Right after Passover* I want you to go there with me, so that you can look him over," he urged and commanded in one tone. To be rid of him she promised to think it over, and edged him out the door. Although he came again and again, he always found her too busy to talk with him.

The approaching holidays kept Mirele occupied in the store, her heavy, pregnant body slowing her motions and delaying the orders, causing some rumbling that made Katynka angry, and in her own way, she calmed those women, explaining that Mirele could not work faster because of her pregnancy. Worse yet, Mirele lost half of the burlap sack of walnuts she bought for the store and was unable to complete the holiday orders without them. She could not understand how they could be missing from the store attic when the entrance to it was only through the store. She asked Avraham to solve the mystery, but like her and her mother, they were all only able to look puzzled.

Not until three days before the holidays did Chaya solve the riddle, when she found nut shells in back of their house when she was hanging the wash. She called in Bena from the store, and asked with whom she had played there recently, and where did they get the walnuts. "Grandma, you know that I couldn't play out there in the last week because I had to help Mama in the store. But I suppose that Yossi and Moyshele played there and that the nuts they had won from me," she simply answered.

"They won walnuts from you? When? Are these the nuts your mother

---

* A Jewish annual holiday commemorating the exodus of the Israelites from slavery in ancient Egypt.

is missing from the attic?" Chaya asked her, though she now divined the answer. "You mean that you were foolish enough to play with the twins that are known as champions of the skull-cap game. Didn't you know that their mother never bought nuts for the holidays because she knew that the two boys will win them away from the children around here and bring to her? Why did you let them take you in to such game? You are indeed a silly girl; you'll never guess what trouble you caused your mother!"

Bena looked at her grandmother timidly and was about to say something but saw that Rachel was about to tease her and not wanting to show how their grandmother's ridicule affected her, shouted, "Why do you make so much fuss of it? It was only half a sack full!! Mama can make believe that she bought only a half sack of nuts this Passover, she won't miss it so much!" And she stuck her tongue out at her sister in defiance.

In the evening when the girls were asleep, Chaya told Mirele and Avraham how the nuts disappeared, and how their daughter reasoned that they could imagine that they bought only 50 pounds instead of a 100-pound sack, and they all had a good laugh over it, somewhat relieved that at least the mystery was cleared up.

Four days after the Passover holidays Mirele gave birth to a dark little girl who resembled Katynka's clay brood. Her cheekbones were high, the eyes slanted and deep-set, and her nose flat. When Avraham saw the child he laughed and told Mirele that for a change, they now had a Kalmyk baby.

"I knew that was going to happen," Chaya cried, "I begged her not to see so much of the balls of lime that woman calls children! But she would not listen to me, and all through the pregnancy she found reasons to go to her house! Would it be a boy, it would not be so bad, but a girl!" Again Avraham had cause to laugh and he asked his mother-in-law why it would not matter if it were a boy. "Well, just so a man looks better than the devil, he is nice enough." Then she saw misery on her daughter's face and quickly altered her agitated tone and added, "Well, well, we will keep her, but you will have to save up a big dowry for her."

Mirele looked down on her infant and tears welled up in her eyes. "It is true, Mother, you did warn me, but Katynka had no one to turn to and I gave it little thought when I knew that she needed me. I had faith that God would protect my child," she agreed with her mother.

"And God did understand and did protect your child and you as well," Avraham assured her. "The infant is well and your delivery came through without any more trouble than with your other children. Don't fret, God is with us and we will marry her off without too much worry. Buroch will not let her remain an old maid," he consoled her. "And if you agree, we will name her Adah."

Buroch did not intend to let Chaya remain a widow much longer. More so, didn't he get her promise to give thought to his proposition? But he bided his time, waiting until the Shavuot* holiday approached, then called on her again. "Chaya, I want you to come with me; you must hear that cantor sing, you will never believe me that he can sing all your cares away. Only when you see and hear him will you be convinced that you are wasting away your life being a widow." He ran out of breath and had to stop talking.

"But I can't leave my daughter now with a newborn infant and so much work in the store before the holidays—a fine time for me to go chasing after some man just to please you," she said impatiently.

"But," Buroch persisted, "we don't have to go before the last day before the holiday, after you have done your cleaning, preparing your baking and even some of the cooking, and believe me, no one will miss you for the few days that we will be away." He stopped for breath again, then continued, "We will hire a wagon and a driver that will take us straight to Zhvanets, and come there just in time for evening worship, then stay the two days in an inn, and come right back to take over the household work again—that is if you don't see things my way."

The long-winded advice cut off his breath again and Chaya quickly took the opportunity to put another rock in his path. "Tell me Buroch, with what will we pay the driver for his wagon and his service and with what will we pay the innkeeper? The money we do not have?" But

---

* Shavuot combines two major religious observances: the grain harvest of the early summer and the giving of the Torah on Mount Sinai seven weeks after the exodus from Egypt.

nothing stopped him from his plans and he assured her not to worry, "as God will provide," while his red beard and eyes went up toward the ceiling in silent supplication. Mirele and Avraham heard them in the store, heard their voices rising and falling as they wrangled with each other, and finally Mirele went into the house to assure her that she could go.

"Mother, you know that Bena loves to take care of little Adah and Rachel is no trouble at all when Avraham is with her. Go and don't worry about us, you deserve a few days away from the housework. And above all keep an open mind."

"My daughter, I think that you are clear out of your mind, sending me after a husband at my age. What do I have need of a husband now—so that he should eat my heart out and shorten my life? I was married, gave birth to three children, and I am blessed with twelve grandchildren, what else do I owe the world? Or are you trying to rid yourself of me?"

Mirele went back to the store a little peeved at her mother's accusation, leaving Buroch triumphant. "See," he pointed a finger in Mirele's direction, "see what a clever daughter you have. She understands more than you do. So I will be back the day before Shavuot and arrange with a driver that he calls for us at daybreak." And he bolted out the door for fear of more objections from Chaya.

Two weeks later he succeeded in bringing her, grumbling, to Zhvanets in a straw-padded wagon. They arrived at the inn at sunset and they already felt the holiday ushering in among the villagers as families of worshippers with their many children, dressed in holiday clothes with faces shining with tender devotion, were on the way to the house of prayer.* The innkeeper merely showed them to their rooms and left them with the instructions how to get to the synagogue. Buroch washed and changed into the only other suit he possessed and wore for the Sabbath as well as holidays and weddings. He went quickly to the guest room to meet Chaya, hoping that she too had hurried so that they could attend all the services, but to his disappointment did not find her there. He sat down to wait, restlessly crossing and

---

* The synagogue.

uncrossing his long legs, stroking his red beard with nervous fingers, and worrying if she had fallen asleep after the day-long wagon ride.

When finally she appeared he eyed her with so much admiration that she gave him a questioning look that made him drop his eyes to the floor. Washed of the road dust, she was dressed in a black velvet skirt that was embroidered with tiny black glass beads on three ruffles at the bottom and a white silk blouse, now turned yellow with the years, which she topped with a cape of the same velvet that also sparkled with tiny beads. She had tucked a silk leaf-patterned kerchief becomingly around the wrinkled, soft face that her eyes dominated and added a black lace scarf on top of her head. She was so transformed that Buroch was overwhelmed! "Chaya, I had almost given you up for lost, but I see that you did remember that I was waiting for you. We will have to hurry, it is already late."

He led her out and stole a look at her now and then, not believing himself that she was the same woman he knew so many years. In the synagogue, Buroch found a place for himself in the men's section downstairs, and Chaya went up to the curtained balcony. She carried her prayer book although she could not read one word in it and stood a while on the top landing looking for a "sayer," a woman worshipper who led those who could not read and did not know when to weep, when to beat their breasts in contrition, and when to say "Amen." She found a seat near one such group, against the curtain that cut them off from the sight of the men below, and sat down ready to join the rest.

She did not wait long before she heard a strong masculine voice opening the services, singing sweet and with much feeling. Chaya parted the curtain a bit and looked down at the cantor, and saw a short, stocky man who looked to be in his early sixties, and as far as she could make out from the distance, pretty handsome. Suddenly she felt a strong tug at her sleeve and turned to find the entire group of women looking at her with reproach; she dropped the curtain feeling a flush of embarrassment spread over her face as she murmured, "Forgive me." She remembered to keep her back turned to the curtain during the prayers although her ears were tuned to his singing.

On the way back to the inn, Buroch tried very tactfully to draw her out and get some inkling as to her mind, but she gave him little satis-faction: she talked about the old building the synagogue was housed in, about the group of women she sat with, about the "sayer" who knew the prayers by heart—but not one word about the cantor! Buroch tried all sorts of diplomatic maneuvers, but she told him nothing, did not let one word drop from her lips. In the inn she somehow managed to be in the company of the innkeeper's wife, so he was forced to wait for an opportunity when he would be alone with her and he boiled with anger when at last they sat down to dinner and she chose a seat far from his, so far that he could not even read her lips when she spoke to people near her.

Not before she was ready to go to her room for the night did he catch up with her. "Chaya, what in God's name did I do to you that you avoid me as if I had the Plague?" he wanted to know. "I think that you owe me some information, after all we did not come all the way out here just so we could spend the holidays here in the inn; tell me what do you think of the cantor?" he almost pleaded with her.

"What could I tell you? That he sings good? That he does! That he is a handsome male? That he is too, but Buroch, for me he is too short! I know well that you men like tall wives but I like a man that's taller than I am, and not that he should reach with his head to my armpits. Do me a favor and prepare to take me home tomorrow night at the appearance of the first star in the heavens." Her eyes twinkled as she spoke.

Buroch was smitten and began to stutter in excitement as he exclaimed, "Too short for you! Look, your own daughter Mirele, many years she should live, and your Hannah too, they are such pretty women, and they were so young when they married and both their husbands are shorter than they are! And don't I remember your husband Simon, may he rest in peace! He was shorter than you and you married him when you were young and straight as a rod. Now when your back is bent and you are so much shorter, you should not be so particular about something so foolish. Listen to me, Chaya, and don't throw away such a golden opportunity and be sorry later in your old age." As he talked he had a feeling that all his words fell on deaf ears.

He waited in great agitation for the next day to pass, watching for a chance to speak again to Chaya, but she gave him none and he began to worry about the time and money he wasted, money he borrowed from the moneylender, giving him for collateral his wife's brass candlesticks, her golden earrings (the inheritance from a grandmother), and two pillows, all with the hope of redeeming those things when the match was tied—knowing that the cantor was a man of means. And now? How can he go back to his wife and tell her that he can't reclaim her candlesticks for Friday night? And the golden earrings she wears with pride when she goes to the synagogue? And how much longer can they sleep without their pillows? He knew that her curses will fall on him like hailstones and he knew that he deserved them! Didn't she tell him not to tamper with Chaya? How many times has she said to him that Chaya was too long independent to want to tie herself to a man now in her advanced years! But did he want to listen to one word she said?

On the way home, Chaya stuck some money into the palm of Buroch's hand, saying, "Here, take this, Mirele gave it to me to give to you. I hope it will cover the expenses." She could not see his face in the dark of the evening, but heard him mumble, "Thank Thee, my Lord," and soon gave way to snores.

When she came home, Mirele wanted to know how she fared in her venture, and Chaya laughed and told her that the cantor was so handsome and sang so well that she did not want to take him away from his congregation, she left him there. And again she took up her household chores and the care of the new baby, but with the difference that now she sang while she worked, something Mirele had not heard her do since she was a young child.

Sometime later, through the store window Mirele watched and wondered why her mother walked so fast and with such agitation, and she went out to meet her. "Look, Mirele, the postman just gave me this letter, and it looks very important, with so many stamps all over the envelope. It must be from your brother Schmuel from America. Come let us get in the house before Avraham goes away so he can read it." Chaya's hands trembled when she handed the letter to Mirele. They made their way into the store and into the house, where they found Avraham about to leave for his rounds of lessons. Mirele gave him the letter and looked so anxious that he laughed and asked them to sit down because they looked as if they were about to hear Moses read the Ten Commandments from Mount Sinai! He drew the letter from the envelope and began to read.

To my dear Mother, Sister, and Brother-in-law,

First of all I want you to know that we are all in the best of health, and hope to hear the same from you. Our voyage was not a good one, what with the high seas, and small cramped sleeping space, and constant banging engines. Worse still was the perilous rolling of the ship that made us down in the steerage quite ill, and unable to keep our food down. We must have looked very emaciated when Yhitta's brother Fivel and his wife came to claim us on Ellis Island, they wondered that the health inspectors allowed us to come into America! They took us to their home in a town called Brownsville, New York, with all our bundles, and kept us there two days. Then Esther found an apartment for us two blocks away from them. My Yhitta is not happy there because to get to our apartment we have to go through an empty store, but I feel sure that she will get used to it after a while. I keep telling her to imagine that the store is our corridor, and as long as we don't have to pay for it, she should be happy with the extra space. Fivel is trying to get some work for me, and says if he cannot get it soon, he will help me turn the empty store into a little tobacco shop. The children are all in school and are learning the new language fast. In the new, blessed country, they don't have to go to school on the Sabbath, for the

religions of all people are respected and honored, not
like in the czarist-cursed land! Thank the Lord that my
children and theirs will not know the misery that the
Jews suffer in Russia. Write us how things are with all of
you, we send our love and many kisses to you and all the
little girls we love so.

Keep well.

Schmuel, Yhitta, and all my children

Mirele looked at Avraham and though she noted an expression of resistance, but not knowing a reason for it, dismissed it from
her mind. Silence hung over the room as all three worked their own
thoughts, till Avraham let out his breath noisily and with it a mumble
that sounded like "infidels!" The women detected anger and ridicule in
the comment, but didn't question, not wanting to destroy the happiness
they felt from the letter that Schmuel's outlook for the future of his
children and himself was full of confidence.

"Avraham, I wonder why he did not mention anything about his
frozen toes. When you answer him, please ask about them," Chaya said.

"No, he did not mention a lot of other things that I expected he
would," Avraham said, and kept his eyes on the newspaper he held.
Anger at his brother-in-law burned on his face and he did not wait
long to answer him.

My dear Brother-in-law,

We were glad to learn that you and your family are
well, and happy, and I can inform you that we too are all
well, thanks to the One above us. Although the winter
was a difficult one, it left us with little to complain about.
Your sister Mirele's pregnancy is a bit hard on her now,
but she bears up pretty well. Adah went through another
one of her spells of lung fever,* and is coughing less
and less. Now I will write to you not like to a brother-
in-law, but like to a brother for whom I have always

---

* Pneumonia.

carried the fondest feelings and highest respect! I had read your last letter with much amazement, and I have found your words of praise of America sound like you have found the promised land, if only that were true! It is not like you, a man who has always lived within our Lord's word, standing watch over every one of His laws, to say untruths! Since you left for America, three other families went from Kamenets to your promised land with the intentions of establishing their families there, and all three families came back again because they could not practice their religion as they did at home. You know those men that I am talking about, but let me remind you of them. Lable's son Itzchok, Ruvn the Tailor from the City, and Motie the Tinsmith. All pious Jews, and as such they wanted to remain to the end of their days. Here at home they do not work on the holidays and Sabbaths as they would have to in the new land. They all told me that in your America one must go to the factory early every morning and work through the day until late evening, leaving no time for one to put on a prayer shawl and phylacteries and pray as our fathers did. Prayers are left out completely as if devotion to our God is the last thing for a Jew! Also that the children there start to learn very late and learn very little of our Torah, not like the children here at home, where they begin at three or three-and-a-half years, so their memories can retain their education through their lives.

How can a true Talmudist like yourself pull up your roots so completely and transplant your religion and culture on foreign soil, to be blind to its pollution? I know that your need to get away from Russia was a great one, and that you had to settle elsewhere, but can you forget that you are a Jew and must do the Lord's bidding? I did not read in your letter anything about a synagogue, about your children's religious education

being continued from where they left off, or what your
thoughts are on Jews working on the Sabbath and
holidays. And what about your wife Yhitta? Does she
still cover her head with a wig as Jewish women do at
home, did she give that up for a nicer living quarters?
Is the air so foul in your newfound paradise that for a
little comfort you give up your Torah? I am glad that
all is well with your family, but I fail to understand
your brand of happiness that you bubble with in your
letter. We send our best wishes to all of you, saying that
God be with you. Write and tell us how your feet feel,
especially the frozen toes.
    Avraham

Two weeks later Mirele gave birth to her child, a male child who
looked very much like a little ape. His body was covered with a down-
like coat of black hair, his black piercing eyes looked out of a wrinkled
face that had the color and texture of parchment, and his head was
covered with a mass of tangled black hair. Avraham and Mirele looked
down very closely at him and asked each other how they could have
produced such a child. Still they felt blessed with having a son at last.
Avraham felt happy and fulfilled, but Mirele was too tired to share
his victory and wondered how she would be able to pull herself from
her confinement bed and function in the store again.

Chaya prepared the traditional raisins and almonds in the infant's
crib so that the little children that come with the parents to the
circumcision can help themselves. She cooked plenty of chickpeas
and baked a large honey cake for the day the child is initiated into the
Jewish faith, and named Isaiah.

Isaiah's body grew slowly, taking on the appearance of a bag of bones
wrapped in a loose skin, though his eyes were always full of wonder.
When he was old enough to crawl on the floor, he got into everything,
took whatever he found apart to see what was inside, then carried it

off to a corner crying, "Mine, mine." The girls eyed him as they would a strange animal, loving him one minute and fearing him the next, when he destroyed a toy they treasured. Adah, closer to his age, was also closer to his play and she watched over him much as a sheepdog. When he was almost three years old he still found himself on all fours and he would out-crawl children much older than himself, making a game of it and always winning. Chaya was troubled to see him on his hands and knees so much, fearing that he would never learn to walk upright, and she feared his constant craving for food as well, despite his filling himself with everything within his reach. Like an animal, his instincts seemed to lead him wherever he could find something to eat, and Mirele or Katynka had to put him out of the store time and again when he reached for everything in sight. His favorite food hunt however was in the Greek bakeshop, where he was never turned away without a sweet cake and a broad smile from the childless Mrs. Nikolaos. He crawled the half-block to the bakery, and up the few stairs to the door and at the counter he raised himself and bellowed, "This, this, want this," until he got what he wanted, which he immediately stuffed into his mouth and crawled back to his mother's store.

His grandmother, seeing his face and lips studded with sweet crumbs, would ask him, "Again? How many times a day do you have to eat! Your guts are without a bottom, maybe it is sewn up. The Devil himself knows where you put so much food!" One day he crawled into the pastry shop and was immediately attracted to a colorful wedding cake that stood on a separate little round table, and he sat gazing at its green and pink sugar roses and the bride and groom, who stood in the center of the cake on a little altar over which hung a shining gold cross. To get a better view of the panorama, he crawled nearer to the table, and tried to raise himself by clutching a fold of the white tablecloth and pulled everything on it to the floor with a loud crash!

Scared, he remained sitting on the floor, knowing that he had done something to cause that ornamental attraction to lay broken and spilled all over the floor, but did not know how and he was unable to ponder on the mystery long, for Mrs. Nikolaos rushed in from the kitchen and seeing the wreck became hysterical and shouted, "Look at what you have done, you little bastard! And tonight is the wedding, what will I do now? You've ruined me, you monkey, get out of here before I lay my hands on you."

What else she might have added, Isaiah did not stop to hear because he stood up on his feet and ran down the steps and the distance to his mother's store as if the Devil himself gave chase. "Mother, come and look, our wonder boy is not only walking upright, he is running like angry wind!" Mirele shouted into the house. Chaya came running to see the panting child and remarked to him, "It looks like you have at last given up being an animal and you are becoming a man, and just as I had about given up too."

It was about this time that Avraham began to teach him his daily prayers and found him a willing and retentive pupil, and in short time began his religious training as well. The boy tagged after his father, plying him with everything that his inquisitive mind found new. He now avoided his grandmother, who always scolds him for playing pranks on the girls and messing up the floor with toys he takes apart while he waits for his father to get home; and she always remarks how much food he eats as if she did not like it. And he had a feeling that she did not like boys because she never said anything about the girls eating too much. He never knew if he liked his mother or not, for he never really knew her and he never knew if his mother liked him, for Mirele was either in the store or laying in bed resting and never played with him.

In his confused feelings he had times when he yearned to put his arms around her but she always looked far away as if she did not see him. The only time he felt her tenderness was on the morning when his father took him for the very first time to the *kheyder,** but that morning he did not want her affection. Why did he have to be awakened so early in the morning while it was still dark outside? He was still so sleepy he could barely keep his head up straight to see his way in the room although the kerosene lamp was on full flame. Then too, he heard his grandmother say to his father that "he better carry the child because

---

* Yiddish for a Hebrew-language school for children prior to their coming of age after which young men attend a yeshiva.

the air is still raw so early in the morning." He was about to protest when his father answered her that a boy going on four who is ready to study Torah did not need to be carried like a baby any longer. Now, Isaiah really began to feel like a man and was sorry to see that the girls were fast asleep and did not hear what his father said. Well, he will tell them when he comes home from *kheyder*. How swelled with pride he felt with the new turn of events. But suddenly his mother picked him up and stood him on a bench to dress him and put her arms around him and tenderly kissed him—reducing him to a baby again.

"My little man, you should learn and grow up to be the pride of your father's life, and a good Jew." And again she kissed him and put a heavy scarf around his neck, tying it in the back and putting him down on the floor.

"I want to go back to sleep," he bellowed suddenly not knowing why. "The poor child can't stand on his feet, perhaps he is still too young to put to such task yet," he heard his grandmother say and to show her how wrong she was, he ran to the door reaching for the doorknob and rattled it vigorously until it opened and Avraham took the boy's hand in his and both braved the cold morning.

Mirele was constantly complaining of being tired. The many child-bearings, deaths of five children, and battles with their poverty wore her down until she had little patience or affection left for her children. Her love for them now turned to concern for their needs. Adah's winter battles with lung fever required a rich diet for her to recover from them. Bena lacked clothes to replace those she outgrew and Isaiah, who began to attend *kheyder* daily, needed warm clothes to face the early morning weather and the cold room of the *kheyder* all day. Where will she get the money with which to provide all those necessities?

Thank God, Rachel gave her no concern on that score. The girl grew like a weed unattended but sturdy, always laughing and singing, running or skipping, which made Chaya scold her to keep her from falling in her play, but it did not change her gait. Her vivid coloring attracted much admiration among the customers in the store, and they commented on her large brown eyes that were a match to her thick, wavy hair and her round, red cheeks that were framed by white skin. The child adored her mother but made her sister Bena unhappy by being so often in the store and drawing their mother's attention to herself.

In the back of their house toward the very end of the courtyard was a lumberyard with thousands of planks piled two and three stories high and the neighborhood children found it an ideal playground. Not only were they able to play hide-and-go-seek, but also "house," the planks offering so much seating capacity and shelving space. Then of course there was that invigorating game where one child touched another and called out "catch" while running up, up, with the other children in pursuit up the wooden planks, till they reached the very top and started down again. As many times as Zelig the owner of the lumberyard chased them away, so many times they came back as soon as his back was turned and they continued their games where they had left off. Nor was the weather a deterrent when rain or snow swelled the planks. Rachel climbed like a boy. She would have beaten out many boys of her age, the six-year-old boys in the Jewish community went to *kheyder* six days a week and on the Sabbath and holidays attended synagogue with their parents. Playing with the girls, she climbed, she tore her clothes, her fingernails, and many times her face, but always came up laughing.

One winter day when the snow was packed down and frozen to the ground, hard ice had formed on the high stacks of lumber and Rachel wanted to show her little friends how to coast down from the very top and slipped, falling down to the ground. The children ran to pick her up; they found her so quiet and motionless that they were scared and ran off. When they passed Katynka's house, she went out to see who was crying and learned of Rachel's fall. Throwing a shawl around herself, she ran to find what looked like the girl's lifeless body. Her face was deep in a little mound of hard snow as if it had sprouted from there. With trembling hands Katynka tore the shawl from her shoulders and wrapped the child in it and ran to her house, there to put her into her bed and cover her with a quilt, and rubbed her wrists and forehead worrying all the while how she could tell Mirele about such misfortune.

Katynka became crazy with panic as some time went by, as well as guilty for keeping her and not knowing how to help her. A muffled sound came from the child, then a low moan, and Katynka bent over her to see her eyelids flutter slowly, and without another thought ran to the store to get Mirele, but found Avraham there, and with a wild, beating heart, told him about his child's fall. He stared at her as if he did not understand and slipped to the floor in collapse. On the way to the house, she met Mirele and, talking very fast and incoherent, informed her of the accident and of Avraham's condition.

"Run fast Katynka and get the doctor, but before that you better get my mother to help my husband," Mirele cried as she ran toward the door. In Katynka's house she approached the bed with dread and found the girl very still. Quickly, she wrapped her snugly into the blanket and carried her back into her house. She removed all her clothes and put a warm night shirt on her and covered her well. Avraham and Chaya came in from the store and stood looking down at the child and tried to comfort each other with, "Do not worry, the Lord is good, he will not let any harm come to her," and, "You will see, she will come out of it soon," and other words, words, and more words that meant little to the three of them.

Katynka soon arrived with the doctor following and Chaya took the children into the store with her. The doctor took a long time with the examination and then took Avraham aside, and seeing Mirele's agitation, came back to where she now sat on the edge of the bed. "Well, your child suffered a bad injury to the brain. Somewhere in her head is a bone pressing, but I do not know the place. We doctors do not have the instruments yet with which we can see what goes on in our heads; perhaps someday we will not be so helpless. In the meantime keep her warm, dry, and watch her constantly for any kind of change. I do not believe that you can get her to take any liquids, but you can try without forcing. Should you see any change, no matter how small—a flutter of an eyelid, movement of her eye—no matter how slight, be sure to call me be it day or night."

He pulled on his fur-lined overcoat, hesitated a while and said to

Avraham, "I also found her to bleed from below. I am certain that the fall broke her hymen, and while it is no danger to her health, you may want to know about it." Avraham stayed the doctor as he was about to leave. "I am glad that you told us about it, Doctor Lazarus, but I need your assurance that it really is so, before I go to our rabbi for a certified statement. It would be a tragedy to a girl of our faith when she becomes of marriageable age. Doctor, are you certain of that injury?" he begged for a negative answer. "I am as certain as any doctor could be without an internal examination, which is impossible for me to subject her to now. I believe that you can ask your rabbi for the certified statement and I will testify to it if he wants me to. Good day."

The gloom that now hung over the house was with little hope of clearing. The three adults spoke in whispers and hushed the children's voices. They took turns in the watch for some sign of life in the wasting little body that had been so robust a short while ago. Mirele gave up trying to put a little milk between her dry lips that she kept closed tight. On the fourth day Avraham felt sure that she was slipping away from them and wrapped her into his prayer shawl, and sat watch all day. The women wrung their hands in despair and wept bitterly and Chaya suggested that they "sell" the girl before it was too late. Selling a sick child into a family with a large brood was a good omen, for among so many children one can be hidden from the Angel of Death.

Avraham scoffed at her idea, but the women had their way and both went to visit Anya the Pauper who was recently widowed and left with eleven children and was due with the twelfth any day now. She lived with her large family in back of a leather storage, in one long damp room that depended on its sole window for light and air and gave the room the illusion of a tunnel. The stench of mustiness and leather hung over the room and now assailed Chaya and Mirele as they neared it. They found Anya at the table cutting into a black radish for the children's lunch. She stood sideways with her dried-up body that boasted her swollen abdomen, which prevented her from coming close to anything.

"I see we have guests, children, move your clothes off the chairs quickly, so our friends can sit down." To her guests, she said, "You came in time to have lunch with us, please sit down." A pack of children with runny noses and torn old clothes that hung on their gaunt bodies almost in shreds, shed everything off the chairs onto the floor exposing the broken seats and disappeared as one into a large packing-case they had played in.

"You look troubled my friends, what is wrong in your home? Would you like something to eat before you talk about it?" She looked close from one to the other.

"No, no, Anya, we do not want any food, we came to you on a mission of mercy," Mirele told her.

"On a mission of mercy from me? What can I do for you? You look so grave, what is it with you that I can help you in some way?"

Chaya told her about Rachel's hopeless illness and asked her to "buy" her and keep her among her own children.

"If that is what you want, I'll gladly do it, if you think it will be of help. How can I refuse you people when you never have let me out of your house empty-handed whenever I told you of my hungry children. Tell me what, and when, you want me to do this thing, and I'll do it."

The same afternoon found the three women sitting at the rabbi's table stiff and tongue-tied looking to each other to begin to talk. Chaya felt that the other two were waiting for her to speak, and with resolve told the rabbi what they wanted to do. Rabbi Mortkhe looked at the perplexed mother and grandmother and asked Anya if she wished to become the mother of one more child. "I would go into fire for those good people if need be. They are kind to the poor, caring with them more than they can, and I want to ease their troubled hearts."

"Then so be it," he said, and made out a "bill of sale" in the form of a petition, a plea to God: keep Rachel, daughter of Avraham and Mirele, among Anya's children and that she, Rachel, consider Anya her godmother, whom she shall address as Mother for the rest of her life.

Chaya looked down at her hands a while and said, "One more thing, Rabbi, when the child fell, she hurt herself below and broke the skin that kept her a maiden, and we are worried against the time when she will be old enough for marriage. Can you give us a document of some sort that the doctor had found her so from the fall, if God lets her live there will be no trouble on that account?" she finished with some anxiety.

"Well, before I issue such certificate, I must talk to the doctor, and when he satisfies the regulations, I will send it on to you. God's blessings on both your households." When the rabbi left the room, Chaya placed a coin on the table and Anya gave a coin to Mirele for the child she bought with it, and the transaction was closed. Rachel remained at home, and if she will live, she is to call Anya mother and give her the respect due a natural mother.

The following days found Rachel very close to death but for the weak breath that she pulled. Mirele did not open the store, sitting at the bedside day and night trying to hold on to the child a little longer. Chaya torn by grief suggested that she get Frayda the Miracle Worker, who claims that she saved many lives on the brink of death. Grabbing and clutching at a straw when drowning gives one hope, Mirele thought, and agreed with her mother, and Chaya quickly left the house and soon returned with Frayda, before Avraham returned from the city.

Mirele watched the woman as if she was bewitched, watched how she boiled water in a basin, then took from her bag a large cake of wax and slipped it slowly into the water, all the time moving her lips in some prayer. She watched the wax dissolve a while, then poured it into another basin very carefully, as if it were precious blood, all the while moving her lips and clenching and unclenching her hands. She stood over the concoction a long time watching the wax taking on different forms as it melted, and it was at these forms that she directed her prayers, they being the "evil" that she was driving out of Rachel's sick little body. At last, she picked up the basin and spilled its contents onto the ground in back of the house, asked a ruble for her services and left. The two women looked at each other but did not speak their thoughts for a long time, but watched over the child for some sign of improvement; then suddenly Chaya said in a choked voice, "Mirele, you know what I would tell you? I would like to bring the other miracle worker too, the new one, Malka. She is spoken of very highly. Anyhow, if one can do the child some good, think of what two can do for her?

What can we lose?" And without waiting for an answer, she rushed out of the door, fearing that Avraham would soon come home.

Mirele remained in her seat and suddenly became conscious of the unnatural quiet in the house and became alarmed, having forgotten that Katynka had taken the other children to her house. Chaya came back followed by the other miracle worker, and again mother and daughter watched as she performed as the first one did, the one exception being that the first miracle worker used hot water and cold wax, the second used cold water and hot wax that she first melted down on the hot stove. Otherwise the procedures were the same. Both went through the same rituals, the same actions with their hands, and the same entreaties to the Lord to drive the evil out of the dying child, and the two grieving women felt drawn into some belief that the child will get better and now live. But Rachel did not show any sign of improving. When Avraham came home from the City, he smelled the wax and surmised what the women had been up to but said nothing, knowing their distress.

On the tenth day, Mirele, worn out and depressed, left the bedside watch to Avraham, and got into the bed with Isaiah, pulling the boy close to her, and fell asleep. She slept through the evening and a good part of the night and was suddenly awakened by something. She opened her eyes to find Bena shaking her sleeping father and shouting close to his face, "Look at her, she is doing it again," and Mirele jumped from the bed. The excited girl told her that she had heard Rachel laugh, thought she was dreaming, then she heard her again and went to see. "And look Ma, she is laughing again!" Rachel was laughing very quietly, her swollen eyes on Bena, and with a puzzled expression on her face with a crooked mouth and dry, splitting lips. Her eyes slowly began to wander around the room and from one person to the other.

Mirele brought the lamp closer to the bed and the girl saw her father looking stupidly at her as if he did not believe his own eyes and she laughed again, the blood running down from her upper lip, but giving testimony of hope for her recovery. Her shrunken face looked like an infant's and when she laughed her cheeks looked like parchment in their dryness. Only her eyes within swollen eyelids looked alive, giving indication of some hope. Chaya stood silently at the bedside watching with the others, then asked Avraham if she should call the doctor, but he told her to wait for the morning. When Doctor Lazarus examined the child, he smiled and said to Avraham, "You must have prayed hard and long, she was a very sick girl. Now you must feed her good food and plenty of it to make up for her loss. Keep her in bed until she gets tired of it, then let her out."

Her buoyant spirit helped to mend her, though her recuperation was long and an uneven process. A week before the Passover holidays, the sun came out clear and warm, melting the icicles that hung from the roof edges all winter long, which began to drip and the snow underfoot to melt. Rachel became restless and complained of staying indoors and Mirele had to dress her warm and sit her on a low stool on the upper stairs of the store. In a short time, many of her little friends came running to see her but stood at a distance plying her with all sorts of questions, then some ran back home and came again with their rag doll and other toys, putting them gently into the folds of the blanket that Mirele had wrapped her.

While the children were renewing their friendship with Rachel, she, in turn, was renewing her life. She was forbidden to play in the lumberyard for a long time but there came the time when no one could hold her back and her laughter full of glee was heard again all the way into the house. She was left with one disturbing edict from her illness: that she had to take on Anya the Pauper for her additional mother, give her the respect due a natural mother but worst of all, whenever she got into a scrap with the other children, they called her Anya the Beggar, Anya the Beggar Bag! Of course, this name calling was never done within earshot of the parents or grandmother. When the taunts became unbearable to the girl, she would try to drown them out by singing so loud that they were forced to give up.

Not soon forgotten was the winter of 1904, when Russia was embroiled in war with Japan. The country suffered misery and destruction, draining from its populace the very necessities of life, and the bitter-cold winter added its share of distress by appearing earlier than was its wont, bringing angry, ponderous winds that led the other elements in mad fury. The small, huddled homes moaned and groaned and crackled with frost and wind storms in discordant crescendos, giving little peace to those within. Children wrapped in tattered rags and torn shoes moved through the snow-laden streets, carrying buckets in the hope of finding some dung with which to fire their stoves, or *grubas*,* but possessors of such animals kept them in their overcrowded homes to shelter them from the cruel winter assault. On the hard-packed, snow-covered streets was heard the thunder of marching troops day and night, bringing panic to young and old in the shuttered and barred doors and windows of their homes.

Mirele kept the store locked and barred for fear of plunder and sat among her children, impatient with the noise in their play and resentful that she was yet carrying another one—hoping that it will come later than she expected. But evidently the infant was ready for the world and she gave birth a few days later to a son. She remained in bed much longer than she had in her other confinements of childbirth, not having the strength nor desire to continue with the struggles tied to her fate.

She felt lifeless despite her efforts to show some elation with possessing five living children—two being sons. The newborn baby had the appearance of a buckwheat pudding that had been rolled in white flour. He was covered from head to toe with a white substance and his little fists held wads of it tightly. Chaya put him into his first bath as she spoke to her daughter across the room. "The pocketfuls of chalk that you ate during the pregnancy sure look good on your son, Mirele. But don't worry, it easily washes off, and he will be handsome just the same when I dry him off." And Mirele had to admit that he was handsome and well formed when she looked him over, though she felt no elation or interest in him. As if from a long distance, she heard herself answering her mother, "I did not eat that chalk because I liked the taste of it, but I felt that it sustained me when I felt too low to go on with my work and worried I was so low toward the end of

* Ukrainian.

my time. I was glad to be forced to close the store before I collapsed."

When Avraham came home in the evening and found his new son, he chuckled with joy and kissed Mirele. "My wife, you have outdone yourself with this child, he is beautiful and looks just like his mother. You could not deny him as your son even with your eyes closed." He looked tenderly at her pale face and downcast eyes.

"How can you tell who he resembles, he is only a few hours old," she asked.

"How can anyone be so blind not to see that sweet face and such big eyes that he just opened to me, not to know he is your son. Only Rachel and this baby have eyes like yours. The other children's are of different shapes and colors entirely. God is good, we are blessed with five lovely children."

But Mirele did not feel His blessedness; she only felt her exhaustion and worry. O Lord, no more babies, no more deliveries, and no more worries for the morrow! Something nagging at the back of her mind that she was unable to bring to the fore was building a wall between Avraham and herself.

While she rested in her bed of confinement, she tried hard to think back to the time when the change between them began, but fear of probing too far and too deep and finding something too ugly for her to endure kept her back. Yet thoughts of events did push to the forefront unbidden and she had to give them attention. Like the time not so long ago when he came home from the City later than was his wont and seemed out of sorts, going to bed without his supper. Why? And when she asked him why he refused his food—if he was ill—she got a gruff answer that could mean a yes or no, and she left it at that, not knowing what to make of it.

And it was during this time that her sister Hannah paid her one of her rare visits, which left her much upset. They exchanged some small talk while Mirele attended two women who came for groceries and then Hannah suddenly remarked, "How I hate men who defame their family's good name for a pretty face!" Mirele looked puzzled. "You don't know what I mean, you, my naive sister," Hannah asked pointedly. What in the world could you be talking about? What's this naive sister remark supposed to mean, Mirele was wondering? "Well can I see that I am speaking to an unsuspecting, blind wife of a good man who does as he pleases!"

"Are you talking of my Avraham?" Mirele now asked, with a disbelieving but fast-beating heart that made her voice quaver. "Who else am I talking about, the chimney sweeper? Of course, I am speaking about your Avraham. I am worried about you two. The other day I walked on the main boulevard of the City, on the way to New Plan, and I was attracted by a very pretty young woman dressed very tastefully in the latest fashion, and as she passed me by I turned to admire her and then saw him." Hannah did not know how to go on.

"Saw who? Why are you so worked up? Why are you telling me all this, are you talking about my husband?"

"Yes, yes, I am talking about him! I saw how the pretty girl ran to meet him with her arms outstretched, and he smiled as if there was intimate understanding between them," she ended in a dead voice.

"So what?" Mirele asked with some heat. "Was he supposed to stick his tongue out to her?"

"Well, I thought you should know about it and as long as you feel so calm about it, I think I should go now and let you understand yourself," Hannah looked hard at her sister, and left without another word.

As soon as Hannah left and Mirele did not have to hide her feelings from people around her, her thoughts began to fly like scared birds from one of his late homecomings to another and she began wondering. She knew that Avraham was a good family man, that he loved his children more than his life, and despite his strange actions of late, she felt that she was deeply embedded in his heart. But then she also knew that he had a great weakness for women's pretty faces! For the first time in their marriage, she now felt herself at a loss for his questionable actions, and no matter how she tried to put her distressed thoughts to the back of her mind, they came seeping through all her cares and other worries.

How was it possible for her husband to act so foolishly? Was he a youngster without responsibilities, without reverence for his God and his family? She battled with her thoughts, believing one minute that Hannah told her the truth and the next she doubted her. But his late homecomings and his seeming coolness to her brought her right back where she started from.

Not being able to keep it to herself much longer, she confided in Chaya her troubles and was shocked to hear that she too, had heard from Hannah about it and would like to find out who the girl was.

"What difference does it matter who she is? If it's the truth, then Avraham is as much at fault as the girl is."

Mirele was not eased by her mother's information.

"Well, I still feel that we should know. Hannah told me that she saw them again, this time standing near a window of a bookstore talking together."

"Look Mother, do you really think that it could not be as bad as Hannah blew it up to be, if they are seen out in the open streets? Is Avraham out of his mind, to openly make a display of himself and some young girl? I don't care what Hannah or you say, I won't believe it," she almost shouted, as if it would help her to understand.

On Saturday, Chaya prepared to go to the house of prayer with Avraham and the children, glad that this time Mirele had to stay at home so that she could breastfeed the baby, for she had to find out more about Hannah's reports about Avraham. And right after the services, she told the girls to wait for their father downstairs and go home with him and Isaiah. "Where are you going yourself, Grandma?" three voices went up as if rehearsed.

"Don't worry, I'll come back soon, I'll have my dinner with your Aunt Hannah, so tell Mama not to wait for me."

"I want to go too!" again three voices like one sang out.

"No, not this time, some other time I'll take you to your Aunt," she promised them and, after stationing them near the men's entrance of the synagogue, left.

In Hannah's house she found it hard to believe that it was the Sabbath, for the smell of cooking and the very many voices in the dining room made her feel that she was at a wedding! She asked one of the servants to call her daughter out from there, and waited a long while. In the meantime three of the youngest children came out crying, "Grandma, Grandma; Mother, Grandma is here," and upon their cries Hannah appeared, dressed in a fine silk dress, and her black wig combed in the latest fashion.

"Gut Shabbos,* Hannah. My but you look pretty in that dress! I hear you have company inside, can I speak to you a moment? But first send the children inside again."

She saw her daughter's forehead wrinkle with annoyance and quickly placated her with, "It will only take a minute of your time."

"But Mother, Fishl invited guests from Moscow, and I can't stay away from the table now, please come back some other time."

"Then just tell me if you found out who that girl is. You promised me to do that, and I must know now."

"Yes, she is the daughter of Gadolia the Wheat Merchant, who lives on the same block where the Plaza begins and her name is Sonia. I really must go now," and without another word ran off.

Chaya lost no time and went to Gadolia the Merchant's house and asked a servant for Sonia. A tall, graceful young woman in her early twenties with a beautiful face and head of jet-black hair combed low on her neck very becomingly made her appearance.

"Yes?" and suddenly added, "Oh, you are Chaya, Hannah Schmyser's mother, aren't you? Gut Shabbos. I am sorry but my parents are not at home, can you tell me what you want of them?"

"I would like to talk to you, but I hear that you have company inside; can we go where we will be out of earshot of anyone?"

Sonia led her into a small parlor and closed the door. "Please sit down," she bid her.

"What I have to say, I can say standing up, and I will say it quickly so that I won't keep you from your friends. Look Sonitchka, I know you since your mother carried you under her heart, although I had never exchanged a word with her. You are a very fortunate girl, you are pretty and rich and very popular in the City with all menfolk, young and old. My son-in-law Avraham Poil is a good and pious man who loves his family, and it would be a sin to have a foolish young girl turn his head. Keep away from him, do not give the townsfolk my children

---

* Yiddish for "Good Sabbath."

to mock. You too will become a gossip piece in the town, and surely your fine family does not deserve to be besmirched in the eyes of the community. Sonitchka, keep away from him and save a lot of heartaches for both our families."

Sonia stood in silence with downcast eyes, but her face changed colors. She saw Chaya turning to go and ran ahead of her to open the door.

Chaya walked homeward so fast that she was out of breath by the time she reached the door and stood there for a long while before she entered the house. The household was quiet; Avraham was asleep on one bed with Isaiah at his side, Mirele on their bed with Raphael sucking at her breast, and the three girls were playing outside somewhere.

Chaya's legs were shaking under her, making her think that it was from not having eaten since early morning, and she took from the stove some meat and sat down to eat, but found that she could not put anything past her lips, she was too upset from the foul piece of work she had done. She hoped that it will have served the aim she had had in mind.

The winter was upon them again with its extreme cold and furious blizzards that caused much hardships for them. The family were locked into the one-room home as if into a world of their own; the sole window cutting off the outside and light by its frosted inlaid patterns of ferns.

The house became a beehive of activity and noise. The children, including Isaiah who was kept home from *kheyder* for the lack of warm clothes, played their fantastical games with so much laughter and commotion that Chaya had to cut into their enthusiasm with threats every so often to balance the room from rocking. The only time the house quieted down somewhat was when the two older girls were out, with the younger children a little at a loss knowing what to do with themselves. But not for long, for children are made of dreams and fancifulness that are inventive and creative and mysterious and so willful that few adults understand them.

Chaya's major worry was Adah, who had recently come through

her fifth illness with lung fever in six winters and she still coughed and looked pale and gaunt. She did not join the others very often in their play, but stood near the frozen window and traced the glacial ferns with a forefinger, or stayed in bed. Sometimes Chaya's urging would bring her away from the window; the child would sit down near Katynka at the stove and watch her mend their clothes and darn their stockings with her slow but sure hands. She watched the flames from the stove grate dancing on the patches of wool that healed the rips and tears like with a curative, the new wool compensating for the worn, handed-down and much-washed stockings.

Katynka asked Adah to play with Isaiah, who was left to his own devices because Chaya had taken the two older girls with her to gather something to hurl in the stove, and Raphael was sound asleep and she was overjoyed to see the girl skip away. This was the first time she moved in a healthy behavior, and Katynka dropped the work in her lap and just sat watching her. She saw into the faint light of distance from her that Isaiah's black glittering eyes danced in his head, while his mouth was working fast, close to Adah's face, which slowly took on a gay expression and some color.

Soon the girl skipped over to her and asked for a pot.

"A pot? What are you going to do with a pot? I had better not touch your grandmother's dishes, she will not like it."

Adah made a dash back to Isaiah, and the two stood whispering a while, as if making a new set of plans, and then Adah went to the low shelf near the stove and took from it a deep pot that Chaya cooked soup in.

"You better put that back. I don't know what you want with it, but whatever it is, you better wait until your grandmother returns and ask her for it," and while she talked to Adah, she looked in Isaiah's direction angrily.

"But you want me to play, don't you! Well, if we cannot have the pot, then I'll just sit here with you instead." And out of Adah came a spiteful cough, knowing well that the ripping sound in her chest will make Katynka give in.

"Your grandmother is keeping two kinds of dishes; I am afraid of doing something that is not kosher with them. Let me go into the store and ask your mother first," and she went, but came back very soon. "I can't talk to her now, she is busy, she has too many people in there. Tell me, do you need a pot that your grandmother cooks meat in, or milk? I'll give you one, but may the Lord have mercy on me," and she crossed herself, and waited for Adah to give some thought to her questions.

"Oh, it really does not make any difference if it's *fleishigs* or *milchigs*,* just so it's a pot!" she flung at her.

But Isaiah, the man, after all he was—his grandmother called him the "Talmud genius" because he already had behind him almost a year of learning and knew more than his sister who was only a girl—shouted, "No, no, it must be a *milchigs* pot."

Katynka reached up to a high shelf and took a pan that she had seen Chaya warm the children's milk in and gave it to them. "Here, but don't play too hard with it, you may break it."

Isaiah removed his pants and his cotton-padded, lice-infested underpants and got up on his bed and stood with his feet far apart, so far that he almost fell off, then, regaining his balance, pushed his small shrunken belly forward and with it his juvenile manhood, his penis.

"Now, go ahead and milk me, mooooooo," he commanded Adah; and she put the pan between his legs and milked his penis as if it were the teat of a cow and he obliged with a hot stream of urine that made a dull sound as it hit the pot!

Katynka clutched her head with both hands and cried, "*Bozhe miy!*† What are you doing there and in a kosher pot too!" She strode across the room to them and stood looking from one to the other.

"Well, you said that I should play with Isaiah, didn't you? So we are playing that he is my cow, and because my baby here," pointing to sleeping Raphael, "needs milk, so I am milking my cow. Why are you so mad at us?"

Katynka just pulled the pan away from Isaiah's outstretched legs,

---

* Kosher dietary laws require two sets of pots and pans, one for meat and one for dairy products.
† Ukrainian for "My God!"

spilled the urine into the snow at the open door, and buried the pan at the side of the house deep inside the snow. When she came back, Adah was helping her brother pull his clothes on again and both were silent. They were interrupted just when they really began to enjoy themselves and now they both felt cranky and did not know what to do with themselves, so they began to fight over a place on the bed, each wanting to sit on the same spot and both screaming at each other.

And so Chaya and the girls found them when they came in loaded down with burlap sacks of wood shavings and paper to burn in the stove.

"What are you two fighting over!" she shouted at them. And Katynka spilled the story of their unique play, and her participation in it, by allowing them to use the pan.

Chaya did not know whether to laugh or punish the children, so she spoke to the two older girls, who were still in their outdoor clothes, loudly, "Why are you still wearing your hats and shawls? What are you waiting for, until we are to go out again, tomorrow maybe? Here, put my coat away Bena, and you, Rachel, put the sack with paper in a corner, don't let it stand in the middle of the floor."

Then turning to Katynka, she said in a low voice, "It's a good thing that you caught up with them when you did, or they would probably have awakened Raphael and fed him some of the so-called milk to sample," and they laughed, both feeling a little closer.

Since the cold weather set in, Katynka spent most days in Chaya's kitchen. In the beginning, when she came in late in the mornings when she knew that Avraham would be gone to the City, one day after the other, Chaya bristled to Mirele, "What is this, a home or a prison I am in? Why do I have to have her, sitting all day and watching me as if I was a prisoner? And the children run to her for anything they want instead of me, as if I were dead already! You don't think that we have enough occupants in the house? I really don't understand you Mirele!"

"Mother, don't be angry, I told her to come and stay as long as she wants to and whenever she wants to, because her house is cold and lonely and she is getting old and is becoming too depressed to be alone. Why does it bother you to have her sit there, in the little corner near the stove for a few hours of the day? She does not watch you like a jailer, she envies your position as a mother, and grandmother, of so many children who revere you, and the children will not run to her so often, as soon they see more of her in the house. Now it is something new to have her in here," Mirele pleaded with her mother and Chaya said no more about it.

But without noticing it on her part, the relationship slowly bettered; and Katynka, feeling it, sat more comfortably many hours of the day near the blazing stove that Chaya fed with anything she found in the store or the streets. The lumberyard was a great help; when she did not find anything to burn elsewhere, she appealed to its owner Zelig, not with words, but simply with her appearance, for when he saw her coming, he turned "the other way" and walked away, for he knew well that he was her last resort or the family would freeze to death.

She would scoop up a sack of sawdust and say to the worker, tell Zelig that I was here and took some sawdust and shavings, and if I'll find some small pieces of planks, I will take them too; I must make the house warm for the children," and she did look for small pieces of wood, but if there were none, she helped herself to the larger planks.

Zelig's wife saw her, and shouted, "We can easily sell what she carries out of here and you pretend that you don't know it!" But Zelig shrugged it off, saying, "She must do what she is doing or they will not survive the winter." He gave orders to his worker never to stop her from taking what she wanted, not only what fell from the saw and the plane, but even if she takes large planks, he is to turn his eyes from her.

Adah's hacking cough sounded like a call to the doomed, and the doctor told Mirele that the child needs building up with rich foods and fresh air, two items that were hard to reach for. The food in the home was scanty, barely sufficient to carry them through the day, and there were no warm clothes that Adah could wear outdoors, so she could breathe fresher air.

One morning Katynka came into the house and told Chaya to follow her into the store and then told her and Mirele about a cousin on the *folvarek*,* on the outskirts of the City, a farmer, and that she was

---

* Russian and Ukrainian for farmland.

going there to find out if she would take Adah for a spell.

"My cousin Evdokiya likes children, and she had a houseful of them, some that are big enough to help with the farm work, and others who help in the house, and if I am not mistaken, she must have had another baby since I saw her last. In her home, Adah will get rich food and warm clothing. Let me go now and I will find out."

"But how can you go such distance in this cold and deep snow?" both women asked in one breath.

"Don't worry, I will take a stout stick with me, and dress as warm as I can and on the way if I get too cold, I'll stop off in peasants' huts for a while. So, I'll go now, and I'll be back sometime tomorrow."

When she left, Chaya asked Mirele if Avraham would allow Adah to stay in a non-Jewish home where she would have to eat the non-kosher food, and saw her look a little confused, as if she had not given it any thought before.

Katynka returned three days later in better style than she had left: her cousin Evdokiya's husband Vasily brought her back in a deep-built sleigh, pulled by a strong, black horse who threw forth great gusts of steam from his nose and made the runners on the glistening snow feel like wings. She herself sat back in the seat alongside Vasily, covered with so many shawls and fur rugs, feeling so warm and snug, that she forgot the distressing cold and loneliness she had suffered walking the long distance to the farm. After she left Vasily off in her house, she went to speak to Mirele and Avraham. After many questions and assurances, Adah was bundled into the shawls that Katynka shed and put into the sleigh and covered with the fur rugs up to her very nose. The child looked on wide-eyed but did not complain—for the idea of riding in a sleigh, and one that was pulled by a horse with bells on, put everything else to the back of her mind and she could hardly wait until they would start moving.

When at last they pulled out of the courtyard, Vasily pulled her head shawl a little higher on her forehead to see more of her eyes and was glad to see that she was not crying, and looked happy and anticipative. He cracked the whip high into the air, and with a shout that sounded to her like "Get-a-wa," he started the horse moving and the sled sped on, on its smooth runners, to the rhythm of the tinkling bells that sounded so joyful and charming to her. But the dying sound in the distance of the very same bells sounded like a death knell to the loved ones she left behind.

The home remained quiet and inactive; the women were in tears and Avraham looked very grieved, even little Raphael seemed to sense a difference in the home and sat hushed and just looked at Isaiah, who was silently tearing a small ragdoll apart. Katynka felt ill at ease, and almost regretted her deed and walked toward the door.

"Where are you going Katynka this early? Your house must be as cold as an icehouse, wait awhile, we are making tea soon, don't go," Mirele begged her, understanding the woman's mixed emotions.

"I don't want you to worry about Adah, she will be warm in the sleigh, and when she comes to the farm, Evdokiya will dress her in some of her girls' warm clothes. There she will get good meat, fresh eggs and rich, warm milk, and before the summer arrives, she will have forgotten her illness"; and with these words, she left the house.

Time, and their busy days, somehow blotted for the parents the fear that the child might be unhappy in a strange home and miss them. Avraham wrote a few times to Vasily asking him about her, and each time he received an answer that Adah was well and happy and was getting nice and fat. Spring was long past due, but it was slow in putting in an appearance, and when it did, the sun took a long time to melt the heavy snows and ice that softened and began to run, making fissures in the locked-in frost and slowly overran the unpaved, narrow streets with muddy water and then turned every inch of ground into mud.

Saturday, Chaya and Mirele, who had left only an hour ago for the synagogue, returned with flushed faces and removed their velvet capes without uttering a word to the children or each other and proceeded to make up the big bed as if for the night. The children stood watching and wondering until they heard voices and laughter, mixed with mocking words being spoken out in the courtyard, and they ran to open the door to look, but Chaya held them back, the voices coming closer and closer until Mirele went to the door and opened it herself. Now they saw their father being carried under his arms by two men;

his shoes that he always kept so clean and shinning dragging in the heavy mud and his alpaca coat that he wore only on the Sabbath and holidays to synagogue in terrible disarray.

But what scared the children into dumbness was the foolish grin that was printed on their father's face and they ran deep into the room and hid near the store entrance. They watched from there how the two men laid him on the bed and silently walked out without looking at either their mother or grandmother. Mirele removed his shoes and struggled to remove his coat too, but gave up after a while because his body was dead weight.

Now the children stepped into the middle of the room, their eyes full of questions, and Bena began to cry. Chaya tried to hush her, but Mirele took them aside, and put her arms around them. "I want you all to promise me something without asking any questions," she told them, and not knowing what she asked of them, they all shook their heads like sheep.

"First of all, I want you to promise me that you will never talk to anyone about this, above all to your father." Now they shook their heads again, but with understanding.

"You know that your father taught and prepared Yaakov Bernstein to be a good Jew, he taught him to pray and believe in the Torah. Today, Yaakov was confirmed, and the Bar Mitzvah was celebrated in the synagogue where his parent's entire family gathered and many of them came to your father with praise for turning out such an apt pupil and drank *l'chaim** and your father had to return a toast to them. But your father can't drink much of any liquor especially whiskey, and so much of it, and when he did, his head turned and he became sick. I am sure that he will feel fine when he sleeps it off, so don't worry anymore about it."

A few days later, Avraham told Mirele that he could not for the life of him remember how, or when, he came home from the synagogue on Saturday, and it was then that she told him the details of her and her mother's embarrassment, and the children's suffering. He lowered his head with shame, realizing what he had done to them and on the very

---

* Hebrew for the toast meaning "To life!"

day when he was praised for his integrity and toasted to his excellent pedagogy and for being such an example as a scholarly Jew. He slowly raised his head and looked at his wife and said, "I promise you Mirele, that will never happen again."

3

A new nest

THE SUMMER CAME AND WENT, and Mirele was again faced with the problems of winter clothes for the family and fuel for the home. Adah was to go back to the farm again, having suffered another attack of lung fever, despite the fact that she had recovered so well from her last bout. And now without warning, the landlord told Avraham that he needed the house and store for his recently widowed daughter, who had to make a living for her six orphaned children! This was a bad blow for them; not only did they have to find another dwelling but also some other means of an income, no matter how hard they had to work for it.

Through one of her wholesalers, Mirele learned that a big tract of land not far from the heart of town, in New Plan, was being turned into a public market, not only for everyday business but also with plans for the monthly fairs to be held there. She lost no time and went to see what they were building there and found that individual stalls, some ten feet apart, were being erected for various wares for home and farm use. She spent some time looking around and asking questions, then rented one of the thirty booths facing the main street.

When she came home and told the family of her decision, Katynka spoke up and suggested that they go to Doctor Popov, a relative of hers, and find out if his attic was still unrented, as he lived almost across from the new market, and the same day found them both in his office.

Doctor Popov was a fifty-year-old widower, handsome and pleasant, and given to much questioning and probing of human motives and actions, as if they were microbes. He questioned much but he was rewarded with few answers as to why the poor had to suffer so much and so badly. When he learned from Katynka what they came after, he looked closely at Mirele and seemed pleased with something he read in her face and showed them the two-room attic above his home; it was light and clean and bigger than the living quarter they now lived in, and Mirele was pleased with it.

"Look Mirele, you can see the entire market from this window, is yours among those in front?" Katynka's voice vibrated with excitement.

"Yes, there it is, the fifth from the corner, the one with the glass window. That's where I will keep the barrel with the pickled apples and watermelon," she told her.

"Well, I see that the attic suits your needs, so I will have to tell you now what you will have to do to live in it. The rental will be in the form of a service from you instead of money. You are to live here rent-free all year round, but in the summer when I go to Crimea for my vacation, and my housekeeper goes to her daughter for the summer, the house must be cared for. I cannot leave it just closed up, it needs to be aired once a week, and dusted occasionally. What do you say, do you think we have a deal here?"

Mirele was dumbfounded, then asked, "But how do you know that you can trust me, you do not know me or my family, and yet you want to leave your beautiful house to my care?"

"You need have no worry on that score, Katynka here would not have brought you to me if you were not the right person for here, would not have this responsibility," said Doctor Popov.

Before the weekend the family settled into the light, clean attic and in the new stall. The entire family worked under Katynka's orders: she seemed to be the wonder of wonders with remembering where the packed things could be found and how and where to place everything.

"Look at that slow, slovenly creature, she works like one possessed. At no time could I guess that she could use mind and muscle with so much speed," Chaya remarked to Mirele, all the while keeping her eyes on Katynka to make sure that she does not mix up the meat and dairy dishes in her valor.

As soon as the house was in order, Mirele and Katynka, with only Bena to send on errands, set to work on the new little booth and in no time it was filled with what Mirele thought to be the most saleable items in a public market and it looked so attractive that passersby stopped to look in and admire the displays. It took no time at all, and a lively trade kept Mirele busy from morning to night and she had to ask Bena to help her a good part of the day.

Busy as she was, she knew that Katynka hovered around them like a mother hen, and that it irked her mother to have her all day and even during the nights when she slept in the kitchen with her and the two older girls.

She waited until she was alone with Katynka, then put her hands on her shoulders with a soft smile on her face and said, "How can I thank you or show my appreciation for what you have done for my family and myself. You have been more of a friend to me than my sister Hannah. With you I share all troubles and never hold back from telling you what is in my heart. Can there be a closer relationship between people than this? But Katynka, now you must go home, you cannot go on staying here much longer. My mother is an old woman, and I do not want her to resent your living with us, she will begin to dislike you, and you don't deserve it. But that does not mean that you are to keep away from us, oh no! You must come often to visit with the whole family or we will miss you very much." Tears filled her friendly soft eyes and Katynka looked away from her. "Yes, my friend, I understand, and I will come as often as I can, but only to see you at the store. I won't get in your mother's way."

Mirele was happy in the little stall and with the change she was forced to make. She had been used to neighborhood trade and here she had trade from transients, from as far away as across the farmlands, and met with many kinds of people who came in carts and wagons and bought from her attractive displays. In the evenings she came home tired but happy, her pockets bursting with silver and her bosom stuffed with paper rubles. "Avraham, the Lord is good to us, he saw the need for the change we had to make. Now we will have an easier life, and we must share it with Anya the Pauper. When you go to the

City tomorrow, take along some of this money to her, let her feel the pleasure of buying what she wants; and tell her how our Rachel is, it will please her to know that the child is thriving and pretty."

Avraham saw a rejuvenated Mirele, someone now fresh and alive, and full of spirit. In the first three weeks she was able to pay for her merchandise, stall rent, and good food in the house. She was able to pay back the money she had borrowed from Fishl that she needed to make the change to the new home and store, and give Anya some money! Her shoulders straightened as the heavy burden lifted from her.

But with one strong, irrational blow, her hard work and hopes were dashed to the ground! It was a Thursday, the fifth week in the new store, and she had prepared the stall for the Sunday fair. Having spent much money and effort to stock the shelves with edibles that appeal to fair visitors, and colorful beads and ribbons, as well as warm shawls that she found profitable commodities for such a day, she then sent Bena up for her lunch. As the girl was about to sit down to the table, she glanced out the window, and gave a bloodcurdling shriek! Chaya ran to her side and was guided by her frozen look and saw flames shooting skyward from the market! "Come, we must get to your mother," she cried, and both ran to the mad cataclysm of the burning stalls. Among the rearing horses wild cursing Cossacks were astride, throwing flaming torches onto the new roofs and knocking over wares with their sabers. Chaya dragging Bena by her hand got in the way of many running people with smudged faces, who cried bitterly and hysterically, and children who were separated from their elders.

At last they came to Mirele's stall and found her eyes streaming with tears while she was trying to put the fire out with apple cider she dipped from a barrel. Chaya ran to her with a curse on her lips, "They should see their mothers and children burn but should be unable to save them, dear God." And she pulled her daughter forcefully out of the stall. Bena barely had time to avoid horses' hooves while she helped drag her mother with strength she could not know she possessed and Chaya pushed them both from behind, till they reached across the street. When they came upstairs, they found the children huddled together and crying. Chaya turned to them and shouted, "Stop it, do you hear me? Stop it right now! What is today, Tisha B'av? The day when the Temple in Jerusalem was sacked. See, here is your mother, and your sister and myself. See, we are all safe," and she set about making tea and took from some hiding place little cakes saved from the last Sabbath and handed them around.

The children held the cakes to their mouths but did not eat them and stole glances at their mother's soot-smeared face and singed wig. Mirele's clothes hung around her in shreds and she sipped her tea with trembling lips. Every now and then a deep sigh escaped her, as she looked at the children's frightened faces. Then suddenly she thought of their father. "Mother," her voice was controlled, but Chaya heard panic in it, "what if we were not the only ones attacked, and the blackguards left for the City? And Avraham is there now."

The children, whose tears were still near the surface, began to cry again, and again their grandmother hushed them. "Stop your crying, you want to attract the Cossacks into the house? Doctor Popov's sign on the door will keep them away from here, but not if they hear your wailing; they know that only Jews cry with so much distress." The children stifled their tears again and sat close to Mirele. She sat with her hands in her lap, her face cold and still as if carved from stone. Her thoughts were now with Avraham and on her misfortune.

Hours passed and darkness began to fall, overtaking the room, but Chaya did not light the lamp, and the two boys fell asleep on the floor. A carriage was approaching the house and they all listened closely as it arrived at the entrance, and soon they heard steps leading to their attic. With wild beating hearts and strained ears, they listened and feared, not knowing. Slowly the sound on the treads came closer and closer and Mirele could stand the strain no longer but rushed to the door and threw it wide open and was pushed aside by a strong hand of a man who walked in. Chaya felt that now they had nothing to lose but their lives. So she lit the lamp and saw a man's face swathed in a woman's shawl and dressed in a peasant's sheepskin coat, his pants tucked into high black boots.

The two women were puzzled, the eyes that peeped out of the shawl looked familiar to them. Rachel walked up to him and looked at his hand that held a cigarette case and shouted, "It's Papa, it's my Papa, look, it's our Papa," as indeed it was. Avraham began to remove his shawl and coat, and laughingly said, "For shame, Mirele. Rachel knew me and you didn't!" He removed the high boots and stood smiling at their worried and puzzled faces, and understanding well what his family had suffered on his account, tried to make light of it.

Everyone was around him now trying to be of some help. Rachel helped pull his socks off. Bena brought warm water in a basin, and the two women busied themselves with putting food on the table. The two boys slept on and were not disturbed. Although no one at the table had eaten since early morning, the food remained on the plates, and the silence grew. "No one is hungry, eh?" Avraham remarked, "Then let me tell you that God is good, and we are all here to prove it. When I left the Bienstok home and walked back toward the bridge, He sent me a guardian angel in the form of Doctor Popov, who passed by me in his carriage, then stopped and shouted for me to get in with him. I wondered what he needed me for, surely not for a medical consultation about a sick patient of his and I joined him. He pulled out a bundle of clothes, those that I wear now, and told me to quickly change into them and throw mine into the river under the bridge as we swiftly pass it. I followed his instructions, understanding that my life was in danger; then he wrapped the shawl around my head and face covering my beard, and told me to feign illness should we be met by anyone.

"And all this not one minute too soon, for before we were halfway across the bridge, we were stopped by two Cossacks. They had galloped so hard after us, that they could hardly keep their horses on the ground. Doctor Popov flashed his license at them and quickly shouted, 'Out of my way, I am taking a man with a contagious disease to the hospital, take your faces out of here, lest you want to catch his sickness,' and those Jew murderers took off fast. But this was not the only time we were stopped, and as many times as we were, his scare worked!" He chuckled and heard the women murmur, "Thank Thee, our loving Father."

Mirele woke up the next morning and stood a long time looking out at the smashed and burnt marketplace that threw so many fami-

lies into terror and need. Half-burnt stalls still showed some color: a fluttering piece of ribbon, half-burnt shawl, and some preserve crocks that stood out stark white against the black burnt wall. But most of the stalls, like her own, were completely demolished and the wares were charred and broken, rolling around with broken window glass that glared back in the sun with defiance.

She felt tears slide down the sides of her face and quickly left the window and prepared tea for the family, and sat down to wait for them to wake. What to do now, she thought. Avraham's earnings will not feed the children, and she was left without means to start all over again and she had no spirit or strength with which to go on. In the afternoon when she was alone with her mother she suddenly said, "You know, Mother, I am seriously thinking of America."

"You have nothing more important to think of, than America? I understand that America is a big country and can think for herself," Chaya bantered, knowing well what her daughter was driving at, and then added, "and such a rich land too."

"That's just it, if a land is so well off, perhaps it will be able to absorb one more family. I am weary of the struggles that batter my life, Mother, and I am beginning to fear for our future here." Chaya looked at her and shook her head in sympathy, Mirele's hard life and fading energy and beauty hurt her, and she made no answer.

In the evening when Avraham came back from the City, she told him that she was thinking of going to America and see if the family could settle there. Avraham's face blanched. "You mean that you can say such thing," he asked in anger, "Did your brother turn your head with his exaggerations of his Promised Land? I told you and proved it too, that it is a land of infidels, yet you long for it like for the very heavens!" She knew how he felt about America, but his anger and shock did not impress her now. She was determined to rescue her children from hunger and pogroms at any cost to herself. She asked him to write to Schmuel and tell him to send her the necessary papers and ticket for the voyage, but he refused, saying that he "did not want to be a partner even to the thought," then added, "Furthermore, should you insist on your wild venture, I must tell you now that you will never see your children again as long as you live, and, I will not allow any of them away from home!"

She shot up from her chair as if hit by a thunderbolt and shouted, "You won't allow them to go! They are only your children, not mine? They are not of my flesh and blood and I did not exert every fiber of my being to raise them? And do I want to go to a foreign land because I expect an easier time for myself, and not because I want to pull them out of this hopeless morass?" The children stopped whatever they were doing and gathered around their parents, looking from one to the other with worried, questioning faces, and Mirele tried to control her emotions and stopped shouting.

She sat down at the table with her throbbing head in her hands, but could not control the tears that fell on her flushed cheeks. She spent the next few days examining her position, trying to find some way out of their poverty; the more she searched her mind, the less possibilities she found, and came to the conclusion that she had to go to America; that there was no other way out for her. She dressed in her Sabbath clothes, and went to visit her sister Hannah in the City. When she came into her home, Hannah was surprised at her appearance, and after looking closely at her, remarked, "Where are you going all dressed up in the middle of the week? Who is getting married that I was not invited to the wedding?"

"I am not going to anyone's wedding, I had to wear my Sabbath clothes to come to you, because my weekday things are not fit for the chimney sweep any longer. Is Fishl home? I would like to see him." Hannah led her into his study where she found him at his huge hand-carved desk, looking bloated with self-importance, working over some accounts of his business. Not only had he improved his big, inherited fortune from the manufacture of reed furniture and luggage, but he also lined his pockets with monies by drawing up notes, making out illegal papers, and falsifying birth certificates. Although he must have heard the two women, he did not raise his head for a long while, and Mirele noticed how fat and grey-haired he looked, the features of his face spread and misshapen and his brow deeply furrowed. "My God," she thought, "Avraham, with all his troubles, looks young enough to be his son."

When he raised his head and saw Mirele, he wondered what she came for, knowing well that her days were full and she was not given to visiting on the weekday. He liked his sister-in-law, he knew her to be clever, not dull like his Hannah, and prettier too, but he hated her poverty like he hated all others, unable to understand why they tolerated it and did not find a way out of it. He closed his account book, and asked her to be seated. "Well, I see that you are all dressed up for some good or festive occasion, and you stopped off to spend some time with us. Where are you on the way to or from?" he asked with some curiosity. "When a poor woman wears clothes instead of tatters, must be for some special reason!"

"Ironically, you are right, but I am not going, or coming from anywhere, but I came to see you about something very important, very special to me."

She saw him stiffen with suspicion and knowing that he feared that she might ask him for a loan of money, she quickly added, "I want you to write to my brother Schmuel in America, asking him to send me a ticket and some money for the voyage, and the necessary papers." She saw him relax but look puzzled.

"You mean that you want to go to America yourself, and leave your family behind? Why?"

"Fishl, Fishl, you who was born with a silver spoon in your mouth, and had a father that spread gold in your path and left you a fortune with which to continue your rich life, know only your world. Do you know what it means not to have enough food for your children? When a pogrom breaks out, are your children exposed to it without the City police standing guard at your door? How much longer can I go on living the life I spent so far? I must go to America where it is possible to educate poor children too, and one can earn his daily bread without so much hardship, and live without fear of being murdered in bed some night or burnt in his home. Avraham is against my going, so he refuses to write the letter for me and if you don't want me to lean on you for our daily crust of dry bread then better don't turn me away, and write it for me. It is impossible to exist on Avraham's small earnings, and I have nowhere to turn but you for help."

He saw challenge in her eyes, and asked angrily, "Why doesn't your husband do something to lessen your poverty? Why are you banging your head against a stone wall while he goes on his merry way without worry?"

"What do you mean he goes on his merry way? Do you think that he does not suffer the same as I do? But what can he do? Your father was a reed furniture manufacturer, you, his son follows his business, my Avraham's father was a Hebrew teacher, he raised his only son to be one too. Did you expect Avraham to be a businessman, a salesman? When he goes out to spend a ruble, it becomes a holiday for the shopkeepers and he comes home with empty hands. And if he had something to sell, he would give it away! Please don't make me talk so much, write to Schmuel and tell him of our misfortunes and that he should act fast and send me a ticket, and the necessary papers, for already my children are getting less food than they need."

He saw how tense she was, and began to clear desk space on which to do her bidding. Hannah came back and asked her to join them for supper, but she thanked her and refused.

She waited until the children as well as her mother were fast asleep and then sat down at the table near Avraham and told him of her visit to Hannah, and that Fishl had written and sent off a letter to her brother in America. He quickly closed his Bible with a hand that shook with agitation and turned an angry face to her and looked with deep hurt into her eyes. So they sat looking at each other, without a word between them while anger and resentment made them too wretched to talk, though they had so much to say to each other. It seemed that an iron wall sprang up between them and cut off all communications from one to the other.

She sighed deeply and left the table and went to bed hoping that sleep will overtake and free the spasms and quivering in her limbs. After changing into a nightshirt, she crawled into bed and covered herself well and slowly began to feel lulled and heavy with sleep. Suddenly, her mind became crystal clear and pangs of pity for Avraham shot through her, causing her to toss and turn until he turned down the wick, thinking that the light of the kerosene lamp disturbed her.

She remained on her side facing him and, from the dimness of her corner, studied him as he sat swaying over the Holy Scriptures, his hand shading his eyes from the nearness of the lamp. She knew that he was confused and distressed, yet he seemed to draw peace and contentment from the holy words. How she envied him his knowledge of the Holy books, which he leaned on for support whenever his life became troubled! And that was so with the Orthodox men who were privileged to study, and feel at home with, the knowledge of the Torah and wisdom of the Talmud, from which they drew so much solace and gratification—a privilege denied their women.

To the women were given the handiwork of their religion to bear and rear children all their lives, to make the Sabbath and holidays festive by special food preparations, special house cleaning, and special worry, where to get the money for their needs at the end of those days, when the men were well rested and in a jovial mood, they had to give themselves to their husbands on Friday nights as Sabbath Brides and on Passover as Queens of the Seder,* and on other holiday nights— because they were holiday nights!

"Yes," Chaya remarked more than once, "the men were a smart lot, they made laws for their own convenience and pleasures, and to make sure that we will obey them, kept us away from the Good Books, and made a religion of their dogmas." The worst of this is that the women had little to lean on. They had to carry most of the burden of earning a livelihood and were exposed to the ugly realities of their lives. Mirele's thoughts spitefully escaped her control, as if they had been kept too long imprisoned, and anger took hold of her. How was she able to live as she did, all those years? She recalled and recalled many bitter events in those years and lived them through again in short minutes, feeling the taste of bitterness run through her.

Slowly the anger in her began to dissipate and some reasonableness took over. Yes, but didn't the women lean on their husbands, who were strengthened by their leanings? And was it their fault that the child-bearing fell to females? And didn't she remember how he suffered when she was in labor with their children? And how he wept when

---

* See Sabbath Brides and Queens of the Seder in the glossary.

they lost a child to the grave, and after he had spent the days in prayer, assuring the Lord of His wisdom! She studied his face and softened toward him; she admired his handsome face that his pointed beard complemented, though it was slowly turning from black to grey, as was his hair.

She noted and loved his personal cleanliness, his clothes always clean, never creased, his shoes looked as if he walked on new carpets instead of dusty and muddy country roads! After many times arguing with him, she gave up, and the girls' hair had to be combed and ribboned before they were taken to the Saturday services at the house of prayer; he counter-arguing that she "be careful and not tear as she combed them, and so it will not be sinful against the Sabbath. Besides, God did not want those He created in His image to look dirty or bedraggled in His House."

He even set an example of dusting his shoes on the first step of the synagogue, before entering, which the children followed, using their handkerchiefs they had tied on their wrists (it being a sin to carry anything on the Sabbath) and she could not stop him. She wondered what it would do to both of them to be so far apart. She now felt a love for him that she had at no time before recognized. She knew suddenly that she had the strength to carry on as she did, because she had him so close and what his closeness meant to her. She knew of his love for her, felt it all those years, warming herself in it, and now feared going from him.

A few weeks later, she received a letter from America. Schmuel wrote that he is sending her under separate cover a steamship ticket and some money; and that she should get help from Fishl to get a passport. Hannah sat with the two, Fishl and Mirele, as he read the letter to Mirele, and then she said to her, "Tell me why must you be the only woman in Kamenets to go to America, instead of your husband?"

"You have heard me say time and again that Avraham does not want to go there and does not want me to go either. I cannot sit by while our destitution grows and my children starve, I must do something about it."

"Yes, but why must you be the only woman in our town to leave a husband and children behind and go to America? I can't understand you."

"No, Hannah, you won't, leave her alone. Don't rub salt into her wounds," Fishl said with some heat. Then he turned to Mirele, "I will make all the necessary papers ready for you, and you make yourself ready to go." She thanked him and left for home, her thoughts in turmoil all the while.

"Make ready to go," sang in her blood, "make yourself ready to go, make yourself ready to go," until she became aware of her swift walking and added to her singing blood, "and fast, so fast that I do not have time to think, or my resolution will come to naught."

At home she had a long talk with her mother, pleading with her to stay on with the children while she tries to make a nest for them in America.

"You speak as if Avraham will let them go to you then. I am afraid that you will not change his mind; and then what will become of you and them? Your life will be torn, and they will grow to manhood and womanhood without you. Mirele, I want to be of help to you and the children, but I fear Avraham's stubbornness in this; he does not even want to listen to himself for fear that he will find himself in the wrong. Maybe you should speak to him again, maybe only you would be friendly with each other and there was not so much anger between you, maybe then he would soften a little." Chaya stopped talking because she saw the pain she was inflicting on her and realized the uselessness of her words.

"But Mother, I still don't know how you feel about remaining here with the children. I know that I am asking a great deal of you, as I did all those years you gave yourself to me for my children's sake. You have done so much for me, that were I to live a thousand years, I could not repay you in deed or otherwise. But if you feel now that you would rather not undertake this hard task, I would hold nothing against you; only I must know now, that I know where I am at."

Chaya saw the desperation in her eyes and hastened to assure her, this should be your only worry. "You know that I will stay on, I will not leave the children to themselves."

"You mean like I intend to do, eh?" Bitterness distorted her voice.

"Now why do you twist the words in my mouth. I only meant that …"

"I know, I know, Mother, forgive me, I know that you did not aim to hurt me, but my soul is raw, and no matter what one says or does, I hurt all over." She sat silently and watched as her mother drew a glass of hot tea from the singing samovar and placed it in front of her, then placed her own glass of hot tea into the palm of her hand. It made her wonder that right hand was still good after so many years of drinking her tea just so.

Chaya sat down across from her, sipping from her glass after she had inserted a lump of sugar between her cheek and upper gum, and did not know what to say to strengthen her daughter's hopes for the future, nor did she know her own feelings about remaining with the children without her around. She felt a little fearful, for she knew that Avraham will not feel too friendly toward her for releasing his wife to go to America, making it easier for her to leave the children. She also expected their poverty to worsen without Mirele's help. Still, she did what she had to do, knowing that Mirele had no other way out.

"Mother, I will go out now and look for another dwelling. With me gone, Doctor Popov will feel the house and its care to be insecure, and being the good man he is, he will not say anything but he will feel very uncomfortable. I will go to the City, I would like to settle you there where you will not be far from Hannah and your sister Baba, and Avraham will be close to his sister Nahama. I feel that in the City, you will also be a little safer should a pogrom break out and Avraham has most of his pupils there too."

That same day she found a two-room house that had a windowless kitchen that was taken up by the big, Russian-style brick stove that left a small space for a work table and a huge room with a wide *gruba*, a straw-burning fireplace, that took up almost half of one wall. Three windows, two facing into the large courtyard and one to the side of the house, brightened the room like a lantern. This was one of eight houses (some a little bigger, others a little smaller) standing in a half-circle in the vast courtyard in back of the Governor's Mansion. One had to pass through half of the Governor's Plaza to get to the narrow cobblestoned street leading down to this courtyard that boasted Zalman Goldstein's enormous house, which stood across the garden, looking much the "rich uncle" with its richly curtained and draped windows and many entrances. A low, spiked fence circled the big garden in the center of the courtyard, which still retained some of the late summer colors in the trees, vines, and shrubs—although it was already early fall—and made it look like yesterday's bouquet.

At home she told her mother and children of her find. "And if, God forbid, a pogrom should break out, the blackguards won't think of crossing the Governor's Plaza, would they? And the courtyard is very safe with its enclosure of a high fence of heavy logs that has a big door to admit vehicles; and within this door is a smaller one that is used for passersby and both are locked late at night by the *dvornik*, the caretaker.* True, the house is not very big, but we are not spoiled for big houses, are we? Oh, that garden, I just can't forget it. Even now, this time of the year, it is still so alive and beautiful that in my wildest dreams, I could not have seen such colors and shapes of its growth! The rear of the governor's house has a piece of land that slopes down into the courtyard with many trees on it that are much taller than the houses, stunting them and making them appear like poor relatives at a rich wedding." Her voice was heavy and tremulous with emotion. Chaya knew that it was not caused by the beauty of the garden nor the safety of their new dwelling; and she sent up a prayer for the day when she will see her daughter gone on her way—before she broke down. Too many days had she watched her look at her children with a heartbreaking hunger, as if she tried to imprint their images in her very blood.

"I wish Avraham would come home, I can't wait to tell him about it," Mirele added, but if she really expected to enthuse him, she was sorely disappointed. For he merely looked at her and did not say one word! His look went through her like a stab wound, reminding her of one other time he had looked upon her with so much anger. That was when she was desperate in their poverty and children's illness, and she wept. But at least he spoke to her then! True, what he had said was not much comfort to her: "You are so afraid of your tomorrows that you fear living today," but at least he spoke his mind, and she was able to

* Russian for concierge or groundskeeper.

make a silent rebuttal—perhaps that was so, but that was because he did not worry for the todays nor the tomorrows!

Bena and Rachel hung around her constantly, their eyes full of unasked questions, afraid of the time when she will leave them behind. And she, knowing it and feeling their hurt, tried to keep a cheerful mood in the house, joking as never before, teasing as never before and making attempts to sing with them but succeeding only in creating more tension in the air. Adah gave her more worry than the others; she feared breaking the news to her when she will go for her at Evdokiya's farm. The doctor had warned her about the child's condition; telling her that seven times lung fever in a child of eight was very serious, and one more attack may prove fatal to her. How upset will she get by the news? She really did not know, for she knew very little of her three youngest children; she was too much taken up with their physical needs.

She awakened from her sleep when it was still dark out and dressed quietly and left the house for Evdokiya's farm, knowing that the next few days will keep her busy with moving the family to the new home, and she was anxious to see Adah. The walk through the still-sleeping New Plan was refreshing, with crisp, sweet air, and by the time she reached the *folvareki*, the farmlands, the sun rose up full and warm like in greeting, and Mirele smiled her appreciation. She always loved the *folvareki* but rarely had time to spend there and now walked along leisurely enjoying everything she saw. Peasants' small huts stood as if with folded arms now that the harvest was in; wooden implements leaned against the walls, resting from their long toil of the summer, and waiting for sharpening and repair for further use. Smoke curling from the chimneys, the only activity around, reclaimed life inside the huts. The vast fields glowed a golden brown from the distance—looking much like a woman soon after the birth of her child—knowing and ready for the next dissemination. Only the cornfields looked dark, with the stubble off the cut cornstalks that looked up at the sun in futility. She passed huge pastures now turning colors, where cattle were grazing and fields with tall bales of hay drying in the sun looked like overdressed children playing games.

Her senses were lulled with the peaceful countryside, and she felt full of energy and alive to her responsibilities. She made mental arrangements for the children's needs and her trip. Feeling almost happy that at last she knew that she was working in the right direction, her spirits soared with new hope. If only Avraham would now let her speak to him, if only he gave her a chance to explain her plans to him and not cause her to leave without an understanding between them. If only his bitterness was not so deep and hurtful, it would not tie them into such tangled knots! But come what may, she must go forward, she must not hesitate now and spoil her plans.

As she neared the farm she heard children's voices in the distance, young laughing and shouting voices, and soon saw a flock of children run toward her with Adah in the lead. "Mama, Mama, I saw you coming up the road from the hayloft. My friends did not know who it was, but I knew you by your wig and the reed basket," she panted hard and threw her arms about her.

"My goodness, whatever did Evdokiya do to you? You look like a stuffed goose." She held her at arm's length and looked her over while the other children stood at a little distance and shyly watched the two.

Evdokiya came to the door and seeing Adah in the arms of a strange woman understood her to be the child's mother, bid her welcome and held the door open for her. "Adah, I see you have a guest, the rest of you children go back to the barn and play with the new puppies."

Mirele entered the kitchen, suddenly felt her head reel from alien cooking smells, and for a short moment thought of how Katynka must have felt stifled upon entering their home the very first time. She looked around the huge room and was impressed with its cleanliness and saw many tin pails mouth down, a wooden rack still wet from a recent washing, probably waiting for the evening milking. Both women felt stiff and shy, stealing glances at each other, having heard so much of each other's goodness from Katynka, and trying to find some opening.

"Sit down, please, you must be tired from the long walk," Evdokiya pulled a chair to the table for her, and Mirele sat down still holding her arms around Adah, but not taking her eyes off Evdokiya, for she was fascinated by her tall and gaunt appearance and charming sun-browned face; her green eyes that slanted outward toward high cheekbones lit up her broad face with deep expression and the heavy black braids were wound and wound around her head into a garland of gloss.

Suddenly Adah put her mouth to her mother's ear and whispered, "Did you come to take me back home?"

"Well, do you want to go?" Mirele asked her. "I don't know, sometimes I miss my father, and grandmother, and Bena and Rachel and Isaiah and even Raphael, but I love my friends here so much."

"And did you ever miss me?" Mirele asked laughingly but Adah ran out before she answered and was heard to call to the children, "Maybe I can stay longer," making both women smile.

"If you ask me and if I would know that you won't be hurt, I would tell you that she did not miss anyone," Evdokiya said, and both women laughed, finding a oneness in their knowledge of children's ability to adjust to more children and some of their restraint fell away. "Adah feels here like at home, at no time did she show unhappiness with anyone or anything except some fear for the horses so that she keeps her distance. Would you like for her to stay on a while longer?" she asked with friendliness.

"No, I came to take her back with me. I suppose that Katynka had told you that I am going to leave for America, and I expect to go in a week or ten days and would like to see the family all together before I go. Evdokiya, let me tell you now how thankful I am to you and your husband for giving so much care to our child when she was so much in need of it. Who knows if she would now be alive if not for your kindness," tears welled up in Mirele's eyes and she reached into her reed basket and took from it a roll of rubles and placed them at the peasant woman's elbow. "I wish I could pay your kindness back with deeds too, but, seeing that I am unable to, please take this money."

"Oh no, don't give me this, you don't owe me so much; you brought me so much cotton goods when you brought Adah here that the girls and the boys will be dressed like City children now that the harvest is in and I can do the sewing. Please put the money away. Katynka told me of your difficulties, you need it more than I do. As for deeds, what you have done for my cousin Katynka is no less than what I have done for your child. Katynka told me of the doctor's warning that Adah must be watched against another attack of lung fever and I want you to know that anytime she needs coming up here, she is welcome." Evdokiya now spoke with the freeness of a friend, her green eyes warm and sincere.

"Yes, of all my worries of going away, Adah's threatened life weighs on me the hardest." The doctor stressed the danger of an eight-year-old child who suffered seven winters with lung fever, and she feared another attack might change her mind and keep her from going, but all she heard were words of assurance from her mother—that her grandmother would want Katynka in the house often as a visitor; that she wouldn't in the least mind her there; and that the children would welcome her with open arms, while Katynka kept nodding her head and weeping.

Then they lowered their voices and whispered to each other so low Adah could not hear a thing, making her feel like she would like to scream, but instead she began to move closer and closer to them and when she was about to hear what they said, she found herself in her mother's lap! The women looked up with some concern at the child and then Mirele raised herself with some difficulty and said, "Come on my child, we must be on our way, it is already dark out and we are both tired." The two friends looked into each other's eyes, kissed and clung to each other while tears washed down their faces, and parted. Again Mirele took the child's hand into hers and started for home.

Being busy with the moving and installing her family in the new dwelling covered her nagging spirit for the next few days and she felt almost happy, but when her hands could find no more work, she became aware of the children's watchful eyes upon her and a deep depression settled once more and took over her being. Seeing her children's distress and her mother's anxiety was punishment enough, but Avraham's silence and his wounded appearance were more than she could bear! She heard Rachel tell him one morning that she wanted him to do something about not letting her go, that "he should shout and even beat her, as Elya the Barrel Mender does his wife when she puts too much salt into the gefilte fish, anything—just so he keeps her home," because she, Rachel, "does not know how she would live without seeing her beautiful mother the very first thing in the morning and the last thing at night!"

Even the girl's heartrending crying did not move him to speech! The boys were the only two in the house who did not seem to be too much disturbed about losing their mother to America. They went on with their studies, their pranks, and friend-making in the courtyard as if nothing of importance was taking place in their lives. Bena's eyes were open to understanding everything, while her face carried an unhealthy flush that did not go well with her forced bounciness. She felt so much older than the rest of her sisters and brothers and tried to act as such, trying to be of help to her mother wherever possible until the very day when all the important papers arrived, and then the wagon that was to take her to the railroad station.

Mirele quickly packed her belongings, working fast before her tears fell, then kissed her children, her mother, and walked with determination to the door although her knees were buckling under her. When she was about to climb into the wagon, she felt Avraham's hand helping her up, and then he handed her a package of food that her mother had prepared for the journey. He looked hard at her, then kissed her burning eyes and bade her Godspeed.

She made herself believe that this was only a dream, that she was not leaving the children, her mother, and an angry husband behind—but the rocking, rolling vehicle did not help her believe too long as it raised itself on protruding rocks and stones and came down again with a force that made the straw on its floor fly. Her thoughts fastened onto the past again with all the hardships and illnesses of the children, as if a hand was raised against their lives and they would follow each other to the grave before they were in their teens.

Aside from those she buried, Adah gave her more trouble than the others, for even though she was well for a spell, she got into all sorts of mischief from which it took her a long time to recover. Like with the straw-covered bottle of acetic acid that was kept for vinegar dilution, with which she almost killed herself. Thinking that it was *kvass*, cider from fermented grain, the child who was always after something sweet managed to reach the high shelf, pull the bottle down, and pour some down her throat and soon fell to the floor screaming.

God was good in His mercy and led Mirele to pour baking oil down the child's throat, while someone ran to get the doctor. When he came he shook his head in helplessness and said, "You did all I could do, let us leave her up to the good Lord for protection." What misery they all suffered the following three months watching the child fade and shrink—and they had to stand by her powerless. Then when the balance tipped in her favor and she was able to take a little cereal, a little milk or an egg, the relentless winter set in and with it another attack of lung fever that nearly carried her off to the other world!

Mirele's thoughts flew from one child to the next, to the boys, to their mischievous pranks, their teasing, their brilliant manipulations to get some things out of their grandmother—and from each other; to Rachel, who gave her much joy with her constant sunny nature and enthusiasm for life; but when she dwelled on Bena, a special warmth spread in her, for she knew the oldest better than the rest, she was the easiest to raise. She always stood at her side, understanding what and when to say and do whenever she was needed or whenever there was stress in the shop or in the home.

If only she did not leave Bena at home now! What chances of marriage will she have with their poverty? All her charm and prettiness will not do her any good unless she could bring her to America before she gets too old. With Avraham so set against it, only God knows what will happen to her. Yes, yes, every child brings its own joy and sorrow to the parents, sooner or later.

She tried to push Avraham from her thoughts, not wanting to feel the deep wound in her heart. Try as she would, his sullen face of the past few months loomed, causing her to weep. How could this come about? How could they become such strangers after so many years of meaning what they were to each other? Was it her fault that their lives were so hard and she had to be the breadwinner for the family and go seek the bread where it was to be found? She searched her soul deeply where she was at fault, and found many reasons for his bitterness other than her going to America. She understood his wretchedness for their poverty, which he tried so hard to cover up with his own clean, neat appearance but could not do so with the family's old, worn things. She understood his feelings of inadequacy as the family's provider and how deep it ran, despite the fact that among the most pious Jews in Russia it was in the main that the woman provided for the family, while the man sat all day in the yeshiva, the house of learning, or just helped her to increase her earnings in some small way.

Avraham used to deride those students of the Talmud, saying that many do so to escape their responsibilities for their families. She felt that she stood out as one that took his place and shrank his ego to a malignancy in the eyes of his family and in the eyes of the more progressive world. And did she help their situation any more by keeping him at arm's length lately? True that she feared another pregnancy and did not want another child who they were not able to feed, but didn't this help intensify his growing acrimony? But how was she to cope with their worsening conditions while with each pregnancy she felt that she would not have the strength to live through it? And why didn't he realize her torture, staying so close to him and yet fearing his nearness? After all the years of knowing each other, knowing and loving each other's bodies as they did, why couldn't he understand, and react with understanding instead of so much spleen? Her thoughts and emotions became mixed, and she was glad when she heard the driver tell her that he wants to stop to water the horses near the little brook. And although she came to no insights in herself, she was glad that he broke into her thoughts, which were causing her so much pain.

She watched as the driver unharnessed the horses and led them to the water and then took from his coat pocket some thin paper and a pouch of tobacco and rolled himself a cigarette with expert fingers. "While we wait, maybe you would want to eat your lunch," he asked her, and she suddenly felt hungry and cramped and wanted to stretch her legs after the long uncomfortable wagon ride. And she rankled because she did not throw back into the driver's teeth his antisemitic question as soon as he asked it, "If it was not so that the Jews go to America to get rich?"

"Dear Lord, if it was to get rich, would I now go so far from my children?" she thought, and a deep depression settled within her that was coupled with guilt that she was deserting her family—and at the same time being deserted herself!

She sat huddled in her lonesomeness not seeing what went on around her; forgetting to walk through the entire station to see its many attractions, as she had promised herself so many times to do. She felt thirst but was too indisposed to move. Not until she felt the heavy impact into her abdomen that caused her to scream with pain did she become alive to her surroundings and saw the round, hard, corn-colored head that ran into her to avoid being caught by an older brother. The older boy stood looking at her with some awkwardness then asked, "Did he hurt you?" all the time holding on to his brother's wrist. And Mirele, seeing the youngster's fear, tried to lessen it by quickly assuring his brother that it was not bad at all, that she had screamed with fright not with pain. At the same time she caressed the well-shaped, corn-colored head—which suddenly jerked away from her and its owner shouted up to his brother, "Let go of me, let go, don't you see she is a Jew—I don't want her to touch me with her hands, let me go. I am afraid of her Jew wig," and he forced his hands free and ran away, with his brother following.

Mirele shook her head and thought of her mother's words: "Little children swallow what adults chew." Although her mood was bitter, she was fully awake and angry and began to look around at her neighbors. She saw the many people through the breadth of the station as so many passengers like herself, but they looked different than she felt—they looked busy with children, with husbands, with wives, and happy! And she saw many non-Jews too, and they were going to America too! Why did the antisemitism have to follow her here to add to her isolation? Or was it to strengthen her conviction that in America all people are equal and everyone's religion is honored and respected, and it is there that she must go to make a place for her family!

4

Grandmother Chaya turns smuggler

AS SOON AS AVRAHAM SAW MIRELE seated in the wagon, he went back into the house and stood a while at the window with unseeing eyes and a conscience that was pricked by guilt and remorse; then absentmindedly picked up his prayer book and sat down at the table with his head bent low over it. Chaya found him that way and a deep sigh escaped her—but what could she say to comfort him? what solace could she offer him? But when she saw the suffering on the children's faces, she worked her face into one of serenity and loudly proclaimed, "Now that your mother, with God's help, is on her way to America, I will bake a fresh batch of bread—that is if you will all help me—then you can eat it with the butter that's been left from breakfast," and she found chores for every one of them down to little Raphael, who was really taken by surprise, for this was the first time his grandmother asked him to bring in the firewood from the back of the woodshed.

Avraham was disturbed by her promise of hot bread and raised his head. "How many times have I told you not to give them hot bread, it will give them cramps in their stomachs? Why do you insist on giving it to them?" His voice sounded petulant.

"Tell me the truth, how many times did I give it to them, and how many times did you hear them complain of bellyaches?" She looked at him with mocking and turned to the children again. "Today is a special day, and besides, we must use up the butter before it gets rancid, we saved it too long."

"Yes, yes, today is a special day, let's wallow in luxury," Avraham grumbled, shaking his head. He went to the closet and exchanged his skullcap for his hat and left the house in a black mood.

Painfully and slowly the household settled down to its habitual activities and to living without Mirele's presence. All suffered in silence with tears shed inward but Rachel, who moaned and groaned in her sleep, "my beautiful Mama," almost nightly and with such distress that it shook those who heard her, bringing to the fore their own deep longing for Mirele.

With her gone, Avraham had a very bad time feeding his family, and Chaya felt sick with the knowledge that the children were suffering hunger and that she will never be able to sate them on her son-in-law's small earnings. She began to ask around and learned from one of her neighbors that in Zalman Goldstein's kitchen they needed help and she lost no time applying there. She was told to come in early Friday mornings and on mornings before holidays to help with cooking and baking, for which she would be able to take home some food. On those mornings she would leave the home in the hands of the mystified children, saying loudly, "Where I go is my business, and when I tell you to clean the house, and prepare for the Sabbath, don't question me, and don't forget to wash the children's heads with kerosene and yours too, Bena and Rachel. I won't be home too late to prepare the supper, don't worry."

She made sure that what she said would reach Avraham's ears too, because she knew that he was more curious than the children. In the kitchen of the rich landlord, where the gleaming copper pots and pans lived on long wide shelves and the smells of the food made her sick with hunger, she plucked dry feathers from chickens and geese, cut them into quarters for soups and roasting, and made them kosher by soaking and salting them. She kneaded dough for *challah*, cakes, and noodles, and when the cook was busy with other work, prepared the desserts.

For this work she was given all the giblets from the fowls she prepared, which she brought home and, together with a few bones and a small piece of meat, cooked suppers with it. This went on for a few weeks and although Avraham wondered how they came in to such good soups and so many chicken gizzards, hearts, and feet, on Friday nights and Saturdays for the Sabbath meals, he hesitated to ask any questions. But once, when she also added a small piece of chicken to the meal—which the cook gave her for staying later than usual—he wanted to know where she got so much money to buy it with. At this Raphael, who sat quietly eating and enjoying his supper, looked up at his grandmother with long, black eyelashes and before he could say a word, Avraham cut him off. "I did not ask you my child, only when one asks you directly should you answer." Chaya knew that he was waiting for her answer, but she became very busy in the kitchen.

She left her meal unfinished and went outdoors and sat down on the house ledge where two neighbors, sisters, soon joined her. Moya, the older of two, the one who received a bigger contribution from her children in America than did Susa, who also had two sons there, was the one more talkative and friendly. "Gut Shabbos, Chaya, I see that you are already finished with supper and out to draw the fresh heavenly air into you." Chaya responded with a shake of her head in response and remained quiet.

"I hope you enjoyed your fish, we did not, and I am aggravated. I told Susa that the fish did not look so fresh to me, but she paid no attention and told the fish man to wrap it up, and he should have heard how the fish tasted after we went through the trouble of chopping, seasoning, and cooking it!"

Susa remained silent; with the small amount she received every month from her sons, she could not afford to live away from her sister and she knew that she had to let her have her way if she was to share her little house with her. She sat with closed lips but her face burned and Chaya was not fooled.

She tried to dispel their bad mood and said, "Better bad fish than no fish at all," and both sisters quickly understood that in their neighbor's house on the Sabbath table there was no fish, and they both shook their heads in understanding and commiseration. The children came out of the house and also sat down on the house ledge, and in no time began such noisy play that the women had to leave them to themselves and went to walk around the garden a few times until Chaya decided to go into the house again.

She found Avraham at the table over his Holy books and sat down across from him with a glassful of hot tea in the palm of her hand. He looked up and with his eyes begged for the answer which she could no longer escape. She slowly and carefully placed the glass of tea on the table and, looking him hard in the face, asked, "Are you then so insensitive to your children's hunger that you can afford to let your Jewish pride stand in the way of their eating a little more food? I cannot stand by and watch their faces and bodies shrink and their eyes get bigger and duller day by day. At such time I cannot think of pride; they are growing children and must have something to grow on or they will join their sisters and brothers in the cemetery. What is wrong if I do a little work and bring into the house some food for it?" Two rings of fire encircled her high cheekbones and her fingers were busy tying and untying her kerchief.

"You still did not tell me for whom you work, what kind of work you do," he reminded her in an icy tone that cut into her and stung her to answer.

"I know that you will not like what I will tell you, but if you must know, I am working for the servant in Zalman Goldstein's kitchen every Friday morning, and for that I get giblets and sometimes even a meat pie." She watched as his face went ashen with anger and wretchedness and added quickly, "My daughter left all that's dear to her so that she could provide a better life for her children, a future where they will not suffer hunger and want and I will do all I can to keep them alive for her." The rings of fire had now spread all over her face making it look sick with fever.

"You mean to tell me that you dared to degrade me so? You went to serve in a kitchen? In my family, no one served anyone else but our Lord! How will I be able to look anyone in the face now? Avraham the Scribe's mother-in-law, a servant's servant! As for your daughter, if she did not hold so much fear for her tomorrows, her todays would be taken care of by the same God that cares for all His children, but no, she had to fly in His face to show Him how strong she was and run off to America. To think that for a few giblets you would take it upon yourself to humiliate me so, and make my children appear as paupers. I know that it is too late, but I expect you to see what you did to my good name and discontinue your 'honorable' work."

He stood up and walked to the window and with his back to her, added, "There will be no more of this in my house. God will provide for us. He does for all His people, and see that I don't have to remind you of it again." He changed his skullcap for his hat and left the house, angry at his mother-in-law, at his wife, and his poverty that wrought so much misery in their lives.

5

Garment shop

ONDAY MORNING BENA AND RACHEL were up at sunrise and quietly left the house without disturbing anyone, and were well out of the courtyard before Bena began to speak. "Now I will tell you where we are bound for. I learned that Ginendle the Shirtmaker in New Plan needs apprentices and if we hurry, we might get hired by her."

"That I would like, I always wanted to know how to work on a machine, and besides, maybe we will earn some money too!" Rachel was all aglow.

"Well, the machine does not interest me one bit, but I am anxious to learn to work it because we must earn something toward our food in the house. I don't know what she will give us but I heard she gives something in addition to the hot lunches that she serves the girls," Bena puffed hard and begged her sister not to walk too fast, because she could not keep up with her.

"You remind me of a bad mother-in-law, to complain of her daughter-in-law when she walked too slow, and called her lazy, and when she walked too fast, she called after her that she is tearing her shoes. You want to get there before someone else gets the job, but you complain that I walk too fast!" Rachel was excited at the prospect of the machine and working with other girls. She loved people and they warmed up to her very fast. "You know, Bena, we should make up between us now that no matter what Ginendle will offer us we should bargain for more, because I heard that she is very unfair to her girls and dishonest with those that she deals with."

"How do you know so much about her, did you ever see her?" Bena wondered.

"Oh, I never saw her, but I heard our neighbor Monya talk to grandma about her and from what I've heard, I can well imagine what kind of boss she is."

"Serves you right, you listened to gossip and now you are frightened of her. I know that she is a pious woman, married to Eecheal the Hasid, and because they are childless, she most probably treats the girls who work for her like her own," Bena said righteously.

"Oh yes, would her own cousin gossip about her? Monya is her first cousin and feels ashamed of her. You know what she does when a peasant or a soldier bargains about the price of a shirt? She puts her hand over a large knob of celluloid that adorns her comb that holds her wig in place and swears that 'this head' should die if the shirt does not cost her more, and the poor victim thinks that she is swearing by her real head wig and believes her and pays her price!" Rachel was indignant.

"Well, we will see for ourselves when we get there," Bena answered and wished that the distance would be swallowed up a little faster.

They were well past the bridge and were approaching the public market that still showed the ravages of the last pogrom, but here and there a hopeful stallholder stood on a ladder hammering nails into smoke-blackened boards or thatching roofs. The only quarters that stood intact were Ginendle's shop, storehouse, and home, which were housed under one roof. For some reason the onslaught of the Cossacks' fury missed this house although it was standing on the very edge of the marketplace and in the way of the wild and destructive force! Some pious Jews in the synagogue believed it was because God wanted to spare the good Hasid Eecheal's home for his purity, others believed it to be a miracle, and others because Ginendle paid off the leader of the assault!

When the girls reached the door, they were hungry and tired, but were anxious to get inside and talk to Ginendle, and Bena led the way in. A smell of cotton materials and machine oil assailed their nostrils as they went into the shop, and there they were met by a tall, buxom woman who walked with a man's long stride and asked them what they wanted.

"We heard that you wanted learners," Bena informed her.

"Yes, I need some new girls, can you sew by machine?"

"No, but we want to learn, that's why we came to you," again Bena spoke up.

"I really needed learners two weeks ago, now I can use girls with experience, but we'll see what I can do with you. Where do you live and who are your parents?" She looked closely at them.

"My father is Avraham the Scribe, and we live in the City in back of the Governor's Mansion."

"Yes, I know your father, your mother went to America didn't she?"

"Yes, she left a few months ago," Rachel answered.

"All right now, I'll show you how to work the machine, then I'll see what you can do; here, sit down near me and watch." She directed them to a bench.

"Before we start, could you tell us what you will pay?" Rachel ventured.

"Like I pay all beginners. The first two years they get lunch every day that they come to work, and a pair of shoes, new ones, for the Passover holidays. In the third year they get 5 rubles in addition for the year." She looked sharply at Rachel, who was looking at Bena expecting her to do some bargaining, but seeing her closed face, remarked, "That's all you pay? Why, we will tear our shoes before the year is up, we come from so far they will wear out in no time; as for the lunches, they too will not feed us for the day. What will we have for our work, can't you do a little better?"

Ginendle saw Rachel's excited face and turned angrily on her, "Look you young snot-nose, I don't need you here, and I didn't send for you to come. Is it my fault that you live so far from here? You can take the job or leave it, it's one thing to me, so don't waste my valuable time." She liked Bena's silence and turned to her, "Why don't you tell your big-mouthed sister not to talk so much? Come on and sit down here and let's begin to work."

Before the day was over the two girls knew how to thread and oil the machine, and learned how to sew the straight seams of the shirts together. Ginendle soon learned to like Rachel, who no sooner learned the work when she became the faster of the two. She sang and laughed all day at the machine, while the rest of the girls began to complain to her that they had trouble catching up and when Bena scolded her for racing with her work, she tried to slow down, but soon forgot herself and made the shop hum again with the fast machine and her loud singing. Bena had learned to put the shirt together with much difficulty, and at the end of the day complained of back pains and came home in a low mood. The hardest part of the day's work for both of them was the walk of eight miles back home, no matter good weather or foul.

Chaya's lot eased up a bit. Two mouths less to feed left more for the younger children, but it was still not enough and she had to find some work that will add a little food in the house. She asked around for a while and then she learned that a rich family from a faraway city had settled on the very edge of the town in a big house and that the household was preparing to marry off the youngest daughter, the last of six children. Well, she thought, here must be some work for me, even if it is for a short time. Avraham does not know them, and they do not know my proud son-in-law, and as soon as the Sabbath is over, I'll take myself off there. And she did, although it took her almost two hours to get there the first time, till she learned of a short cut that brought her back within an hour. There she learned from the kitchen help that they did not need her in the kitchen, but did want someone to pluck down from goose feathers for new pillows for the bride.

She eagerly accepted the work and there spent two to three hours a day, not telling anyone but Adah where she was going and bribed her into silence with sweets she brought back for her. The few rubles she earned, she spent on staples such as buckwheat groats, flour, and beans and hoarded them in the attic against the coming winter. When she used some while she was still working, she did so with a sparing hand, for fear of seeing her "little store" dwindle down or, still worse, arousing her son-in-law's suspicion.

The very first letter that came from Mirele was a big event for the entire family, for she was gone more than two months and until this letter they had heard nothing from her and they had worried. Avraham came home holding the letter in his hand, asked if the two older girls had come from work yet, and upon being told that they had not, he slyly put the letter on the table, looking disappointed, and said, "We'll wait for them!" The two boys looked so curiously at the envelope that Avraham could not help remarking, "Watch out, a rabbit may jump out of there!" and while they all laughed, Chaya turned from fear of what might be in the letter one minute, to the next, the hope that Mirele had found what she went looking for in America.

At last the girls came in and Avraham sat down near the lighted lamp and read it to them.

> My dear family,
>
> I am well, and I hope our Lord kept you all well and happy. My trip across the ocean was not a good one; most of the passengers were sick with what the doctor termed dysentery, and many died of it. I was well but seeing all that misery around me made my trip a nightmare. At present I am living with my brother Sam (Schmuel) and I found work in a factory where coats are made for ladies. Imagine, I—who had always been so clumsy with a needle, who could not even make a decent patch on a child's piece of clothing—have now learned to sew linings into coats, sew buttons on them and even sew collars of fur on them. I am called a "cloak-finisher" in the trade, and I make as much as 15 dollars a week. I am able to pay off my ship's ticket, pay Yhitta for my meals, and I am putting away for another ship's ticket as much as I can. I am doing pretty well, dear ones, and I am looking forward to the day when we will all be together again.
>
> Avraham, I want you to send Bena to me as soon as I send you some additional money to the draft of the 10 dollars I enclosed and her ship's ticket. Together with her, we can work and save up enough money to bring

the family across so much sooner, while the children are still young and will have an opportunity to go to school. Bena is no youngster any more, she is of an age when we must think of marriage for her, and what chance has she got where she is now without a dowry? Surely you don't want her to marry a widower with a house full of children or a cripple, God forbid! In America dowries play a small role among the working people, unless a girl is far gone in years or is deformed in some way. Everyone wants to marry a lawyer or a doctor, she puts herself into the hands of a matchmaker and it winds up in a business deal.

Bena can easily get a fine workman (without a dowry), who will make a good living for her. Avraham, please don't make it too difficult for our daughter, help her get away from home; give her a chance, she is a good child, but she needs our help to see her on the way to a future. Sam and his entire family send their love to all of you, and they too hope to see you soon in America.

Your wife, Mirele

Avraham raised his eyes and looked around at his assembly's flushed faces and shinning eyes and knew that they were waiting for him to say something. He only folded the letter slowly, and put it together with the money draft back in the envelope and with sudden anger threw it hard on the table. All, down to the little "lost-soul" Raphael, felt his bitterness but asked no questions of him. When all had gone to bed, and the lamp was put out, very few eyes were shut in sleep.

Avraham lay in the dark going over and over what he had read in the letter and could not forgive his wife for having taken the reins completely and with such strong determination tried to direct the whole family's lives. Did she think that he was going to follow her directions just because she gives them in a soft, pleading voice? He knew her scheme. He knew that if he allowed Bena to go, it would take but a short time and she would ask for the rest of the children!

No, he had told her before she went away that the children will stay with him as long as he is alive. That he was not going to allow even one child to cross the ocean to America. Then why was she asking him to send Bena? He had made sure that she understood him well and that he meant every word he had said to her. Then what makes her think that he was going to do her bidding, that he has changed his mind? Does she think him so weak-minded that he has already forgotten? Well, then he will have to convince her once and for all that he meant everything he told her then, by not answering her letters now! Yes, let her do all the letter-writing she wants, he will never answer a one, not a single one! Let her stay on in her glorious America, alone, till she gets tired of its golden opportunities, being without her husband and her children and decides to come home! Yes, he will give her a chance to look around and find what a foolish venture she went on. He will not answer any of her letters, nary a one. Let her wait, and worry, and write, and wonder, and worry and boil in torment as she made him do!

Even while his thoughts were working in anger and rage, something inside him failed to register or relieve his passion. He felt like one hit by buckshot instead of expected bullets and became confused. He stretched his arm and picked up the cigarette box from the table and pulled one out, but refrained from lighting it for fear of awakening Raphael, who held on fast to his chest with a claw-like grip. He put the cigarette back on the table and tried to force some sleep from his distressed being and he shut his eyes very tight, trying to shut out everything, including the moonlight that had moved on to his bed. But his mind played a contradictory battle now and did not let him sleep.

He opened his eyes again and began to send up a plea to the One above. He needed help, but in the midst of the appeal he found himself unable to clarify his thoughts, for his anger seemed to float around him in the air, trapped in absorbent cotton, making all sorts of faces at him! He sat up quickly, feeling that his mind was failing him, almost throwing Raphael on top of Isaiah, and began to rub his forehead.

He sat thus a long while, then without being aware what he was doing, found himself separating and examining the circumstances of his dilemma. He turned his thoughts to the girls and grudgingly admitted to himself that their future did not seem too rosy, particularly Bena's, as she had become too quiet, too much introverted in the last few years. He knew that she carried more hurt than the other children. Since she was very young she had felt the poverty and the hardships of the family, and helped as much as her underfed body was able, to take the punishment.

Her chances for a good marriage were doubtful here at home, but how could he send her off to America, knowing that he will never see her again? "Then you want to make her a sacrifice on your altar of selfishness?" a laughing face of anger swam in front of his eyes and he put his hand up and tried to sweep it away, now knowing that anger obscured his thinking. He got off the bed and felt around the lamp on the table and found the letter where he knew he had thrown it earlier in the evening, and sat down on the bed again and tried to reread it by the light of the moon. He was unable to see it, but he knew every word that had goaded him into his madness in that letter and decided to tell Bena to go to the tailor and have the clothes made.

He knew Mirele's strength, he knew that she will never return to Kamenets-Podolski. But, he knows that he too is strong in his convictions; and he will show her that he is also fair in dealing with her, fairer than she tries to deal with him. He will send her Bena, but no other child! He will show her that he could care for his children so that eventually he will raise them and make good men and women of them, so much so that she will hear all the way to her newly adopted land of them, and feel proud of them even though she did nothing to help in their development!

In the morning he told Bena to order a pair of shoes in addition to her clothes and gave her the 10 dollar draft. Chaya and the girls were surprised at his change of mood but did not question or talk about it, leaving good enough alone. He went about making the preparations for the journey.

Unexpected discord, however, rose in the house. The boys began to show off their nastiness by making faces at everyone, fighting with each other, asking all sorts of crazy questions, and demanding food every few minutes of the day! Adah, back only a short time from the farm, begged to sleep with Bena every night but Rachel refused to give up her usual place with Bena, and Adah followed her around the house every minute she was home, then suddenly blew up at the supper table one night and threw her spoon down with a clatter onto the table and shouted, "I want Bena to go away from the table, want her to go now," and sobbed as if her heart would break!

"What in the world is the matter with you," Chaya asked, "Why should your sister go away from the table, are you afraid that she will eat too much?"

"I want her to go away now, do you hear me? Right now!" and became hysterical, and Avraham nodded to Bena to leave the table.

She went away and sat down near the window, feeling hurt and bitter and turned to her father, "I have only three more days to spend with all of you here, and who knows how long it will be before I see any of you again, and everybody in the house acts as if you can't wait until you get rid of me!"

"Why do you say such thing? Who wants to get rid of you? Do you know what it means to me to lose you to America?" Avraham tried covering his guilt for giving in to his wife.

"Everybody! No, not grandma, she too sees how my dear sisters and brothers are carrying on since the letter came! The boys are acting like idiots all day and even in the evening when your back is turned, and Adah who was so close to me always, now took her turn to show me how much she loves me. Of Rachel's action, these last few days I am ashamed to talk even. She stopped talking to me as if I am taking her place with Mama by force and not out of necessity. Does she really think that she could sit in a shop and work like an adult? After all, I am eight years older than her! As for you, Papa, I am well aware why it costs you so much anguish to send me to America but I am also fully aware why you let me go, then need I tell you how it makes me feel?" She saw his face blanch and his hand that held the water glass tremble; she saw the untouched food on the table that turned cold, and the faces all around that were wretched and silent, and felt that she wanted to run, run anywhere where she could get that picture out of her mind.

She threw a shawl around her shoulders and walked slowly, not wanting to show her agitation, out of the house. When it became too cold for the shawl to keep her warm, she returned from her desolate, depressing walk which calmed her a bit, and was just about to enter the house, when she heard Rachel's voice, "Don't boss me around, I am not Bena who you chased from the table. I told you a hundred times before that I don't like to sleep on the oven. I have time to do that when I get to be a grandmother or even a great-grandmother." Seeing that she reduced Adah to tears again, Rachel added, "Go ahead and cry, you're as crazy as a bedbug. One minute you drive Bena from the table, the next, you insist on sleeping with her! No, for such bosh I don't give up my sleeping place."

Bena walked in and looked at Adah's tear-swollen face with some interest but kept her silence. The house had become chilly and the two boys were already in bed, fast asleep, but no one else made a move to make night, everyone looked too much awake and too keen, as if the day was first beginning.

Chaya took in the bedding to the kitchen at last, and after a few minutes came back and beckoned Adah, "Come on, get undressed and go to sleep before it gets much colder. I made up your bed with a warm cover, get under it fast," and was answered with another flood of hot tears and a chest thumping with hiccups. Avraham walked over to her and patted her head and, while looking at the two older girls, said, "Stop crying, I am sure that Rachel won't mind giving up her place to you for one or two nights; get undressed, and creep into Bena's bed." Rachel's face flamed and she was about to say something. Bena quickly shook her head in agreement and silenced her.

Another night was spent tossing and turning by all but the boys. Although the stove had not been fired that day and the bricks were ice-cold, Rachel, in her fury, tossed all night as if on hot coals, burning as if in fever. Chaya did not sleep for fear that Avraham will yet change his mind and stop Bena from going because she had opened her mouth for once to him. If not stop her, then he will make it difficult for her, and everyone around her, especially her mother, who he wanted to be the main target. Avraham's sleep was disturbed with the very opposite of Chaya's thinking. He felt ashamed and very sorry for Bena, his quiet daughter, who he never gave much credit to for deep thinking and that she was able to put two and two together and understand his reasons for sending her off! How bad she must have felt not having heard once from him that he was doing so for her own good! But he was! Couldn't she see that? Or was it for his good? True, he had his other reasons for keeping her with him but it was for her too that he came to the last conclusion!

And as soon as Bena got into bed, Adah put her arms around her and hugged her so close that neither were able to breath, and whispered, "Bena, I can't let you go, I won't let you go. You know that I can't remain here without you! All that time that you went away to work at Ginendle's, I counted the hours and minutes for you to come back. I didn't want to play with anybody I felt so crazy. And since we got that letter from Mama, and know that you are leaving us, I can't even explain how I feel! I tried hard to hate you, maybe I won't care if you go, but it didn't do any good, because maybe I don't know how to hate so good. Please Bena, don't go, please? I promise to be so good that no one will know I am around, and I promise I'll never fight with anybody!"

"Shush, you are keeping everybody from sleeping right now; you better go to sleep and let the others sleep." Bena tried to pacify and hold her very close while she choked with tears.

And the day came when she had to leave and everyone tried to keep a stiff upper lip, not wanting to send her away under a shower of tears. They helped her gather and pack the last few things she would need on the way and then dress her in her new shoes and clothes that made her look so beautiful that Raphael shouted, "She looks like a bride, Grandma, she just needs a veil on her head, yes, a veil on her head, Grandma, she looks just like a bride!" Although slight of build, she carried herself with grace. Her face retained her childhood sweetness at the same time as her young wisdom, reminding Avraham and Chaya of Mirele in her youth. Now, like her mother, she too kissed the family quickly and walked out to the waiting wagon with fast steps and made room for her father, who was taking her to the station.

They made small talk, covering up the vast distance because they could not tell each other what was in their hearts. She resented his matter-of-fact manner in which he seemed to ship her off to America for God knows how long, perhaps never to see her again, without telling her that he might miss her, even to tell her that he hated to lose her to her mother, anything! How could Avraham tell her of his hurt that she was going away and that he feels that he already misses her? How could he tell her that she is and has always been very dear to him, that he understands her parting pains for the family and himself? But he felt that she would have no faith in his words because she misunderstood him completely and it would only add to her pain. They had but a short wait for the train, kissed hastily, and she was off! He came back to the wagon with tear-flooded eyes and sat silent all the way home.

Once again the little house became silent, as if its occupants were mourning for someone. Rachel did not sing so much now and her steps lost their spring on the road to work, with no fast, dancing step that Bena so often complained to her about because she could not keep up with her. Adah's usual laughter was hushed for long periods of time, causing Chaya's eyes to wander the house in search of her. Only the boys went on with their normal amount of play and educational work as if nothing unusual had happened. Isaiah, his big black eyes laughing, wanted to know why grandma and the girls were so tearful just because Bena went to America, then became even more puzzled because his father gave him an angry look and left the house in haste without telling him.

6

The bitter and
the sweet of it

ANOTHER SEVERE WINTER WAS AT LAST ending and the courtyard was a swimming mess of mud and ice. The April sun
had softened the six-month-old layer of frozen winter and
it let go everywhere. The garbage heap steamed and gave off smells
of fresh greens and decaying rags. Mud sucked in the footwear of
those that came and went anywhere in the courtyard. Every rooftop
that faced the sun dripped their long-accumulated winter crowns
and the house windows, long dressed in frozen ice patterns, at last
allowed the sun to make a warm, clear appearance. The three younger
children were forced to stay indoors all winter long for lack of warm
clothes, and when the thaw began and they were itching to go out
and dance in the mud and sun, they had to stay in because they
had no overshoes. It was no easy task for Chaya to stand up against.

The children were cranky most of the time and no matter how much
food she gave them, they begged for more. In desperation she would
shout at them, imitating, "I want something to eat, I want something
to eat," making pitiful faces at them, "that's all I hear from you all day
long. I am sick and tired of hearing it. Where should I get so much
food for you? You eat as if it's your last day on this earth. I do not want
to hear you beg for food anymore, you hear me? The worms should
eat you as you eat the heart out of me." At other times she would, in

anger, get a hold of a boy's sleeve, without the flesh of his arm, and wring it real hard and scream, "If I hear you again asking for food, I'll twist your arm right out of its socket, you hear me?" The children heard her, but in a short time forgot and pleaded again for more food, and she begged them, "Have you no pity on me? What do you want me to do, cut myself into little pieces and feed you with them?" However, Adah, she would steer to the stove, and there in a loud voice tell her to lay down and rest on the oven and at the same time shove a piece of coveted sugar into her hand.

The evenings were the best time for the family. The house was warm and light, thanks to Katynka's cousin Evdokiya's gift of cordwood and kerosene oil. After the skimpy meals, Avraham sat down with the two boys at the table and read religious legends from the Hebrew books, then later asked them questions to see how much they absorbed and understood. Adah always managed to worm her way in between the boys and her father and watch their faces as they swallowed each word that passed their fathers lips. How she envied her brothers! All three conversed freely in Hebrew, but she did not understand one word of it. Every time she begged Avraham to teach her, "No," he always answered, "girls don't have to know Hebrew," making her wild with anger.

But when he began to teach the boys Yiddish reading and writing, she made a commotion, insisting on being included in the group and Avraham had to undertake to instruct her too. Not only that, but she made him promise to give her instruction in Hebrew also. This was a promise she looked forward to seeing, but in the meantime she was not going to sit and wait. When Raphael made his homework or had his father listen to his lessons, which were beginner's, she sat with him, listening, and asking questions and learning along with him, till she was able to read Hebrew fluently, though she understood no word of it!

Rachel was away at work most days, depending on the weather, and when she came home there was little of the evening left for her. She found the supper already eaten by the family and had to sit alone at her bowl of food, the sessions of study were over, and the household was almost ready to creep under the warm covers for the night. Still, she loved the evenings, for they brought them all together, and she was able to talk her heart out about the shop, and all would listen. She left at daybreak and came back far into the night to bake herself in the family's intimate glow of love, troubles, and the daily happenings.

After many times urging her father, he began to give her lessons too, as he gave Adah. But try as he would, he could make no headway with her. She was unable to remember her lessons from one night to the other, though he took many pains with her. He watched her head nodding in sleep and her tired body trying to hold itself erect and knew that it would be impossible to get any learning through her and he gave up.

Adah wondered why it was so hard for her sister to retain her lessons and asked if she would like her help, so that if Father gave her lessons again, she would be able to remember because she would be better prepared. Rachel became excited and cried, "Would you really help me? Would you? I know that you can, I can see how well you write and read, even the Hebrew, just like the boys. I'll tell you what—if you help me with my homework on the days when I can't go to work, I'll teach you some nice songs that I learned from the girls in the shop, all right?" And so they began to work together on Rachel's days when it was too cold or blustery to put a foot outdoors and little by little she began to make some progress and Avraham resumed her lessons.

The first time that Rachel began to teach Adah some songs was on a Saturday, after their grandmother and father took the boys to the services. First, they straightened the house, set the table for the Sabbath meal, and made themselves presentable in their Sabbath clothes. Then they began with Rachel standing in front of Adah, "First we will begin with an easy one, one that is being sung in every home, but to make sure that you know all the words, we will go over it." And they sang the old folk song known to all Jews:

On the hearth
burns a small fire
and the house is hot
the Rabbi sits there with the little children
teaching them the ABCs.

Their young voices rang out in simple sweetness that lends itself to folk songs close to the heart. Then Rachel introduced Adah to Yoysef Bovshover's *Song of bread*, its beautiful lyrics calling to the poor to self-help and a better future. How long they practiced their songs, they did not know, until they heard their father and grandmother and the boys at the door. They were surprised and felt a little uncomfortable and foolish and stopped midway, looking at each other with grins. Avraham laughed and said, "Had I known that my daughters had such good voices, I would have trained them to be cantors! And how come, dear Rachel, that you remember the songs so well, but not your lessons?"

Then came a time when Adah tried to renege on their agreement and upset Rachel's hope of attaining a little learning. She argued with and bullied the stubborn, predictable Adah to no avail, then she tried to reason and plead with her until a fight broke out between them, which Chaya had to quash. After a few days, Rachel came home from work with a new strategy and slowly approached Adah with it. "You see, if you were not so obstinate, I would teach you a poem that would make you the envy of all the children you play with. But then, why should I, are you so good to me? I guess I can teach it to your friend Rayzil instead!" and she pretended a calm she did not feel.

"What poem?" Adah asked.

"Why do I have to tell you, what poem? When you will hear it among the children in the courtyard, then you will know." She saw Adah's interest rise, but ignored it, and Adah became silent for the next few days and watched Rachel's every step.

Four days later, when Rachel could not go to work because of the heavy snowfall, Adah suddenly screamed, "So why can't you teach me that rotten poem, why do you want to teach it to Rayzil," and Rachel thought it was time to spring the trap on her now, while she was so agitated, and lifting one shoulder a little higher, said, "Well, it all depends. If you think that you can keep a promise, then I will teach it to you, one line at a time, after you help me with one page in my book." Adah looked bewildered, she felt that she was drawn into a trap, but could not afford to withdraw from it and every time that she learned a line of the poem, Rachel gained a full page of learning from her.

The whole household became interested in Rachel's poem, owing that she herself made it up, and waited from one line to the next wondering what she would add to it. Not that anyone understood one line of it—or even one word! But the lines, which consisted only of two words each, were so funny and playful and had such fast rhythm that amused the children, that they caused them to laugh until the tears rolled down their faces. Rachel herself never knew what would pop into her mind next but she dragged it out as long as she could to get what benefit she could from Adah's help. In the meantime, she gained, making progress with her reading and writing. When at last her mind went dry on her so-called poem and she had nothing more to offer Adah, the agreement was broken. Both however were satisfied that it had brought them good results. Rachel was able to chalk up an advance in her studies and Adah possessed a written copy of the poem, which read like this:

Moydi onya
Zatza panya
Panya zatza
Koopa matza
Matza koopa
Mendle doopa
Zoktm mendle
Bendle zock
Kishki buck
Buck kishki
Holi vishki
Vishki holi
Chusin kolli
Kolli chusin
Rabbi nussin
Nussin rabbi
A kitski na tabi!

Chaya took pride in Rachel's new knowledge. She admired her

wont of it and her insistence on getting it even at the very cost of her strength and sleep that she could little afford, what with her hard day's work and long distances to and from work. When the boys tried to tease her once because she did not know how to spell the word *flame*, Chaya shouted at them, "You, swollen heads with learning, watch out, it's the illiterate ones that will one day sell you for a bale of hay," and turning to Rachel, she consoled her, "Don't you worry about them pestering you, you will get married even though you don't know as much as they do what is written in the Talmud. Show the smart boys the new shoes you earned within a few months."

7

Kolmin-Dodya

THE THIN BODIES AND PALE FACES of the three younger children worried their father and grandmother, fearing the sicknesses and epidemics that usually break out at the end of every winter. There was little Chaya could do to fortify them against any illness that they might get, but Avraham was a believer in the good of cod-liver oil and he tried to pour lots of it down the children's throats. Every night at bedtime, the same wrangle would break out, when he went to the closet to get the big bottle of pale, golden liquid, with the picture of a fisherman dressed in heavy rubber clothes dragging a very big codfish from the sea. The children would scatter and find hiding places under the beds, in the beds, the oven, or even make an attempt to go outdoors.

Avraham would wait until his mother-in-law would go out to the cold, dark water shed and then he would sit down with the large soupspoon and call out, "I am waiting, come on children," but the house was quiet, except for Rachel's low laughter. And he would call them again, but on the third call when they do not respond, he angrily threatens a spanking. This brings them from their hiding places, looking disheveled and fearful at their father while he pours the thick mess from bottle to spoon and tells one of them to step forward and drink it. Drink it they do while their arms beat shuttle-wise across their tear-stained faces in the struggle to avoid meeting the hateful spoonful and taste and smell the heavy, sharp, oily mess that they have to swallow.

If only the weather would become mild and give the children a chance to go outdoors! When Rachel sat near her sister and brothers, her red cheeks looked like ripened fall apples among their pale, green faces: the contrast stood out so boldly that it worried Avraham and Chaya no end. One night at bedtime after a hard tussle with the children's oil-taking, Avraham sat down heavily on a bench and asked Raphael, who was still blowing his nose that was loaded from his crying, to call his grandmother into the house. Chaya came in, all the while wiping the boys' noses with a corner of her apron, looking chilled. Avraham then asked the children how they would like to visit with Uncle Kolmin-Dodya and was greeted with shouts of joy. But Chaya looked doubtful and Avraham understood why.

"Well, I don't mean right now, especially after the good time you just gave me. The weather is still unsettled most of the time and it is still too cold to undertake such long walk. We will have to wait until it gets warmer and dry underfoot. But this I promise you, the very first Saturday that we get a warm, clear sun, and the snow is completely sunk in the roads, we go!" Chaya nodded her head in agreement, and added, "Yes, and you better stop fighting the fish oil every night, and take as much as your father gives you so that you don't get sick, or we won't be able to go."

Raphael looked at her with hostility and answered her quickly, "Grandma, you too should take some oil, cause you want to go with us and you might get sick if you don't." Isaiah added, "Taste the oil? You know that Grandma can't even smell or eat herring! She almost faints every time she has to cut some up for us, and you ask her to take fish oil!" All the children laughed, while Chaya looked affronted and Avraham amused.

However, it was not until three weeks later on a Saturday that the weather showed itself as if made to order and they were able to undertake the walk to the Dolina,* where Avraham's distant relative lived with his family. After they came up through the narrow, hilly street to the Governor's Plaza, they stopped near the Governor's Mansion for a while to catch their breath. Across the plaza, the Russian Orthodox

---

* Russian and Ukrainian for valley, canyon, or lowland.

Church, with its awe-inspiring, curious-sized gilded domes that glistened in the sun, struck terror into the hearts of the young children and dampened their interest in the day's outing.

The Christian Russian Easter, only a short time back, renewed the former Easter holidays when Jewish children had to be kept indoors and in window-locked homes, with shut blinds and in darkness, in fear of molesting or maiming by the ardent church-goers. The two boys tugged at Avraham to go ahead, and when they did, they had to pass the firehouse where eight big-eyed black horses drank from a trough and puffed noisily through their mouths and noses and scared Raphael (and perhaps the too-silent Isaiah too) so badly that they had to walk away in great haste. If their promenade through the Plaza was unpleasant and hurried, the rest of the way was leisurely and enjoyable for all of them, for it took them along a crest of a high ridge overlooking the Smotrich River, all the way to the Dolina.

The river now looked white and calm, but were it able to speak, would boast among other of its capacities of its rampageousness that is powerful enough to carry off the poor belongings of the huts around it and when it really wants to show off its potency the poor little homes too! Yet, in the summertime, when the sun lends its luminosity that slowly and playfully colors it as it ripples with fresh waters cascading from ridges and mountains around it, one would attribute willful craftiness to it. Not even in the fall, when its waters turned cold and gray because the sun's rays are unable to animate it any longer—even then, one looks back at the pleasures it had given so generously all summer long and looks forward with keen pleasure to the winter sports ahead that it offers. But with approaching spring, the same river turns into a brute beast, converting ice and snow into a turbulent river that causes much havoc.

And despite the priest of the Russian Orthodox Church together with the City dignitaries' efforts, as soon as the ice is heard to crack, they come out under the bridge* that spans across from the end of the City to the beginnings of New Plan and there, while the onlookers elbow each other for a better place, they cut a twelve-foot cross into

---

* Then known by its Russian-language name, the Novoplanovsky Bridge.

the ice, sprinkle it with holy water, and pray for the safety of the inhabitants. But as if overnight, a wrangle starts between the end of the winter and the budding of summer, both unable to see eye-to-eye, their conflict setting off louder and louder cracking noises, until the cracks become long and wide fissures that swallow the snow like a hungry beast.

In a short time the sun comes out and hangs warm and laughingly over the weakened ice that, as if shame-faced as it tries to escape it by running away very fast, comes alive with high rushing waters and big blocks of ice that beat against each other in the race to get ahead. This is the signal for the dwellers nearby to abandon their homes, and those heeding the warning carry off to friends and relatives as much of their belongings as possible, while the rest they leave in the hands of God. The swelling river overflows its banks, creeps up and into the little houses that stand helpless and lonesome, and laps at whatever has been left for it. Soon it floods and carries off the "leftovers" down into the raging flow many times, together with the homes. Many houses, like the one that Kolmin-Dodya lived in also around the river, were huts, built on earth-bound ledges that stood far to the back of the others'; those were considered fortunate although they too suffered some flooding, and some of those houses also contributed some of their contents to the bobbing display, which looked like children's toys in the water.

The children had heard many times from their grandmother how their parents' home, their very first one, was washed away in the Dolina and how they had to go live with their grandmother Rachel. At such times Avraham would repeat, "And you should have seen your mother's face when she came back from the City, and saw the vacant lot our house stood on! What hurt her more than losing our home was the loss of all her wedding gifts. She stood up on the steps and watched as her noodle board and rolling pin danced up and down in the water and cried bitterly. All that was left of our home was a broken pitcher half-stuck in the mud and the featherbed that my mother made for us as a wedding present that a neighbor rescued before it was washed down into the river."

Although the children had heard the same story many times, it sounded new whenever they heard it again. At the end of their long walk, near the steps that led down to the river, Rachel detached herself from the family and ran down to her uncle's house, and found it very quiet. Uncle Kolmin-Dodya was fast asleep on a couch much too short for his long legs, with his mouth wide open, and Aunt Gittel, her kerchief low over her forehead, was sitting at the window with a prayer book in her lap, drowsily nodding her head.

Raphael came in and made his presence known by trying to grab the cat and got a deep scratch on his hand for his troubles. Aunt Gittel came to with a start, jumped from her chair and in her soft voice, said, "And I thought that I was dreaming when I saw you Rachel." She went to the door and welcomed the rest of the family with a warm smile, "Come in, come in, so long since I have seen any of you. Thank God, you all look so well after the long hard winter!"

Her greetings brought Kolmin-Dodya to his feet and he stretched his hand to Avraham in a "*shalom aleichem*, peace be upon you, as I live and breathe and am a good Jew, look who is here! God sent you to me, Avraham, I would have come to you soon. I needed you so badly for a long time, but I suffered one illness after the other all winter long, and my Gittel here didn't let me outdoors!"

A horde of children stampeded the house, and seeing their cousins, became elated and so noisy that the adults were unable to hear each other. Aunt Gittel went into the kitchen and returned with a bagful of sunflower seeds and gave them to Rachel, who was the oldest of all of them, and told her to share them with the rest of the children, but outside of the house.

When the house became quiet again, the four looked at each other and smiled with relief, then Kolmin-Dodya said, "Yes, Avraham, God sent you to me now, I have a lot of troubles on my mind and my heart is heavy." Avraham turned to Gittel with a smile, "He's probably worried because I am a poor man," but he noted the worried expression on her face, and added, "Did you have too bad a time with the river, a few weeks back? I see it left many pieces of land vacant, but around your house it is dry and the earth seems firm and unscooped."

Kolmin-Dodya quickly answered, "No, it has nothing to do with the river, well it is about the river, but nothing about being flooded; to the contrary, we were able to help many of the unfortunate families around here, because the water did not reach us at all. Sit down. I have a bitter story to tell you. You know the big windmill water outlet that is directly underneath the bank staircase? Well, it's been dry for some seventy or eighty years, except after an exceptionally heavy thaw, or rainfall, when its waters pour out into the river. In the summertime we bathe near there, because the water is not too deep and we are far from being good swimmers—we are still waiting for a medal from our good Czar for bravery in the river. For more years than I can remember, the children have played in the brick-lined tunnel from which the windmill waters used to go through because it was so safe and dry.

"Well, last fall, when it was already quite cold, we suddenly were treated to a sun that warmed like a dear mother, and the devil must have put into me a desire to prolong the summer. I shed my clothes and walked into the water that was even warmer than the air, dived further into its warm depth and my hands touched what felt like a heap of some kind of metal. I came up, and again dived down, this time bringing up two fistfuls of rubles! In my bewilderment I drew on my pants and ran to tell Gittel about it, but soon remembered that she had gone to her sister's house to help her make some preserves and had taken the children with her. I stood in my dripping pants feeling chilly and weak not knowing what to do, then decided to pick some of it up and later ask Gittel what to do with it.

"I found a flour sack and with it went back and found the very spot I wanted and without difficulty filled it half full. It was very heavy to carry it back to the house. And for some reason I felt like a thief, I ran with all my might until I got into the house again. By then, I was so exhausted and chilled and upset that I could not think any further and sank onto the couch and fell asleep. When Gittel and the children returned, I woke up in a terrible panic but had to wait until the little ones were asleep until I could tell her, then show her where I put the sack with silver. She wrung her hands in panic and paled like a corpse and told me to get rid of it before it brings down great misfortune on our family, not to forget that we are Jews.

"To this day I cannot understand her premonition—she cried that it will bring a curse on our house, and indeed it did! We cannot rest, we are afraid of anyone learning of it, we are afraid to leave the house, and we are afraid to be in the house with it! What can we do? Suppose our enemies who want to make a raid on our community planted it there for this purpose? What an excuse that would give them to give us a bloodbath! The only way we were able to wash ourselves clean of it, was to throw it back into the water—but I was so torn with the temptation of a better life for our children, to save them from the poverty and hunger, sickness and antisemitism that we suffer all our lives. I am no longer a young man, the children's future is not very promising, and I dreamed that the half sack of silver would change our present way of life. I debated with myself so long, until the river froze like a sheet of steel, and I was unable to put it back—had I decided to do so."

Avraham and Chaya sat as if frozen in their silence until Kolmin-Dodya finished, and he and his wife looked at them, both, for a panacea, and then Avraham asked, "And now?"

"You mean that I should put it back now?"

"Yes, why not?" Avraham asked pointedly.

"I am afraid, I have a feeling that someone is watching me day and night and wants to catch me with it, in my hands, so that they can let loose their pogrom on our helpless people."

"You leave me wondering if that is the only reason. Perhaps your fears are self-made."

"Avraham, so help me God, that is what it is. I would now gladly give it up, realize what a mistake I made delaying it so long, but how did so much silver, and there is more there, get into the river without some evil intent? You know that silver does not grow in the river! Yes, my fears have reason, you know they do!"

They were interrupted by the children's return for more seeds, and Gittel went to the kitchen and brought back another bagful, added some cookies for them too, and instructed them to go back outside. They tramped out and sat down on the big rock near the water again, and Moishe, the oldest boy in the group, sat facing them all and began to tell his cousins about the goat who came as a guest to a Seder.* He began by asking, "Did you know that a goat can take the place of Elijah the Prophet?" This made all the children laugh, then Isaiah looked at Moishe as if he were mad. "What kind of a joke is that supposed to be at the expense of our Prophet," he asked him. "Well then, listen to what I'll tell you and you will hear," Moishe answered.

"The second Seder night of last Passover, after we went through half of the rituals from the Haggadah† and we came to the part where Papa had to refill all the wineglasses, he refilled also the glass that was reserved for the Prophet Elijah, then he sent my brother Motel to open the door wide and let him in as our guest.

"Motel did as he was told and returned to the table and we began to read the invitation prayer, and before we knew what hit us, our neighbor Herschel's goat was on the table! He stood in the middle of all the food and licked from the plates as fast as he could swallow! We remained sitting as if turned to stone until my mother got the broom, and did she let him have it. (My mother was very disturbed, she said that it was a bad omen, and though my father disagreed with her, he too looked upset.) But we could not look at each other without breaking into laughter, could we?" he asked his sister and brothers, who shook their heads in agreement, and he continued, "and that made my father mad, he was so angry that he almost deprived us of finding the *afikoman*.‡

"But after a while he relented and allowed us to look for it—and of all the people in the world, who do you think found it? Imagine, we, the older children, knew of so many places that he hid it during the years we grew up but couldn't find it, but little Yentl, our baby, found it and got the prize! And to think that she is a girl too!"

"I am not a baby, I am going on five, and anyhow, I needed the new pair of shoes that Papa bought for me," she told them wisely.

In the house the conversation between the two men still went on, while Chaya and Gittel sat listening with strained nerves, having no words to add. "Well Avraham, what do you say, do you still think that

---

* Jewish ritual service and ceremonial dinner for the first two nights of Passover.

† Hebrew for the prayer book used at the Passover Seder.

‡ Hebrew for a piece of matzoh, unleavened bread, that is hidden by the father during the Seder; when the youngest son finds it afterward, a reward is exchanged for it.

I am making too much of it," Kolmin-Dodya begged of him.

"Can I see some of the silver and gold pieces? I want to see the dates on them," Avraham asked, and the two men went to the water shed and Kolmin-Dodya pulled a large flat stone away from a corner of the shed and revealed the sack with money. Avraham pulled some out and went to the kitchen window to examine it, turning it back and forth in his hand, then said, "This is silver and gold money all right, but it looks to be some hundreds of years old. Look, it has foreign faces on it, not at all Russian, and no dates on it either. I would suggest that you turn the whole lot of it over to the governor and put your mind and house at ease."

"How can you tell that the faces are not Russian, and the governor will not accuse me of stealing it?" Kolmin-Dodya asked, with fear in his voice again.

"Look closely at those faces and you will find them strange to us. Would you want me to go to the governor for you? I feel that I can convince him of the truth. Last week I was called to his office because he wanted me to translate a document from Hebrew for him, and when I finished, wanted to know who had printed it. I didn't know, and had I known, would I have told him? But he was very pleasant to me to the very end."

"What kind of document was it?" Kolmin-Dodya was anxious to know and Avraham told him that it was from a Zionist organization, explaining to Jews why they should work toward their own homeland.

"Actually, it was not what you or I would call a document, but only a thin pamphlet, but you know that our high-and-mighty rulers call every scrap of paper a document," he explained.

"Seeing that you have already had the great 'honor' to talk to that pig, I would be very happy to have you represent me there. I would be scared to death to speak to him and would bungle everything so badly that it would appear that I did steal the money. When do you want to go?"

"Monday would be a good time, and in the meantime do not sit and worry yourself, God will help you," Avraham assured him. The sun was beginning to set and the air was turning cold. The children came in again and looked for a place at the stove that was banked the day before. The adults looked at them and smiled, and Avraham told them that they must be on the way home before it gets cold and dark, fighting off Gittel's invitation to stay for supper. All the children begged, pleaded, and even let a few tears fall, to convince Avraham that they should stay, but he saw that as a good reason for leaving sooner.

On the way home, Raphael had to be carried by his father and grandmother for most of the way, he was that tired and sleepy from the day's events. Chaya had something on her mind, but waited until the other children were out of earshot before she said to Avraham, "You know, my son-in-law, I am not one bit happy about you going to the governor. It is true that he has some respect for you, but don't forget that you are a Jew, and at present, with so many demonstrations that the students carry on against the rule of the Czar, the blame is put on scapegoats, and I don't think that this is a time for you to show yourself too much there."

Avraham did not answer her but kept turning it over in his mind a while—coming to the conclusion that his mother-in-law was a woman, and as such, she lives in fear.

Monday morning after prayers and breakfast, he left the house without even looking at Chaya, and three hours later two policemen stormed into the house just as Chaya was about to leave and asked her where she hid the money. Like a flash she knew that they were already in deep trouble! She pleadingly explained that she had no money, but they looked with ridicule at her and turned the house upside down; mattresses were ripped apart, drawers pulled out of their pockets and contents spilled all over the floor, and dishes were broken into smithereens. Chaya watched as hot tears spilled down her face, seeing the poverty-stricken home being destroyed, but at the same time felt thankful that the children were out of the house. Her anger at her son-in-law was so great that she had little room to worry about his whereabouts. When at last the police left, some neighbors came in to help her put the house back into a semblance of a home—all the while sighing and cursing the Czar. Not one neighbor asked Chaya why she was subjected to that upheaval; they knew well that no Jew was immune to those sudden searches.

In these times then, the land was rotting and tottering on its crutches with pogroms, the students in the universities spread all kind of revolutionary leaflets and pamphlets among the city masses and illiterate peasants as well. No one would say how those pieces of propaganda reached into the houses or huts, but they were found regularly, with the same call for revolutionary action. Besides raiding homes that were of suspicious character (because they showed light late into the night), the police also swooped down into houses where there was much comings and goings, many times finding sickness or death there, but leaving without a word of regret.

Chaya gave the children tea and bread for their supper and told them that she had lost her purse and was unable to buy food today, and when they questioned her over and over again where their father was, she let loose her day of wretchedness on their heads, "If you don't want to get the beating of your lives, you better go to bed and stop driving me crazy. I told you more than a dozen times that I had lost my purse, and that your father went around to the various places that I've been to, to see if he could find it. Go to sleep, I don't want to hear another word from any of you. When you'll wake up in the morning, you will find your father in his bed as you always do!"

The younger children tried to swallow that bit of gall, but not Rachel who, seeing her grandmother's flushed face and burning eyes, seeing her hands shaking when she tried to hold her tea glass, waited until the other children were asleep, then asked her why she was so upset. Now, Chaya broke down, crying softly while she told Rachel what she had lived through all day, and now God knows where her father was. The two stayed up all night waiting, running to the door every time they thought they heard something. At daybreak Chaya put up the samovar to boil and cut up some of the bread into thin slices for the children's breakfast. Rachel sat with closed eyes, fearing to open them and see her father's place vacant in his bed.

After a while the singing of the boiling samovar awoke the children, and they hopped out of bed looking for their father and when they did not see him, looked aggrieved. Rachel felt their hurt and tried to ease it. "I will stay home from work and go to Aunt Nahama, perhaps she would know where Papa is," but this only brought more apprehensiveness. Never had their father failed to come home to them at the end of the day and now they missed him distressingly. Raphael began to whimper, then put his head down on the table and cried as if his heart would break, and Adah with Isaiah followed his example, the difference, that they put their heads on each other's shoulders instead of the table.

"Sit up all of you, and eat, you are drowning me in your tears. You always find something to cry about, its nothing new, one time it's because you lost a kopek and now it's because you think you lost your father. Don't worry, he'll turn up, go ahead and eat up your breakfast."

They sat up and ate, all the while looking angrily at their grandmother. Chaya sat with her glassful of tea in the palm of her hand, tried to swallow some to show the children that she was not worried, then said to Adah, "You will spend the day with Aunt Baba and I will call for you in the evening." Adah was about to raise an objection, then the door opened and her father stepped into the house. He looked tired and pale, his heretofore clean clothes muddy and in disarray. He was immediately surrounded and plied with all sorts of questions. He found a seat on a bench and looked at them fondly. "Sit down, don't disturb your meal, I will in good time tell you all about it."

They felt his hesitation and too sat down and made an attempt to eat, while their eyes were upon him. Only Chaya, burning with anger, had not uttered one word. She waited to hear what other troubles they can expect from his venture. Avraham went into the water shed and there removed most of his clothes and washed his body with the cold water from the barrel, dressed, and came back looking refreshed. He put his *tallis* and *tefillin* on and stood a long time with his prayer book in deep supplication.*

When he finished, he folded his *tallis*, and said, "I know how much worry I caused you last night with my absence, but there was no way that I was able to get word to you. I had an appointment with the

---

* *Tallis*: Hebrew for the prayer shawl worn by pious Jewish men usually when in prayer; *tefillin*: Hebrew for phylacteries, small leather boxes with Torah verses inside that pious Jewish men strap to their arm and/or their brow before morning prayers.

governor yesterday, I wanted to tell him something that I thought he would be interested to know—and at the beginning he looked interested and very friendly to me. He even seemed happy that I brought him the information, but, my dear children, we are Jews—and in czarist Russia that's a crime! I was shut into a little room at first, then taken to the jail until they would prove that I told him the truth."

Rachel was watching him as he spoke and saw that he was beaten around his head, and that his hands too had black-and-blue splotches on them and asked with concern, "Oh, Papa, why did you have to go to the governor with that information, don't we Jews have enough enemies who point fingers at us? Look at you, they beat you, didn't they? And look at your muddy clothes and shoes!"

"Point a finger? I did not go to him to inform on anyone; on the contrary, I thought that I will take the worry off your Uncle Kolmin-Dodya; he had nothing to hide, did not steal anything, do anything illegal—but his fears made him so nervous that I was afraid that he would make some mistake and put blame on himself." He began to remove his shoes, and continued, "What, did you expect that I should have come home dressed, as if for a wedding? In the jail they put me in the same cell with two drunks. The cell was a mud hole and I had to sit on the floor all night. Here, Adah, take my shoes outside and clean them for me. And you, Rachel, will hang my clothes outside until the mud dries and then give them a thorough brushing."

Although the children were curious to know what kind of information their father had brought to the governor, they did not ask, but watched as he changed into his Sabbath clothes, and then left to give his students their lessons. Chaya looked down on her hands, and said, "If we don't have enough of our own troubles, he goes out of his way to take on others'."

8

Nahama, Avraham's sister

C HAYA DECIDED TO PAY A VISIT to Nahama and talk some of her troubles off her chest. She told the youngsters to play outdoors until she gets back and went off. The walk took her up the narrow, tree-lined street with its budding gardens, past the Governor's Mansion and through the Plaza that looked so spacious to her always. Then began the residential section of the City which was the pride of Kamenets-Podolski. Some of the houses faced the street, although the entrances were through courtyards. The wide, tree-lined, clean streets boasted many professional offices that opened their doors from the front. So did the well-to-do businesses that catered to their well-to-do clientele.

A little distance from the Plaza, a courtyard with five fine houses and a large garden complemented the beautiful area around it. This property belonged to the Goshenbergs, who were known throughout Ukraine for the manufacture of fine furniture. The head of this family, Eaheal, Nahama's husband, was a fine family man and a good Talmudist who was fond of modern education, which his children benefited from. Two boys he sent to Kiev University, and his three daughters he educated at home by employing a tutor for them. With all the wealth that he accumulated from his business and investments, his good character did not change a bit. He carried a warm and sympathetic feeling for his brother-in-law Avraham, and loved him dearly. Eaheal was a very gentle human being, although his height and thickly bearded face gave him the appearance of a wild giant and he made babies cry for fear of him.

His wife Nahama, on the other hand, was short, stout, and very clear-skinned, and was considered a pretty woman who carried herself with the grace of a queen. The good marriage she made, coupled with the comforts of her life that she surrounded herself with, spoiled her and made her vain. Chaya found her in the kitchen where she was watching her three daughters polishing the silverware and brass utensils in preparation for her oldest daughter Riva's wedding.

Riva was inspecting the samovar when she heard the door open and, seeing Chaya enter, wondered what she came for but smiled and bade her welcome. Chaya stepped into the sunny kitchen that was as large as her own living quarters and furnished with expensive furniture and gleaming copper utensils that hung from the wall near the stove. She greeted them all but turned to Nahama and said, "I am troubled, and want to see if you can help me, perhaps Eaheal can. Your brother is in need of someone's advice, he will get into deep trouble and drag the family into it too. I did not sleep a wink last Monday night." She related the trouble he had at the jail and she at the house and added that she feels that is not the end of it, and wished that Eaheal would put some sense into him.

Nahama began to bristle, looking at Chaya with animosity, but did not answer her. Riva, who was very fond of Chaya and pitied her for her lot, was irked by her mother's silence and gently said, "Yes, Chaya, we know all about your difficulties with the police, and my uncle's bad experiences with the governor. Uncle was here a little while back and told us all about it. He is now on the way to Kolmin-Dodya to see what may have happened there. Don't worry, it will all blow over and be forgotten."

Now Nahama interfered with excited gestures. "My brother has more sense than you and your daughter give him credit for, needs no helpful advice from anyone on how to keep out of trouble. What he knows when he is fast asleep—others should learn from him when they are awake! I hope that you do not go around town spreading what you know."

This insult, adding to her anxiety and empty stomach, was all she needed to explode loudly. "Your brother needs some sense knocked into him, he does not worry about his children! When I bring something to the table to eat, he examines it closely and wants to know if I did not embarrass his family name by getting it. Would it be better if the children sickened and died like the others? I am not a woman of the streets—when I bring something extra for the children to eat, it's from hard work that I do in other people's home and while he is away. I have to do it on the sly, behind his back, and believe me it's hard!

"Mirele is sacrificing her life, in a strange land far from her family, to keep those children alive and all he thinks about is his precious family name! Did you ever see children hungry? Can you understand their misery? Do your children come to you every few minutes and tell you that they want something to eat and you knowing that their guts are empty and have to turn them away with a curse—because they are cursed? What do you know about going without anything you want? The smells in your kitchen of cooked and baked foods are enough to keep you in your smug little world.

"You, Nahama, surely don't understand what it means to do without, you wouldn't have given my daughter Mirele that famous recipe for cookies before she left for America! For shame! Telling her that if she had no eggs she should use water, and if she had no butter, she should use water, and if she had no raisins, she should use a drop of cinnamon. I'll bet you had expected those cookies to melt in her mouth like yours, with all the butter and eggs and the rest of good ingredients you put into them!"

Nahama's cheeks were burning and she looked ready to answer her, but Riva pulled a chair to the round kitchen table and led Chaya to it. "Please sit down and have tea with us, and here, have some butter and cherry preserves with it," she pushed the fresh-baked bread near her and a bowl of large black cherries preserved from their own garden and began pouring tea for all of them from a silver samovar. The two younger girls went to wash and Nahama stood up, not wanting to sit at the same table with Chaya, with glazed eyes, looking at the white-patterned tablecloth, her cheeks aflame. Riva seeing the situation, simply put her arms around her mother and led her to a chair and gently pressured her into it, then asked her to cut the bread.

Nahama picked up the fresh bread and holding it close to her breast cut even slices and put them on a white cloth napkin, then moved it to the center of the table. To quiet her hungry stomach, Chaya drank some hot tea and, when the girls urged her to eat, she told them that she had eaten a heavy breakfast before she left home.

Riva looked at her and smiled, "You know, Chaya, I am going to settle in Proskurov after I am married and I already feel homesick, and Mama sheds tears every time we talk about it."

Chaya looked at Nahama and saw the well-fed, well-cared-for creature and almost felt pity for her, but was unable to hold back from saying, "Your mother sheds tears and I shed blood when I think of my poor daughter so far away and alone, and working so hard. God knows when I will see her."

She got up from the table and tied her head kerchief more securely and bid them well and left. All the way home she repeated to herself that she was happy that she told that little creature off, that it will help a little; what help she expected, she really did not know, her anger not having subsided fully yet and her thoughts still running. "That cow, should she have the misfortunes that Mirele has had all her life, she might better understand why tears are shed!" For Chaya to curse when she was agitated was as natural as for her to breathe; the curses fell from her lips like polished diamonds without her even being aware.

When she came into the courtyard at home, the children were nowhere in sight, not a one, and she had told them to play outside until she returned. Well, they will now catch it from her! She heard no sound around the house and peered into the window, to be met by a strange sight: Adah was on her bed, with many pillows on her, and the two boys were on the floor asleep. She became worried and called out to them they should come and unlatch the door, and both boys ran and let her in.

"Since when do you boys and Adah sleep in the daytime?" she asked, and saw them look scared. "Is there something wrong with you, did you get into some mischief and are hiding from someone and why is Adah asleep?" She got no words from them and looked around the room.

She saw the wet floor, as if recently washed, and the room as tidy as if cleaned for the Passover holidays. She wrinkled her forehead in puzzlement and insisted that the boys tell her what had happened while she was gone. In a slow start Isaiah began to tell her that Adah had gotten sick, right after she had left, and had vomited first in the courtyard, then after she came into the house for water, in the house too, all over the floor. When she felt better, she scrubbed and cleaned it up, then cleaned the house to make it look nice, then as she was about finished, she suddenly fell to the floor and could not get up. They tried to help her, but she was too heavy for them and so limp, they were unable even to move her, and he told Raphael to run outside for help, and that's when Katynka came in. She put Adah on the bed and is now getting the doctor.

Chaya looked down on the girl's flushed face and removed some of the pillows that covered her, then felt how cold and clammy her hands were. In desperation she shouted at the boys as if they were at fault, "Who asked her to wash the floor? Or to clean the house, what is today, a holiday? That girl will drive me mad with her self-destructive bent. She is her own worst enemy! And why were you sleeping, are you sick too?" She wrung her hands in despair.

"Grandma, we were not asleep, just pretending to be. Before Katynka left, she made us promise to try to go to sleep, cause she did not want us to bother Adah, or leave her alone in the house. So, we tried very hard to sleep, didn't we, Isaiah?" The six year old tried to reassure her, then added, "But we are not sick, are we, Isaiah?" and his brother nodded in agreement.

Katynka walked in followed by Doctor Popov, their former landlord. He looked around and smiled a greeting to all of them, examined Adah a long time, then told Chaya that the girl came down with scarlet fever, but not to worry that she will be fine in a short time. He wrote out a prescription and said that he will leave it at the pharmacy in the City and that someone should call for the medicine within the hour. Katynka dug some silver out of her purse and tried to pay him for the visit, but he refused it, assuring her that at the end of the child's illness, he will give them a bill. After he left, the two women looked at each other, worried for the girl's sickness or the money for the medication and how they will pay Doctor Popov's bill later on.

The doctor came more often than he himself expected to, but she was a very sick girl and he was afraid of neglecting her. When Avraham tried to pay him some money toward the bill, he turned it back, "What good can money do for me? I have more than I can use up in my lifetime even if I lived to be 100 years old. What did me a lot of good was that I was able to save your daughter. She was so full of complications that I thought that they would never end, and what was worse, half of them I did not understand. She paid up the bill in full by fighting off her troubles, let us shake hands and call it a fair exchange." When the door closed on him, Chaya remarked with a great deal of warmth, "He is a Gentile with a Jewish heart!" But Avraham contradicted her, "No, a Christian, with a heart of gold."

Adah lay propped up on two pillows and witnessed all the activities in the room, but she was so spent that she thought she was dreaming. Every now and then she tried to say something, but nothing issued from her mouth; she tried again and again to shout "Papa," until he turned to her with his *tallis* and *tefillin* on, and motioned for her to wait, a broad smile playing on his face. Avraham finished the morning worship and came to her bed and looked happily on her, patting her face, and said, "So my little girl decided to wake up at last, good, and pretty soon you will be able to walk around as you did before, and with God's help you will be running around the courtyard as you have before you took sick."

Isaiah and Raphael stood near the bed and watched their sister; they edged closer and closer, all the time staring into her face until Raphael remarked to her, "Take off your cap, we want to see how you look without your hair." She looked at him without understanding what he had said. Then Isaiah added, "Yes, take off Grandma's *tschipik**" and you will find a big surprise."

Chaya shooed the boys away from the bed and sat down on its edge

---

* Yiddish for a soft, shirred cap worn by some ultra-Orthodox Jewish women under their scarf or kerchief after their heads were shaved for marriage.

with a steaming glassful of tea in the palm of her hand, and between sips, told her, "You see, child, you were gravely ill, your fever was so high I could have baked bread on your body and of course that is the best place for lice to multiply, and that they did to such great numbers that I was afraid that they would eat you up alive."

Adah began to whimper, but Chaya continued, "Doctor Popov told us a few times that if we don't cut and shave your hair then he will take you to the hospital and have it done there. You came very close to going there anyhow, not because of the lice, but because your chest was full of mucus and he had to open a hole into your throat so that you could breathe better, but we begged so hard not to take you away, that he did whatever he could for you right here. Now don't fuss about your hair, it will grow in again before you'll know it and most probably blacker and longer than it was before."

Chaya went to a drawer and took from it a colorful piece of material and showed it to her.

"Your sister Rachel brought it from the shop, and Saturday night we will sew a new *tschipik* for you to wear until your hair grows back." Her grandmother's nearness and Rachel's promise of a new *tschipik* to make her look pretty pacified the invalid and she laid back on her pillow with a sigh of relief.

"Little ones swallow what grownups chew."
Jewish aphorism

Dressed in a new cotton dress and her new, colorful *tschipik*, Adah, drawn and pale, sat on the house ledge sunning herself the first day out. The children in the courtyard stood around her, looking curiously at her headgear and asked all sorts of questions, such as, Why were you sick, did it hurt much? And above all, What happened to your hair? That fancy-looking *tschipik* on a young girl was something new and they stood around waiting to find out why she had to wear it. Her dear friend Rayzil came along and saw how they were torturing Adah, and she made a wide movement with her hands, as if driving chickens in front of her, and shouted at them, "Come on kids, leave her alone, you make her crazy with all your silly questions, go on all of you, and leave her alone!"

Very reluctantly they broke up the circle around Adah and drifted off. That is, all but the seven-year-old Boris, who tried to keep some of the children with him until she answered the questions put to her, mainly, Why she hid her head in the *tschipik*. He shouted, "I will stay here all day until you tell me why you wear that thing on your head," and not getting an answer, shouted, "Is it because they had to cut your hair off because you are a dirty Jew?" Those children who remained within earshot, all Jewish, stiffened and looked queerly at their Gentile friend, for "dirty Jew" was a hidden terror for them: it meant beatings, house searches, arrests, and beards torn off old, pious grandfathers. These two words were associated with all that is destructive to the lives of Jews. They sucked this knowledge in with the milk from their mother's breasts. They looked at Adah and Rayzil for some answer, but they were both silent, except that they saw Adah's body stiffen, too, and her breathing come with some difficulty.

Both girls were in their tenth year. Rayzil was taller and prettier than Adah, but when they had to make some decision in the course of their play, she always turned to Adah. This time, however, she did not ask or wait to hear what she would but she drew a ball from the basket and threw it as far as she was able, and told the children it will belong to the one who gets to it first. As they ran for the ball, she turned to Adah and asked her if she would care to play house, and opened the straw basket she always carried around with her and pulled out three straw stuffed dolls, some tin tea dishes, and many pieces of colorful broken plates, that they had collected on the garbage heap before Adah took sick. She placed all those imaginary household furnishings near Adah and asked her to be the mother this time, and that she had just given birth to a baby. That way she didn't have to get up from her seat on the ledge. But she got no answer, just a moody shake of the head. Something inside of Adah kept pounding over and over again, that sounded like "dirty Jew, dirty Jew, dirty Jew," over and over slowly but in rhythm, like in a disturbed dream.

"Don't you want to be the mother, don't you feel like playing now?"

Rayzil asked, seeing her friend's ill humor.

"I don't feel like playing now, but maybe later I will," she told her, and Rayzil put all the toys back into the basket and sat down near her, talking excitingly about the coming summer. "Soon we will be able to hide in the cherry trees again and eat until we are stuffed with them, and the carrots and cucumbers will be up in a week or so too. My brother Dovid ought to come back from Kiev with some beautiful rose plants and put them near the corner where we have the tea roses, and you should see them! He also brought back some plants that will grow tomatoes, though my grandmother says that they cannot be eaten because they are not kosher. Just the same, Dovid planted them, laughs at her, and says that it's rubbish to say that about any vegetable. Anyhow, when they come up on the vines, we will taste them and find out if we like them. I think my grandmother is getting old and fanatical, she goes around all day and worries everyone about this or that not being kosher. Is your grandmother like that too?" she asked anxiously.

"I don't know because I don't know what fanatical means." Adah told her.

"I don't know either, but I heard my brothers call her that when she didn't want Dovid to plant the tomato vines." And they both laughed.

Rayzil was the youngest of the Goldstein children and was tutored at home because her mother felt the house getting too big for the dwindling family after they had sent off the older children to universities in Kiev. Miryam, their mother, was a tiny-built woman whose step in the house and in the courtyard was light and fast, always on the way to do something for someone who needed her help. She never sat idle although the house was cared for by servants. At no time did she give her opinion or make a decision, or reprimand a child; she said very little and did much. She dressed clean and neat, her wig combed to conform to her face that was gentle but plain. And one felt at home and comfortable in her presence. When her youngest, Rayzil, became of school age, Miryam came to her husband Zalman and told him that she wants her youngest with her. "We can't remain in an empty house, it will echo of the children's voices. We need Rayzil to remind us that we were not barren, that we raised a family and gave a good part of our lives to them." Zalman listened not so much to what she said, but the tone she said it in, and heard in that voice that she needed the child at home to bask her motherhood in, and fully agreed. "Yes, and it is about time we asked Avraham the Scribe to start her on her Yiddish and Hebrew lessons too," he added to her satisfaction.

Miryam spent a lot of her time among the Jewish and Russian classics and had introduced her children to them at an early age. She was an educated woman, having come from a rich family that lived by the Torah and Talmud. She was the only girl among eight brothers, and her will to learn was so great that the parents allowed her to go with them to the house of learning for many years, and when she became too big a girl to be among growing boys, she continued with a teacher at home. When she married and the children began to come and kept her busy at home, she made it her business to continue with as much reading as was possible for her. The home of the Goldsteins ran on oiled wheels of education, Zalman's mother used to say.

Saturdays, Miryam gave over to reading from Graetz's *History of the Jews* to her children as they grew up. And now she was left with Rayzil, to whom she read and enchanted with the history and many of its legends. On Wednesdays, she would have the child read to her from the Russian books and enjoyed her clear voice and diction. Rayzil invited Adah many times to join her when Miryam read, and now again reminded her that she should come to the house on Saturday for a reading, and Adah said she will, if Rayzil will call for her.

Now Rayzil stalled for time, hoping that her friend will change her mind and want to play with her. "So don't forget you made a promise that you'll come to my house Saturday, so don't forget," she talked on. "I said I will come, I will come, why do you have to talk so much about it?" Adah said in irritation.

"Well, why can't I talk about it? My goodness you sound so quarrelsome. Are you mad at me or something just because I said that you should be the mother before?"

"Why should I be mad at you? I am not, but I feel sick inside. Don't you?"

"Why should I feel sick inside? I didn't have the scarlet fever, you had it, and I thought you were already better." The puzzled girl looked at her friend with fear.

"I don't mean sick with scarlet fever, I mean sick inside me, since I heard Boris say 'dirty Jew'," Adah corrected Rayzil.

"Oh that," Rayzil answered with some annoyance, "He's only a kid, what does he know? He really does not know what he is talking about, he probably heard someone say it and is repeating it. Anyhow, I must go into my house for my milk now. I'll see you later," and she ran away.

Adah did not feel any better that day or that night; her father heard her turning and moaning, and watched her restlessness with concern and asked her once if she wanted something but she only stared at him with blank eyes, and he went back to his bed. In the morning before breakfast, she went out into the courtyard and began to look for something, not really knowing what she wanted to find. Her grandmother missed her at the table and sent Isaiah to look for her. He found her just roaming around, and shouted to her, "Your cornmeal mush is getting cold, you better come in or I will eat it up for you." They went back into the house and she ate her cereal with hot milk, and when she was done, she slipped out of the house again and this time she saw Boris standing in the doorway two houses away.

This small house had a tenant on the ground floor, and one on the first floor, both Turks, who worked in the kitchens of the Governor's Mansion and were seldom home. For the children the hallway was a haven when it rained or snowed, when they played hide-and-go seek. Now, Boris stood in its doorway looking bored and, seeing Adah, began walking toward her, and as soon as she saw him, she knew what she wanted. With a tensed body, she walked over to him and asked him to come into the hallway and he, not knowing what she had in mind, followed her in and suddenly found that she was dragging him to the very rear of the long hall. And there she beat him about the face with all her strength. He felt one slap, then another, and another, all the while she was saying in a high-pitched voice, "And don't call me 'dirty Jew' any more, I am much cleaner than you, you filthy pig."

He tried to get away from her but was unable to push her out of his way and, in hot anger, shouted back at her, "Dirty Jew, Dirty Jew," again and again, the spittle dripping from his enraged mouth. They both became locked in each other's arms, both crying, and trying to get the best of each other. Then Boris managed to get a leg into position and kicked Adah hard, hurting her so badly that she had to turn him loose for a second. That was the second he hoped for, and he began to run, only to be caught again by his enemy and dragged back to the rear. The boy was wild with rage, and tried to fling out at her again but could not, so he screamed "Dirty Jew," at her, in a voice that was trembling with hate and partly muffled by his heavy breathing, but with so much venom that she tried hard to shut his mouth with her hand, but in the struggle buried her nails into his cheeks, tearing the skin in long, bloody lines. When at last she let go of him—rather, when he managed to break away from her, the blood spurted all over him as he ran home crying. Adah walked out of the hallway spent, triumphant, without the hurt inside of her.

Boris's nine-year-old sister Maria had just finished scrubbing the floor and the dirty water in the pail still stood at the doorway with the wash rag and scrub broom in it, when in dashed Boris, blind with anger and pain, overturning the pail and spilling the water all over the floor. "You better get on your knees and wipe up all that water that you spilled on that clean floor," his angry sister roared.

"And if I won't?" he shouted back, sticking his tongue out.

"Then don't, but just wait until Mama gets back. Oh, will you catch it from her." As she spoke to him she saw for the first time his bleeding face, meant to take a closer look and walked a little nearer to him and frightened him away; sure that she was going to hit him, he dodged her and ran out of the house.

The two children's mother, recently widowed, worked as a condiment preparer in a meat smokehouse. At the end of a sixty-five-hour week, she brought home 5 rubles, with which she had to feed and house the children and herself. She was happy when she found this one-room house with the protective courtyard where she was able to leave the children all day and feel at peace. One other reason for being happy about her living quarters was that her friends who rented the place for her told her that the landlord Goldstein was a "good" Jew, and if she falls back in her rent sometimes, would wait until she had it. She needed that security with the little money she brought home. Her little Maria was a help to her; young as that girl was, she kept the house spotlessly clean, and when she, Olga, came home with feet swollen almost twice their size from standing on a damp cement floor all day, with her stomach grumbling from hunger, she found the house clean and warm and her little son fast asleep with exhaustion on the floor.

Then she had to cook something for their supper, the main meal, and awaken the boy to eat. However, this evening, Boris was not in the house, not on his usual place on the floor, and Maria told her mother about his bleeding cheeks, and also about the pail of water that he spilled all over the floor and then ran out on her. The two went out to look for him, but the evening was cloudy and it was quiet and dark outside. They went all around the courtyard calling his name but found no response. Olga sent Maria back into the house to watch the supper cooking, and she herself walked slowly from hallway to hallway and all around the garden calling his name, but she could not find him because he fell asleep in the forbidden berry patch in Zalman Goldstein's garden.

Chaya bolted the door, and as she was the last one to get to bed, she also put the kerosene lamp out, and was prepared for a night's rest. When the household was on the brink of sleep, all as one suddenly sat up in their beds, their hearts wildly pounding because of the loud and steady knocking and banging on their door. Voices were heard mingled with a child's sobbing. Avraham pulled his sleeping robe on and lit the lamp again. He pulled the bolt out and before he had a chance to open it, the door was pushed in on him from the outside by a policeman who was followed by the neighbor Olga Stretitskaya, who held on to Boris's hand. Both Olga and the policeman were shouting at the top of their lungs, but no one could make out why.

"What is wrong?" Avraham asked, looking from one to the other.

"You don't know what's wrong? Look what your girl did to my boy's face," Olga wailed, "and him without a father, my poor orphan!" and she turned the boy's face toward Avraham to see. It was so raw and bloody that he could not believe that a child of his could do such thing.

He turned around and looked at all his children, who in turn looked at each other, wondering who the guilty one could be. "Who do you say hurt you so badly?" he asked Boris, and the sobbing boy pointed to Adah, "That's her, that one without the hair, she did it." Adah, white as if she were lifeless, huddled herself into the bedclothes as deep as she could go and from there answered in a muffled voice, "I didn't do it," and began to cry. Chaya had thrown a shawl around her, but her teeth were chattering. She went to the girl's bed, sat down on the edge, and begged her not to cry. "You can see for yourselves that the boy is lying. How could she harm even a fly when she got up from such bad illness only a little while ago? I don't know what your boy is up to, but you, Olga, are a mother, and you know how weak a child is after being so many weeks in bed with a bad case of scarlet fever. She is a quiet child, she never fights with anyone, why should she do such a thing to your boy?"

She turned to Boris and looked into his tear-swollen eyes and asked, "Tell me, Boris, why do you say she hurt you like this? Tell me the truth, why would she want to do this to you, why?" Boris began to answer, "She did, she did it to me because—" He stopped; he had been watching two pairs of black eyes, angry hostile eyes, that belonged to Adah's brothers, when Chaya was talking to him, and he was afraid of further punishment from them in days to come. "Well," the policeman prodded him, "tell us why she tore your cheeks so bad. Boris tell me, don't stand there like a dummy, with a mouth full of water."

"I went to the trouble to go for Yashik here, and now you stand like a dead tree trunk and won't talk. Boy, you made up this story and tore your face in the berry patch I found you sleeping in," Olga exclaimed. "I'll skin you alive. All the troubles you cause me. Did you go to the garden for fruit and were caught and torn by the briars there? Talk up, boy, I want to know what happened to you!"

Boris stood silent and beaten and made no answer. "Well, let's be on our way," Yashik said, as he turned and walked to the door. Olga followed, pushing Boris in front of her, mumbled something, and stepped out of the house on her swollen tired feet. "A black year on them," Chaya sent after them. "For them we are not human beings.

Any time of day or night, any excuse at all no matter how small or if it's only a lie, they tear our doors open and we have to bare our souls to them!"

When the household quieted down and Chaya was about to blow the lamp out again, Avraham stayed her hand with a look and asked Adah to come to the table and sit down near him. He turned the wick down and quietly asked her, "Tell me what happened between you and Boris today." Adah began to cry again and between sobs told him how he called her "dirty Jew," and how it hurt her insides and how she brooded all of last night over it.

"Then why did you deny it?" he asked her. "Because I was afraid to tell them the truth, was afraid to start trouble because the policeman was there."

He saw her shake with a chill or fear, and knew how troubled she was, and he smiled at her saying, "You have the true mark of the Jew in you: pride and fear. Go back to bed now and have a good night's rest." He kissed her and she felt forgiven.

9

Aunt Sima

"CHILDREN, WE WILL HAVE TO CHANGE our sleeping places tonight, our Aunt Sima is coming to spend two days with us again. I expect her sometime this afternoon, probably late in the afternoon, I guess. I know that you boys don't like to sleep on the floor, but it is only for two nights. You should know by now that she does not come to us for a good time. Where else could she spend the two nights when she comes all the way from Smotrich to see the doctor here?" Chaya spoke to all the children, but appealed to Isaiah especially. Isaiah's glittering eyes were dancing as he turned and said to Raphael, "Well, my brother, tonight will be your turn to sleep next to the wall and my turn to choose which of the two corners we will bed our mattress in."

Raphael made a face, and said, "Yes, and we can't sleep with Papa again. I know that he hated to sleep in Grandma's bed when she and Aunt Sima sleeps in ours." He looked very disappointed and Isaiah tried to help. "Would you like to sleep in a bed that makes noise like an accordion with every move you make?"

"That's enough, Talmud genius, just make sure that your Aunt Sima does not hear your so-called funny jokes, you will make her feel like an intruder in our house," his grandmother admonished him.

Aunt Sima was a guest in the home every six weeks when she comes from her little hometown to Kamenets-Podolski to see her doctor. Doctor Popov tries to help her get well from a sickness no one knew about. No one knew what he was trying to cure her of, but one of her symptoms stood out in full view for anybody to see. Both her right shoulder and right side of her head jerk upward while her face assumes a weak grin giving the impression that she was calling someone to be followed. This muscular spasm appears every 4 or 5 minutes, even when she sleeps.

She was an only child of a Hasidic couple. Her father held a position as head bookkeeper in a bank in a nearby town where he stayed all week and just came home for the Sabbath and holidays. His homecomings were celebrated by his Hasidic friends with singing and dancing in ecstasy to their God. Sima's mother Zlota was very proud of her daughter and held high hopes for her future. Small wonder, Sima was the type of beauty one does not often see; she was called "the Sultana" because of her olive complexion and graceful way of carrying herself.

When she was sixteen years old, Leyble, the town's *shadkhan*, began to suffer from sleepless nights—and when he did doze off, suffered nightmares because of her. No matter when he approached Sima's mother with the name of a suitable applicant for her daughter, her answer was always the same, "For such match, we can wait a little longer, she is too young yet," and turned him out of the house. What really worried Zlota was that they did not have a kopek put away toward Sima's dowry. No matter how often she begged her husband to keep a little of his earnings aside, that they could marry their daughter off some day, he had the same answer to her, "Don't worry, God will not neglect her, he knows what I do with our money, and when the good and right time comes, he will not embarrass our child."

Leyble, of course did not know the real reason for the mother's delay and he always talked to himself of the match that hangs in the air, "For who knows, a beauty like her, nowadays, can take it into her head to find a husband herself. Girls nowadays take it into their heads to marry without a matchmaker, because they fall in love, they think— as if they know what it means. Who knows what their newfangled ideas can do to a profession like mine! They go off to the big cities and see theater and get all sorts of ideas of how to run their lives! Such empty heads—and they want to get married without the advice of a *shadkhan*, God forbid!" But eventually, Leyble got his chance. Sima's father, on his way home for the Sabbath, tripped on the road and fell, hitting his head on a rock, and spilled his life's blood out without a human being near him.

His wife and daughter were in near collapse with grief. Leyble waited while the seven days of *shiva** passed, during the time staying away while the family and close Hasidic friends came to console them that their loved one was now in Heaven and that with his pious record from the earth, that he will surely petition the Lord, personally, for his wife and child. On the fifth day he, Leyble, too, came to offer his condolences, and listened while the women wept, but he stood in the background, not being a relative nor a Hasidic friend, only the small town's *shadkhan*.

But seven days later, after the women had raised themselves in their stockinged feet from the low wooden boxes that were prescribed for Jewish mourners, combed their hair, and once more sat at the table for their meals, he turned up, this time for pure business, and without much waiting began to talk to the mother. "Zlota, believe me, I come to you now as your benefactor. You shouldn't wait any longer, you need an old maid on your hands, God forbid? Don't play with fire; today I have someone worthy of your daughter," but he was unable to deny her staying hand, stopped talking, and listened to her, "Not now, please, not now. You must give us a chance to come to ourselves before we can talk about that. You must leave us in peace for a while yet," she pleaded with him.

"You want me to give you a chance until your daughter becomes an old maid, God forbid? Why do you insist on playing with fire? Today I have someone for you, someone who would suit her just right, and tomorrow? Who knows, God forbid, a smart girl might get the idea that he is a good catch and who knows if he will be around here again? You better listen to a smart man and do what I tell you, don't wait!"

He urged with so much intensity that she had to tell him now the real reason why she can't talk about her daughter's marriage possibilities. "You must understand that Sima and I are penniless since my

---

* The period of seven days' formal morning for the dead begining immediately after a Jewish funeral.

husband died. Not only do we not have what to live on, but I do not have a ruble put away for my child's dowry," she talked in a quiet voice, but tears formed in her eyes, and he looked at her bewildered, lost for words for a moment.

Then, he regained his composure and tried to laugh. "Go on, I believe you are fooling with me, because you ran out of your stock of excuses, and now you are telling me nonsense. How would such a pious man like your husband, God rest his soul, leave his one and only child without a dowry, his good wife penniless, when he made such a good wage at the bank? Why, he supported all the paupers in the town, and he would not be considerate of his own dear ones?" But while he was talking to her, he began to read from her face that his words were in vain, that she really meant what she told him. He was unable to keep from asking her, "You mean that he really gave away his money to all those paupers and left you and his only child so poor?"

"Yes, it's true, every word of it. I used to plead with him constantly to put some money away for Sima, but he did with the money whatever he wanted and now the two of us are the biggest paupers of all around here." Now Leyble really lost his tongue, just sat looking at her a moment, then said good-bye and left the house.

In a short time Zlota became an invalid, and the two moved from their home to a one-room dwelling they rented from a neighbor and lived from the little money they got for their home and its furnishings. Knowing that her time was running out, she sent for Leyble and now pleaded with him to find a husband for Sima. Yes, she knew that her daughter will have to marry beneath her station, she being an orphan now, most probably it will have to be a widower with a houseful of children, a cripple, or a man of a trade instead of the Torah, an unlearned man.

Leyble was now clean of any doubt that he might have felt, began to feel sorry for the two and started searching for a good match. It took a while, but he came at last to Zlota and told her that he had found a young man who is good to man and God, and they made the arrangement for the meeting for Saturday night. The mother saw to it that Sima was dressed in her Sabbath clothes all day and into the evening, though she did not tell her why and she put on her long gold *chai*,* the only piece of jewelry she still kept for her daughter.

When Leyble came in with his "find," they found Zlota sitting in an armchair despite the doctor's orders, for she did not want the young man to see that she was an invalid; but when she saw him, her heart almost stopped! So that was the good match that Leyble found and talked so much about? And it turned out that this was the man. It took Zlota a long time, first, to convince herself, then Sima, that she had to marry him. When Sima cried and argued that she did not want him, that she would rather remain unwed, the mother too, cried and argued that she would rather die right now than go to the grave knowing that her only child was still unmarried. Velvl, however, was a fine person, although with a limited education that he put to use earning a living. He was built like a ten-year-old boy and was frail of health, and became a Hebrew teacher in a *kheyder* for young boys.

No matter how many tears were shed by mother and daughter, within three months the beautiful girl was married to Leyble's best match and Zlota went to her grave feeling fulfilled only a few months later, knowing that her daughter was carrying the fruit of her marriage under her heart. Velvl was a gentle, quiet man seventeen years older than Sima, whom he loved dearly. He worshipped her to the extent that the men in the small town called him a "rag." Sima made few demands on him nor did she undertake to make the family decisions; still those same men and some of the women told each other that "she wore the pants, not her husband." However, Sima seemed to shrink daily since she married him and now four years later, after she had given birth to two sons, she was constantly ill, and came to Kamenets on regular visits to Doctor Popov.

Not so with Velvl. He became a happier man since their marriage and when they were blessed with the two boys, felt his cup overflowing. Only his wife's constant ailing depressed him and he begged her to tell him if she was unhappy, to which she always answered, "Why should I be unhappy? You are a good man and you are good to me, and our

* Pendants made up of the two-letter Hebrew word for life; worn since the late 19th century.

children give us much joy, what more can I ask for? It is too bad that my mother is not alive to see my happiness."

But slowly, so slowly that one cannot remember when and then it began, she changed. Her right shoulder and head began to twitch, the foolish grin appeared with it when the spasms came. It was a queer motion, and the townspeople began to talk that she looks like a girl calling men to her attention and indeed the spasms gave her just that appearance. After her second child was born, she begged her husband to keep away from her, not to force her to be wife to him, if she is to stay alive. And the gentle, meek man, without understanding and without asking, did as she bid him, though as a religious man he felt the hurt.

Still Sima sickened and he then told her to go see a doctor in Kamenets. She did just that, but still did not seem any better. She never told him, that fine, considerate husband, that Doctor Popov told her that as long as she will live with him, she will be sick. But she kept returning every six weeks just the same.

The wagon brought their guest Aunt Sima, and Chaya, hearing the wagon-clatter grind to a stop, went out to meet her and relieve her of the small bundle she was carrying. Avraham and the children stood at the window and watched the two women outside and Raphael turned his face up to his father and asked, "Papa, where Aunt Sima lives, don't they have doctors?"

"Sure, they have," Isaiah laughed, "but she likes Doctor Popov better."

Yes, Avraham thought, she likes Doctor Popov better and I had hopes that she gave him up already. Sometimes I wonder if she really comes here for his help or to talk all night long with my mother-in-law. Avraham had a legitimate question there, for whenever the two women got into his bed, the whispering starts and lasted well into the night. Many times the whispering fell on Chaya's half-deaf ears and she would answer Sima half asleep, sounding as if she was fully awake for she knew all of Sima's troubles by heart.

Now the children were seated at the table while Chaya portioned out the evening meal and tried to keep their eyes off their aunt, not to make her self-conscious of the spasms that played around her head and shoulder. Instead, they told Rachel, who had been at work all day, about the big mistake that their grandmother had made this very afternoon when it rained. Chaya heard them in the kitchen and came in, looking angry. "That's not so," she told them, "I did not make any mistake, you better eat your supper and go outside and play." The three youngsters looked at each other mischievously, but finished their supper in silence and went out into the courtyard and made so much noise while playing that it was with difficulty that the adults inside heard each other.

Late in the evening when everyone turned into their allotted sleeping places, the lamp was turned down very low by Avraham while he read from the Torah at the table. It became very quiet in the room; only the steady breathing of those already asleep could be heard. Avraham thought that there was something wrong between the two women; they too seemed to sleep and he wondered if they could be angry at each other after they had spent such a friendly evening together. However, when he tired and went to bed, he became aware that there was communication by the two women; the usual whispering went on all night. Well, he thought, that's normal, and he turned on his side and fell asleep.

Chaya, tired from the day's work, listened only with half an ear now while Sima poured her heart out to her and she soaked up her outpouring in a half-asleep, relaxed drowsiness until she heard that she was going on with the same complaints that she had voiced a few months back. Then she listened a little closer and heard her say, "But I can't forgive them for doing that to me. I know that you told me that all pious women of the Jewish faith must do it, but I can't see why."

Now sure that it was going to be like that all night, Chaya felt that she did not have to be on the alert; she knew well what happened on the second day of Sima's marriage, when the women came to cut her hair and shave her head. "Does she think she's a Gentile?"

"All Jewish brides know that as soon as they are married, they have to have that done to them, then wear either a wig or a kerchief for the rest of their lives. Most day-old brides kick up a fuss when they are approached with the scissors, but did she have to carry on as if they were going to cut her throat? It was an ashamed face that her mother had to show in the town when it got around and, to make things worse, Zlota could not stop her daughter from weeping when people were around. Sure Sima looked changed, and her friends did not recognize her on the street when they finally came across her and her shaved head. But did she really think that she was going to keep her thick black hair all her life? The men way back in our religion saw to it that we don't. They made the laws and we must obey them like the rest of the edicts that they made in their favor."

That Sima looked like a little girl playing house no one could dispute, but so did all the new brides, with the exception of the older girls much past Sima's age. So why did she have to make more fuss than anyone else and have the rabbi's wife tell her that it was unbecoming for a Hasid's daughter. What else could that good woman tell her? That she, too, did not like it and cried when the women came to cut off her heavy blond hair and, when the blond curls fell to the floor, that she fainted?

"Yes, yes, I am listening to you, I hear you," Chaya assured her. "I heard what you said but I didn't want to interrupt you." And again the voice went on and on and then suddenly Chaya came out of her drowsy state and asked Sima to repeat what she had just said.

Sima sounded peeved now as she said, "I felt for a long time that you were not listening to me. Now listen, I said that the last time when I went to the doctor, I told him that I feel sick every time I lay with my husband, and guess what he told me?"

"I don't know," Chaya answered with some misgivings.

"Well, he told me to leave Velvl, that I mustn't live with him as a wife! Why do you think he tells me that?" Now Chaya became wide awake, turned her face closer to Sima, and asked in a low whisper if the doctor told her why she feels sick every time she is with Velvl.

"No, but I did tell him that we now sleep in separate rooms and that he keeps away from me. But he told me that I will never get well unless I leave my husband and marry a strong man, a man who knows how to live with a wife. I don't know what he is talking about. What about our children?"

Chaya listened and kept turning the bit of news in her mind for quite a while until she came to some understanding of it, then simply said, "The doctor knows what he is talking about but we Jewish women don't leave a husband or break up the family for such things. No matter how strong a man is, our Jewish men, they don't concern themselves with their wives' feelings other than to impregnate them, that's their obligation in our religion." Sima listened and now thought that she understood what the doctor told her—but agreed with Chaya's rationalization.

She turned to another subject now. "Velvl's talking of going to America, says that he will ask his cousin who is there now to send him a ticket. He wants to go by himself and when he settles there and finds something that he can make a living at, he will then send for me and the children. To me it's one and the same thing, here or in America. If I'll be sick in one place when I am with him, I'll be sick in the next. You know what the world says, 'that no matter where one puts the sick, they moan.'"

"Let's talk about that tomorrow, to sleep now," but Chaya never knew when her bed partner stopped whispering; sleep overtook her and she had to give in to it. In the morning Sima, half asleep, walked to the doctor's office, and from there went to her hometown feeling a little bit better because she knew that in six weeks she will come back again.

10

Wrong prayers, wrong winnings

ISAIAH AND RAPHAEL KEPT TEASING THEIR grandmother about the wrong prayers she made when it rained the day that Aunt Sima came. Their grandmother stood it as long as she could and then promised them a good beating if they keep at it much longer. But the children's testimony to her limited knowledge of her everyday prayers annoyed her. She had learned her prayers like all other illiterate women of her time: by rote, from her mother. Now she stood washing clothes in the wooden tub trying to think back, step by step, leading up to the time and at the time, just what she had said. It worried her that the boys should know the prayers and not her.

"Is it possible that my memory is failing me already? I have said prayers since I was a very young child and now I get caught by two young rascals with the wrong one. Let me see, I cleaned the house for the Sabbath, because Sima was coming, and I stacked the pillows nicely into a pyramid shape with the smallest on top and warned the boys that at no time should they throw it over in their rough play. Then when I was about to fire the samovar, suddenly I heard the clap of thunder, and I remember that I was thinking that that was just like poor Sima's luck, as she will probably get soaking wet in the wagon on the way to us. Soon there was lightning, and the rain came down as if to start another flood to float the Ark."

Chaya closed the door and window and told the boys to be sure and put their skullcaps on and say a prayer to the thunder and lightning and not to be afraid because God was watching over them. Suddenly there came a crash of thunder as if the world was coming to an end and she buried her head under the pyramid of pillows in her fright, saying, " 'Blessed art Thou, O Lord, King of the Universe, who hast produced the works of creation.' Now, what's wrong with that? I must remember to ask Avraham to set his two Talmud geniuses straight with their prayers, for I am sure I know mine." After her mental gymnastics, her ego was somewhat healed, and she would have forgotten about the whole business if the boys had not made her angry over something again, at night. All evening they were busy with some puzzle or riddle they kept asking each other and no matter what went on in the house they were deaf and blind to it. Their palaver was so great that when Rachel came in from work with the news that Papa had won the lottery, she could barely make herself heard. "If you boys don't stop that noise and make ready for bed, I will tell your father about the smart style you treated your grandmother with these last few days."

But before Rachel had a chance to continue with the news, they again got lost in their play and continued with the noise they left off a minute ago shouting over each other. Then Avraham, who had arrived, called a halt to their excitement. "Both of you come over here. Do you want to go to bed crying tonight? I want to know what you did today to make your grandmother angry. How many times have I told you that respect for your elders is a part of your religion. Tell me what happened between you and your grandmother." He looked from one to the other with anger.

Isaiah pushed his brother, saying, "You tell him, Raphael," but the younger child looked smitten by the way his father looked at him and for the first time that day closed his mouth voluntarily. Tears appeared on his long lashes and his mouth trembled a little. Isaiah began to feel that the lot fell to him, so he slowly started to tell his father all about it. "You see, Grandma said the wrong prayer when it thundered this morning and it was funny, cause she hid her head under the pillows, the pillows she had stacked up on top of each other. I guess that she knew that God could not hear her muffled voice, so she prayed so loud and it came out so muffled that we could not help laughing at her. And Papa, she said the wrong prayers too, we told her about it, that's all we did and now she is mad at us for it," he finished with a grievance.

"What makes you wiseheads think that they were the wrong prayers?" Chaya asked them, a little unsure of herself. "Well Grandma, you said the prayer for the lightning instead of the thunder that sent you hiding under those pillows," one explained slowly.

"How would you know?" Avraham asked him. "Thunder follows lightning, how would you know in the short time that one follows the other for which she was saying the prayer?"

Isaiah looked at his brother for support, but quickly rallied. "We could tell, couldn't we Raphael? First, Grandma is afraid of thunder and when it is very strong, she hides her head under the pillows, so we knew that she was saying the thunder prayer, we thought, until we had a big flash of lightening, and we heard her say the thunder prayer, which means that she had said the lightening prayer first."

By this time both brothers felt relieved and a little hopeful that their father will forgive them. But Avraham still looked stern and asked pointedly, "Since when do we laugh at people who know less than we do?" and made them feel really bad, because they could not very well tell him the main reason for their laughter. But their father still had an insistent look in his eyes, and they felt that they will have to make a clean breast of the whole thing, and Isaiah undertook to do it. "Papa, I will tell what really looked funny to us, and why we laughed. When Grandma made the bed this morning, she warned us not to upset the pillows that she built up halfway to the ceiling, but when the thunder went, she dived under them so fast that we had no chance to remind her that she was upsetting them. And on top of that, Raphael wanted to know why was her head afraid of the thunder and not the rest of her. What if it hit where she stuck out of the pillows? Anyhow, it looked so funny to us then, but not now—does it Raphael?" Raphael shook his head in agreement with whatever Isaiah wanted him to agree; and Isaiah went on very seriously, "I, for one, and I am sure that Raphael too, feel sorry that we made Grandma mad. Aren't you, Raphael?" and

Raphael shook his head again.

Both looked as if they meant it; though if one looked close at them, he would see a little speck of laughter still clinging to their long black eyelashes. Chaya listened while they spoke to Avraham, feeling that they were really speaking to her. And when they, on their father's recommendation, begged her forgiveness, she smiled at them and shook her head; she was now worried with something else.

Raphael was not satisfied with her answer, and kept asking if she really forgave them, over and over again. "Yes, yes, I forgive you, I know that you won't do that again so you will find something else with which to shorten my life. Yes, I am sure that you will be good—good when you are asleep. I said I forgive you, now show me will you mean what you said, and go to sleep or you will not be able to raise your all-knowing heads in the morning."

When the children were asleep, she sat down near her son-in-law and said quietly, "You know Avraham, the children confused me, and now I don't know one prayer from the other. Will you listen to me and put me straight?" She recited the prayer for thunder that she said under the stack of pillows, which was really for lightening, and Avraham said, "Whose strength and might fill the world."

"Then I was wrong. I did say the wrong words and the boys knew that I was wrong and still they begged for my forgiveness. You know Avraham, it is not the first time that I mixed up the words, I must have done that a long time because they seemed so right to me. I hope He will forgive me, sinful old woman, I meant well but done wrong." She looked down, feeling badly about the whole thing, especially the children's self-reproach. Avraham saw her mood and told her, "You don't have to feel contrite, He knows you meant well."

Chaya slept well that night, the boys too; but not the girls nor Avraham, for they were too excited about the prize they won in the lottery. They pushed the night with their sleeplessness toward the morning, with impatience to get to the office where they had to collect the winnings.

11

The raffle

NEXT TO GOD, THE RAFFLE WAS a little hope for the pious Jew, for it carried a double value. First, if God is good to you, He sees to it that you win, so that you can pay the tuition for your son's religious education and if there is a little something left, then you put it away for your oldest daughter's dowry. The second value is carried within the shade of the first, called luck: for who that believes in God, does not say, "With God's help, I will have good luck"? So in either case, help from God—or when He is too busy with more important business than to pay personal attention to you—then it is with "good luck" that He may endow you. Armed with this philosophy, the sale of the raffle was held twice a year, with huge success.

Not only religious Jews were its victims but also Jews who only had faith in "luck"; they too, contributed to the Combine, who became richer with every drawing of the prizes. The Combine had its big headquarters in Kiev and their agents in all the small towns as well as the big cities, where they carried on with their business with the slogan "Who knows, it may be your turn."

Years back, when Mirele first learned that Avraham, too, was giving away their food money for raffles, she pleaded with him to give it up without being aware that it was now some ten years or so that his hopes had been dashed with every drawing. And it had surprised her when he quickly agreed with her and so easily. When he next turned down the agent's sale it was with a feeling of relief; now he did not have to live with false hope until the next drawing. Too many castles in the air were smashed for him. However, when the time for the drawing came, his interest drew him to the agent's office to see who won what. As he approached the office, he saw men with flushed faces hurrying out and talking in excited voices. He pushed his way in and found out that Motel the Barber had won a purse of 100 rubles! One hundred rubles! At no time had a prize been so big, not even a quarter of that amount had ever been won before; and this was the time that he had to listen to Mirele and stay out of the chance!

Well, he thought, I'll know better the next time the raffle comes around, I'll not listen to her again, and take my chances as other Jews do. Women are not meant to know how to speculate even with a few rubles.

And each time he made the sacrifice to the lottery was at the expense of a much-needed pair of shoes or food in the house. Until the last chance he took, he bought the raffle in his name, but after Bena left for America, he bought the last one in her name hoping that she will win and have it toward a marriage there.

When Rachel came home with the news that he won, he went to the office the next morning to claim his winnings but the agent told him that it had not arrived from Kiev yet; that it can be expected in a day or two. The family in the meanwhile was in a turmoil all day long and in the evening when Avraham came home, he was weary and silent and told them that they will have to wait for tomorrow or even until the day after. Rachel stayed home from work the next day and the boys from the *kheyder*. Chaya told them that only once in their lifetime will they have such holiday as this. Who knows, but the office may send someone after them today, and with their father away, the agent may find some excuse and ship their prize back to Kiev. Chaya's reckoning was logical; she disliked and distrusted the "Complain"—as she called the Combine—because she heard of the many times that they withheld the prize from a recipient for one excuse or another.

Toward the evening, after Avraham's rounds of his students, he went to the office, again telling himself not to be too expectant, that he will not find anything there yet, but he did: he found his mother-in-law and children in the office waiting for him, all with happy, shining faces. He wondered why and approached the agent at the counter who stuck a fast hand out to him and jubilantly congratulated him.

"I just told your children what a lucky father they have. Here take your prize, it's all yours on that lucky daughter's ticket. Send it on to her with our best wishes. Let them see in America how we treat our own here. You deserve this happiness, you had faith all these years, first in God, then in us, and your prayers were answered at last!" and he took a large package from the shelf under the counter that was well wrapped in a colorful paper and held many stamps on it and handed it to the winner. "Please take it home and open it there, I must leave now for another town to make another family happy and it's getting late." He almost forced them out of the office. The children walked home like they were walking on clouds. After all, it was not an everyday affair that a father wins a lottery, as their father did.

Rachel urged her father to stop near a high fence and open the package because she was dying to see what it contained; all she wanted was a glimpse into it, to see if it was money. He refused, saying in a weak voice that if she did not die all day, she wouldn't die if she waited until they reached home. Then Chaya put in her pitch, "You know what I'll tell you, Avraham, I have a feeling that there is nothing of value in that package, it's too big. And my heart tells me that the reason that the agent hurried us from the office was because he knew that the contents are worthless."

Now Avraham understood why he felt so depressed; he too felt what she had just voiced. At long last they reached home and Rachel ran into the house and lit the lamp, found the bread knife, and asked who will have the honor of cutting the strings. Avraham looked around at the excited children and told her to give the knife to Isaiah, who made sure to show off by making all kinds of ceremonious gesticulations before cutting away the strings, then tearing off the many papers, and at last opening the box. There, reposing in a bed of white tissue paper that was artistically draped around it, was a looking glass, staring back at them!

There in that box was their disappointment, their dead dreams, their futile hopes of needed shoes and warm clothes for the winter! Yes, there was the expected treasure at last before their very eyes, and what could they do with it? They stood around the table without a word; each with his own bafflement, his own defeat, until Raphael began to laugh at his image that looked back at him and he asked his father to raise the mirror so that he could see himself better. Avraham carefully raised the 12 × 18 inch mirror from the box, and found that it was cut in all four corners with a leaf pattern and in the middle of each pattern was a knob of cut glass that was the screw head that held the front and back together. In its wooden back, in its very center, was a keyhole and a little key in it that was engraved in gold, as was the metal that it could rest on as a stand. All six heads were bent over the table watching their prize package, but not one moved to find out what would happen if they turned the little golden key. They were so disheartened that they put it aside and went to bed without wanting any food.

Rachel came home the following night with news that whoever saw her wanted to know what they had won, and although she disliked to, she had to tell them of their disappointment and then suffer their words of sympathy. "Papa, would you send the looking glass to America for Bena?" she asked, and he shook his head and with a satirical smile, answered her, "Yes, I'll send it on for her, she won it."

Now that they were a little used to their chagrin, they all found something to say about it. Raphael wanted to know if they could find out what the little key is for and asked if he could turn it and Isaiah, his eyes dancing with adventure, asked his father what he would do if he turned the key and a million rubles fell out all over the room, then added that he, Isaiah, would dance like Uncle Menashe after a few drinks he takes at a bar mitzvah in the synagogue.

Chaya stood at the table ladling the soup into plates and told them all to wash for supper. Avraham put the mirror on the big bed and told the boys not to touch it until they were through with their meal and then they will find out if it contains rubles or rags. Never did the children eat so fast and in silence without knowing just what they did eat. Avraham had a hard time keeping up with them, and they had to wait for him to finish his meal so that they could join him in saying the blessing. And here too they had difficulty, for they began saying the prayer too fast and their father had to raise his finger to stop them many times and begin all over again. While he was the first one to say, "Blessed be our God, He of Whose bounty we have partaken, and Whose goodness we live," the two boys stood up and answered, "Blessed be He and blessed be His name," showing a great impatience, but just the same keeping their eyes on their father for permission to leave the table. Needless to say, they ran to the bed then to put the mirror back on the table and begged Avraham to operate it. Avraham looked at the silent Adah, and then handed her the key and told her to turn it in the lock, not to be scared of it, that no cat will jump out at her.

As soon as she twisted the key once, the mirror gave out a fine musical tune that they knew as a mazurka. They all stood and listened, entranced, and soon the two girls began to sway to its rhythm while the boys laughed at them as they watched.

"Well, it is a happy mirror at any rate, that is until I look into it," Chaya said and grinned, and Raphael wanted to know why, and was after her to tell him. "When you look into the mirror, it is pretty, because you are young and you have the whole world before you, but when I look into it, it gets old and full of wrinkles and it wonders how much longer it will last. Now you know why, my little 'lost soul'."

She told Adah to turn the key again when it finished the first song and instead of hearing it repeated, it played another melodious tune that one could dance to, and the third, a different one still; in all, three different tunes. They could not get enough of the music and played it over and over again before they were ready to send it off to their sister in America. Meanwhile Avraham made a promise with himself that this mirror was going to be his cure from the Combine, that never again will he be caught so absurdly.

12

Come, let us meet
the Sabbath

T HEY NEEDED AND WANTED MORE PLAY, not the controlled stride of their elders who stopped so often to greet each other and talk about their affairs. But the youngsters managed to find some merit even in the stops: they used that time to look each other over, talk, tease, and even try to flex a muscle once in a while, then raise such commotion that their parents were forced to go on. Isaiah and Raphael too would have liked to join just such a group of noisemakers but they knew that their father would disapprove and instead stood by until he was ready to go, then walked on with him in manly gait.

Chaya, dressed in her black velvet skirt and cape, with the silk, yellowed head kerchief tied becomingly around her soft face, was looking in the bookcase for her prayer book, all the while issuing orders to the girls. "Rachel, don't forget to grate the black-skinned radish very fine, but don't leave your skin on the grater. If you want ever to get married you must learn that the radish is the poor man's vegetable and must be handled with respect, so watch your fingers, and don't bloody up the radish with your effort." Then she turned to Adah, "And you, Adah, can go this afternoon to hear Rayzil's mother read—that is, if you don't run around and get yourself too tired to live while I am gone." At last she came up with what she was looking for and left the house. In the courtyard she met the two neighboring sisters and together they went on to the house of worship.

When they entered the house of prayer the usual smell of decay mixed with the offensive smell of urine hit their nostrils and the rickety steps groaned under their feet as they walked up to the balcony to the women's section. If only I were as rich as some of these men who come here to pray, she thought, would we have to worship our God in such an unfit place? She asked herself this question every time she came to the synagogue, but then smiled when she remembered the proverbial saying that "every pauper is a would-be charity giver." When she reached the top step, she looked around until she found Dvoyre, the "sayer."

Dvoyre was the wife of the winemaker and looked as if she was its taster too, for her cheeks were red, and round, and two deep dimples always played in her cheeks as she read from the prayer book and she was always of good cheer, making the women around her feel the goodness of the Sabbath. If, God forbid, she took sick and was unable to attend the services, then the entire section of the illiterate women would be forced to depend on the only other sayer, Rivka, the widow of the former *shamas** of the synagogue. And to see and hear Rivka the Widow pray was to witness a funeral of a dear one. She would sit with her listeners around her in a semicircle, rocking back and forth, beating her sunken breast in contrition, and crying rivers of tears that ran down the sides of her nose into her mouth and distorted every word that she issued, and the women around her followed her every action.

Which of them did not bring the past week's struggles and bitterness along with the hope of dispelling them with their prayers? On one such Saturday, when Chaya and her son-in-law were leaving the synagogue together, she said to him, "It is a sin to our Lord, that Rivka carries on so, on our beloved Sabbath, our day of rest. Is she the only one that is cursed with troubles? Do we know one family without, be it sickness, poverty, or death! Is she the only one that has a lame child? And to think that all those women around her sit there and help her turn the Sabbath into a day of mourning!" She walked faster than Avraham in her agitation.

---

* Hebrew for a beadle or caretaker, an assistant, in the synagogue who ensures things run smoothly.

"Then you don't sit with her?" he asked with some interest.

"Why should I! I sit with Dvoyre, to sit with her is like listening to the Song of Songs. I cannot live on tears alone!"

"But what do you do when Dvoyre is not there?" he wanted to know.

"Well, then I sit very far away from Rivka, and keep my ears open to the men below and try to follow the best I know how, God forgive me."

But this was a joyful Saturday for Chaya and the women she sat with, for Dvoyre was with them and they did not have to sit with Rivka and hear her lamentations. When they were about at the end of their prayers, they heard a hard rap on the lectern below and soon heard their seventy-eight-year-old rabbi make an announcement to which they closely listened. "My brothers, this is the day we have long waited for, to be exact, ten years almost to the day, and I am happy to bring you the good news, and to thank our Lord for letting me live to this day to be able to bring with all of you together our Torah to the Jews on the *folvarek*,* who waited for long for it." The excitement shook the small frame of the pious man and he had to stop a while before he was able to go on.

"We had to wait a long time for the governor to grant us the permit for the march with our Torah, but we got it, and we can now go without fear, for he promised to give us police protection all the way. Tonight, after the Abdalah,† we will all assemble in the courtyard of Reb Asher,‡ the Holy scribe, and with thankfulness to our God at last carry the Torah to its long-awaiting ark," he finished. A happy murmur ran through the synagogue, the women up in the balcony parted the curtains and looked down at the happy faces of the men and watched them congratulate each other while they quickly folded their prayer shawls as if to run and proclaim the good news to the entire world.

Chaya was busy thinking and did not intend to walk home with anyone, so she hung back, standing and tying and untying her kerchief until most of the congregation had left. Now alone, she walked homeward, slowly working a plan in her mind how to keep the two girls

---

* Russian and Ukrainian for farmland.

† The benediction for the end of the Sabbath and beginning of the working week.

‡ Reb is a Hebrew and Yiddish honorific among Orthodox Jews meaning Mister.

away from the procession tonight. She knew that she was unable to even make the attempt to keep the boys back, but the girls she must! If only she could feel the joy Avraham felt: to be the giver of the Holy word to his brethren while his sons witnessed it! But she still carried the memory of ten years back, when a Torah had been carried to the same ark, to the same community, by the same congregation, and it smothered today's joy for her.

She was unable to forget the bloody fighting that had taken place not far away from the Governor's Mansion, at the end of the Plaza, when two men, one a City clerk and the other a visiting Cossack from the steppes who had met in town in a tavern and drank more than they could hold, seeing the procession decided to follow it. Both were without shirts although it was cool evening, both had their trousers open, exposing their flesh. It was a moonlit evening with a star-studded sky, and every Jew was dressed in their Sabbath best, and because of this special occasion, some women wore the bits of jewelry that they still hid in their poverty.

The procession tried to ignore the two intruders, tried not to see them, and walked a little faster, trying to lose them but instead soon found themselves engulfed by a big crowd who began to shout at them, "We scorn you, dirty Jews," "Your scurvy heads are your mark," "Go hide in your dirty houses," and other mocking jeers that raised anger in the young and tears in the old, who tried to keep the others back from answering with their fists. Now the walking slowed down and attracted the police, but they watched and grinned and walked on. Because the paraders were held back by their elders, through fear for the women and children, and did not answer back, the disturbers boiled in anger that they were not shown the resentment they expected and walked on in drunken seething. Suddenly the silence was like at a funeral: the only sounds coming from the shuffling of feet on the dusty road and the insults that flew now and then from the antisemites. Yakov, the son of a peasant, who lived on the *folvarek*, was on his way home from the City, when he unexpectedly came on this scene and wondering at its grotesque behavior, shouted loudly, "Hey, what's going on here!" and did not go any further, for his few words touched off the raging madness of the men, women, and children and the mass of humanity became one clenched fist of anger!

The morning found the road spattered with blood, torn clothes lie trampled in the soft dust, hats and skullcaps moved around the ground at the will of the gentle wind with no one to claim them. The trampled grass wanted to tell what it knew about the mothers who ran with their young to safeguard them from sure death, about the young men who ran carrying in their arms the fragile grandfathers who were built like children and were too old to run for their safety, but there was no one around to listen. Ah, the trees too had some things to tell, they had still a better story than the grass, but it was told instead by Rabbi Ezekiel, the seventy-eight-year-old pious man. "I still do not know who picked me up together with the Torah I held in my arms, then sat me down in a thick clump of trees without one word and disappeared. But whoever it was, may God's blessings be on his head." That was what the trees had seen, and wanted to tell also, how they, the trees, protected the frail little Rabbi all night; and how early in the morning, the little gray-headed grandfather took off, holding the Torah close to his breast.

The entire community lived in fear for the next few weeks, and because the Torah was mishandled, and desecrated, it was interred in consecrated ground. It took Reb Asher, the Holy scribe who is losing his eyesight, close to ten years to write this new Torah, to replace the other one.

Chaya came home still turned inward with her thoughts and upon entering the house found the family already waiting dinner for her. "What kept you so late, Grandma!" the children asked. And Chaya had her plans all set, she served the food and at the same time unrolled her strategy that she had worked so hard on. "You will never guess who I met up with, so I'll tell you. First, I met my sister Baba coming from the Hasidic synagogue, alone, because your Uncle Dovid is away to his Rabbi for the weekend," this was the first volley she threw at them.

Then Isaiah looked at her with a puzzled face, "Grandma, we know that he is away for the weekend, he told us last week, don't you remember?"

"Yes, yes, I forgot, my Talmud genius that you know about it, but if you'll allow an old woman the privilege to speak, I may tell you something you do not know. Your Aunt Baba is alone and does not feel so good. Would we have a good bed for her here, I would ask her to come sleep with us, but as we know we don't, we cannot let her sleep all alone in the house; someone will have to spend the night with her, or maybe two nights, until Uncle Dovid comes home."

Chaya knew well that the silence that suddenly became so loud was not due to the food they were eating but because they were all thinking of tonight's march to the *folvarek*. She knew that the girls were already informed, because she heard that Raphael could not get into the house fast enough to beat Isaiah to telling them. So, she continued, "Rachel, I thought that you should go, but I met Ruvn the Barrel Mender and he told me that there is some trouble going on in Kolmin-Dodya's home and that the family there want to see me. It's nothing about the money they found, that has quieted down after they asked him a few questions. You know that I can't find the way that is the short way there; and with the long way, I'll be all day on the road just going there and I'll never make it back in the dark. Rachel, I want you to come with me." She looked at her pleadingly. Still an unnatural silence for such a noisy crew.

She went on, "And knowing that you boys will go with your father tonight, then Adah, you will go to your Aunt Baba." She saw the girl's unhappy face and quickly added, "You needn't go before nightfall. Your father and brothers can walk you to her house while they are on the way to Rayzil's house. You can still go to Rayzil's house after dinner and listen with her while Miryam reads from her good books."

Avraham had been listening all the while to her. Now he looked up from his food and looked at the two girls and saw Rachel look puzzled and Adah disappointed. The boys were both silent but betrayed their inner happiness through their shinning eyes and the careful handling of their food. Chaya waited to hear from her son-in-law but he sat and ate as if he had no care in the world. He understood well her machinations and understood her reasons for them.

Ten years ago, Mirele was sick in bed with a bad burning rash and the two girls, Bena and Rachel, were down with the measles, and she, his mother-in-law, had to stay home with them, leaving him the only one of the entire family to enjoy the festival. However, for many years after, he thanked God that he was the only one there. True, now Rabbi Ezekiel got an assurance from the governor that he would get all the protection from the police that was needed, going to and from the *folvarek*, but who can trust the Czar's servants? Perhaps it's for the best that the girls don't come tonight. And this day and night was a time not to be forgotten by the family for a long time to come, as they went in three different directions at the one time.

After their meal, Chaya and Rachel left for the Dolina to see the Kolmin-Dodya family. Rachel led her grandmother, who knew the shortcut as well as she did, through the park with its flowering bushes and beautifully curving path that brought them to the back gate from where they emerged and entered the broad fields of corn and wheat, which waved their golden treasures that shimmered in the sun.

"I must remove my shoes now, Grandma, I love to walk on the field road and feel the soft earth under my feet," Rachel said, and looked for a stone to sit on.

"But on the Sabbath?" Chaya reminded her, but in the same breath added, "Well, your feet aren't too strong, they ache so often. Go ahead and take them off." That was all Rachel had to hear, and she pulled off her shoes and stockings with a sigh of relief, standing first on one foot, then on the other and proceeded down the road. Chaya listened to the girl's chatter and could but admire her laughing liveliness.

When she ran out of the workshop stories, she found new songs to sing to her; and here and there she found something to point out, that she, Chaya, was not aware of. "Now, just look at the nodding stalks of the wheat, don't they look like they are dancing a polka? And now look over there, at the cornfields, don't their stalks look like stuffed dolls all standing or dancing farther in a row? You know, Grandmother, if I were not a Jewess, I would marry a peasant because I love to work the earth and watch how it produces with so much color from little seeds. And would I grow flowers! I would plant so much that there would hardly be a barren spot on this earth! Too bad that Jews can't be peasants, so I guess that I can't have my wish," she ended sadly, making her grandmother smile.

"Yes, too bad, a peasant in the family we need yet. We have everything else, but not the misery of a peasant yet. Do you think that their lives are to be envied? All the food that they raise does not feed their families. Their children go hungry more often than you and your sisters and brothers. They cannot see the beauty of the fields as you do, because the sweat of their hard labor blinds them. They live in worse ignorance and poverty, they are nothing more than serfs to their master, the Czar and his family."

The Dolina came into view and Rachel's feet began to dance in anticipation to wade in its cold, swift running waters. Men, women, and children were bobbing up and down and swimming all along the banks where the adults had left their sheets upon entering the river in their nudeness. The entire stretch of land along the river was papered with small dwellings that seemed to be bursting with children and dogs, which ran in and out of the houses and the river shouting and chasing each other. Rachel walked ankle-deep in the water and now and then was forced to run because the big boys, recognizing them as Jews, made sure to splash their Sabbath dresses. Chaya too felt like walking with her bare feet in the water but felt foolish in the presence of her granddaughter and satisfied her urge by dipping her handkerchief in the river and washing her face with it.

As they approached the house of their cousins, they had to go up a hill to the stairway that was built over the outlet of the mill-water many years ago. Rachel ran up the hill and then began to hop down the stone stairs two at a time but stopped short. She stood looking down toward her cousins' house and wondered why it looked so caved in, with a neglected appearance around it. Chaya, who was still on the stairway, saw Rachel's sudden hesitation and hurried down to her. "Why are you standing there, why don't you go farther down?" she asked her. "I don't think that any one is at home. Look, Grandma, there is so much earth laying around the house and the door hangs halfway off." And they both hurried down the rest of the stairs and ran toward the house.

Chaya, the taller of the two, raised herself on her toes and peered through a window, and was met by a sight that frightened her too much to say anything to Rachel. "What is it, Grandma!" Rachel asked her, but instead of answering her, she took her hand and both walked to the door and stood looking in. They did not believe their eyes that told them of the furniture that was piled up one on top of the other in the center of the room and the floor that was dug up all around it so deep that puddles of water stood in many places! They looked and looked, words failing them.

Then Chaya began to wring her hands and tears gathered in her eyes, and she said, "Rachel, a tragedy happened here, and there is no one around that we can ask, woe is me!"

"But Grandma, you said that you met with Ruvn the Barrel Mender and that he told you that they wanted to see you, didn't he tell you anything about them? Didn't he tell you why they wanted to see you?" Rachel looked hard at her and saw her grandmother looking away from her and her face reddening. She asked no more, for she felt the truth and knew that she was making her uncomfortable. Chaya recovered her balance and still holding her hand, said, "Come let us go down a piece and see if we can find someone to tell us about them." They walked quite a stretch before they came to a Jewish house, recognized by the mezuzah on the door, and knocked and a full-bosomed woman came to the door. Chaya looked at her and said, "Tell me, can you tell me where I can find anyone of the Kolmin-Dodya family? There is not a soul in the house and I can't see anyone around it either." The neighbor looked Chaya and Rachel over and decided to tell them.

"Come in, I see that you are strangers around here. We are newcomers ourselves," and the three went inside the house. Chaya's face was now burning with anxiety and when the woman asked them to sit down, she begged her to give them whatever information she had so that they could go. But the woman, anxious to talk to someone, began a long story of how they moved from the little town where she was born, how they came to find this house, and how she found the people around her unfriendly and unwound and unwound until Rachel felt like she would jump out of her skin and stopped her. "Please tell us what happened to our relatives, that is, if you know anything about them, or else tell us that you do not know anything about them and we will leave you in peace and go," and she made as if going to the door.

"Wait, don't go, don't rush off like that, sit down, I have something to tell you and your grandmother. But I must have your promise that you will not tell anyone that I told you this, because I am not supposed to know about it."

"Last Saturday after my husband and three sons left for the syna-gogue, which I could not attend because of a toothache that had kept me up all that night, I fell asleep in a chair near this window, and after a while the prayer book slipped from my lap to the floor and you know how it is."

But Rachel did not let her go any further and shouted in rage, "Either you don't know what happened here, or you don't intend to tell us. Come on Grandma, let's go home," and she pulled her grandma to her feet.

The woman got up fast and pushed both back into their seats, saying, "I really don't want to tell you, but you will hear it from someone else anyhow, so I might as well do it. Just as I said, I fell asleep on the chair, and the fall of the good book brought me to my feet, and that's when I heard a clanking noise as of metal against metal. I went out of the house to look around for its cause, but did not have to go too far for a strange scene met my eyes! In the very front of your relatives' house stood six or seven policemen, talking and smoking and holding shovels and heavy burlap sacks.

"I was puzzled and wanted to go farther but then I became aware that I was the only one around outside and I quickly returned to the house and bolted the door. What went on in that house I didn't know, but I sat and waited until my husband and sons came home, and it was then that we all heard a terrible sound and we ran to the window and saw their oldest daughter Donya, who had returned from the house of prayer first, I suppose, to prepare the table for dinner; they are such a big family, God bless them! And it was when she tried to get into the house that she saw the wreck they made of it. She screamed with so much rage that we could not think of eating our Sabbath meal, so

I beckoned to her from the window, but either she did not see me or did not want to see me. At any rate, she stood leaning against their house until her parents came home with her sisters and brothers."

She stopped to draw a much-deserved breath now, but her two agitated listeners waited with impatience and tried to hurry her up. "Yes, yes, so what happened then?" Chaya and Rachel prodded her as if they were rehearsed.

"Well, for two hours, I didn't know what was going on because they all had gone inside, and it was quiet, with the exception of the steady sound of shovels, like steel biting into hard earth. Much later we saw the police leaving the house, some with the burlap sacks over their arms and some with the shovels over their shoulders like soldiers carrying guns. Then we heard the crying of the women and boys like it was the Day of Atonement. My husband and I waited until there was no sign of the police anywhere and then we went to see how we can help them. It was not easy to get into the house because the floor was like a river by then, with the earth dug up all around the house near the walls, stood up in wet piles. When we came in, the girls were just bringing the mother out of a dead faint and the boys stood around their father, trying to pacify him while he was cursing the Czar with every breath he drew.

"To make this long, tragic story short, it seems that those blackguards were looking for gold or silver that was supposed to be buried in that house." She stopped a while and looked at her listeners questioningly, while Chaya murmured, "They should bury their dead ones like they bury our every hope in us, dear God. Now please tell us where we can find them."

"Please let me finish first. We came in and when we saw their misery, we begged them to let our boys help them put the house in some order, and my husband talked to your relative Kolmin-Dodya a long time, trying to convince him that they should forget that they were 'visited' and go on with their lives as before, but like one, the entire family were against staying on in that house. A few days later, they gave away the furniture that was not too badly broken to some poor family up the river, and they themselves went to live with kin of theirs on the *folvarek* until they can get some kind of papers with which they can go to America."

The woman now sat spent, while Chaya and Rachel remained in their seats thinking what to do next until a thought struck Rachel, and she said, "You know, Grandma, we can still join the marchers to the *folvarek* tonight and see if we can find them at the synagogue when we get there. Let us go home right now, so we will be in time to join Papa and the boys."

They thanked the woman for her time and information and left. Much as Chaya wanted to do as her grandchild suggested, to go with the marchers to the *folvarek*, she did not want to expose her to the dangers that such a march held for her, and made sure they would come much too late. She walked slow, claiming that her feet hurt and that she felt tired, and by the time they came to the park gate, it was locked for the night, being it was already sundown. For Chaya it was fine, now they had to walk the long way and she was sure that they will miss the marchers by at least an hour.

Rachel was disappointed and she somehow guessed that her grandmother wanted to keep her from going to the march, so she grumbled discontentedly most of the way. "If only that woman did not talk so much of her business and had gone straight to the point, we would have made it in good time. But no, she had to go next door by the way of China, she had to draw every detail out for us as if we were little children."

"And if we did come home earlier, would our feet still be able to carry us to the *folvarek*, you foolish girl!" Chaya tried to make light of it.

"I suppose you would have to stay home, but my feet are not tired, I still can walk there and back if only it was not too late!" Rachel said with some heat.

Late that night when Avraham and his sons came home, Rachel was already fast asleep but Chaya, tired and worried from her afternoon's experience, could not close her eyes. When she did doze off for a while, she awoke with a start, wondering if she did not hear something. Are they coming back alive? Why did he have to take the children with him? All these and other such questions came into her mind and did not let her rest. A few times she was sure that she heard the children's voices in the courtyard and jumped off her bed and ran to the door only to find the night staring into her face. Why did he have to take the children with him, must they taste the bitterness of being Jews so soon? Much later when she began to fight her tired body from the sleep it begged for, she heard the sound of voices she was sure of at last and quickly threw her shawl around her and in her bare feet crossed the courtyard where she saw Avraham with the two boys, and Zalman Goldstein. She stepped behind a tree and waited until they passed her by, still talking of the evening's adventure. "Thank God," she thought, "they are safe at home and they sound happy too." And when their landlord walked into his house, she came out from under the tree and followed them into their house. "What are you doing up so late?" the surprised Avraham asked her.

She smiled happily and told him that she went out to look at the moon and peeled off the clothes from the two tired boys and tucked them into bed as if they were babies. Avraham still wondered why she had been outside so late but seeing that in her present mood she will not give a straight answer he thought it wise to wait until the morning when she will get over whatever it was she had to get over, and then he will tell her and the girls all about the good news. With that the household now settled into sleep.

Very early in the morning Adah banged on the bolted door with her two small fists and when Avraham admitted her into the house, she was crying and mumbling something under her breath that no one understood. Chaya, aroused from her few hours' sleep, jumped out of bed and seeing the distressed girl tried to put her arms about her, but Adah pushed her away with angry force while she kept on talking and blubbering.

"Just what is the matter with you! Why don't you blow your nose and tell us what is the matter with you!" Rachel asked her, but Avraham motioned to her not to ask her any more questions and leave her to him.

Chaya washed and began cooking breakfast, all the while keeping an eye on the "lost soul" as she called Raphael, who looked so tired with so little sleep; no wonder, a six year old walking such distances!

When they were all at the table, Avraham sent Adah to wash her hands and face that was swollen from tears and advised the others not to talk about the experiences of the day before until they were finished with the meal. And so it was, and because Rachel had to leave for work, he told her to be the first one to talk.

She looked at him a little confused. "Papa, didn't I tell you that I don't have to go to work today! Sure, I told you that Ginendle went with her husband to the rabbi for the weekend and that they won't be back until sometime tonight, don't you remember!" And seeing her father shaking his head in recollection, she continued, "But if you want me to tell you about yesterday first, then I will."

"Well as long as you do not have to leave the house now, suppose we start with the youngest and go on to your grandmother to finish. Raphael, what have you to tell us!" Avraham asked. Called on to speak, when so many at once paid attention to him, was a new experience for the "lost soul". Up to the present minute his immediate wants were listened to, but his opinions of a special event? That was news to him! True, he was bubbling with news about the parade, about the little flags he carried—he got two instead of one—and about the questions everybody asked him, especially the ones that were so silly like, "Do you miss your mother?" How would he know if he misses his mother, so he didn't answer, and the women, especially the women, patted him on the cheeks for not answering! And when he became too tired to walk, how the big boys, very big boys, carried him on their shoulders; hoisted him real high so that he could see over everybody's head. That was fun, because then he could see even better than Isaiah, who had to walk.

"Raphael, we are waiting to hear from you," Avraham prodded him. And when he started to talk, somehow all his thoughts became tangled and nothing came out of his mouth. Oh, yes, something did come out of that knot, but not through his mouth but from his eyes! While his thoughts battled to make themselves heard, his eyes shed big round tears of vexation in sympathy for his difficulties. The flags, the broad shoulders of the big boys he rode on, Torah, the singing, everything tangled into one big hopeless knot, and he did not know how to untangle it!

"I think that we should start with the oldest and come down to him, maybe by then he will find his tongue." Rachel came to his defense and all agreed that Grandma should be the first to begin.

And Chaya had no difficulty with her speech but in her emotions, as she told what she and Rachel had witnessed and heard from the neighbor the day before. She ended by asking Avraham if he saw any of the family at the synagogue or anyone that knew anything about them.

Avraham smiled and followed with, "Now that I am the next one to speak, I am glad to bring you good news of the family. They were all there, Kolmin-Dodya, Gittel, and all the children, and they told me the very same story as you did. However, they are happy that it is all over and they decided to go to America. Kolmin-Dodya now tells me that it is for the best that this thing happened because his brother was after him for years to make up his mind and bring his family to America, but he fought it, and now they are all determined to go! Well, to me it was a great shock that Kolmin-Dodya would think of going, that he should even wait to listen to his brother. All his life's studying and his children's learnings will go up in thin air there. Of course, we could not talk at great length because of the noise in the synagogue, but they promised to pay us a visit shortly and then we will be able to talk of everything. In the meantime, we know that they are well and living with a good friend who is very happy to have them with her." Avraham ended and asked Rachel if she wanted to add something to what her grandmother had told.

"No, both you and Grandma had said as much as I know, but I am still mad at that woman for talking so much, she can pull a story until your guts hurt. If not for her, I too could have been with you to the procession and on the *folvarek*."

Avraham smiled at her and said, "You, my daughter, should not be so critical of others, you too can talk your head off. Now you can see how one looks to the other when proportion is not used. You too should learn to control your tongue. Look at Adah, do you hear her talk as much as you do?" Before Rachel was about to say something in her defense, he turned to Adah and gently said, "Now you can tell us what made you cry so hard this morning when you came from Aunt Baba's house."

Adah sat very quiet and did not feel like talking now, but saw that all were looking at her with expectation and she felt that she had to defend the uncontrollable weeping of the morning; she began very slowly to unfold her story. "Aunt Baba was surprised to see me at her house because she thought that I would be with you, Papa, in the procession on the way to the *folvarek*. She wondered how Grandma knew that she was not feeling well, because she felt very good, she said, but she wanted me to tell you and Grandma that she sends her thanks for your consideration and my company."

While Adah spoke, Avraham looked at his mother-in-law and she looked down at the table and he was now sure that she found ways to keep the girls from going with him last night. Adah's voice became thick with tears again and she was hindered in talking anew. Suddenly she shouted, "I wish you hadn't sent me there! You knew what Aunt Baba did when I was asleep? I was suddenly awakened during the night because there was a light shining in my eyes and I was so scared that I wanted to scream but I was afraid." Now she really blubbered at the memory of her fright and Avraham tried to console her. "For a light you got scared, and with your own aunt in the house!" He tried to laugh it off, but Adah was unyielding and continued her story.

"When I opened my eyes, I saw Aunt Baba standing near the bed with a candle in her hand whispering something that I could not understand. Oh, how I wanted to scream, but I was afraid to and pretended that I was asleep. Do you know what she did? She went around to all the corners of the room and stopped to call names that I never heard in our family before, and in the same low voice murmured something, sobbing all the time! But in every corner of the room, she did the very same thing."

She stopped a while to wipe her runny nose, then went on. "At first, I thought that I was dreaming, but as she went on, her sobbing reminded me of the way Moishe's mother did at his funeral, and I was so shaken up that I was about to run out of the bed and run out of the house in the middle of the night and come home. But suddenly she put the candle out and came back into the bed and tried to put her arms around me, but I moved all the way to the wall because I thought if she touched me, I would die!" She spoke with excitement and her voice was now pitched high and her hands were hard at work trying to express her feelings that she felt her mouth failed to do. Avraham looked at his mother-in-law again and saw her eyes downcast and felt sorry for her. To sooth his child he went close to her and patted her head, saying, "Never mind, if you don't want to go there again, you need not do so; no one will force you to."

"Grandma, why do you think Aunt Baba would do such things!" Rachel asked.

"When you get a little older, I will tell you all about it. In the meantime forget it and don't talk to anyone about it," she said to Rachel and looked around at the rest of the children, knowing well that they all labored under a strong curiosity now. She remained at the table, thinking they're much too young yet to understand that a human being can be stronger than iron. She thought of her sister Baba, who was two years younger than herself, and when she was only ten years old, she was already a head taller than her. Her body had blossomed forth as if a seventeen year old. How her laughter rang through the house then! Of course, she was scolded and many times slapped for it, because it was not in accord with Jewish traditions for a young girl to carry on so, giving the impression that she was all ready for the *shadkhan* to find her a husband—especially when there was still an older, unmarried sister in the house.

And the poor, young, blossoming child could not understand why her parents wanted to stifle her laughter, or her singing, or her dancing in the courtyard like all other girls of her age did and why they found so many reasons for hiding her from people when she felt like putting her young supple arms around the whole world and laugh and sing the day away. Yes, Chaya thought, she should have laughed and danced and sung then, and to her heart's content, because now all that is stilled in her. Instead, her soul cries out to the twenty children that she buried despite gentle husband Dovid the Hasid, who tries so hard to convince her that God is compassionate, that He is forbearing after all. Did He not let them keep their firstborn son, Moishe? And their sixth child born, a girl, Chava? How can she help her constant thinking of the others, especially when she is left alone with her thoughts? Then she relives their births, their illnesses, and their deaths. Small wonder that she goes around looking for them at night, the wonder being—that she is still alive!

Chaya realized that she was turned inward with her thoughts after she heard a question that someone asked, repeated to her; and she shook off her preoccupation and looked around, then saw her Talmud genius talking.

"Grandma, are you listening? I said that I wished that you had been with us last night so that you too could have enjoyed yourself as good as we did. When the parade began Rabbi Ezekiel walked in front carrying the Torah and all the boys of bar mitzvah age were close around him for protection from anyone who may want to harm him, but who would want to harm an old rabbi who carries a Torah? The rest of us followed, carrying little white and blue flags, singing all the way to the synagogue, and you should have seen how many people were waiting for us there! And Grandma, if you saw all the kissing and congratulations that went on there, you surely would have thought that you were at a wedding! Then Rabbi Tomasz of that synagogue made the blessings and did we dance in a big circle! So many things happened, I will probably remind myself later of more and then I'll tell you."

Chaya's face beamed with joy but she could not keep from a question that was always in the back of her mind and asked him, "Tell me, did you have the police with you, and did they guard you well?"

"Yes, there were police with us all the way, but they did not come into the *shul*,* they stayed outside with the other non-Jews, who laughed at us and called us *Zhyd pachok*, cradle heads.† Then when we were on the way home, the same police came with us. What did we need the police for? No one would hurt us." Now the "lost soul" began to struggle with himself and finally broke through, yes, "And why don't you tell them about all the wine the men drank and all the honey cake the women

---

* Yiddish for synagogue, the Jewish house of prayer.

† Ukrainian derogatory term; *Zhyd* translates as "Yid."

forced you to eat! And about the man who drank to so many *l'chaims**
that he fell down the few steps from the women's balcony!"

"Well, it looks like our tongue-tied boy has at last found his tongue
again and has something to say too. What else do you remember, tell
us?" Avraham immediately saw that he made a mistake, for Raphael
seemed to shrink at his words, and he began to stammer and look lost.

"I ... I ... want to ... I ... didn't ... I don't know. No, I ... I want to
tell ... more. There was ..." His tongue became mutinous and refused
to produce his thoughts.

"I guess it will be like Isaiah said before, and Raphael too will think
of some more to tell us later on," Chaya said to console the boy.

---

* Hebrew for "To life!"

13

Who can choose?

SOME DAYS LATER AVRAHAM came home and told Rachel of the letter that he received from her mother. He saw her eyes light up with pleasure and she shouted, "Let me see it, let me see it," and she took it from his hand and kissed it.

Chaya, who had been in the kitchen trying to kindle the fire in the samovar, came running to hear what caused the girl's gaiety all of a sudden and when she learned of the letter, she understood why he had looked so downcast when he came home. She sat down to wait until he opened it and read it.

Avraham looked around and found all four children waiting for him, so he was unable to hesitate any longer, and began to read:

> To My Dear Husband, Mother, and Children,
>
> First, I want you to know that Bena and myself are in the best of health, and I hope that this letter finds you all healthy and happy. This is the fourth letter that I am sending on to you, but I do not understand Avraham, why you do not answer me? I would be worried about you, but because you returned my money that I sent to you a few times, I gather that you are all well but that you are still angry at me. I believe that we should now consider it time to have an open discussion with each other about our situation, even

though you are in Kamenets-Podolski and I am in America.

I was ready with money to send for all of you two years ago, although that money I was ready to borrow and pay off as I worked. In America this is possible. As I said, I was ready then and you refused to come or send the children on and I did not press you because I wanted time to convince you how wrong you are. I pray that by now your better judgement came to the fore and you will agree to prepare yourselves, all of you. I am sending you under separate cover a money order with which you can clothe and shoe the entire family and make ready to go. In the meantime, I would like you to set the date so that I can order the ship's tickets for that time, and I will also send you the necessary papers you will need for the journey.

I beg of you Avraham, don't keep our children much longer in Russia, bring them to America while they are still young; they will still have the opportunity to attend school and learn good trades. Forget the nonsense that in America Jews forget their religion, because those that want to maintain it do so because no one gets in their way. Bena too pleads with you, she misses you badly. And you, my Mother, and children, help your Father make the right decision and bring you all to me quickly because I miss you all. Please, Avraham do not send the money order back to me, but do with it what I beg you to do.

My heart goes out to all of you, and I live with the hope of seeing you soon.

We send you all our love,
Mirele and Bena

P.S. Avraham, this letter was written for me by a young American girl from a Jewish religious family. I too was born into a Jewish religious family in Kamenets-Podolski, but I cannot even sign my name in the language of my people.

    Mirele

Avraham ended, and the room remained quiet. He looked around from one to the other expecting them to go to work on him, but no one spoke. They held back because of the hurt look in his eyes, although they were all bursting with a desire to speak. Chaya was about to go back to the kitchen to finish what she had started before, but he held her back and asked her to speak her mind while they were here, all together.

She looked queerly at him. "My son-in-law, we are not all together. Your wife, the mother of your children, and their oldest sister of whom they are so fond, are not with us. It is my opinion that you should hurry a letter to Mirele and tell her that we are all ready to come and that she should send out the papers that we need and fast!" She ended on a high-pitched tone and with emphasis. He blanched under her words but controlled his voice and turned to the children. "And you, my children, have nothing to say? Do you miss going to America? Would you want to leave behind all your aunts, uncles, cousins and the many friends you have, and go to a strange land?"

He looked into each face, noticing their high color after the letter was read. "Papa, you know that we don't miss America, how can we when we were never there? But I know that I miss Mama so badly that in the midst of my singing or laughing, a cloud settles over me. Since she left, I don't think that I missed one night that I didn't see her in my dreams," Rachel told him.

"And you, Adah, would you like to go to America and leave your father behind?" and before Adah could answer, Raphael ran over to his father and threw his thin arms around his neck and cried, "Not me, Papa, not me. I don't want to leave you, I don't want to go to America, I don't remember my Mama, and I want to stay here with you." Hot tears washed down his face and he had a bad time with his full nose.

Chaya tried to draw him to her, "So you will stay here, but now come over here to me and let me help you blow your nose, my poor 'lost soul'. You do not miss your mother, because you don't remember her and you don't know her. Here, blow hard, again, now once more." She pitied the child, who was the only one among the children who really did not know Mirele as a mother. "Well, I see that I will be able to keep at least one of my children with me. I see that you, Adah and Isaiah, agree with Rachel, you want to go to your mother." He spoke patiently, but he brought tears to Adah's eyes and she did not answer him; but the miserable-looking Isaiah did.

"Papa, you put it to us to choose between you and Mama, and we want both of you. Don't you see, Papa, we want both you and Mama," and the "Talmud genius" closed his upper lip over the lower one so that no one would guess that he wanted to cry. Adah's weeping was deep at the start, but it slowed after a while and soon completely stopped.

Avraham waited, and then asked; "Now that you had your cry, supposing you tell me now why you did?"

"You know why, Papa. You want to keep us here, and Mama wants us there. What about us? Can't we be like other children who have both father and mother at the same time in the same place with them? I didn't see my mother for so long I forgot what she looked like. Many times I try to picture her face but I just can't remember it any more. And I miss Bena too something awful, that's why I cried before." And her chin began to tremble again, but she kept her tears under control this time.

Avraham had asked the questions with the hope of receiving different, entirely different, responses, and he felt very bitter now because he had made up his mind that he was going to ask Mirele for the last time to come back home to the family fold or agree to a divorce. No more mention was made by any of them of the letter and he did not answer it. When the money came, he did not tell the children, but the very same day sent it back. The letter he wanted to write to her, he postponed from day to day until he forgot about it, though it was always in the back of his mind as something that he will do when he gets around to it. It was not important to give himself to it now.

Time went on, season followed season, and they waited, facing an unusually early winter. The tall oak trees that were covered with dancing green leaves all summer abruptly found themselves standing naked and colorless. Within a few sudden very cold nights, the green leaves had turned a bright red, then gold, and soon a dull brown and began making their journey to the soft earth around there, to await their rebirth next spring. The stark nakedness of the trees and the grass that turned hard and brown together with the fall that died so prematurely surely foretold of a long and bitter-cold winter.

14

Chaya and Katynka

RACHEL SWALLOWED HER LAST BITE and had one arm in the sleeve of her coat while she tried to tie her kerchief. She was late getting to work and her grandmother kept talking to her. Chaya stood near the door and talked on. "It is a few weeks now since we saw her, I want you to go and find out why she does not show her nose into the house here. And tell Katynka that …" but Rachel opened the door and ran out. "Did you hear what I told you to do?" she shouted after her.

"I heard you, but I won't do it." Rachel's voice trailed in the distance.

Chaya wondered, she knew that the children all liked Katynka, especially Rachel, who always managed to bring home to her little squares of the materials that were cut away from the outsides of the shirts and Katynka made pillowcases from them. Well, she had to wait until she came back from work and then find out. She gave Rachel a chance to wash up and eat some of her supper before she asked her if she had been to see Katynka.

"Grandma, I told you this morning that I won't go to see her," she answered with annoyance.

"But why not? What have you against that poor soul?" Chaya wanted to know.

"You should go to her! You insulted her, not me." Rachel's face was red now.

"Just what are you talking about, what kind of insults did I make to her and where and when?" Chaya's face too was now red with anger.

"You don't know when!" Rachel laughed sarcastically. "What are you talking about? If I knew why, would I ask you?"

"Well then I will have to remind you because you should know! It is now three weeks that Katynka took sick, and she had sent for you twice, but you did not think it important to go to see her! A girl that works in my shop told me that her little sister came twice to call you, and you ignored Katynka's cry for help both times!"

"Oh Grandma, how could you?"

"My enemies should know from a good day, if I knew about her illness. What little girl brought what message to me? May I never see your mother again, if I saw a girl that Katynka was supposed to send to me for help. Tell me what is wrong with Katynka, what is she sick with? If you knew all the time, why didn't you say something to me before? At no time could anyone accuse you of keeping your mouth shut for very long—but now, when a friend is sick, you keep it to yourself, and then you get mad because I did not go to see her!"

Chaya was badly upset but did not say anymore. The following morning, she took her shopping basket off the hook and put into it a homemade bread, a glass of preserves (that she hoarded for the winter) and a glass of rendered beef fat, then added a little box of tea leaves and looked around the kitchen to see what else she could add. Oh, yes, she better take some sugar too, she knew how Katynka loved sugar. She used to say that it takes the bitterness out of her life. When she neared her home, she was happy to see that a thin, light smoke was coming from the chimney of her house. God is with her, she is getting some help, she thought, but where did she get the kindling with which to start the fire in the stove!

She hastened her steps and reached the door hurriedly, to find inside the house Katynka, sitting hunched-up in a chair near the stove, dressed in almost every bit of clothing she possessed. "Good morning, Katynka, my but you are dressed up, are you that cold or do you feel sick?" She knew the answer before she asked the question just by looking at her sunken yellow face, and the tears that rolled down slowly as if unbidden. Without another word, she looked around and decided what she must do: rolled her sleeves to the elbow and first went to the bed that was all tangled up with the bedclothes and straightened it out. Then she removed Katynka's outer clothes, leaving her only in her nightshirt, and led her into the comfortable bed and covered her with as many quilts as she had. While Katynka stretched herself in the new warmth and comfort, Chaya boiled water, made tea for her, then added some of the preserves to it and brought it to the invalid, and bade her drink it.

In the meantime, Chaya made soup of the remaining water and the rendered beef fat, which gave off an aroma of a good cooked meal. Katynka slowly drank the tea, all the while sniffing at the soup, and watched as Chaya was peeling an onion to add to it, and for the first time since she took sick, felt a good sensation settle around her being and she silently thanked God that she was not alone anymore. "Grandmother Chaya, I am sorry that I have to be a bother to you, but I feel too weak to protest too strongly," she told her.

"Is it a bother when one human being helps another? Don't you help others when they are in need? But tell me, who took care of you when you became ill?" Then looking closer at her, Chaya added, "Tell me, just what is wrong with you, did you call a doctor?"

"I fainted on the street a few weeks ago, and when I came to, I found myself in Doctor Popov's office, and him letting blood from me with leeches. I was so scared that I thought that I was screaming, but while my mouth was opened, I was unable to issue one word. Later he told me that there is something wrong with my heart and that I must stay in bed a long time." She rested a while, and seeing Chaya's questioning eyes on her, she continued. "When I had fainted, I was picked up by two women who were on the way to the new marketplace in their wagon and the very same women brought me back here from the doctor's office, made a fire in the stove, and then left quickly because they had merchandise to sell. A few minutes after they had closed the door on me, it opened again and the smith's little girl Eidele came in and asked me if there is something that she could do for me. She showed me the half ruble that she had in the palm of her hand that the women had given her, so that she would not leave me alone in the house for too long. What could a seven year old do for me! She sits near my bed most of the day, only runs home for her meals. I felt so sick, I thought that I was going to die, so I sent for you, and the child came back and told me that you had your own troubles and couldn't come, and that you said that I was not to send for you anymore."

Worn by so much talk and her emotions, she leaned back on her pillows and rested a while, then continued, "I am not angry, I know that you do have enough troubles to suffer in your own house, and besides, why should you help me? I am not of your people."

"So, that is what you are thinking? You think that we Jews are so low that I want you to die like a dog, all alone? Don't talk like a child. Jew or no Jew, when we need each other, we are just human beings in trouble. I would like to see that child that you sent to me for help, I would like to ask her something."

She got up from the chair, and swept the floor, then sat down on the edge of the bed. Katynka fell asleep somewhat comforted and secure for the first time since she took to her bed. Chaya sat on, and wondered what she could do with her; she could not leave her alone, for who would take care of her, who would make a meal or change the bedclothes for her? There must be some way, she must find someone who can help her even if it would be only for a few hours a day. Her thoughts flew from one to the other as she ruled out the poor, who could not, and then the rich, who would not. Then she played with a strange idea.

Why not, she thought. The wise men say that he who goes on an errand of mercy is protected from all evil. She played with thoughts that were indeed strange for her kind, then her hand flew up to her head and with one finger she tapped her forehead while she smiled wisely. Well, if I am to do a good deed, then I must not delay but go on my way, she thought, and quietly let herself out of the house, and walked very fast the few blocks from Katynka's house to the church she worshiped in. She kept looking back over her shoulder to see if anyone was watching her while she turned the corner to enter at the side of the church, into Father Servuich's living quarters. Again she turned her head, and seeing no one she knew, she knocked on his door, half hoping that he was not there for she was not at all certain that she was doing the right thing, and besides, she felt awestruck at the church seeing it so close.

But soon Father Servuich came to the door, and seeing a Jewish woman, showed his surprise and asked what she wanted with him. At no time did she feel so much panic, for at no time did she stand so close to a church or a priest! Since her childhood, and through her adulthood, she held fear of the Church, feared the Russian Easters that were celebrated with bloodletting of the Jewish people, feared the priest's encouragement to beat the Christ-killers, when they were close to the Church. She now felt the great division of the Christian and her own religion as never before and felt like she was on the brink of an abyss and Father Servuich saw her confusion and wondered how she came to his door.

"You want to talk to me about something?" he asked.

"Yes, I came to talk to you about a woman of your Church, you know her, she is the widow of the Petty Officer Stepan Gorezdykh. She, Katynka, is very sick and the doctor told her to stay in bed for a long time, but she has neither kith nor kin to look after her. She herself cannot make a bite of food for herself or keep a fire going in the stove or bring something from the store that she may need, and I don't know to whom to go for help for her. I myself would be glad to help her, but I have a big family to take care of, and I do some work outside of the home, in other people's houses. Besides, I live all the way in the City, near the Governor's Plaza, and it's hard for me to go to Katynka very often. Maybe you can get her into the hospital or get someone to come to her house every day to help her."

She waited while Father Servuich stood in deep thought a while, then he told her that he will try to get someone to care for Katynka and in the meantime, would she continue her help.

He added as she was about to turn away, "The Lord be good to you."

She went back in high hopes, surely in a church with so many worshipers it will not be hard to find someone that will have pity on a helpless invalid. She opened the door of Katynka's house very slowly not wanting to awaken her, but found the little girl on her bed and crying. This frightened Chaya badly, and she ran to the bed to see if Katynka was alive, and she saw that she too was crying softly.

"What is this, why are you both weeping, did you think that I deserted you?" she asked with concern.

The little girl jumped off the bed and was on the way to the door as if the Devil was after her. But Katynka called her back and then held onto her wrists. "Here, sit down again," she ordered her. "Tell this Grandma what you just told me, don't be afraid, she will not scold you, I just want her to hear the truth." But all her urging was in vain. Eidele sat with downcast eyes and worked a circle with one swinging leg, the foot touching the earthen floor. Chaya saw how ill at ease the child was and told her to go home, but come back a little later.

When she left, Katynka raised herself on an elbow and looking Chaya straight in the face said, "We know each other a long time and I believe that you know that I feel closer to your family than to my own people. When I became sick, you were the only person that I wanted badly near me and when Eidele told me that you refused to come to me, I felt no anger for you, but only self-pity and the fear of dying and laying here all alone, until the stink of my carcass would call to the outside." She rested a while, then continued, "Well, she did not go for you after all, she lied to me."

Chaya listened and understood, and forced Katynka to lay down and have a nap again. Later on she gave Katynka some of the soup that she had made and then told her where she had been; and of the priest's promise to send someone to her as soon as he can find such a woman, or else he will see if he can't. Chaya talked on, Katynka was anxious to tell her about the little girl Eidele, but she could get little chance, because of Chaya's rambling about Mirele's letter, the boys' pranks and their advancement in their studies and even of the neighbors in the courtyard who had some argument over a kitten. Anything just to keep the invalid at rest.

At long last Katynka broke through, holding Chaya's eyes with her own, and began to tell her about the young child. "Eidele's mother died when she gave life to the child, and she was raised by her father in the smithy while her big sisters and brothers went to work. Eidele was left to herself, the sparks of her father's anvil were the only toys for her childish imagination. When the women sent her to me, she adopted me for her mother. She was afraid that you will take over, she would be put out by you, and lied. Chaya, her clinging to me is so pleasant! I feel as if she was my own flesh and blood. Imagine what that child did with the half ruble that the women gave her, can you guess? No? Well, she went to the store for candy, she told me, but came back with kindling wood and matches! How she cried before you came in. Then she told me why she lied. She was afraid that I'll put her out of the house. What am I to do with her?"

"What can you do with her! Let her stay with you as long as she wants to. I don't know how long it will be before you will get somebody in here, in the meantime it's good that the child is around. Katynka, now I must go. I didn't tell you, but I went back to work to the kitchen of my landlord, only now I go in Thursday afternoons for a few hours and Friday mornings for a few hours, so that my son-in-law cannot catch me when he comes home. It's getting late, I must go to make the cake and *challah* dough mixture so that the cook can start baking in the morning."

"But Grandmother Chaya, will they still pay you with the fowl giblets as they did before?" Katynka knew of the bad time she drew from Avraham then.

"No, no. I told them that now I want them to pay me with money, so they give me a ruble and a half every week, and I use that money to buy staples that I put away in the attic for the winter, and of course there is a little more food in the house now too. I hope that I can keep on working there until I buy some warm underclothes for the children. All right, I am going now, and I will be back in a few days to see if you have someone with you."

She left, but returned in a few minutes, and went to the stove to see if the fire was still burning, and how much soup she left for her. "I'll tell you, if I don't come up to see you tomorrow, then Rachel will be here, and I want you to give her this half ruble and let her buy for you whatever food you'll need. But I guess I might be up here myself." She pressed the money into Katynka's hand and left hurriedly.

But almost a week passed and neither Chaya nor Rachel came and Katynka was cared for by little Eidele. The weather did not wait for the poor to provide themselves with fuel or warm clothing, but took a bitter cold turn and soon brought along sleet and snow. The streets became deserted, and those that were forced to be on them hurried as if driven by beasts. Chaya was unable to rest, she constantly worried about Katynka and she was unable to send Rachel to her because she suffered pains in her legs and had to stay at home from work. One morning she got up determined to go to New Plan, and no matter how much discouragement she got from Avraham and the children, she dressed and went. For her to go to Katynka in that weather was like going uphill on a glacier. Her coat was worn and thinned with the years' wear, the shoes on her feet were torn at the soles and made walking the slippery roads and bypasses hard while the wind tore at her shawl around her head and made her breathing difficult. Her nostrils became full of frozen steam from her labored breathing and her ears burned from the frost. On the way she stopped off to buy some meat and a few groceries that she knew Katynka needed.

When she finally reached the house, she was worn and frozen to the bone, but satisfied that she "made it."

Katynka stared at her, then shouted, "Are you out of your mind Grandmother Chaya! In such weather you dared walk such a long distance."

Chaya was too exhausted to answer, but she slowly removed her shawl, her coat and stockings that were almost worn through at the soles. It took her a while until she was able to adjust her sight to the objects in the room because her eyes were streaming; then she saw Eidele sitting on the edge of the bed, feeding some hot milk to Katynka by large spoonfuls.

"How do you feel, Katynka. I am sorry that I could not come before, but my son-in-law is sick and I must take care of him. Rachel too is not well, she has bad pains in her legs and must stay in bed."

While she spoke, her eyes wandered around the room and she saw the disorder that was there. "I can see that you were alone all this time, that no one came to keep you company."

"Father Servuich was here, and he said that he was trying very hard to send someone to me but this cold weather discourages anybody from leaving a warm home. The poor man came in here looking like a frozen broomstick and he left me some money from which Eidele bought me eggs and milk; what else can a poor soul ask for, I am well fed, and warm."

"Yes, what else? Perhaps we get so little because we ask for little. You should be in a hospital. When Doctor Popov comes to see my son-in-law tomorrow, I will get after him to find a bed for you in the hospital." She busied herself with the packages she brought until she found the orange and brought it to the invalid and told her that her people believe that an orange is the best medicine for a woman after the birth of a child and for a sick person.

She brought tears to Katynka's eyes. "You should not have bought it for me Grandmother Chaya, it probably cost you two days' work! Where could you have gotten it in this weather! I wish you didn't bring it to me." And now the tears fell.

"You see what I mean when I said that we ask for too little! When you get something that's bigger than little, you want to turn it back. Go on, eat it. It will do you good." She turned her back on her and began to prepare soup for her. She worked almost the day through washing bedclothes, sheets, and whatever she found that needed cleaned. She also cooked soup, made tea, and cleaned the room.

She saw to it that Eidele combed and braided her adopted mother's hair, while she, too, chewed on some of the orange that Katynka stuck into her mouth.

"But you still did not tell me what was wrong with your son-in-law, Grandma Chaya."

"What should I tell you! What is not wrong with him! First of all, as you know him for a long time, he is a mule! No—what did I say—not a mule, he is a donkey—stubborn and stupid! He can live to a ripe old age if he took better care of himself, but instead, he is chasing around trying to make a living.

"He, with his rheumatic heart, does not believe in rest or less trouble on his mind, because he has to show his wife that he can remain here and carry on by himself. Such a stubborn man one can find only once in a lifetime, and his pride will drive him to an early grave. Mirele sends him money and he sends it back the same day! Now he came down with something that looks like a rose on his ankle, the doctor said it is 'erysipelas' or something. He is in pain and has a fever. I hope that he will get better soon," she ended with a sigh.

"Did you buy an orange for him too?" Katynka asked seriously.

"What, and have him accuse me of doing some shameful work for which I got the money for it? No, I am very careful that he does not find out about my work." She laughed roguishly, dressed herself, tied her shawl securely around her head and left, after telling Katynka that she will see to it that she is taken to the hospital.

And two days later Doctor Popov came and took her to the hospital, all the while assuring her that she need have no worry about the payments there, because he got her a free bed in a ward. With Eidele's help, he bundled her into as many covers as he found there, then went out and padded the bottom of his roomy sled with a fur cover and placed a pillow for her head. When he brought her out, Eidele followed with a feather blanket that she had brought from her home and they both covered and tucked her in.

Katynka peeped out of her covers and said to the child, "When I get better and come home, I'll ask your father if I may keep you for good with me. In the meantime, don't run out into the cold too often and take care of yourself." She raised herself and kissed the girl, feeling her soft, flushed face.

The sled had a bad time going on the high drifts that piled up while the snow was dancing to the fury of the wind. Doctor Popov had difficulties seeing more than a few feet away and with the horses who slipped now and then, but he was glad that at least he was able to get her to the hospital, for he knew that to wait until the weather cleared meant her death.

15

Clutching at a straw

THE WINTER WAS MERCILESS TO AVRAHAM and his family. He was unable to leave his house for many weeks, the illness having left him weak and in fear of another attack. Rachel felt better, but was unable to go to work during the bad winter months; the road to and from the shop was paved with ice and snow and was impassible in most places. Adah was well, but her winter cough returned and her "hacking" went on day and night. She brooded and fought with the boys, who refused to let her into their games The only time she seemed content was when she sat close to her father while the boys read to him from the Holy Scriptures, from the Gemara,* and chapters on civil law. First, they read in the Hebrew, then translated into the Jewish language. She was fascinated by the historical "stories" that seemed so simple and opened another world to her. When the boys' translations were too fast for her to grasp, she did not ask them to stop or explain anything to her, because she did not want them to tell her that "it was not for girls to understand such things."

At one such time, when they did tell her so, and before Avraham had a chance to admonish them, Chaya, tired of their teasing, stood over them and loudly proclaimed, "And many times it is not easy for girls to understand 'such things,' and that is because all the Torah's knowledge is stuffed into your heads and none is left for the girls. But

---

* The Gemara is the part of the Talmud comprising rabbinical analysis of, and commentary on, the Mishnah. The Mishnah is the first major written collection of the Jewish oral traditions, also known as the Oral Torah.

some day women too will get to know what the Good Books say and then you 'Talmud geniuses' will not be able to sneer at us." She patted Adah's head. "I may not live that long to see this, but you my child are young yet, you will."

But this did not satisfy Adah, for her imagination was fired by the Jewish histories that she heard in the home and when Rayzil's mother read to them on a Saturday. After those readings, the girl had some difficulty to come back to the present, and daydreamed of the time past that gave birth to the present. Chaya understood the girl's daydreams, and forgave her when she did not respond to her call.

But the boys' isolation during the winter cramped their activities, and they found some outlets in teasing, wherever they were able to do so. Of course, when they saw Adah turned inward, they would not lose the opportunity, and one or the other would start something.

"Look Raphael, your sister Adah swallowed a Sabbath reading and can't digest it so her ears are folding up."

And their laughter filled the room, until Rachel boxed their ears, for she too was restless and bored with her confinement and the boys' teasing annoyed her. She missed the activity of the shop, the girls' gossip of the town and their singing at the machines. The girls were mostly of her age but better developed and better informed and they talked openly about their body development, their dreams for the future. From them she learned not to be afraid when she began to ovulate, and about sex.

She wondered where they had gotten all this secret information and why it was a taboo in their own home, and why she herself never knew or questioned where she or her sisters and brothers came from. Sure, she knew that somehow her parents were involved—but how, where, or when had not been a mystery to her because no action or word spoken in the house ever aroused her young curiosity, until she heard the girls in the shop talking. Now in her forced idleness at home, she looked back at the time when she and Bena began to work, and as soon as they became friendly with the girls in the shop, and became aware of some very strange talk among them and when she turned to Bena for an explanation, Bena would look uncomfortable and tell her not to listen to them. Was it because Bena too heard talk about sex for the first time? And perhaps was at first puzzled about the very words they used! Well, then, she was only a kid, but now—now she was close to fourteen years old, and she learned a few things, and had a strong desire to talk about them to someone that would understand, someone that she could ask questions of without fearing ridicule. She longed for her mother and wondered how much longer it will be before she will see her beautiful face again?

Why was it that other girls could make plans for their future, for their marriage (as if they had much of a say in that), or go with one of their parents to America, while she had to live inside a tangled web in which she was so tightly bound that she dared not even question her condition. And there was little use talking to her grandmother; for she too was floating from day to day in her misery without much hope. Sickness and hunger and a tight-lipped man from whom she had to hide the little money she earned, or the food that she bought with it, stilled much of her former self; she lost much of her wit, and became taciturn, too impatient with the situation around her.

Rachel, for the first time, began to become aware of many things in the house she was not conscious of during her working day. She looked around the one room that served as bedroom, dining room, and kitchen, and saw the old furniture, broken, scratched, and inadequate. Why can't they have a good bed to sleep in, or a decent bench to sit on! Her Aunt Hannah had chairs by the hundred that they manufactured, but she, Rachel, never sat in one in her own house! She always sat on the rickety benches, as did the other members of the family. As if for the first time, she now saw the stark poverty in their lives. Not one child had warm clothes. The patches that her grandmother made on their clothes covered such large areas, it was hard to tell which were the patches and which were the original garment.

She sat brooding, her eyes roving all over, all over, taking in the poverty she grew up in, now in a different light and with great pain. When her eyes rested on her father, he too looked different to her than ever before. What was it about him that looked so strange now! When he stood with his face to the wall his back bent and swaying in the prayer shawl, she wanted him to turn around so that she could make sure that it was him, and not a stranger, although she had seen him in this position all her life. For the first time, she saw how cleanly brushed his clothes were, but how worn and frayed they were too, and at his knees almost threadbare.

Her eyes ran over him again and again and made her wonder why she is first now seeing that his hair and his beard were almost white. It was true that she always saw it, but with her eyes only—not as now with an adult's hurt. Indeed, he looked old, although he was still a young man, only in his early fifties; and she began to feel old too, and the walls seemed to close in on her. She must do something to change this way of their lives; how did they go on living like that up to now? And how much longer could they go on with this kind of life? There must be some way out—if only she could think of something!

Chaya watched her mood, and although she was afraid of letting her go outdoors, she was anxious to disturb it and insisted that she go out. "How many more times do I have to tell you to go out for some dung. The house is like an icehouse, but you sit as if you were as warm as in your mother's womb! Better go out now, later you will not be able to stick your nose outside." She gave her many things to wear and tied her own shawl securely around her head and shoulders.

Once out, Rachel could barely breath. The frost was dry and sharp in her nostrils and the skin of her face seemed to crawl. The bucket handle stuck to her bare hand, made it raw, and the whiteness of the snow hurt her eyes but she was glad to be out of the house and feel the cruel elements beat the inner misery out of her. Her mind cleared and young blood pounded in her veins and she longed for someone at whom she could throw a snowball!

She walked out of the courtyard and into the narrow street, leading downhill toward the field patch, where the peasant Stepan kept his three cows, but her errand was in vain—the cows were no doubt in Stepan's hut—for who had the heart to let them out in this weather.

She walked on, slipping and catching her balance until she came to the field that looked like an ironed sheet without a single wrinkle, and of course without a single hoof print, in it. She turned back, for further down was but forest, and up the hill was the Plaza, which was swept clean of dung by the street sweepers. She turned back feeling worried; how could they go through another night as the last one!

The cold made the house creak and the chimney moan all night, and her grandmother had pulled everything from the drawers and piled them on for more warmth; but they still shook with the cold, although they kept their bodies hard by each other, and the morning was a curse!

To get out of bed meant throwing off the covers and separate the nearness from each other in the house, which had been in the grip of frost and wind all night. It was unbearable!

She watched her grandmother get out of her bed and go to the kitchen to fire the samovar for tea, but the water in the barrel was frozen solid into a round brick of ice and she could not make a dent in it. Then she looked around for something to burn in the stove, but could find nothing and a look of fear spread on her face and she heard her murmur, "I must run to Hannah for help, I can't let them die." And she pulled some clothes on and made for the door; but not before she told the children to remain in their beds because there was nothing to get up for anyhow. How long she was away could only be measured by the misery she left behind her. Then old spines and empty stomachs did not bite into them as did the guilt of seeing and letting their grandmother go out in such a fierce cold winter morning. And her father? He stayed in the bed between the two boys who clung to him with wide open eyes, but did nothing to stop her!

True, he was unable to go outdoors himself in this cold, the doctor forbade him, but he should have stopped her just the same! He stopped her from doing many things before—why didn't he do it now? Like a few weeks back while he was sick, and he saw her going out Thursday and Friday mornings and he insisted on knowing where she was going, and she had to give up that work she was doing at the Goldsteins' home! Yes, he stopped her many times, but not when her life was in danger!

Oh, Rachel thought, how bad I feel, I wish that I could die!

But suddenly the door opened, and Chaya walked in, her eyes streaming from the cold and panting for breath, looking as if she had turned into a block of ice. Quickly but clumsily she removed her heavy outdoor things and went into the kitchen without looking at anyone, and with resoluteness, attacked the ladder that led up to the attic with the heavy press iron: she banged away at it until it fell apart like a child's toy. The sticks flew in every direction but she gathered them up and carefully put them in a corner, handling them as if they were sick babies.

Avraham and the children were still in bed and they looked on with mixed feelings. She had attacked the ladder with such suddenness and fury it left them dumbfounded; yet they felt security in her action. They watched as she tried to break the two long boards that held the steps together, as she rested one end on the floor and with her knee tried to break it in the center.

"Grandma wait, you can't do that, you'll break your knee, wait a minute, I am getting up," Rachel told her, and began to emerge from the bundle of covers, but her father told her to go back to bed, then asked her grandmother why she didn't tell him what she meant to do, asked like he felt guilty, and dressed and went to the kitchen and helped her break up the big boards. Then grandmother lit a fire in the stove and asked Avraham to chop some water from the barrel and she busied herself making tea for breakfast.

The little home became warm and they were all around the table eating what was left of yesterday's bread with unsweetened tea. The small amount of staples that her grandmother had managed to smuggle up to the attic was almost depleted, and the bread of her last baking she doled out in thin slices. Rachel wondered how they will go on living when that little bit is gone too.

She walked into the courtyard with an empty bucket and a heavy heart, because her grandmother was saving what was left of the ladder for the bitter cold mornings; but what are they to do for the rest of the day and the evening? The house is already cold, despite the warming it came by this morning, although the sun was out and no one but herself opened the door to let the cold air in.

Everything in the courtyard was snow-covered: the roofs, the walls of the houses, the garbage dump, the toilets and the garden fences, as were the tall courtyard door and gate! Everything was white and the sun was looking at the whiteness with a cold hard eye! She was trembling with the cold, but could not help admiring the tall trees that held the snow on their branches so tenderly, especially the trees on the land in back of the Governor's Mansion and while she looked at them with admiration, one eye seemed to stray and behold something that forced it to call the other to witness. Look, wood, and indeed Rachel saw two thick branches that for some reason had refused to lend themselves to the snow, or perhaps did and then shook it off, beckoning to her as if with two arms. She had to mount a hill of snow and ice to get up to it, and slipped many times, but finally she was near, and without worrying that the trees belong to the governor, she began to break the branches off. Her hands and knees were raw from the friction of the snow and her breathing was fast and hard, but a smile spread on her frozen face from inner satisfaction, for now she will not go home empty-handed. The trees that had looked so tall from the courtyard were really short enough for her to reach the lower branches that were thin and closely clustered. She broke them off and they did not protest with the noise of a snap because of the damp, and perhaps they understood.

When she came home with the big load on her back, her face was almost purple and her hands were torn, but her eyes sparkled!

"And there is more where this came from," she told her grandmother with a grin.

Chaya and Avraham looked at each other in wonder, then they released her from her burden and outdoor clothes. Avraham removed her shoes and stockings and chafed at her frozen feet and torn hands while Chaya prepared hot tea for her.

The house was kept warm now, but the food rations were becoming smaller with each meal. Chaya and Avraham lived on sugarless tea and soon Rachel too began to live on this hot water diet. But Adah, who coughed all day and a good part of the night, was the recipient of some food. Chaya managed to keep back some sugar and what was left of the preserves she had made during the summer. When the girl's cough became very bad, Chaya would motion her into the kitchen and feed her preserves.

16

Help from the family

AVRAHAM DECIDED TO VISIT REB DOVID. Opening the door, Baba said, "You should have come with the children and my sister. We had made up our minds to pay you a visit last Saturday, but our Moyshele and his wife came to us for the Sabbath."

Before he could collect his thoughts to answer her, Reb Dovid, Baba's Hasidic husband, came in. He was a short, underdeveloped man, more like a boy of twelve years, but with white curly hair and a long white beard that dwarfed his stature. His walk, as all his movements were, was fast and with precision. Being a good mathematician although a known Hasid, who lived for his God and his Rabbi, he was employed by the City bank as its chief bookkeeper. His spirit was the spirit of one that does not live for now but for later life in Heaven, no matter the beatings one takes now, it is God's way of testing your strength. Money that was left over from their frugal way of living he brought to his Rabbi to be used to expand the houses of learning.

When he opened the door and saw Avraham, his face lit up with pleasure and he ran in, a hand extended in greeting. "*Shalom aleichem*, Avraham. My but I am glad to see you, it's been so long since you visited us. Tell me how are the children, and Chaya? What brings you here in the very middle of the week and in such dog weather?"

"*Aleichem shalom*," Avraham answered. "I know that you have to go back to the bank soon so don't let me detain you; I passed by, and stopped in to see if all is well with both of you," he lied.

Reb Dovid removed his heavy coat and stood awhile looking at his kin, then said, "You know, my dear friend, you do not look so good to me. I know that you were sick but a 'rose' on your foot should not make you so pale and gaunt. Something tells me that you are a stubborn Jew. To me you look like you do not eat too well nowadays. If it is so, why didn't you come and tell us so that we could give you some money to tide you over whatever bad spell you suffer? Why are you so secretive about your situation? How many Jews are not in some sort of material need every so often, and need a helping hand from his kin? Come now, let's wash for the midday meal, we can talk at the table."

Avraham followed him as if he was under a spell; he washed then joined Reb Dovid in prayers. In the meantime, Baba had set another place at the table and put a steaming tureen of soup upon it, in which meat-filled *kreplekh* floated on top. And again Avraham was assailed by nausea and he rose to leave the table, but Reb Dovid placed a gentle hand on his arm and restrained him.

"Sit down again and eat Avraham. But a little bit at a time, rest, and try to swallow some more. By your looks, I can see that you celebrated a week of fast days. Take some of the soup without the *kreplekh*, and acquaint your stomach with it first, then you will be able to eat the solid food."

With his coaxing and his own effort, he managed to eat a few spoonfuls of the soup; then Baba cut a *kreplekh* into small pieces and put them onto his plate.

"Now try to eat the pieces but chew them slowly, no, no, not so fast at the beginning," she warned him. Tears welled up in the eyes of all three at the table but they continued their meal in silence.

Baba removed the dishes from the table and the men said grace for their meal. Reb Dovid rose, and again put his gentle hand on Avraham's arm and said quietly, "I have another 20 minutes before I get back to the bank, so I must leave now, would you like to wait for me here until I come back from work? Or, if you want to go home, would you take Baba with you, and I will call for her when I am through at the bank? What do you say?" and in the meantime he stuck a 10-ruble note into his hand.

Avraham thought a while, then said, "No, I must go home, I have been away a long time and must get back, and I'll take Baba with me."

Get back, get back to what, to find them in their great misery that he left them in while he filled his own belly full? He was troubled with new guilt.

As soon as Reb Dovid left, Baba got dressed in her fur-lined coat and tied her bewigged head into a warm shawl and they started out. The walk was unpleasant for both; she needed an arm for support on the slippery snow and he knew of her need, but felt uncomfortable to touch her, the wife of a Hasid. When they reached the house, they saw a sled with two lively horses standing at the door and they wondered who the visitor or visitors might be. The house lamp was lit and it sent out a welcome beacon to them and the house was nice and warm.

"What is going on here?" Avraham asked, and then he saw his niece Riva sitting tailor-fashion on Chaya's bed and knitting what looked to be a stocking.

"This day is full of surprises," Rachel said when she saw her Aunt Baba. "First Riva, and now you, Aunt Baba. My, it's just like a holiday today."

The three younger children were very busy in a corner of the room and Avraham wondered why they were that quiet, but soon discovered that they were hard at work feasting on something that looked like the roast he had seen at Baba's table, earlier in the day. Chaya gave them tea to wash down the meat, while Rachel stood by watching with gleaming eyes.

"It is indeed a holiday, look, I brought you your aunt to visit with you," and Avraham was puzzled that Riva came, and wondered what brought her here when she saw him only a little while back and had not mentioned anything about a visit to the house.

After Chaya removed her sister's coat and overshoes, they all sat around the table and drank tea from the singing samovar and talked of the weather, of the illnesses in the community, and of many other, small, but important things that the lives of these six people centered around. During a short lull in the conversation, Riva told them about her coming marriage.

"It is too bad that I cannot have the wedding here, in Kamenets-Podolski, but my future mother-in-law is a very sick woman and can't travel the distance between here and Proskurov. Besides, she feels that as long as we will settle there, we might as well have the wedding there too and not drag all his family to our home just for the wedding. Mama was a little put out about it, but my sisters and brothers are very happy about it because they could travel to a bigger city than ours. And of course, with Papa, no matter what I do it is good, he leaves those things to me. I am leaving as soon as it gets warmer, so that I can help with all the arrangements."

She saw that her uncle wanted to say something, but that he did not want to interrupt her, so she ended, and looked at him waiting for him to speak.

"Riva, those horses out there will freeze to death, where is the driver of that sled?" he asked her.

"Don't worry he went into your neighbor Olga's house for a while, he will probably be back soon to put them into a barn until I am ready to go home."

She put him at ease, and continued with her plans, telling them of her bridegroom's family and what she looks forward to by living so close to them. Then she turned the subject to him, and his children's future. He tried to block her but did not succeed; she insisted on knowing of his plans and, along the line, kept asking why he did not take the children to America, where their lives would be better spent.

"I know many people that went away and remained there, in America, and are raising their children with less fear and effort than they would have here. True, some go and come back, but they are always the few that cannot be satisfied with any change, no matter how small. What can you judge from the distance?" she asked, and talked a long time in this same vein, but felt that her words were hitting a stone wall.

When Reb Dovid came at the end of the day, they were back on the same subject again and he agreed fully with Riva. "Avraham, you, as well as I, know that the survival of the Jews, after all the torment we took and still take, is because we stubbornly guard our religion. In every country in the world, we worship the same God, perhaps in a different manner, but all with the same fervor. There, one can perhaps find many more sects of our religion than here, and worshipers of many different countries who practice their spiritual rituals in different fashions, but those that hold God dear are one, throughout the entire world. Sure, you will find some Jews, especially of the younger generation, who are not up to our ways, but, look right here at home, don't we have young people who were raised in homes where Orthodox Jewish tradition and high learning is the breath of life, and they go the other way? You, yourself, told me of the heartache you have of your many students, who refuse their fathers' pious beliefs, of the younger ones whom you found straying away from all you and their fathers taught them, before they are even of bar mitzvah age! What about the boy that put his *tefillin* on the house cat two days after his bar mitzvah? And that, the son of the good, and God-fearing, Hasid, Yisroel!"

All the children had their eyes on Avraham's face, but could not guess what was going through his mind. He listened, but offered no indication of his opinions or feelings, and Reb Dovid continued speaking.

"Oh yes, I meant to tell you and almost forgot, Kolmin-Dodya was in the bank this afternoon to deposit a money order he received from his brother in America. They are waiting for some papers they need from the governor and they are having some trouble about a child's birth certificate. In the meantime, they are marking time until they get all the legal credentials together and in order and then swoosh! Then he and his family too will go to America!" He ended talking and looked into Avraham's eyes but found a blank expression in answer.

Toward evening Isaiah was bundled into his outgrown overcoat and grandmother's shawl and sent off to get the sled driver in Olga's house. Then Riva bundled Aunt Baba and Uncle Reb Dovid into the back seat, covered them well with the many shawls and took a seat with the driver in front. The clouds hung very low and looked angry and active.

"Look at that sky," Reb Dovid said to the women, it looks as if it will shed ink blots soon," and the sled sped away leaving the sounds of the tinkling bells around the horses' necks to linger a while in the courtyard.

17

The last straw

AVRAHAM HAD A BAD NIGHT, HE tossed and turned the night through, and his mind ran with many thoughts; the evening's conversations came back to confuse and torment him and prevent him from sleeping. He got up, lit a cigarette, and stood near the ice-encrusted window and tried to look outside. What could he say to anyone to make them understand his abhorrence to America. He too had heard about it and what he did was not good. People came back because they refused to go along with the Sabbath-breakers, the money-chasers, and the neglecters of their religion and cultural background. Yes, he heard this from many who returned from the "golden land" when it was hard for them, they ran from here, but they did not know what they will find there until they saw? No, he did not want to do that; how can he go to America feeling as he does? And everyone is after him, maybe they know better about America but not his feelings! Here, he has his sister and her family, and much kin through his marriage, and many friends that know and respect him as a learned man, and his religion and that of the children is kept as God meant it to be; and his parents are at their eternal rest here, his roots are deeply entrenched, he just can't pull them up and transplant them elsewhere!

The cigarette butt burned his fingers, and he dropped it to the floor, stamped it out with his shoe, and remained standing in the same place, his mind in a jumble. Other thoughts pushed themselves to the front of his mind that he was unable to negate: he did know a few learned and pious men that went with their families to America and remained there! The turmoil in him was so great that he was unable to separate and examine each side of his problems and come to some conclusion. His body began to tremble from the cold that pervaded the house and he went back into the bed to the same restlessness, and waited with great impatience for the dawn to break.

When he opened his eyes, he realized that he had been asleep for a long time, that it was quite late in the morning or early afternoon, because Chaya and the children were around the table and eating what looked like a good lunch. The room was warm and the samovar gave out a musical sound from its innards. He looked around the room and hated to disturb its tranquility, so he closed his eyes again and rested until he heard Rachel say that he must be sick again for it was not like him to sleep the morning away.

"No, no, I am not sick, I just overslept. Had you been as noisy as you always are, I would have been up a long time ago."

And to the tune of the belated babble he dressed and washed and put his phylacteries and prayer shawl on and began his morning prayers. He was halfway through when he was aware of some disturbance outside the door and turned in time to see Isaiah open it. The boy began to shout, "Look who is here, look who is here!" and Kolmin-Dodya, Aunt Gittel, and a string of youngsters streamed into the house.

Chaya and Rachel quickly closed Avraham's bed, and made room at the table for them all the while Chaya kept on saying "My, what guests we have," and looking very pleased.

"Don't fuss, don't fuss, please don't, we can't stay here long, we just wanted to spend an hour or so with you," Kolmin-Dodya and Gittel begged.

Avraham smiled a warm welcome to them, but continued with his prayers. "Go on, don't worry about us, finish your prayers, we will wait for you," Kolmin-Dodya said to him and in the meantime caught Raphael by the back of his pants, and sat him on his knees. "Tell me, young man, how does it go with the Gemara? Are you learning as fast as Isaiah is?" And the bashful child was feeling very happy sitting on his uncle's knee and wondering how a man can get so tall. He looked at him and gave his gentle, shy smile, for he liked this giant of an uncle who was always laughing and asking questions about how much you learned—but never really waited for an answer.

While Avraham was busy putting his prayer shawl and phylacteries away, Chaya brought to the table a feast that almost knocked him off his feet when he saw it! She begged Kolmin-Dodya to wash for lunch and together with his family join Avraham, who had not yet eaten. Avraham wondered where in the world she had gotten chicken to cook, and in the middle of the week too! And so much! He looked around the room and noticed a white cloth, covering what looked like a big mound on the chest of drawers near the kitchen entrance; and saw his mother-in-law bring from it such delicacies like cheesecake, rose jam, and oranges (oranges this time of year and in his poverty-stricken house!). He was bewildered when he saw her bring all this forth with grace as if it was a daily occurrence in his house.

But when she also brought a tall straw-covered bottle of wine to the table, he could contain himself no longer and asked, rather loudly, "What is today, Simchat Torah?"* He asked this of Chaya, but then turned to his kin and added, "Or did you Kolmin-Dodya get so foolish that you brought all this along with you?"

"Me, no, but I am so glad to see all this in your home. I see that you are not so bad, thank God, it's about time. We are living very close to the earth now, we are saving every kopek we can for our long journey ahead. I thought that you got advance notice from someone that we were coming, before we leave for America," and he laughed with the joy of a child and Avraham saw that his children laughed too while they looked at each other.

Chaya sat close to Gittel, with her habitual glassful of hot tea in the palm of her hand, and urged her to taste the rose jam. "You see, everything turns out for the best. If I did not have all this good food near, we would all feel bad, for your going away is certainly no consolation to us, so at least we have a party. Our family is dwindling down, some marry and leave us to go to other cities, others go to settle in America, and so many died in recent years that they could fill a city by

---

* Jewish holiday celebrating the Torah.

themselves! Pretty soon we will not have anyone to invite when the girls marry and the boys are bar mitzvah. So you see that this being the last time we will probably see you, I am happy that we are able to be so hospitable now. All this good food comes from Nahama, and her daughter Riva brought it to us only yesterday. She too is leaving us soon. She is marrying a Proskurov young man and will settle there. Even the wedding is going to be in Proskurov. She knows well that we won't be able to attend, what with buying of new clothes and shoes and other expenses so she brought us a wedding feast yesterday. I begged her not to leave it with us. I somehow felt as if we were like strangers at her wedding, but she insisted and almost cried for me to take it, and now that you are all here, and we are able to enjoy it with you, I am glad that I did."

Avraham listened to his mother-in-law rattle off all that about Riva's wedding and experienced a stab of depression in his soul. His sister Nahama did not even take the pains of asking him if he would be able to attend the wedding! She did not even give him a chance to express his regrets and wish her and Eaheal to live to see much joy from their first child that will marry! And nor did Riva think of inviting them! No, she just sat yesterday and talked of many things, but never asked or questioned if they would be able to attend her wedding! Why did his mother-in-law have to accept her food, when she herself felt the indignation? Were he at home she would not have dared do such a thing, and if she did, he would have refused her gratuity! No, this could not be Riva's idea, she is too sensitive a person to other people's hurt, this must be Nahama's machinations!

"As I was saying Avraham, I want you to give me Mirele's address, and as soon as I see her, I will write you a letter and tell you how the two women get along there."

Avraham came out of his angry absorption with a slight start when he heard Kolmin-Dodya speak and went to a drawer in the chest from which he took an envelope with the return address where Mirele and Bena lived and gave it to him. Kolmin-Dodya still held Raphael on his lap, plied him with all sorts of questions, tickled him, and asked him to solve some riddles; then he wanted to know if he would like it if he stuffed him into his pocket and brought him along to America, to his mother. This gave the boy such a jolt that he slid off his esteemed uncle's knees and ran to bury his head into his father's chest until the guests left.

Many questions burned on Avraham's tongue when he handed Mirele's address to Kolmin-Dodya but he kept them to himself, because he knew that everyone defends her actions and that Kolmin-Dodya will too. He did not ask him to carry a message to his wife and daughter either, for what could he say to them through someone else that he did not already say through the letters he sent them? The babble of children was so loud it was difficult for the adults to hear each other but they were happy to witness the friendship that tied them so strongly. When the visit came to an end, and the families were to part, all were in tears. It was hard for the women to see the two men bid each other farewell in broken voices while they themselves shed tears as if it was their daily practice. The houseful of youngsters were laughing and crying and wishing each other the very best for their lives and then the household became unnaturally quiet with the last tinkle of the bells from the long sleigh.

The winter stretched on with its icy cold program. The overcast sky would part two or three times a week to let the sun peek through. So much snow was piled up in the streets that no one ventured out. The courtyard's little houses were buried so deep that one had difficulty finding a door. Every house was a world in itself; no one came in or went out. The only indication that there was life within was the smoke from the chimneys.

The short day came to a close with the twilight's approach of a dying sun, that darkened the pages of the book, *Speech of Truth*, that Isaiah was reading from, and he complained to his grandmother. "I can't see a word anymore, how can I read? Can't we have a light in here?"

But his grandmother looked angrily at his father and did not answer. She knew that Avraham knew too that there was not a drop of kerosene oil in the house for the lamp but did he show any concern?

"Put away the book, we can continue tomorrow," Avraham told his son and got up to stand near the frost-encrusted window and let his thoughts overtake him. How long, dear God, how long can we remain alive here? Please show me the way, he prayed, I cannot see the hunger in my children's faces any longer; and I am killing an old woman that is giving of herself like a sacrificial lamb. What should I do, what should I do? He pressed his forehead to the cold window pane, but did not feel the frost bite into him.

A while later he became aware of a light in back of him and turned to see his mother-in-law holding a fresh-lit candle in her hand; when he threw a puzzled look at her, she said, with her eyes downcast, "May God forgive me, this is the last candle with which I am to bless and usher in the Sabbath on Friday night." She bent over the crying Adah and put a gentle arm around her. "Here, look, we have light, stop crying. What's so unusual about a dark house, don't we always sleep in the dark?" and then she pushed her into the kitchen, still carrying the candle with her.

"Grandma, must she have a light to see how to eat the sugar?" Isaiah said, with a smirk.

"Just give me a piece of sugar and I'll show you that I can eat it in the dark," said Isaiah, and in the dark, he felt his father's disapproval of the taunt.

The morning found Avraham with pen in hand, his forehead furrowed, writing a letter to Mirele in America.

18

And the sun
pierces the clouds

AVRAHAM CAME AWAY from the post office very much disappointed and bent his steps homeward, his thoughts with Mirele. It was five or six weeks since he had sent off the last letter to her and so far received no answer. Was she or Bena suffering from a sickness? Two women, alone in a strange land away from their family, anything could happen to them. He felt depressed and hurried on but his thoughts gave him no peace, and soon went on another tack. Was it possible that Mirele had changed her mind and wants to come home again! On the other hand, perhaps his letter came too late and she decided to divorce him because she became used to being without him? And that despite his willingness to bend to her wishes and bring the children and her mother to America? His last letter should have convinced her he wants to come there, that he is willing to forgo his own feelings and do her bidding in any case, why didn't she answer one way or another? He needs to know one way or another!

His agitation grew with every step he took, and panic befell him at the thought of being severed from his wife, completely. By the time he reached his door he was all tangled up in anger, remorse, and self-pity. He saw Adah fling the door open and heard her shout, "Papa, Papa, we have a letter from mother, hurry, come read it to us."

But it took him a while to shake off his chagrin and understand just what she was saying, and its meaning. He saw how they all sat in readiness, waiting probably since the postman gave them the letter early afternoon. His hands shook a little as he removed his outdoor things, but he tried to calm himself and then asked for the letter which was laying on the table as big as life for everyone to see. Adah jumped for it before the boys and handed it to him and watched as he opened the bulky envelope and extracted from it a letter, a draft from an American bank for money, and a batch of ship's tickets for the entire family! Now his knees began to give way and he let himself down onto a bench and in a voice that he was unable to control, he read the letter which was short and to the point:

> Dear Avraham,
>   Bena and myself are well, and we hope that this letter finds all of you in good health too. I am sending you the tickets and money that you will need for the journey. You have time until the end of next month so that you can prepare yourselves with the necessary clothes, and documents from the governor and health department. Should you have any trouble with the children's birth certificates, ask Fishl to help you with them, he knows how to go about such things. We send our love, and pray that your journey be a good one.
>   Mirele

He looked up to see the children's puzzled faces, and Chaya's eyes, which looked out from the burning patches on her face, searching him for more information. Rachel, who had been home from work with a festering finger and had spent the night moaning and groaning, now stood quietly by and pierced him with her eyes for some enlightenment.

"Well, why are you all so tense for you know that you have a mother in America don't you! And you know that she wanted us all to come there and that you all want to go there! So she sent us the tickets and money, and we will have to begin to do our planning very soon, because we do not have too much time," he spoke playfully, trying to soften the situation.

"But Father, what about you!" Adah almost screamed at him, while Raphael neared himself closer to him and edged himself onto his knees and put his head on his father's chest. "Papa, I will stay with you, here," the child murmured, "I don't want to go to that funny country, America, I don't like it, I like you."

Rachel was unable to control herself much longer, and soon screamed, "I don't care who wants to go, or who does not want to go, I want to see my mother and I want to go as soon as I can."

"And you, my oldest son, you too want to go to America," he asked the troubled-looking Isaiah, who looked from one to the other.

"Yes, Father, I too want to go to Mother, but not without you. If you don't go, then I will stay here with you," he said with tears in his voice.

Chaya felt that there was more to the situation than met her eye. She wondered and rightly guessed that he had probably written to Mirele that he decided to bring the family to her.

Avraham saw her burning face, and felt a son's pity for his mother, and he wanted to pacify her agitation. "No need to be so excited, children, you want your mother and she wants you, and you know that I cannot live without any of you, so I will come along too."

One could feel the tenseness go from the children's underfed bodies and smiles appeared on their faces. Both Chaya and Avraham were unable to control them from the noisy hilarity all evening and the little house rocked with it until they were all asleep. Only then, when it was quiet, and the lamp was turned out, did Avraham light his cigarette and lay on his back and give thought to Mirele's letter that was dripping with ice water. True, it was rich with money, tickets, and directions, but the words, and the tone were short and cold. No mention why she kept his last letter unanswered so long, no mention whether she was glad or happy because he agreed to come to her. She felt no special need to put herself out to say how happy she was to have him. His feelings were hurt, and they led him from one reason of anger to another until he could stand it no longer and he got out of bed, lit the lamp again, and turned the wick low, just giving him light enough to read some chapters from the Torah until he felt somehow released from his anger.

The following morning, they all sat around the table listing what they needed most for the journey, what bedding they were to take along, and what identification papers they had to have. They sat and talked until they covered a good deal of their plans, and then Avraham told them that they will not be able to go, after all, because if they were to buy all those things that they think they must have, then they will not have enough for the journey.

He had to pay some debts he made and that he was not going to run away with someone else's money! When they began to look upset, he told them to wait a day or so, by then he may know what they could or could not do. That night there was no sleep in him, his worry of the money he owed Dovid, Doctor Popov, and Zalman Goldstein, for so much back rent tormented him and he began to think of writing to Mirele again and tell her of his debts that are keeping him from going. But what could he expect her to do! He knew that the streets were really not paved with gold in America, as they say, and if that was what she sent, that was probably all she could send.

Feeling that this night would give him little rest, he dressed and went out of the house to walk around the garden in the courtyard. It was a "white night," the moon was almost full and the stars twinkled. He lit a cigarette and continued walking around and around the garden, with his heavy heart and baffled thoughts, without being aware of its beauty. The early spring lilac bushes gave off a pleasant, delicate fragrance, as did the rose bushes that glistened with the night dew, but nothing reached him. When he finally tired, he went back to the house and sat down at the window to watch the dawn come. Yes, he thought, I must tell my children and my mother-in-law that we can spend very little money on shoes and clothes if we want to go; very little, in fact almost nothing; that they will have to make do with what they have until they get to the "land of great opportunity." They must learn too, that we cannot leave here with money that is not ours, that it was loaned to us by good friends when we needed it and it must be paid back before we go.

There was nothing much Chaya or the children could say or do when they learned of their choice of either doing without new things or staying home but had to accept Avraham's proposal to pay their obligations and go with what they had. Then began the hustle and bustle of washing, mending, and sorting what clothes they were to wear and which they were to take along for an entrance into America.

The two boys stayed out of the way of the girls and their grandmother; as a matter of fact, they stayed out of the house for fear of drawing their grandmother's ire upon them at a time like this. But too much of a good thing needs examining, and Adah, who had less to do than the others, was sent to see how the boys were spending so much of their time outside. She walked around the yard and asked the children for her brothers, but no one knew where they went, no, they did not see them this morning at all. But a few minutes later Adah dashed into the house and told her grandmother that she saw Isaiah crouching and moving his bowels in back of the house.

Chaya became angry and shouted, "Why in back of the house! Is he too lazy to go to the privy across the courtyard. Send him in to me, I'll teach him not to be so lazy next time."

"But Grandma, something is the matter with him, he looks awful sick and Raphael sits near him all the time and looks very frightened. I'll send him in but Grandma, you better don't beat him, if you do, I'll tell Papa." Adah was gone quite a while, then finally came in with both boys.

Chaya was busy in the kitchen and Rachel looked up from the washing, she saw Isaiah, she called to her grandmother, "Look at him, eyes and no face and what is face is as green as grass!"

Indeed, the boy looked sick. Chaya quickly dried her hands on her apron and took him by his hand and led him to a bench and sat him down. "Tell me what happened to you, what hurts you? Answer me, don't look at me with anger."

She put her hand on his forehead and let a sigh escape her, "Woe is to me, he is burning like fire! Now, of all time, he has to get sick!"

The sick boy made a dash to the door and was out before she could hold him back. She followed him to the back of the house and found him in a stooped position pressing his very guts out; his face was red with the exertion and his arms were stiff at his sides. She saw the little heaps of excrement all around him, here and there blood showing on top. She became alarmed and gently urged him not to press so hard, and then come into the house. Isaiah straightened himself with some difficulty, buttoned his pants and followed her, with Raphael following him like a shadow. No sooner were they inside, when another spasm assailed him and he ran out again.

Chaya did not know what to do, but tried to calm him, and begged him to get back into the house and stay in bed until he felt better. She tried to give him some tea, but he roiled in pain, moaning all the time. In the evening when Avraham came home, and found him in this condition, he was beside himself with grief, and looked to Chaya and Rachel for some suggestion to ease the boy's suffering, but they felt as helpless as he did because they knew that Doctor Popov was in the hospital with a broken leg for the past week. He stood thinking a while, then told Rachel to run and get Doctor Voroniuk, whose office was near the Plaza.

Rachel hesitated a minute then told her father that she will go, but she felt sure that he would not come.

"Go, don't waste any time, and don't come back without him!"

She left the house and walked slowly up the narrow street, thinking that her effort was wasted because she knew well that the doctor was an antisemite who hated to give his services to Jews. She wondered what had made her father think that he would privilege their home with a visit? Still, she began to walk a little faster because she knew that Isaiah must have help and very soon or he will die. And of all time, he had to get sick in the midst of their readying for the journey! Her feet seemed to work faster than her will, for before long she found herself on the Plaza one block away from the doctor's house. But what is she to say to him to make him come! Something must be thought of, she must bring him with her no matter what!

After she pulled the doorbell, a servant opened the door for her and immediately told her that the doctor was not at home. Ah, Rachel thought, she smelled Jew in me, and she pushed the woman out of her way. "Doctor Voroniuk, please, I must see you, it's a matter of life or death!" she screamed into a well-lit room.

The doctor came out of his chair, angry that anyone dared to break the tranquility of his home and office. Rachel was upon him before he was a foot away from his desk, and she was glad to see that he was alone.

"What is the meaning of this?" he asked, his nostrils quivering with anger, and it was at this moment that it came to her for the very first time that she must do something very drastic to make him go home with her—and she screamed very loud at him, "A little Christian boy, your kind, an orphan, was left at our house because his mother had to go to the hospital and he took very sick and we do not know what to do for him. You must go with me and see if you can help him or he will die!" She looked wild, her face was full of excitement and flushed with it, while her mind was a network of confusion.

The doctor peered over his pince-nez at her and wondered why a Gentile child would be left at a Jewish home and came to the conclusion that either the mother was dying or the girl was a big liar. In any case, he went along with Rachel because he believed her that a child was very ill—and who knows if it might be a Christian child!

Sitting in the two-seater carriage alongside the doctor, Rachel's mind plotted her course. She will run into the house first, whisper to Isaiah not to tell the doctor anything about his mother, and then wink at her father and grandmother to substantiate her tale, and everything will turn out fine; and by the time they reached the house she had the plan well in hand.

Avraham came to the door when he heard the carriage approach and felt thankful that Rachel was successful. "Good evening, Doctor Voroniuk, I am very glad that you were able to leave your office to come to help my son who is terribly sick," Avraham greeted the doctor and then wondered why he looked at Rachel with hateful fury, but led him to the sickbed where Isaiah lay, with a flushed face and clenched hands, moaning. Doctor Voromiuk asked him many questions while he examined him, and meantime Rachel worked her way outside the house, not wanting to hear should he ask about his mother.

At last, finished, he came away from the bed and told Avraham that Isaiah had a bad case of dysentery, that he must stay in bed until he is recovered from it. "Be sure that he does not go out of the bed even when he has to evacuate, keep something near him at all times. For the next few days give him nothing but weak tea and the medicine I am now prescribing, and be sure to keep that other boy away from him. Two rubles please."

While he pocketed the money, his eyes roamed the room for Rachel, but he had to leave without seeing her, not saying a word to her father about the story that she had cooked up.

Rachel stood in back of the house and watched how he got into his carriage and heard him mumble, "Zhyd," and she felt like running to him and spitting into his face despite the help he may have been to her brother.

Isaiah caused the household much work and worry. What if he should still be sick when they were to go! And should he be able to go, will America let him in with his green face and emaciated body. Chaya heard from others that America turned back even little children that had some trouble with their eyes. It must be a country of healthy giants she thought, so how will they allow such a sick-looking boy to enter! Her thoughts ran on in spite of her busy hands as she washed Isaiah with the tenderness given to a new born, and changed his underwear for the third time that day and begged him to call her as soon as he felt the need for the receptacle.

Rachel took over the clothes washing from her grandmother although her recuperating finger still felt sensitive to come in touch with. Adah was busy with putting fine darning stitches on the socks and stockings they will wear to travel in. She sat near the open window with the pile to be darned in her lap, and her friend Rayzil watched her from the outside sill, making patches look so much like the socks that they hardly showed a difference. "I wish my mother would teach me how to mend my stockings like that," she said in admiration.

"You are crazy like a bedbug, since when do rich people do such things? You people wear your stockings until they get dirty and then throw them away, you don't even wear a hole in them. But poor people must know everything because we cannot throw anything away, there is always someone poorer to give it to. Now you see how crazy you are?

Did you ever wear anything that was not new from the beginning? Did you have to wait until your older sister or younger sister wore and wore and wore the clothes before you finally got them?"

Rayzil looked at her very best friend and laughed. "So when you get to America you too will be rich, and what will you do with all those stockings you are mending now? And what will you do with all the things you say poor people know that rich people don't? But maybe you will find some poor people there too, just a few, and because they are not from our country maybe they don't know as much as you do so you can teach them," she consoled her.

"Well, I'm not sure that there are any poor people there, because I heard that they live in houses that are five stories high, and you know that the rich families here don't live higher than the second or the third landing. Even your family, and my two rich aunts and uncles, live but on the first, so if they live on such high landings, they must be very rich! And that makes me believe that if there are poor people in America, they must be so few in numbers that even they live on the first landings!" Adah reasoned.

"Oh, dear God, please take into your ears whatever just came out of this foolish child's mouth and for once make this rainbow painter's daydreams come true," Rachel joined in from her place at the washtubs.

Raphael sat all day long at Isaiah's bedside and watched his every move much like a dog his injured master, despite his grandmother's constant reminder of the doctor's warning. But, he argued, Isaiah needed him, could not do without him at all and he argued his point while shaking his head up and down fast, and looking at his sick brother for concurrence, for which he got a weak confirmation or a slow up-and-down head shaking. For poor Isaiah did not care one way or the other, he just wanted to be left in peace. But that was enough for the "little lost soul," as his grandmother called Raphael, to feel a warmth spread all over him and he would think, see he does need me! He does want me close to him, just like I want to be close to him all the time.

And why not? Aren't we always together? Do we ever go any place without each other? Or do we ever do anything interesting by ourselves alone? That's why we are called the two *blazn** by everyone. Because we know how to work together when we make jokes or play pranks on others. We know how to be a team because we can surmise each other's thoughts. Raphael knew well that without Isaiah he was a nothing. That he would be unable to draw laughter from anybody or even look anyone in the face because of his shyness; but on the other hand, he had a feeling and a bit of guilty satisfaction that Isaiah too would not be so well without him and that pleased him.

When Chaya succeeded in prying him away from Isaiah's bed and shooing him outdoors, he stayed out a short time and came back with the excuse that there were no children in the courtyard to play with, although the clamor of their play was heard into the house.

Rachel was finished with the washing and now sat down to mending clothes for their journey and was worried because Isaiah had no pants, weekday or holiday, with which to go to America. He outgrew both pairs and although she can alter them for Raphael, it did not solve Isaiah's problem. Surely he could not come to America looking like a pauper. Mama will be unhappy enough to see her oldest son looking so emaciated and sick, without him looking like a scarecrow, sticking out of his outgrown clothes. She sat worrying for a long time, wondering where she could get her hands on a piece of material and came to the conclusion that she would go to one of her aunts and ask for money for the material which she herself will sew into a pair of pants.

At first she thought of going to her Aunt Nahama, after all she is so rich that the little bit of money she will ask for would not mean a thing to her, but then she reminded herself how outraged she was because her only brother was leaving her for the rest of his life, and she quickly changed her plans to go to her other rich aunt, Aunt Hannah. Sure, Aunt Hannah will not turn her down, after all wasn't she her mother's only sister! And didn't she know how poor the family was and wouldn't she want her sister's children's own mother, and even her brother-in-law, to look decent when they went to America? Surely, she will give her the money as a going away present if for no other reason.

And as soon as Rachel assured herself of success, she dropped

---

* Yiddish for clowns.

whatever she was doing and was on her way. But one had to have luck to get help from others and Rachel's lucky streaks always needed improvement, she never seemed to ask for something at the right time. It's true Hannah was never given to grant favors to anyone, but now was really not the time to expect one, no matter how important it was to Rachel, for the last six months was nothing but a calendar of misery within that rich home. The misery was so great that the rich furniture, the very deep expensive carpets, and heavy brocaded drapes looked out of place in a house of deep trouble and mourning.

True, Rachel knew that her cousin Yisroel, the oldest of her aunt's children (who came after some of her other children died of tuberculosis), died six months ago, and she felt very badly about it, so badly that she fainted twice at the funeral and had to be brought home and put to bed. But it was all she knew and when she asked the family how Yisroel died, of what sickness, no one seemed to know and no two people gave her the same answer. A few did know but kept the information among themselves.

Those few people knew that the twenty-nine-year-old handsome, clever university student of high learning, was also a leader in the revolutionary underground movement, with his headquarters in the attic of his parents' home. And he met his death while delivering some important secretive papers to a group at New Plan. He chose to go under the bridge, on the frozen river, to avoid meeting anyone that might follow him to his rendezvous. When he was halfway across, he became aware that he was being followed and began to run and collapsed—not having known that it was one of his collaborators that had walked a distance from him for his protection. And when the young man tried to help him up, he discovered that his friend was dead.

Under the cover of night, he removed all the papers around Yisroel's body and pockets, delivered them to the right place and brought back a friend with him who helped him place the body in a wagon that carried it to his home, to Hannah!

She became a mad, raging fury with grief and anger. Her Yisroel, her oldest son, the most handsome, educated, good-natured son! It could not be, it could not be! No, she was going mad, she was just imagining that he was in his coffin! But why! Why did he die? How did he die? Why did his friends bring him home in a wagon as if he had been a peasant! Hannah tore at her hair, her face, and her flesh for weeks.

She refused to see anybody, even her mother. But slowly she learned from her husband the truth of Yisroel's revolutionary activities and the cause of his death, which was probably heart failure from panic.

Anger overtook her grief and she screamed at her husband, the all-knowing Fishl Schmyser, to whom all came for advice, "Tell me, how is it that you allowed such things to go on under our very noses? Why do our children who have everything, need a revolution! Don't they get enough food or clothes or have a bad home! Don't you send them to the very best universities where only rich children can go, where you pay twice the tuition money of any non-Jew! Tell me, tell me. Yes, tell me why do we Jews have to put our heads on the chopping block, don't we have enough troubles because we were born Jews? My children, revolutionists! And you knew all the time, you, who are supposed to be the first hand to the governor for legal advice where Jews are concerned! Don't you think that it will get out somehow and the rest of our children's lives will be in jeopardy? And how about your standing with the governor, do you think that you will get by with it?" she cried bitterly.

And he listened to her with a strange calmness while he watched her tear-worn eyes and the strange way she examined the back of her hands of late. He did not tell her that he learned of the children's underground participation only a few days after his son's tragic death, when his younger son Moishe, told him, because he felt that his father must know now. The shock of this was very great to him and he tried to reason with them to give it up before the rest of them end up like their brother, but the reasoning, the angry threats, only strengthened the little band of revolutionists and they kept up their work for they knew that he would not expose them, as he threatened to do, to the police.

The only entrance to the attic was through a small hallway from the outside door and it was always being watched by one or the other of the youths, who would signal when policemen came into the courtyard, then the two constantly going typewriters would be silenced. For a long time, Hannah had been hearing those machines running, but never having seen one, and not being able to locate where the sound came from, and being a nervous woman, believed that she heard what no one else did. She was ashamed to say anything.

Six weeks after Yisroel's death, her daughter Chava came to her with the sad news that she must go away to America with her husband if he is to escape the military service. This was another hard blow to the parents and Hannah tried to raise all sorts of objections, but had to give in at last when Chava confessed that the real reason for their hurried departure is that she also became implicated in the underground work and remaining home will mean exposure for their friends, and Siberia for her and her husband, in the very least.

Hannah listened to her and looked her hard in the face and cried, "You too. No wonder my hands are bleeding so bad. Look, see right here on top." Chava looked at her mother's clean hands that were free of blood, then at her, and saw that she was broken within. Hannah's eyes were constantly on the back of her hands, "seeing the blood" that was never there, her eyes were seldom dry.

In the living room of the house that they took over from Fishl's parents when his father died, Hannah had found a very deep closet that her mother-in-law must have used for linens, for the shelves that were built from ceiling to floor were spacious and beautifully carved at the edges. This closet Hannah converted into a sort of luxury pantry in which she stocked preserves of all kinds, baked cakes and cookies, jellies from the most exotic fruits she was able to get, as well as candies, and all this she put under lock and key. No child was allowed to open its door unless she stood right there to see what was taken from it. But now, the door to that wealth of indulgence stood unlocked but no child went near it.

In the afternoons her youngest child, Royza, a beautiful red-cheeked girl of eight years, would come to the kitchen for food for the group in the attic, and the family servant who was with them more than thirty years, would knowingly fill a straw basket full of bread, meat, and fruit, without asking any questions of Hannah. When Hannah added a few candies or some preserves, or cookies, they returned it, no one wanted it! This caused more tears to flow from Hannah's eyes, and she saw more blood on her hands.

Rachel knew of Yisroel's death and Chava's quick departure, but was ignorant of anything else that was plaguing her aunt and came into her aunt's house with her usual fast steps and vigorous movements, slamming the door hard behind her. Hannah was badly startled and ran to the door.

"Good God, it's you, I thought they came for them, didn't they," she asked in a hushed voice and the tears always on the surface streamed down her face.

"Who came for whom, Auntie?" Rachel asked, but by now Hannah recovered somewhat, remembering that no one must know of the tragedy that was hanging over their home and she turned her face away and placatingly said, "Nothing, nothing, I am worried about my Chava, we received only two letters from her since she left home, so I am nervous. Look at my hands Rachel, do you see blood on them too?" she asked with some hope that she will confirm what she herself saw.

"Blood? Where do you see blood, there is no blood on your hands. Why would there be? And why do you cry about Chava not writing more often to you. She must be busy settling in the new country, she will never forget you, you are her mother aren't you? Give her a little more time and she will write you all about her new life.

"Look, Aunt Hannah we are soon leaving for America, in about two weeks. Aunt Hannah, I need a favor from you. My mother sent us some money with which to buy new clothes for the journey, but we had to use it to pay off debts we made while Papa was sick, so we have to make the clothes do that we have, and we are not too bad off, that is, all but Isaiah. He is badly in need of new pants because he outgrew everything he had, and I would gladly make him a pair, but we have no money for the material. Would you buy it for me or give me the money and I will buy it? When we get to America and I find work, I will return the money to you." she pleaded her cause.

She saw her aunt's face getting redder and redder with anger and bitterness that spread over her. And by the time she finished her request, the bitter face opened like a running sore, and screamed, "So, that's what you came for! You are always begging. Since I know your father, he never provided his family with their need, and now after he forced my poor sister to run away to America, he is carrying my mother off too! He is taking my nearest family away from me. Money you came for? Well, you won't get 1 kopek from me for anything. Let your father bring you to America looking like the paupers you are, for all I care!"

Hannah began walking from the room they were in, into the living room and Rachel ran after her shouting, "My father is a better man than your husband, and you know it yourself. My father does not have men working for him twelve hours a day for next to nothing. If my uncle had to earn his living by labor, he too would be a poor man like my father." Rachel's face was a red flame and her breath was short from excitement.

"Go, go, don't stand here and shout; I hate your father and your poverty and you!" and again Hannah tried to run from her, but Rachel was too enraged to drop the argument and shouted again at her, "Ha, now you bemoan our mother's leaving for America, where were you all the years when she needed shoes on her feet? Did you ever ask her if she needed a few kopeks for the bathhouse, or for a doctor? The only time you asked her to your house was when you needed her in the kitchen when there was some special occasion in your home! Now you suddenly miss your only sister after all the years of misery my poor mother had here, under your nose; you never stretched out a helping hand to her."

Rachel threw everything she harbored for her aunt out in hot anger and intensity, as she continued, "You need not worry, we will not present ourselves to my mother looking any worse than the other immigrants on the boat. Our clothes that we have will be clean, well mended, and she will suffer no embarrassment because of us!"

Hannah had now edged herself close to the closet that contained the household delicacies. And the rich aroma wafting from it called the girl's attention, and although she was almost emptied of her mad irritation, she now added, "I can't help telling you Aunt Hannah that that closet in back of you reminds me of you. It too holds good, rich things that can satisfy, gratify, and please but no one, not even your own children, can help themselves to its contents. You keep it locked up like yourself. But someday soon someone's will stronger than your own will break it wide open, and then, then, everyone will share in it."

She ran from the house very fast and from the courtyard still faster, until she reached the street, and there stopped a while until she calmed down somehow. Now, where? she thought. I do not dare go to my Aunt Nahama for money, because it will get back to father, and he will make a scandal in the house, but, what else can I think of? However, she began walking home with a slow stride, feeling depressed and discouraged. But by the time she was halfway to the house, she cheered herself up a bit and thought that she will surely think of something (and she did, even though it earned her a scolding from her grandmother that she was unable to live down for many a day.)

Chaya had been gone since sunrise, walking more than three miles to the cemetery to the graves of her family. Knowing that this will be her last visit, she stopped for a long time at each grave to recall the lives she had known so well, before they went from this world. Her visit to the graves of her parents, her sister, and brothers did not move her so deeply as did the twenty little eternal resting places of her sister Baba's children. Each one of the little infants, the young babies, as well as those children that lived long enough to begin walking, moved vividly through her memory; she even recalled many of the children's names and for how long they lived until they were cut down and broke Baba's heart and soul.

Then she found her grandchildren's hideaways, so many, so many, and talked to them, the hot tears washing down her face again. When she came to the grave of her husband, gone so many years, his head-stone almost buried with him, she bent low to the ground, as if to be sure that he will hear her and to him spilled out all her bitterness of her widowed life. As if her speaking was not enough, she caressed the jutting gravestone, and pleaded with its owner to invoke a better life "for his children and grandchildren."

"So much heartache my dear Simon. So much, it is hard for a body to endure it. Sometimes I envy you your peaceful sleep. All the afflictions that I had to witness from my children's lives while you just wasted, as if they were not yours too! Now, do you think that it is any better with them? No, my dear Simon, it is not better, it is even worse than before, and I must have your help to see them through their present miseries. I am an old woman, Simon, and I am leaving soon for a strange land. I will not be able to visit with you anymore, but this I must tell you, you must intercede for them, you must help, you cannot just lay in all your glory and not help your children."

She straightened up, a sharp pain of hunger shot through her, and she remembered that she had not eaten anything today and decided to leave. But first she bent down again over the headstone, and once more caressed it, and murmured, "Forgive me for disturbing you," and kissed it. She became aware of the cold sun's rays and realized that it was already setting, that the sun was deep toward the west, looking much like an angry relative. I must hurry, she thought. I have a long walk back, but she stood a long while in the same place, and looked around her, her eyes searching everywhere, and then hurried to the gate. Her walk homeward was slow and tiresome, and although she passed Hannah's house, she did not stop there for a glass of tea, knowing that Fishl, her son-in-law, was home this time of evening.

When she reached her house at last, she found Adah serving out evening supper to the family, and at no time did the *kasha** smell so good to her. She found a deep bowl and filled it full and garnished it with a spoonful of rendered fat and sat down at the table to enjoy it.

"Why are you serving supper Adah and where is Rachel," she asked. "Rachel, oh, she went to Ginendle to sew up a pair of pants for Isaiah, but first she cooked the *kasha*," Adah answered.

Raphael could not contain himself any longer and put his word in too, "And Grandma, he will have the nicest pants in the world, they will be made from velvet, black velvet! not plain cotton like mine!"

"Where in the world did she get black velvet from, where did she get the money for it?" Chaya asked, looking around her with probing eyes. But the children were all quiet, the boys waited for Adah to tell, and she became busy with pouring tea in the kitchen and serving it to the table.

---

* Yiddish for cooked grain, typically boiled.

Avraham waited until she was empty-handed, then pulled her near him, "Tell me, Adah, where did Rachel get the money for expensive material?" She tried to stall him for a while by lifting her shoulder in an "I don't know" gesture, hoping that he will begin to say grace for the meal and forget his question.

But if he forgot, it was only for a moment.

Raphael's chest was bursting and at last had to burst out while pointing his finger at Chaya, "Your skirt, Grandma, your skirt, the one that you wear to go on the Sabbaths, Grandma!"

Chaya looked at Adah, whose eyes were down to the floor, and asked, "Adah, what are you hiding from me? What is the 'lost soul' trying to tell me? What skirt is he talking about? My God, don't tell me that she cut up my velvet skirt for his pants! Tell me she didn't do it—did she?"

"Well Grandma, it was like this, she took the skirt out of the closet and looked at it...." She was interrupted by Rachel's entrance, who hurried in with a bundle in her arms, her face rosy from the long walk in the early spring air and happy with her accomplishment.

She sniffed, "Oh, I see you have had your supper already. Am I starved! I hope that you left something that smells so good for me too, and a lot of it. She put the bundle on the bed and went to the kitchen to see what she could find in the pots.

Chaya raised herself from the bench and, with misgivings, went to the bed to see what the tied bundle contained; all eyes were upon her except Rachel's, because she was busy nosing around in the pots for food. They saw their grandmother pull out a pair of black velvet pants which she quickly threw down on the bed again, and she began to wail, "My very best skirt, the only one I have that I can wear among people and feel like a decent human being. The only skirt I could wear when I go to America. What am I to wear now! Must I show the whole world that I am a poor woman? How dare she do such thing! Not enough that I give her my body and soul, does she also have to take the rags off my back!" Chaya wept and wept and Rachel stood near her as if petrified, holding her plate of *kasha* in her hands and looking at her and for the first time in her life could not find words, until her father asked her why she cut up her grandmother's skirt.

She looked bewildered and said to him, "I didn't think that she would mind. I took only one ruffle off, I didn't think she would care! Papa, I even sewed on the small beads that I took off the ruffle to the place from where I ripped it, so that the stitches won't show. I didn't touch the other two ruffles because I had enough for his pants from the one."

She put her plate on the table, went to the closet, and brought the skirt back to her grandmother, but Chaya refused to look at it. "Why don't you see for yourself now." Rachel began to cry. "Had I known that you would feel so bad about it, I never would have touched it. Look Papa, does it look so bad? Grandma, I am sure that if you would see it, if you would only look at it, you would find it better than you think it is."

Rachel was wild with remorse and anger at the same time; she hung the skirt back into the closet, and sat down again but did not eat her food. Isaiah began to laugh and Raphael joined him, not even knowing why his brother thought that this was a funny time to make jokes. "You shut up, Isaiah," Rachel shouted, glad at last for someone to let out her anger. "I made the pants for you. You didn't think it so funny when you saw me working so hard covering the marks in the velvet that the stitches left with those tiny beads that almost made me blind. Since you began to feel better, you get on my nerves with your rotten jokes, so shut up!"

Isaiah tried to wipe the laughter off his face, but the laughing Raphael kept feeling sure that if it was worth it for Isaiah to do something, it was worthwhile to support it, and he guessed right, because he soon heard Isaiah follow up with, "Rachel, I was not laughing at you, or making jokes about you, I was only laughing because I think it is funny that a skirt gave birth to a pair of pants!" He defended himself and his eyes danced merrily.

"That's enough, that's enough, my Talmud genius, why don't you let your sister eat her food, she is hungry," Chaya said to Isaiah, showing her forgiveness to Rachel at last.

19

With faces toward
the rainbow

S O MUCH TEARS, AND GOOD WISHES, were exchanged in
the last two weeks not only with family and close friends, but
with Chaya's synagogue supplicants, Avraham's students, and
their parents, his synagogue acquaintances here and in the City, and
those that he knew from New Plan.

And, of course, Rachel spent a few hours in Ginendle's shop where
she cried and laughed together with the girls, reminding each other
of the things they learned from each other, the songs they sang at
work, the hardships of their lives and their forgotten young dreams.
They kissed and kissed each other while Ginendle served them a good
hot lunch, adding this time meat-stuffed *kreplekh* well-greased with
chicken fat to the usual lunch she fed them, and Rachel promised
them all that she will write about the wonders of America, as soon as
she sees them.

The younger children did not cry when they parted from their
friends in the courtyard, for they were too exhilarated by the prospects
of their long journey by trains and boats; nevertheless, they too felt
sorry that they had to leave them behind and wished them the best,
as they kissed each other and shook hands like grownups.

And now the straw-padded wagon with the family in it, with all
the bundles of clothes, bedding, and food, began to move away from

the house, the neighbors and their children, getting out of the way of the two patient horses, watched as the wagon turned to leave the empty, forsaken house and the courtyard behind, and began shouting parting good wishes, farewells, and reminders to be sure to write. The women wiped the tears from their eyes; they hated to see the family go from that friendly group of families, yet were happy for them too that they could go to the land of great opportunities where their lot may be bettered.

Adah's best friend Rayzil stood in the very front of the gathering and cried bitterly and loudly, but Adah was unable to see or hear her because she had her head on her father's lap and was sobbing her heart out. Not until they were past the City, and New Plan, did they relax and bend with the motion of the wagon.

The horses trod the soft earthen road with steady rhythm and lulled them all into a sleepy silence. Avraham's arm was around Adah's shoulders, but he said nothing to pacify her big hurt when she had to leave her very dear friend Rayzil. Knowing her for a quiet child that never showed her emotions, he was glad that she gave vent to her feelings of distress. He himself could find no peace since tearing himself away from everyone that he held so dear to his life. He tried to lift the heavy mood he was in but he was not equal to the task.

Chaya's eyes were closed to the sun that was baking her body with warm rays, and swaying with the vehicle's movements, her hands folded in her lap, feeling a strange taste of peace, the peace a mother feels after she married off the last of her brood. She was not asleep, yet not awake either, but her mind was dull and a secure feeling enveloped her. She heard the children's voices but not what they said, and she made no effort to hear. She knew that they were close to her and their father, safe.

But one voice seemed louder than the others, and she was somewhat annoyed with it and raised one eyelid to see where it came from, at the same time becoming more attentive, and heard Rachel shouting across to her, "You were not sleeping Grandma, were you? I didn't wake you up, did I?"

"How can a body sleep with you shouting so? You made sure that I should not sleep, you made enough noise to wake the dead," she told her granddaughter with resentment.

The two boys came out of their lethargy and imitated Rachel teasingly, "I didn't wake you, did I, Grandma?" and burst out with a shout of laughter.

"You clowns be quiet, I did not speak to you. Grandma, I wanted to ask you about Dvoyre, why did she carry on so when she was in the cemetery to bury her husband? Everyone said that she acted as if she was crazy with grief."

"So why should she not have carried on so? He was her husband was he not?" she answered her lightly.

"Yes, I know, but he treated her so badly, he drank away her little earnings, and beat her and her children, and had to go without food many times, because he would not work. If I had such a husband and he died, I would be glad." Rachel told her.

"Who knows, maybe she is glad too, maybe she carried on so at the cemetery because she didn't bury him before? Who can tell what's in someone else's heart? Just the same, that he was, he was; now he is no longer with the living and we don't have to talk of him with disfavor," she admonished her with a raised forefinger.

"That's right, now that he is dead, he turned into a sack of sugar and we cannot remember him as he was," Rachel answered with some heat, and added, "And you tell me why we Jews believe that when a person dies he becomes holy, and we cannot say anything bad about them no matter how much harm he did in his life?"

"I can tell you that you talk too much, and you should give your mouth a rest. Look at your sister, does she ever talk as much as you do? She sits quietly and does not worry about anyone's business." Chaya now was angry at so much talk.

"Yes, I know that Adah is quiet, too darn quiet, even when she is filled to bursting; when you smacked her across her mouth when you could not answer her question she asked you. She still carried around with her a feeling that she committed a sin for asking such a terrible question. She is a fool, why does she go to you and not to me for anything she wants to know? I would tell her everything she wants to know."

By this time Avraham had had enough of their chatter and told Rachel to leave her grandmother in peace.

"Papa, if you knew why she slapped Adah, maybe you would be mad too. I wish you would ask her, Adah, I mean." With that she seemed to close the subject.

Avraham wondered what could have brought his mother-in-law to allow herself such free indulgence. She never before raised a hand to his children, less to threaten them with a beating, but it only remained a threat.

And what could have Adah asked to deserve being slapped by her? He bent closer to his child and asked her to tell him about it. She raised her head and looked around and saw her grandmother drowsing off again and her sister busy with making a wreath out of the wagon bedding. The boys, however, seemed much too attentive to her and her father, they looked as if they stretched their ears way out of proportion toward them, and she did not want to tell her father anything because of them. She knew that she would have a hard time to live down their taunts and teasing if they heard her talk to her father about it. But when he suggested that they go off the wagon and follow for some distance, she agreed, in a double score; first, she would tell him what he wanted to know, and then she would give her brothers something to be envious of.

When the boys wanted to go with them, their father forbade them and helped only Adah off the wagon. "It's good to stretch your legs for a while, isn't it? Now tell me, why did your grandmother slap you, why did you get that angry?

The girl hesitated a while, then said, "Papa when she took me to the baths last week, I heard someone in the room next to ours calling, kosher, kosher, three times, and I wanted to know why and asked her, and she slapped me so hard that Rachel saw the marks of her fingers on my face when we came home. Papa, was it a sin to ask her that question?" She looked fearfully at him.

"It is never sinful to ask questions, the world would be a bad place to live in if we did not want to know everything." He smiled at her trying to ease her anxiety.

"Then why did she hit me for?"

"Who can say why? Perhaps because she had many things on her mind and you asked at the wrong time. Surely, she did not mean to hurt you, forget it."

"So, you tell me why someone in the hall across our room called kosher, kosher, kosher, this three times?" She pressed him and he became uncomfortable.

Fathers don't talk to their daughters about such things. How can he, a young girl not yet twelve years old? Anger at his mother-in-law, his wife, and himself began to eat him. How was he to explain to her about the ritual that pious Jewish women had to go through every month, the *mikvah*,* to cleanse themselves of the menses?

"You know of course that kosher means clean, don't you?" he asked her.

"Yes, so why were they, the other room, told so many times that they were clean? Anyone that goes to the baths are clean when they are finished, then why did they have to make so much noise about it?"

"They have a special attendant in the *mikvah* who sees to it that they are very clean and that's the way they let them know about it."

Before she could ask him another question, he told her that now that she will soon be together with her mother, she should remember to ask her anything else that she wants to know. Avraham was angry at himself for not having explained to her what she wanted to know with more ease and clear account, angry at his mother-in-law who could have saved him from this disturbing situation, and most of all, at his wife, who he felt should have been with his girls until they learned from her what girls learn from their mothers.

Adah saw him look at the back of their wagon as if he wanted to get back into it in a hurry and wondered why her question brought such hardship to both her grandmother and father in answering it. Still, he did tell her that she should ask questions when she wanted to know anything. Well, she thought, as she ran to head off the wagon, when I get to America, will ask so many questions that I will know as

---

* Hebrew for the flowing pool to be used, among other things, by women observing the laws of *niddah* (menstrual purity).

much as Rachel does. Then she laughed out loud while she climbed into the wagon to convince her brothers that she had a good time with her father.

Once again, the family sat together and each with his own thoughts, and the road to America growing shorter with every turn of the wheels. Isaiah seemed the happiest of the lot. He lay on his belly on top of a bundle of bedding, daydreaming of the past and building castles in the air for the future. He remembered hearing that in America a "good" head like his own can go far, maybe become a fireman even! He saw pictures of American firemen and they wore such nice uniforms, with two rows of shiny buttons on their jackets and nice hats that look like the gymnasium students wear, with black shiny visors. His dreams were not entirely without some disturbance though, here and there they produced some little obstacles, which he tried to push out of his way. For instance, there was the question if Jews are allowed to be firemen in America, or are they forbidden like here at home? Then too his father held out hopes for him to become a rabbi and somehow, the two don't go together. This made him feel depressed, but not for long, for his will to conquer those obstacles gave him the strength to push them away, and it helped, for soon he was able to see himself both as rabbi and fireman. This, he reasoned with himself, will please him, and his father too.

But then "reason" thrust itself on him with a dangerously pointing finger at his dream bubble, and wanted to know how one can be both a rabbi who must be in the house of prayer on the Sabbath and holidays and a fireman who may have to run to put out a fire on the very same days? True, the dreamer said, but a good Talmudist should be able to filter out such things; didn't I learn that no argument should be lost, no decision made, until every angle of a problem is closely examined from every view. This he did, very carefully, and came to the conclusion that what he heard of America, it can happen that he can become both! Suddenly he became aware that the wagon stopped rolling and that everyone was climbing out of it.

The driver had stopped the horses close to a streamlet that reflected the young trees around it and freed them of their harness and blinders.

Raphael, the first one to jump out, ran to the horses who were now standing ankle deep in the water drinking. If only I could reach to get up on that brown shiny horse, my smart brother would then be convinced that I am not afraid of horses anymore, he thought.

Both horses trod back and forth in the water poking with their mouths about for something to eat. Raphael's favorite one, the brown one, edged closer to a rock, and in a flash felt something land on his back. Being a horse that pulled men's burdens but not directly on his back, he resented the uninvited guest, and trying to escape him galloped into the middle of the stream, the water reaching up to his belly. The cold water shocked him into confusion and he stood there not knowing what to do. He just stood throwing his head up and down furiously and snorting with anger!

When the family saw the "lost soul" on the back of the horse with his arms around his mane and clinging to him tenaciously, they cried in terror, while the driver put his lunch down and stood near the water grinning. "You Jews are all afraid of horses, don't worry, this horse will not hurt him, he is even too old to drive a fly off himself with his tail. Hey, you out there, smack your hand hard on his behind, and he will take you out of the water."

But no direction could reach the petrified hero; he just hung on to the horse not knowing what to do or what to hope for. The driver picked up a stone, rather a large one, and aimed it at the water near the horse; it hit him on his hind quarters instead. The sting of the stone added to the rest of his troubles, made the animal rear and throw his burden into the water, and then he ran out to roll in the new grass.

Rachel ran into the cold water, and brought her almost drowning brother out, struggling in her arms. He wanted to get out of her arms, he refused to be carried like a baby, was a big boy of six, and he was not going to have his brother tease him for the rest of his life because a girl carried him out of the water. His lips were blue and his body was shaking from the cold, but he kept his tears back so hard they burned his eyes. But Rachel was not going to let him fall into the water again, they had enough troubles from him for one day, and she carried him over to a piece of soft ground and put him down.

It was when his grandmother brought him dry clothes to change into that his resolutions fell apart, and one could hear him scream from quite a distance. He kicked and screamed and refused to let her take his wet clothes off, and yet he himself was not up to the job. "Don't be worried about him, he will cry himself out," his father said and then added, "It is better that he cry, than if he had drowned and we would cry for him."

When Avraham saw him laying spent, only intermittent spasms shaking him, he tried to raise him to change his clothes, but the boy was reluctant and held back. "Come on, Raphael, we must go on our way if we are not to miss the train to America. If you will let me change your clothes, I will ask the driver to let you sit with him in the front, what do you think of that?" Slowly the boy raised himself and with his father's help changed into his dry clothes and soon found himself in the front seat next to the driver's, facing the horses.

He rubbed his tear-swollen face and smiled. He was beside himself with happiness and turned to see if Isaiah was watching him and wondered at what he thought of him sitting up there with the driver, but if Isaiah had any ideas, or envy, he did not display it, so he turned back to watch the horses being reharnessed. His admiration of the driver became deeper than even for the horses, when he climbed up to his seat and gave his guest a long twig that looked like a whip. Then they started; how the horses ate up the road! He was so thrilled that he almost fell out of his seat when the wagon hit a rock and jumped up and then down with real force. His eyes wandered all over the horses, watching their bobbing heads and the intricate work of their legs. How do they know which one to put forth first he wondered, and then assumed that they were smarter than people gave them credit for.

Suddenly he became aware that the driver was whipping them all the time, and felt sorry for them. Does he not know that they are God's creatures and that we must protect them? It is even written in the Good Books that we are not allowed to harm animals, he thought, as the whip kept coming down on the horses' backs, and his admiration for him began to wane. Does he expect them to run like the fire engine horses that strike fire with their hoofs on the cobblestones in the city?

Again the whip came down, and on his favorite horse too, and made the boy wince, and a feeling of sadness settled on him.

The sun began to set and the air became cold so that Raphael felt uncomfortable sitting in the unprotected seat, and he wondered if he would not be better off among the bundles of bedding in the wagon. The horses seemed to know their way past the fields and forests and little villages with small houses that were almost hidden by hats of straw-thatched roofs. It grew dark, the stars began to play, and Raphael began to count them, but in the midst of a large number of them, shouted, "Papa, Papa, I am scared, take me to you, I don't want to sit here, take me to you." Rachel reached over and pulled him off his seat and handed him to his father. No sooner did he feel the comfort and warmth of his father when he fell into a deep sleep.

20

The train ride

RAPHAEL SLEPT SO SOUNDLY that he missed everything that was going on in the railroad station. His father had to carry him into the smoke-filled room and lay him down on the bundles of bedding. Avraham looked around the noisy room and wondered where so many men, women, and children came from, and almost all that he saw were Jews. The huge room smelled of kerosene and human sweat, and was dimly lit.

"So many people, wonder where they are all going," Chaya remarked.

"What do you mean where? They are all going to America, can't you see that they all have their bedding with them? Where else do we take bedding to, if not to America?" Rachel asked.

"Why do we have to take bedding there, don't they have geese in that country?" Isaiah wanted to know.

Avraham warned them not to leave their place at the wall where they sat on the floor, and walked off to get some information about the train arrival. He walked toward an official at a desk wearing a red uniform and bellowing information over the noise of the adults and children. The youngsters ran around shouting at each other and climbing on anything that presented itself. It was no easy task to cross that room, what with the children underfoot and bundles that were ready to trip you every step of the way. He picked up the sounds of many dialects as he went, hearing that they were from Lithuania and Galicia, as well as from Ukraine.

When he was informed that the train will be in an hour, he hastily but with much caution picked his way back, and found his family eating bread that they washed down with hot tea. "Where in the world did you get tea?" he asked, but everybody was busy blowing on their tea to cool it off. Chaya cut a slice off the bread and handed it to him, then poured some tea out of the kettle he forbade her to drag along because it was so old and banged up, and gave it to him.

"Look, children we must eat and be ready, for the train will be here soon for us, and it will not wait for anyone." He was glad to have the tea, his throat was parched from the dust of the road.

"Papa, don't you think that we should wake Raphael, he must be hungry too," Adah asked, and they all looked at the curled-up boy, flushed with sleep.

"I think that we should leave him be, when he will be hungry he will let us know soon enough," and they all shook their heads in agreement. Chaya closed the food hamper and tied it with a cord so that nothing could slip out, and told the girls to tie the knots in the bundles a little tighter; then they all settled on the floor with their backs hard against the wall and were ready to board the train as soon as it arrives.

All around them were men and women, their faces lined with fatigue, sitting lax with their heads on something or someone, just hanging loosely, ready to fall where it will. The heretofore noise of the children died down slowly, some of them already asleep. Many were sprawled on the floor, some on benches, and the very young in the arms of their mothers, sucking at their breasts. Time did not hang heavy for the children, only served to bring out of their night, day, that they could continue with their play.

The hour ran out and the travelers were restless, every stir brought them to attention. They fought off sleep as they listened closely. At the end of the second hour, they gave up the struggle and sank into torpid sleep. With the coming of the dawn, the train sped into the station, its chimney spitting up black smoke enveloping the station room with its soot. Not until the official in the red uniform shouted through a rolled-up paper to magnify his voice, "All aboard, all aboard," did anyone know that their train had at last arrived.

At once the room became a beehive of activity. Bleary-eyed mothers with sleep-swollen faces and aching limbs began to hurry their children, to become fully awake at the very first call, and had they been left to their own schemes, would have been the first ones aboard. From all directions came cries of caution and panic.

"Yonkile, where are you?"

"Rokhl, hold on to your brother's hat, don't lose him."

"This is not your bundle, you are mistaken."

"Oh my God, Mother, you can't get sick now, the train is waiting for us."

But slowly the din in the room lost its strength to the waiting train.

Everyone wanted to get into the train's compartments and settle with their belongings, but were slowed by those in front who were laden with bundles and flocks of children. Fear was dominant among those passengers who never saw a train before, and not knowing what to expect inside, made their way with lagging steps and fast-beating hearts, retarding those in back of them. To the great irritation of many women, their husbands and sons insisted on examining the train from the outside, from the wheels to the engine that was now puffing steam and smoke from its innards with a show of impatience. Inside the cars the confusion was great, everyone was pushing someone else. Bundles fell apart and children cried, and the conductor's "Hurry, hurry," added to the clamor.

Chaya cut a path across all this confusion calling behind her, "Follow me, follow me, or you will get lost," until she found a good-sized space on a bench and told them to put their bundles under it and sit down. When they were all seated they missed their father, and Raphael who was in his brother's charge, began to cry, "Papa, Papa, don't go home again, come with us."

"Stop crying, he will be here soon, probably got carried away with the crowd and will find us, don't you worry. Look what you made of your face, you look like Mendl the Chimney Sweep with all that soot." Chaya cleaned his face while she spoke to him.

Not until the train started did Avraham put in his appearance and still their anxiety. He sank into the seat that Isaiah vacated for him and sat breathing hard. Adah saw that his face was scratched and bleeding into his beard, and in alarm asked him about it, and he smiled trying to make light of it. "Tell me, when is a person the happiest?" he asked her, and she shook her head. "I don't know, are you happy now?" "Yes, I am happy now. I have lost something, and found it again; that makes me happy."

"But where did you get your face so badly scratched up?" she insisted, while she applied his handkerchief to stay the blood.

"Well, if you must know, then I will have to tell you. When I stepped up to the platform of the car, a man leaned very close to me and I was about to tell him that he was crushing me, when I saw that he was pulling my wallet out of my breast pocket. Well, I screamed out loud and tried to get it back, and as you see, I have it right here, because some good people around me helped me recover it. You didn't expect him to give it up willingly, did you! My face will heal up, don't you worry about it."

The boys listened to him too, but their eyes were staring out of the window. There was so much to see! Everything ran past them, fields, rivers, and so many cows out in the pastures! Farmhouses with pigpens near them, hens with many little chicks following, and they disappeared from view so fast as if they had not seen them. Chaya held out some bread and apple butter to them, here, "Take this my 'lost soul', don't be so busy at the window. Isaiah, how many more times will I have to offer you the bread?"

They took the bread out of her hands and turned back to the window. So many things to see and the train rushed by so fast it was hard to behold all the wonders, but of all things, the telegraph poles flew past as if the Devil gave them hot chase! Isaiah tried to count them but soon found that he could not keep up with them, while Raphael did not even make the attempt, he was scared enough with their size and nearness.

More than two weeks of riding and transferring from one destination to another waned the boys' interest at the windows, and they turned their attention to the children in the trains. Here they found boys their age, and their interests. Friends they were to meet yet again and again in the transferred trains and, later on, on the boat to America. Their happiness was at a great height when they met again after each parting and their play was continuous.

The very last train they transferred into was to the German border, and the travel-weary passengers feeling the nearness of their destination perked up, and spoke to each other of their plans with great animation, for the nearness of Hamburg, where the ship is waiting for them. They spoke of their hopes in the new country over and over again as if to assure themselves that at last their dreams were about to materialize.

Most of the passengers did cross into Hamburg, Germany, but some did not, among them Avraham and his family. The reasons were many, among them the lack of necessary identification papers. Avraham's family passport contained all the names of the family, except Rachel's. How or why it was left out was a riddle no one could guess. Together with other families who were turned back, they went to the town's Jewish inn to gather their wits. The mournful groups entered, all talking at once, most of the women crying.

"You see we are not alone in our troubles," Avraham said to the crying Rachel who was bitter and angry. "But Papa you are consoling me with smelling salts. They have their troubles and we have ours. I wonder if my dear, rich Uncle Fishl didn't fix it like that, he hates me," she told her father.

"That's not nice, you can't accuse anyone of a misdeed because he did you a favor. I would not have known what kind of papers to take with me had he not gone to the trouble to advise me where to go and what to ask for." He led his family to a round table and told them to leave the bundles on the floor and to wash for lunch.

The room was crowded and noisy and the innkeeper, a tall, bearded Jew, went around taking orders and promising fast service to everyone. Avraham's table was the last to be served by the innkeeper himself, who sat down with them holding a glass of tea in his hand, asking the reason for their troubles.

"Only God can help us," Avraham told him with a wrinkled forehead, "One of my children, this girl here, was left out of my family passport and they would not listen to any reason at the office, and I can't go on."

"God can help you, but someone will have to do the work for Him, He is too busy with more important work for Him to do it Himself. Did you ever hear of people smuggling at the border? Well, here it is nothing new. Families come all the way from other countries to this town so that they can go to America by Hamburg, and for one reason or another they are turned back. Well, we help them here, and they get to America in good time. Do you want me to tell you how it is done?" he ended, looking around the room.

"Please tell me how you can help us." Avraham pleaded with him.

"Well, you and the rest of the family go and cross the border on the passport that you have. The girl here, he pointed to Rachel, leave with me. When it will get dark, a man will carry her across the river and bring her to the inn where you and your family will be waiting for her." He stopped and then added, "Of course, that will cost you 10 rubles for the services of the man and myself."

Many things troubled them now: how could they leave a young girl in a strange place with strange people, and to some stranger who would carry her across the river? And all men too, for so far Avraham nor Chaya hadn't seen the innkeeper's wife or any other female that belonged to this establishment. And one heard so much about child snatchers, white slavers, these days! She can even be shot crossing the river at night. They had very little money left and they had so much journey ahead of themselves, and now with the 10 rubles that the innkeeper wanted, it will leave them penniless.

The man stood waiting, and knew well what worried the father and grandmother, and said, "I know what is running through your minds, in your place I would feel worried too. You don't know me and you are uneasy to leave your daughter with me. What is worse, I can't convince you that no harm will come to her, but if you want her in Hamburg you will have to trust me. She will not be the only one to go across tonight. Most of these people here too are waiting for such help. Decide and let me know, I must make arrangements."

The cooked hot food they so much craved after so many days without it now stood on the table untouched and cold. The two boys did not understand the seriousness of the situation, but the tensions of their father and grandmother took their appetites away.

"I believe what that man told us, it's the only thing we can do. We can't go back, so we must go ahead."

"But Papa, do you have 10 rubles to give him?" Rachel asked.

"I have altogether about 12 rubles, and we still have a long way to go, but that's not the trouble, I hate to leave you here alone among strangers."

"Don't worry Papa, no one will want her, she eats too much and she talks too much, and if someone will steal her they will bring her back soon enough," Isaiah tried to console his father.

After much talk, they had to make the decision, and Rachel was left behind. Avraham had no trouble to pass with his family into Hamburg and asked his way to an inn that the innkeeper sent him to, to wait for Rachel until midnight. "You and many others," the new innkeeper told him. "This house makes its business during the nights. We draw a living from the immigrants who are troubled by the borderline and help them with whatever it is possible!"

The old Jew, bent with age, spoke with a German dialect that amused the children. "Like a man from another world," Adah said to her grandmother, and she shook her head in agreement. He led them to a side room, talking all the while. "In the meantime, you can get cleaned up, there is water and towels in the room behind, and at sundown we will have a *minyan** for the evening prayers in the main room. Then we will have supper and then you can all go to sleep until your daughter comes, and then I will wake you." He opened a door to a huge room in which stood six beds and a table and left them to themselves.

The worry about Rachel and the lack of money did not let Avraham sleep, and every little noise in the lodge would bring him to his feet, only to find out that it came from stirring in other rooms. In desperation he slipped into his clothes and went to the main room, and found a few people sitting around a table and quietly talking.

He turned back to look for the innkeeper and in the semi-darkness bumped into someone who in a hushed tone said, "Papa, it's me. You

* Hebrew for the customary gathering of at least ten men for daily prayers.

gave me a scare. I am here a long time already but I did not want to disturb your rest," as she led him back to the main room.

"Papa, I have so much to tell you but my clothes are wet and I am so sleepy that I can't stand on my feet. Should we sit in here to wait until morning, do you want to get back to your bed? If you don't want to sit here yourself, I'll stay with you."

"No, you go inside quietly and I will stay here a while longer, then maybe I will be able to rest better." His heart felt the joy of having his child safe with him again.

Not before late noon did Chaya find it in her heart to wake the sleeping girl. Twice before had she gone in to wake her and went out without doing so, but time was passing fast, and only two hours' time was left for them to get to the pier and board the ship. "Come on, lazy girl, the day is almost past and you don't show a sign of wakefulness. Your father and the boys with Adah have already been two times to see the ship we will go to America on, and you missed it all. Get up, we have little time and you must eat something too."

"Believe me Grandma, I did not miss a thing. I had enough excitement to last me a lifetime. I can tell you something I witnessed last night that will make you wonder how I remained sane. But maybe you have already heard about the baby that was drowned because it began to cry while we were halfway across the river. Then too the mother …"

But Chaya did not let her finish. "I know all about the tragedy. They brought the mother here, raving and tearing her hair from her head. We went through Gehenna* before she was taken away and put into the basement and locked up there so that the police don't get her. What good will America do for that young couple now with the loss of their first born, for whom they built all their dreams. Come, let's go now, I want you to eat something," she ended, tying her head kerchief tighter around her face.

---

* Yiddish and Hebrew for Hell, the abode of the damned in the afterlife in Jewish and Christian theology. The metaphor comes from ancient Gehenna, a valley near Jerusalem where children were burned as sacrifices to the pagan god Moloch by some Israelites before the Babylonian Exile in the 6th century BC.

21

The ship

TOGETHER WITH A GREAT MANY families going to America on the same boat, Avraham and his family loaded with bundles trudged to the pier. All walked in family groups, usually with father, if there was a father, loaded down with heavy bundles ahead, the children following, and the mother with the infant in her arms bringing up the rear. Avraham and his family were the last of these groups.

Chaya, also loaded with many bundles, walked near the distraught mother of the drowned infant and spoke to her softly. "You are still a young woman, God will bless you with another child, nay, many more, don't mourn so for the one God wanted, it's a sin." She knew that she talked in vain. She learned that the young woman's name was Leah, and her husband's was Daniel, and that they came from a little town near Kamenets, "so that makes us *landslayt*,"* she said to the husband, and promised to spend more time with his wife when they settle in the ship.

To get "settled" in the ship meant pushing and shoving and losing each other in the crowd and not being able to hear each other in the clamber of the people and the commotion of the ship's engines; everyone held on to their bundles and with flaming faces tried to understand where to go. Avraham shouted questions in Jewish-German dialect and asked an officer, who made some sense out of his questions, where he was to take his family and was pleased to see

---

* Yiddish for countrymen.

him give orders to a sailor to lead them to the third class in the ship and to their bunks.

Adah was very proud of her father, who seemed to be the only one of the immigrants who made himself understood. She looked up at him and smiled and tripped over someone's bundle of bedding. "Can't you see where you are going? If a cow was in your way, you would fall over him too," an irate woman shouted at her. The sailor opened a door and motioned to them to follow him down a long flight of stairs, and there they were swallowed into a long, narrow hallway. He looked for a number on the doors until he found it and, pointing to it, left, taking the lantern with him.

They stood in semi-darkness until Avraham pushed the door open. Inside, one small light bulb lit up the tiny room that contained six narrow bunks that looked much as if they sprouted out of the tree walls. Chaya stepped in and looked at the bare mattresses, dirty blankets, and pillows naked of pillow cases, and shook her head. "We cannot sleep on these dirty rags; Adah, you and Rachel help me untie the bedding, and Isaiah and you, Raphael, climb into these things they gave us for beds and take all the pillows and blankets and put them underneath the beds, we will use our own."

When the bunks were made up, the little room appeared homelike and the small lightbulb seemed to shed a brighter light. Avraham stood near the door watching and then told them to follow him up to the deck for some fresh air. Suddenly there was a loud rumble as if it came from beneath the floor they stood on, and instead of the clatter of wheels they heard up to now, there came to them a tortuous clamour and movement that almost threw them off their feet. People ran like drunks to and from their cubicles, fear of the unknown causing them to shriek. Avraham gained his balance and held on to the frightened Raphael, who was crying loudly. "Just hold on to each other and let us go upstairs. I believe that the boat is beginning to leave the wharf and we must not miss it."

Isaiah was the first one on the way up with the others following, and they found most of the immigrants already there, standing as if turned to stone with disbelief that at last the ship they were on was really now leaving for America. Sailors ran to and fro attending to the ship's emergence into the broad waters. The chimneys spat black smoke that rained its residue in every direction. Gradually the passengers seemed to relax feeling the ship moving with resolution, cutting its way for their destination.

"Papa, I feel happy now. At last I feel that we are really going to America, my beautiful mother and my sister Bena, and to fulfill all my good dreams. I will go to school there and learn like all the other children, and I will learn fast to make up for all the time that I lost." Rachel talked fast, two round tears sliding down her flushed cheeks, which she wiped with the sleeves of her coat.

"Yes, my daughter, America is waiting for you, she will give you everything you dreamed of, she will throw the horn of plenty into your lap to play with, as soon as she sees you," he bantered with her.

Food was served three times a day in a large dining room, but very little of it was eaten by the pious Jewish immigrants for whom no kosher food was prepared. Baked potatoes in their jackets, herring, and eggs from the shell were the mainstay of the young and the sick, and not even the bread was eaten from the kitchen because its ingredients were not known. Family groups spread blankets on the floor of the deck and ate their meals of bread brought from home, which they washed down with hot tea. For this time of year, when on land the sun only begins, it was pleasantly warm and healing, giving the days a holiday impression. Laughter was heard from one end of the deck to another and friendships were tied to last a lifetime by some of the passengers. "Ship sisters" and "ship brothers" became as close as their own kin. Promises of meeting in the cities they were bound for were going to be kept and the wish to see each other prosper and help one another was strong. Stories were told and listened to by young and old, all ending with the aspirations and hopes that in America their former poverty and misery will be wiped out and forgotten.

Avraham kept apart from his fellow travelers except at prayer time when he would, together with his sons, join the *minyan* of worshipers. Once finished, he would sit with the boys on deck and continue with their studies. But Chaya and the girls made up for his aloofness by making friends with everyone that gave them the chance. Chaya found women who spent hours each day relating their live's tales and making promises to each other to meet in "Nevyork" when they get settled there. Chaya tried to help Daniel care for his mournful wife, but saw that she only got in the way.

Rachel had no difficulty making friends; her pretty face and hearty laughter drew everyone's attention, more so the attention of young men who stood at a distance and admired her, wishing they had the nerve to approach her, but knew well that both her father and grandmother kept an eye on her. Adah was happy on the ship, she seemed to have found the kind of work she liked. She walked around most of the day and helped the sick with hot tea from their banged-up tea kettle and cold water she carried around in a pitcher. When a mother was too sick to care for her infant, Adah took it away from her until she was better. When she found herself without being in need on deck, she would go downstairs to the long hallway and listen if someone was vomiting or moaning or calling for help. The passengers named her *malekh.** "Here comes the *malekh*," they would say, and it made the girl feel grown-up, but shy, and she would busy herself to hide her bashfulness.

Most of the days on the ocean were as if made to order. The mornings and evenings were cold, but the middays were so warm that the heavy winter clothes had to be shed. Only one day gave them a bad time: the ninth; the day after they all had enjoyed its salty air, the sun's warm rays that imparted so much joy and laughter to all, so much so that the first-class passengers, who were bored with the sameness of their good lives, were thinking of visiting the third class, to see how the poor fared. Had they gone on that day, they would have met a different situation, but a languid spell seemed to hold them and they waited for the following day.

They came from the second and first class; rich women dressed in expensive clothes and carrying bonbons and fruit baskets holding fruits that were out of season and luxurious, with which to treat "those people below." They walked about, rich, well fed, seeking fun, while speaking many languages and looking at the ill-dressed underfed

---

* Yiddish for angel.

throng sprawled all over the deck. They offered the sweets first to the adults, who refused them, and then to the children, who first looked to their mothers or fathers and, getting a nod from them, took as much as their little fists were able to hold. This made the slumming madams smile with happiness and they called to each other to tell of their success.

Suddenly the sun went down and the ship seemed to glide on unknown waters, and soon stood up on one end, sending everyone and everything into one heap, before anyone could get up they were sent to the front of the boat, as if in one mass. Rain pelted down, thick long hurtling spears of it, and lightning split the sky, while ear-splitting thunder added to the confusion. Men, women, and children, rich and poor, Jew and Gentile all laying in one knot, and no one could help himself. Although it was mid-morning, it was dark as night. Children were crying, adults moaned, while the ship went from fore to aft and back again, and almost in upright position. The sailors held onto the ropes as they tried to get their bearings and tried to shut vents and doors but with no success.

Passengers caught below decks tried to climb to the top, sure that the ship was sinking, and found themselves swept off their feet and thrown at the ship's will, to and fro. So slow did the thunder and lightning abate that no one knew when it disappeared altogether, but the rain continued to fall now a little gentler and the boat steadied itself gradually, giving the heap of humanity a chance to disentangle itself; one by one they got to their feet while daylight returned and the immigrants went below to change into dry clothes, and their visitors went back "home."

"Why do you have to cry like a baby?" Rachel teased her sister. "Look, Raphael stopped and you still keep at it. Don't forget there are sick people waiting for you; come on put on my blouse and let's get out of here." But Adah was not to be stopped, she did not want to change into dry clothes and did not want to go up to the deck. "Papa and the boys have to change and you are keeping them in their wet clothes standing in the drafty hallway." Rachel lost her patience and stomped outside. "I can't do a thing with her, she lays there like a wet sponge and won't come out," she shouted.

"Leave her to me, you go up and stay with your grandmother, and don't go too far away from her so we won't have to look for you," her father told her and went inside to see Adah.

"Papa I feel better now, but do you know why I felt so sick before?"

"Well, I am glad that you feel better, just get into those clothes Rachel left for you, and go up to the deck, the boys and I must change too." And he began to walk out, but she caught his arm and held it. "No, don't go until I tell you why I felt so sick. One of the ladies from the upper decks held a box of bonbons close to me while we were all in a heap in the front of the ship, and I laid there and ate up the entire boxful of them. Then while we were cast from one end to the other, the box was still under my nose and I could not help eating them all. Now my belly feels like it's full of lead. I wish I could do something to get rid of it, vomit like other people do, I feel that sick." She slipped into Rachel's blouse and waited for her father to say something to her, but he only smiled and told her to hurry into her dry clothes and go up on deck to try to throw that feeling of sickness off herself.

When she at last came out, Isaiah shouted at her, "My goodness, who do you think you are? You hold up everybody as if you were the Queen of Sheba. We are wet too, and we had to stand here and wait until you decided to come out at your own good time."

"Oh, shut your silly mouth," she shouted back at him, and food and the bonbons she stuffed herself with came gushing out of her mouth and made her reel.

"Quick Isaiah, Adah is going to die, let's get Papa." Raphael ran to bang on the door of the bunk, while Isaiah went to his sister and not knowing what to do for her, pleaded, "Adah, stop, please stop, I will not say anything mean to you again. I swear I did not mean to make you this mad." He held her forehead while she struggled with her breath, her face almost blue. Avraham ran out and saw Adah's troubles and smiled so broad it puzzled the boys.

"Now you will feel better," he told her while he wiped the sweat off her brow and told the boys to find some rags in the bunk and clean up the mess. At no time did they obey with so much willingness, and so much helpfulness. Up on deck, no one was now sitting on the deck floor as it was still wet, and many of the wet passengers were standing against the sun to dry their clothes saving those in their trunks for America. The sky was clear and the sun began to show a sinking face, calling the Jews to Maariv,* and Avraham stood near his two daughters waiting for his sons to come up and join him in the room where a large group of men were already waiting.

* Hebrew for evening prayers.

New York City

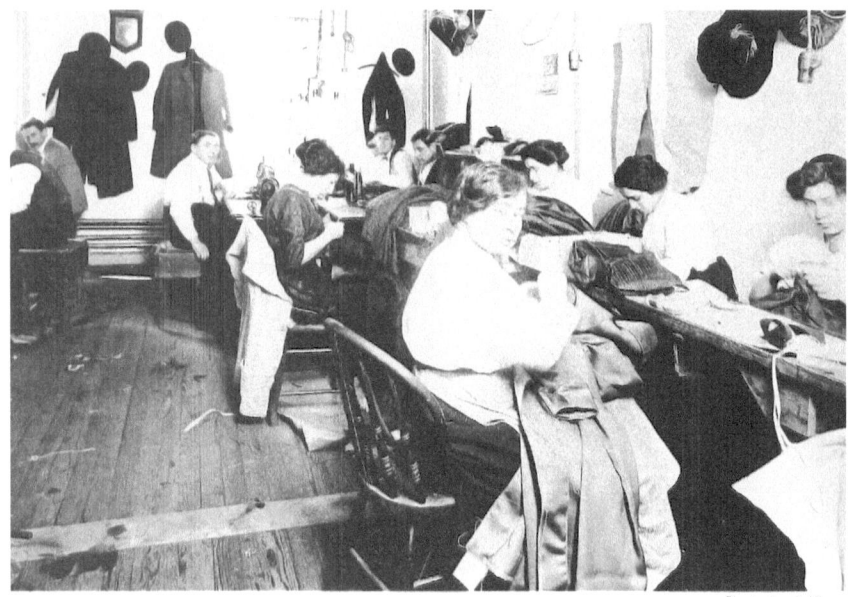

Garment workers in New York City, 1910

The machines in the shop roar so wildly
that often I forget in the roar that I am;
I am lost in the terrible tumult, my ego
disappears, I am a machine. I work, and
work, and work without end; I am busy,
and busy, and busy at all time. For what?
and for whom? I know not, I ask not!
How should a machine ever come to think?

– Morris Rosenfeld, "In the Sweatshop"

22

The cloak shop

ANKLE-DEEP TRASH and the dim light in the old tenement hallway forced one to look more than once before locating the wooden narrow staircase leading up to the "bedroom" shop, on the third floor, where Schwartz and Lefkowitz operated their cloak and suit factory. Having reached and opened their door, one is confronted by a dark, ominous tunnel formed by two walls facing each other, piled high to the ceiling with bolts of woolens. Those passing through to and from the shop and the little office tiptoed in fear of disturbing the precarious positions of the material, and be swallowed up by it.

The approach to the factory was heralded by the whirl and hum of machines, and as one got closer, by the shouting of one voice, loud and rancorous. Herschel, the factory foreman, ran from one machine to another screaming for workers to work faster and faster. Most of the operators were immigrants, middle-aged, bearded men wearing skullcaps, and came from small cities and towns where they had never seen a machine or been inside a factory. Making a living was in God's hands and, with the help of their wives' small earnings, they were able to sit in the house of learning and study the Talmud. It was only when the poverty became unbearable and the pogroms a threat to their lives that they left their families and came to America to make a new and better life for them. The younger men who operated the machines, also immigrants, ran from their homes to escape the military service and the poverty they saw in their homes.

All sat bent over their work, the low lights hanging from the ceiling burning their eyes and the dust and lint eating at their lungs. Coughing and spitting was the only relief they found for their mucous-laden throats.

"Come on, come on, you bunch of greenhorns, what do you think you are here for? To say your prayers? Hurry, hurry, I need the work. Maybe if I will cut your beards, you will be able to work a little faster." The foreman Herschel didn't spare the women who did the coat finishing. That is except Rosa, the prostitute, for he knew better than to start something with her. Just a cross look in her direction was enough for him to earn a barrage of curses that would follow him to his grave. To avoid "falling into her mouth," one had to make believe that she was not there, but at times, the younger men in boredom at their machines, would hurl a barb at her and a dirty and blasphemous stream of curses would spill from her thin blue lips and make the women around her shudder. The older men would shout at the young workers to keep their tongues under control, and pleaded with Rosa to be quiet, but this only added fuel to the bitter woman, and she let the curses fall from her mouth like snakes, until she ran out of breath.

Her pet grievance was Mirele. She hated all the women there, the quiet gentle Bena, but Mirele made her blood boil. She would look at her with piercing eyes and curse her in her heart. Look, she would say to herself, look at her, she looks as if she were in constant prayer, she never looks at a man, wears a pious wig and looks like a *rabbanit*,* and the way she keeps an eye on her daughter and shields her, one would think that she was the only virgin on this earth.

Now Herschel came near the group of finishers, Jewish and Italian women, some big with pregnancy, sat bent over their work as if they were spineless. Their heads low and brows drawn against the low ceiling lights, working faster when they became aware of his presence. "Come on, don't be afraid to work a little faster, you won't lose your bambinos. How do you expect to get paid if you crawl with your work so," Herschel shouted with cause and without, all day long. He bellowed when he came home at night to his family. He continued

* Hebrew for the wife of a rabbi.

as if in spite of himself. When his neighbors heard him late at night they would say, "Aha, he is home" to the windows.

Carla, one of the finishers, kept her infant son in a wash basket at her side and heard him crying, but seeing Herschel nearby kept at her work as if she did not hear him. Mirele too heard the child wailing, and called to her, "Carla, your son needs to be fed. Pick him up, don't let him cry so long, he is hungry. Don't worry about that loudmouth, the boss told you that he will allow you to nurse the baby when he is hungry, didn't he? Go ahead nurse him."

Carla gave Mirele a grateful look and dropped on her knees near her child and exposed her breast to him. While the baby was suckling, she took time to wipe the tears from his eyes and the sweat from his little face and admired his very black hair, like his father's, that already began to curl.

"It is so close to the lunch hour, couldn't you wait a while longer to feed him." Herschel stood over her, his eyes on her bare breast; and suddenly it came to him that although his wife had borne him four children and he was sure that she had nursed all of them, yet he could not remember ever seeing her do so! And before he was able to think of the reason, he knew the answer! Sure, didn't he want to show his brother the lawyer, that he too could "make good" in America? So he worked all day and at night he went to school. But while his brother forged ahead, he failed to make the grade. All this while his family was increasing, and he had to "make good" in some other way. If he could not become a lawyer, then he would work hard and save money, so that his children will have the means of becoming doctors and lawyers. And he was working hard days and half into the night every day, every holiday, missing the pleasure of seeing his children grow from infants to youths, hardly seeing them even when they were sick.

He tore himself away from Carla, and ran in the direction of the pressers, shouting at them, "You should burn like the press irons, why are you tickling the garments so gently! You think they are the rumps of young girls! The season will pass before you hang those coats on the racks. Come on, hurry, hurry."

The midday whistle blew and brought the workers to their feet. Like one, they all rushed to the one wash basin to clean their hands, but Bena took her mother's coat off the hook near the pressers' table, and put it on her and led her up to the roof of the building. "I know that it is not too warm today but it is better than spending the half hour down here in the dust. Come on, I brought along a wet and dry towel so we can clean our hands."

She hooked her arm into her mother's and helped her up the flight of stairs. Where the sun did not reach because of the shadows of the water tank and chimneys, there were heaps of frozen snow and in the center of the roof were puddles of water filmed over with thin ice. They walked over to the big chimney that faced to the south, and stood there with the sun on their faces, eating their lunch they brought from home.

"See, isn't it better here than in the dirty, smelly madhouse?" Bena asked.

"Yes, it is much better, and what a wonderful day it is, and it's so early in the year yet. I hope and pray that our greenhorns are having it so nice on the high seas. Thank God, in another week we will all be together again."

Mirele's soft expression changed and she continued, "My happiness would be complete now had you married before your father came to this country. Did you see that new operator that was hired this morning? He looks like very nice, if he tries to talk to you don't go hiding under my skirt for you will remain an old maid for the rest of your life," she warned her.

"Oh, Mama, I am only twenty years old and in America that's not old." Bena laughed at her mother's tears.

"That's true, that here it is not old, but you are too bashful to meet young men, and when they talk to you, you seem to shrink from them," Mirele complained.

If only my mother would know, Bena thought, as she walked down the stairs with her mother, what Aaron means to me, she would not lecture me about other men. How can she know how I melt when he puts his hand over mine to guide me to form the capital letters, or when he accidently touches me, she would feel hurt on my account. Little does she know how shaken up I feel whenever he comes into the house, and that I feel his nearness for the rest of that night. If this is love, then that's what I want.

Two hours later, Mirele felt ill and wondered why her hands shook so badly and had difficulty threading her needle. Again she put the thread between her lips, rolled it between her fingers and tried to push it through the eye of the needle and failed again. She got up to get some water, but quickly sat down again. Bena was aware of her mother's difficulties, she had seen the pallor in her face since morning, and feared that she would not be able to finish the day in the shop, but not wanting to panic her, she just watched, waiting for her to indicate if she needed help. When she saw her struggle to get up and then sit down again, she got to her feet and ran for water.

How in the world did she know that my head was swimming so, Mirele thought, and with that, lost consciousness, falling from the chair and landing under the table. Bena heard the workers screaming and ran back with the water and heard Herschel shrieking, "Again you did it, why do you come to work in the shop when you should sit at a warm stove!" then shouted in the direction of the pressers, "Hey you, come give me a help to put her back on her chair."

Mr. Lefkowitz heard the commotion and ran in with a raised hand to stop the pressers, and told Herschel to help him carry her into the office, and put her on a couch, and tried to pour some whiskey into her. When she opened her eyes, she saw Bena's frightened face and she smiled to her.

"It's nothing, I just felt a little tired," she assured her.

Mr. Lefkowitz told Bena to go back to work and let her mother rest on the couch a while longer. "Tell me, Mirele, why don't you give up your work now? In the past few years when we picked you up from the floor after those faints and wanted to send you home, you pleaded with me to let you go on because your children at home were starving. Now I hear that they are on the way to America, so you want them to come and find you dead? Why don't you stop working while you still have some life in you?"

He stood twirling his gold watch that hung on a gold chain across his protruding abdomen, all the while keeping his eyes on her pale face, wondering what inner spark kept her frail body alive. Mirele kept her eyelids down not answering, although feeling his pressure. Then she got up and straightened her wig, her skirt, and made ready to leave the room; then she saw that he was still standing as if waiting for an answer.

"Mr. Lefkowitz," she pleaded, "you must have a little more patience with me now that my husband and children are coming. I will get some help in a little while, but not immediately. And in the meantime, I must pay rent, I must buy food, and pay off for the furniture and their ship's tickets. I must go on working a little longer, so that they can have some time to get their bearings in the new country. Then I'll stop. Today being Friday, I will leave pretty soon for home and have a good rest until tomorrow night. Then I'll come back here. I feel better already, and I must hurry to finish the work on my bench." She got up and stood a while as to test herself, then walked out holding her head high as if she had a medal for valor and he muttered, "Pioneer woman."

As she passed by, Rosa looked up from her work and noticed how pale and drawn her face looked, and a deep depression settled in her. She did not understand this feeling, nor did she make an attempt to understand why she had to feel so low because Mirele looked ill, but her needle flew faster and faster, drawing blood from her toughened fingers. And not until she saw the pious Jewish workers make ready to leave the shop did she suddenly understand the reason for her deep depression.

Like a flashback, her youth appeared before her and reminded her of the time not so long ago when she too had a father who came home on Fridays earlier than the other days. That he too was a pious man and came home so that he could bathe and wash off the hard work and worries with the dirt that he lived with all week and be ready to usher in the Sabbath by the time Mama lit and blessed the candles that were stuck in gleaming brass candlesticks. How her younger sisters and brothers carried on with their babble and laughter until Papa threatened to send them to bed before he made the Kiddush!* It was not so long ago—yet her own lifetime ago! Her mother too wore

---

* Hebrew prayer recited over a cup of wine immediately before the dinner starting the Sabbath.

a wig like Mirele's, and she was known by all in the tenements on the East Side for her piety and charity.

How many times did she help poor families with food or rent money, while she went without a much-needed pair of new shoes, or dress, for some special holiday? And when Papa remonstrated, she laughed and said that she was dressed in gracious thankfulness to Him for seeing her fit to help His less fortunate children. When on a Saturday, or on a holiday, she went together with Papa to the synagogue how straight her back, and how high her head, and how serene her face was. Yes, just as Mirele carried herself even here, in this hellhole. Poor Papa was a fur worker, then he became a housepainter too, and tried to work at both trades so that when it was slow at one, he could work at the other. And with both of his trades, we had so little to eat.

And when he was but a young man of thirty-five, he was cut down by both trades that invaded his lungs with their poisoning dye, hairs, and lead, and he was forced to give them up. But he lived on a long time as if to see how Mama and the children will exist without his meager pay envelopes. Yes, he lived on as if to spite the Angel of Death's impatience, all the while spitting up his lungs and wasting away from day to day. He refused to die; hoping for some miracle that will provide food and shelter for his family until he lived to see poor Mama bringing home "bundles" from a blouse factory, and sit day and night over the machine, bent and pale, eking out a few dollars a week that barely satisfied their hunger and then he had decided to give up, and died.

What does Mirele with her self-righteous face know of troubles; what does she know of broken family life? Did her daughter Bena have to become a prostitute at the age of fourteen? And again she stuck the needle into a bleeding finger and "A black year on you," escaped through her dry, cracked lips.

But her thoughts continued to plague her and inwardly asked: would that bewigged woman understand why I was glad when the boss of the blouse factory, where I brought back the finished work, raped me? Yes, and when I left the stockroom, I held a fistful of money that was more than Mama made at the machine in two weeks. When she wanted to know where I got it, I told her that I had found it, and whenever I went back with the work, I prayed that he would take me to the stockroom again and do it to me. When Mama too began to cough like Papa did when he first took sick, the welfare society sent her to a home for consumptives, where she lived on only for three weeks. If only those bastards had left me in charge of the children, but no, they took them away to some home, far from the East Side, and I could not see them because I had no fare for the streetcar. And then the "good lady" from the welfare found a job for me in a button factory where, for 2 dollars a week, I sat counting and putting buttons into little boxes 10 hours a day. Was it my fault that I was unable to keep my mind on the work! Oh, how I longed for my family! I longed for them so badly, she remembered, that she felt lost most of the time, until Rivka, the "lady" of a "house" took pity on her and took her and made her one of her "girls."

Funny thing, she said to herself, I can't even remember what any of my sisters and brothers looked like any more, that is except Mama, but that's only because Mirele reminds me of her. I wish I knew what became of them, my little sisters and brothers, now grown men and women. No, no, I don't. What good would it do me or them now! I would not want them to see me as I am and look with pity at me. I don't need pity. I took care of myself before, and I will in the future. No, I don't want them to see me alone and half eaten up by syphilis.

She blew her nose noisily, and looked up to find Herschel standing near her. "Well, what do you want, why the hell are you standing here, why are you standing over me. I owe you something?"

"No, you don't owe me a thing, I just wanted to remind you that it is late. Do you want to stay here until tomorrow night? Look, there is not a soul in the place anymore, and you here still sitting there."

She looked around and saw the finishers' tables deserted, the machines covered, and the pressers' irons silenced. The silent loft looked strange. "Get away from me, go back where you come from. Why did you wait until now to tell me to go home? Your wife and children should wait for you a lifetime and you should not be able to go home? A black year on you and all those you love, bastard. Why were you waiting until now to remind me to go home? Was it because you wanted to play with me a while? You should play with the Angel of Death. I would not be touched by your dirty hands."

Herschel stood away from her, afraid of her curses, afraid to answer her. She was bursting with anger and anything he would say, and would bring on more and more.

Rosa gathered her tools and walked past him in the narrow hallway, nudging out a bolt of woolens here and there, causing some of the walls to give and fall to the floor. With a satisfied grin, she turned to look at the chaos she caused, and watched a while as Herschel silently got down on his knees and began the wearisome job of rebuilding the spaces in the walls that would probably take him half the night to finish.

23

Great expectations

THEIR ARMS LOADED DOWN with all sorts of packages, Mirele and Bena reached the fourth floor gasping for breath. All the way up they could hear and smell the preparations for the Sabbath in the tenement building. Mothers were heard screaming at their children to finish their chores and change into Sabbath clothes, while they themselves tasted their gefilte fish and chicken soup, that it should taste good enough for the angels. The smell of fresh-baked challah and sweet cakes permeated the entire building.

Bena unlocked the door to their apartment and kicked it open with one foot. "Only our house does not smell of good cooking and baking," she remarked.

"Don't feel so bad about it; in a week or so, your grandmother will make the house a home when she sets her foot into it, and you will get the cooked and the baked food along with the good smells," Mirele laughingly told her.

"If you are trying to console me, better tell me that when the family arrives, and Papa and Rachel find jobs, and you will forget the shop and become the housekeeper, instead of grandmother. You know that Doctor Friedman told you to rest, nay, that you must rest, and even in the house you should not overdo it. Mother are you listening to me, or am I talking to myself?" Bena said in anger.

Mirele was busy at the large round kitchen table opening the packages and tried not to answer her daughter.

Tuesday at the crack of dawn found both awake, but not wanting to disturb each other they pretended to be asleep. Bena inwardly cursed herself for sharing her mother's bed that night; had she slept in her own, she could now get up and stretch her limbs to the full and not feel imprisoned against her will. Furtively, she looked at her mother and with an aching heart saw how white her hair had become, and the color of her skin so sallow. They will not recognize her, she is so changed, she thought, and a deep sigh escaped her, compelling her mother to open her eyes.

"Did you have a bad dream that you sighed so? Today is the day for happiness, let us get up and begin to enjoy it."

Bena seeing that urging her to go back to sleep will be futile, jumped out of the bed, and they both began to dress. "It's good that we are getting up this early, why should we sleep away the very day we waited so long for?" Mirele said laughingly and with a forced slowness put the coffee on to boil.

They ate with a slowness that bespoke the lie of their desire to begin their journey, knowing well that it was much too early to think of it. Bena cocked her head and listened, and then went to the door, and turned to her mother, "Yes, it is for us they are calling. Who can it be so early in the morning?"

A shadow fell on both of them as Bena ran to answer the telephone in the candy store. She took the receiver with trembling hands and with a quivering voice asked who it was. A man's voice shouted into her ear, "If this is Mrs. Poil, it's about time you came to answer the phone. Now listen, this is the company that sold you the tickets for your family, and if you remember, a brother of yours suggested that you pay us an additional 5 dollars, which you did, so that we will send an agent to take them off the boat. He will clear all the information so that you need not go there. I called to make sure that you will be home to receive them when he brings them home. Understand? Good-bye." Bena heard the click before she could ask anything from him. She stood with the receiver in her hand, her face showing disappointment. Then she saw her mother standing near her looking with misgivings at the earpiece. Quickly she hung it back into place and led her out of the store, telling her what she had been told.

"Is that all? I was worried that you got some bad news, what upsets you so? Thank God they are safe, and now I remember that we did make those arrangements; my brother Schmuel thought it would be better than if we should have to answer all sorts of questions." Although Mirele sounded as if she made light of the changed plans, the day hung around them like heavy chains. Every bit of noise in the building, a child calling or crying, people walking the stairs, brought them quickly to their feet, and to the door.

Joe the iceman was making the rounds in the tenement building with the wooden tubful of ice on one shoulder and remembered that he owed the missus, as he called his women customers, some change, and knocked on the door to give it to her now. Within a second the door was flung wide open and he was confronted with two wild-eyed, excited women. "Wazza matter, you need ice already again?" but they only shook their heads and looked blank at him. "Here is the change I didn't have yesterday for you," and he counted nickels and dimes into Mirele's palm, wondering at her woeful face.

"You know, whenever you and grandma became desperate, she used to say that 'before we reach our goal, we lose our soul,' and that's how I feel right now. It is almost four o'clock and they are still somewhere on the way," Bena complained to her mother.

Just then, had they lived in a front apartment, and would have either in expectation or boredom looked down from their window, they would have seen the fallacy of Chaya's byword. For right down in the middle of that street, not on the sidewalk, led by a tall man carrying the biggest of their bundles on his back, was the goal of Mirele's entire being. But they did not see them through a window, and so missed the joy at the sight of them, but in compensation for that, they were spared the misery of calling for them at the "Isle of Tears".*

---

* A well-known reference to Ellis Island, in New York Harbor, where millions of immigrants arrived and were processed in its heyday between 1892 and the First World War. Hundreds of thousands were deported, mainly for health or political reasons.

24

Isle of Tears

HAD THEY GONE THERE as they planned, they would have had to witness Avraham's fears of stepping onto the new land. He looked so upset that the children and his mother-in-law panicked that he would not pass the doctor's examinations. Chaya tried to keep the children away from him and let him rest, but that only seemed to increase his anxiety. Chaya's eyes were roving all over the people and saw many adults and children turned back to their native lands because of some illness or eye disease. Many families were broken up, families that went with little to eat to get to the "Promised Land." Fear struck her when at last they called out their names to go to the doctor's room. She was sure that if Isaiah with his green, emaciated face will pass, her son-in-law will not. They walked into a large room with many partitioned booths and were told to wait until their names were called again. This room was noisy, with children crying and excited parents talking loud and fast as if to drown out their nervous heartbeats.

At last Avraham was called into one of the little booths and Chaya and the children remained waiting, for they were next. Suddenly she became aware of an adult sobbing, and turned to find in a corner of the room her ship friend Leike. Her first impulse was to run to help her, but seeing that her head was buried into her tall, strong husband's chest, she remained standing in her place with a thundering in her head. "Rachel, I am afraid something happened to that family. Look she is crying like she lost all hope. You stand here and I will go over to them." She released Raphael's hand, linking it with hers.

"No, Grandma, don't go," Rachel begged her. "If there is trouble with them, there is nothing you can do about it, and they may not even want anyone to bother them now. Besides, the doctor may call any of us soon, and I would not know what to do or say there." Chaya became angry at being stopped, but Rachel's fear of being left alone with the children held her back, muttering, "You are all afraid that I'll carry off the teat."

Chaya liked Leike, who she met on the boat, and they became good friends immediately. Chaya would mind her little boy when she wanted to go with her husband to another part of the ship, or wanted to rest. They told each other the lives they lived and they expected to live in the new land. Chaya was entranced by the young couple's life, the resistance they had to put up against his pious parents, who wanted him to divorce her because she was not able to bear him a child!

Although the couple were brought together in the usual manner by a *shadkhan*, they fell in love with each other on first sight, and nothing but death would part them. They became husband, wife, and parents to each other at the same time. She mothered the big, lumbering red-bearded man, as if he was a helpless little boy, catering to his every whim. He would carry her around in his strong arms and laughingly tease her about one thing or another.

It was at one such time while he carried her around and laughed because she had burnt some bread she baked, that he felt a movement in her thin little body, and in bewilderment asked her about it. "Now," she laughed, "you are really making fun at me. Did you really think that at forty-two I was going to have a child? Do you think I am the biblical Sarah, who gave birth to a child at ninety?"

But four months later she gave birth to a tiny baby, and a man-child! Their happiness was without bounds. Now the four-year-old boy grew tall and strong, they decided to leave the backwardness of his parents, and the poverty they suffered, and go where they would be able to raise him in the country that holds forth so much opportunity.

Chaya's thoughts were interrupted by a call for the two boys. Quickly she took each by a hand, and was about to enter the doctor's booth, when a young man stepped in and told her that he was sent to see that they come through all the examinations, and take care of their belongings, and then bring them to their home. He told her to wait outside the booth, that he will go in with the boys, and with a sense of distrust, she walked back to where the girls stood and consoled herself with the fact that the man was a Jew, and he would not do them any harm.

She stood a long time waiting before she decided to ignore Rachel's fears of remaining without her and quickly walked over to Leike, who had run out of tears and now stood with a wooden face, holding on to her child's hand. "Where is your husband?" she asked, and the little boy answered that his papa went to get something to eat for him. Not wanting to leave without knowing what tragedy they are living through, she tried to draw her friend out of her numbness, and soon learned that she was turned back because they found something wrong with her lungs. "What are you saying?" Chaya shouted with alarm. "How could they tell you such thing? Didn't they examine you before you came aboard the ship and found you to be in good health?" she wrung her hands in sorrow, while Leike stood looking as if she had turned to stone and told her that now they must all go back, although her husband and child can go through into the country, but they refuse to do so without her.

Again the young woman broke down and cried with a hopeless bitterness, and the child not knowing why she cried so much, cried too. Chaya stood in misery without being able to offer her friend one word of consolation, not one word! She stood rooted to the spot, forgetting the children, forgetting that she was anxious about Isaiah, and stood trying to find something to lessen her friend's agitation. But what could she say to her when so many of her dreams were ended. How can one go on living without some hope?

Adah tugged at her sleeve and told her that they were called and that she must hurry back. Chaya went, telling her friend that she will see her as soon as she is finished "in there." Inside the doctor's booth she was surprised to hear the doctor asking the children questions in Yiddish and begged him to do something for her friend, who was rejected because she has a little something not so good with her lungs.

The doctor smiled and told her that if all the troubles on this island were just a little, it would be much pleasanter to work here. This did not satisfy her, and she pressed him to examine her himself, "Who knows maybe a young doctor did the examination, and he does not know to what troubles he is putting that family, I am sure that if a man with your experience looked her over, you would very soon find the mistake!" Her eyes begged him, her soft wrinkled skin tried hard to smile, but only succeeded to break her up into tears.

"My good woman," the doctor said, "I was the 'young' doctor that rejected her, if you mean that little woman with the handsome four-year-old boy. There is nothing I or any other doctor could do for her now, she is sicker than she knows. Please take a seat, I want to examine your chest."

Chaya was a bundle of nerves, her mind was on the two boys, her son-in-law, and Leike, and the doctor heard the nervous pounding of her heart with understanding and passed her, along with the two girls.

Avraham and the boys were waiting for while "that young man" went to get their baggage off the boat, and when Chaya looked at them, she saw that they were ready to enter America.

Soon they were on the way out of the "Isle of Tears," Chaya with a bitterness in her mouth because she was unable to see Leike again. No matter how much and to how many people she appealed, she could not see her, not even to say good-bye. For her to leave without seeing the little family again was to cloud the happiness she felt on entering America, this long-awaited day. The young man carrying the largest of their bundles was followed by the family into a horse-drawn streetcar, where the passengers looked at them with smiles and understanding. Chaya turned to Avraham and said, "Look, not one antisemite," and although he wanted to agree with her, said instead, "No, because they are probably all Jews themselves." She sniffed with dissatisfaction and turned back to the children.

The streetcar ran along Avenue C and when it reached 3rd Street, the young man told the conductor to let them off. Some of the passengers helped them with the bundles from the floor, but were not thanked for their troubles by the shy children nor their father, but Chaya, always in search of the milk of human kindness, not only thanked them, but flashed her warm smile too. They crossed over to the north side of 3rd Street and followed their guide toward Avenue D. The street was full of children, pushcarts piled high with fruit, vegetables, and dry goods lined the two sides of the street. Although the sun was brilliant, making the pre-spring day a welcome sight, on this street it did not show its face; the tenement houses, five stories high, shut it out, and most of the windows and fire escapes were laden with airing bedding.

"Why do we have to walk on the road instead of the sidewalk?" Avraham asked his guide, and the young man smiled and said that they are saving time on the roadway because the sidewalks are too crowded. If the sidewalk was crowded, so was the road, and more so. Horse-drawn wagons laden with commodities for home and trade tangled with children dancing to the music of a hurdy-gurdy. Men pushing tin ovens shouted, "Sweet potatoes, sweet potatoes, a penny and two." Bags of garbage lay along the gutters and children made play kicking them around into the road. Strong black horses laden with beer and wine barrels drove by.

Adah and the two boys were wide-eyed with the wonder of it all, but Rachel only looked at the girls dancing, many her own age, and her steps were in time with the music. She looked at them with a wish to join them, and in her fervor, collided with anyone that came near her. At last, their "Moses" found the number of the house and signified for them to follow. This was not easy to do as they were in the middle of the block and the pushcarts that lined the street did not allow much passageway, but with a little shouting at each other, the venders moved their "stores" a little and let them go through, shouting after them laughingly, "Greenhorns!"

They came to a doorway that was flanked by a candy store on one side and a butcher store on the other. The front little foyer boasted brightly polished brass boxes on the facing wall, with what looked like a little button at the end of a nameplate on each one. They stood and watched their leader push one such button and soon heard a fast clicking in answer. "Come on, they are waiting for you, let's go a little faster," he ordered with a smile that lit up his face for the first time since they were in his company.

25

Mirele's goal - I

"MAMA, THEY ARE HERE, you stay upstairs, I will go down to meet them," Bena said, as she ran down the stairway, legs almost giving way under her in her excitement. She met them on the second landing, and was immediately surrounded by the entire family, that is, almost the entire family, for Rachel could not contain herself any longer and ran up the stairs to her mother and flinging herself into her arms, cried, "My beautiful mother, at last I see you again. I could not wait much longer. I would have died if we didn't come to America now. It was so hard to pass the days without you, to fall asleep at night was the hardest, I was afraid that I will die in my sleep and never see you again." She sobbed.

"And for me it was easy to wait so long until I would see you again?" Mirele tried to calm her excited child all the while fondling her head and kissing her.

Bena came up with the rest of the family, and because the neighbors crowded around them so, they made their way into the house before they had a chance to embrace each other. The young man who guided them all day just put his bundle down on the kitchen floor and left the house silently and unnoticed.

Mirele was so overcome with joy that she did not know who to greet first, but ran from one to the other, hugging this one, that one, her wig askew and her face flushed. She looked at Avraham's hair and beard, which had turned completely white, and remarked, "You, too, and I thought that only my hair turned grey so fast." At her mother she looked with some wonder, for in her, she saw little change. If her back did not show a bit more bend, she would find no change in her at all despite the hardships she left her with. Her eyes still held the same brilliant sparkle and were full of mirth.

"Mother, how do you do it? How do you manage to keep so young, or don't you want to give away your secret?" and she was happy that her mother did not show the wear and tear of the two years' struggle.

Then she took her children close to her and examined each one carefully. When she saw Adah's rounded body and flushed face, she hugged her once more, and turned her attention to the two boys. She was disturbed by their slow growth and thin bodies, and Isaiah's bad color gave her grave concern, but she thought to herself, "I'll not worry now, because I know that they did not eat to the full while they grew, but now I will stuff them like geese to make up for it and they will grow tall and strong. She hugged them to her, and felt her youngest child rebuff her closeness, and she let them go.

Rachel did not leave her mother's side, she hovered around her like a shadow, never far away, and she saw her mother's look of confusion when Raphael tensed his little body against hers. "Don't mind that little shy goat, he does that with everyone that wants to be his friend." Mirele watched him go to his father and link his hand into his, and followed him around the house. "That poor child looks like a lost soul, is it any wonder he pushed me from him, he does not even remember having had a mother."

Adah looked at the round kitchen table that was laden with so much food and covered with a white tablecloth on a mere weekday! On a tray piled high were white rolls, some with poppy seeds all over their tops, others braided and shining with egg white that browned them to pleasing crust, and the smell of the rest of the food made her hungry.

Another thing that raised her curiosity were dresses that hung from the bedroom door. Beautiful dresses, they looked like they could be worn at weddings, and she did not hear anyone say that they are, so they must be for Sabbath wear for Rachel and herself! She could not tear herself away from the vivid prints that looked so soft and inviting to the touch.

"How many more times will Mama have to call you to the table?" Rachel asked her, and she became aware that she was the only one not seated, and took her place near Bena, giving her a tight hug. What a meal! It looked to her indeed like a wedding feast. On a weekday, chicken soup and chicken? But what are those glasses with cloudy water her mother told them to drink?

Mama placed a plateful of cut-up oranges and told them to eat them as soon as they drank the Epsom salts. It was indeed bitter to swallow, and they all kicked up a big fuss, but finished and grabbed at the oranges as if for life preservers.

Grandma Chaya laughed, and wished them all that this bitterness should be the only one they should know of the rest of their lives, and from now on they should be only sweet. The drink never the less spoiled Adah's holiday mood, even though it ended up with baked apples and cake for dessert. A constant stream of information went on at the table, both sides giving news about family and friends.

Avraham stealthily looked at his wife and sighed deeply. She looked so different, her skin once so fair was now yellowish, the stars that glittered in her large brown eyes looked spent in spite of her present excitement. In the hugging and kissing so many of her loved ones, her wig came askew and he saw that her hair was all white too; however, she still carried herself straight, her head high, and her abdomen still stuck out a wee bit.

Mirele caught his glances at her and turned her head away like a shy girl, but felt the happiness of her younger days when her husband used to say that he "drank" her beauty with his eyes. When they were finished with the meal, Avraham and the boys remained at the table to say grace for the food, their sing-song filling the home with the benediction.

Chaya looked at her daughter, and saw a smile of contentment on her face, and felt the security of her children and silently thanked the Lord. Later they sat in the "front room," which was as a rule preserved for special occasions in America, such as weddings, parties, and funerals. But in the poorer homes they also served as bedrooms at night. Beds that stood covered and folded behind doors all day would open to use at night. Mirele's front room was "pretty" as Adah named it: the two windows were hung with lace curtains, the newly bought furniture was highly polished and the imitation fruit looked real, in the cut-glass bowl that stood at the center of the table.

Avraham was attracted to a bookcase that held a set of books of poems by Morris Rosenfeld, the Jewish labor poet, and wondered who in the house was able to read them. The boys stood at one of the windows and looked down into the "canyon" four stories below and sorely wished that they could spit down and see how far their spittle would go. At Bena's insistence, Mirele sat in the rocking chair and rested while she watched the activities in her house that was so full now. Avraham stood with a book of the poems in his hand and then put it into Adah's hand, asking her to read from it. She looked at the page he held open for her and for the first time saw anything written in verse, with form that ended in rhythm. She had never seen it written so, although she heard her sister recite many poems without knowing how and why they were so formulated.

She bent her head over the book and read with fascination, her father feeling pride in her. She walked into the kitchen with the book and sat at the table pouring over it, enthralled by the sound of it. The boys came in, and stood watching her face for a while, then got tired of the meaninglessness of what she read, and began to imitate her in a sing-song manner. This gave them some release for their restlessness and they shouted with laughter, which brought their father's threat of punishment, and they quieted down for a while.

"Mother, you remember that you have a brother-in-law in America, don't you?" And when she saw her mother's wrinkled brow in bewilderment, Mirele went on. "He is my father's brother Ephraim, don't you remember him?"

Now Chaya became interested and shook her head, remarking slowly, "So many years have passed, so many years! That's right, he ran away to this country when the children were still young."

"Well, let me tell you about them. Uncle Ephraim is as tall and strong as a tree and works very hard, but Aunt Gittel passed a little more than a year ago, may God rest her soul. Mother, I have seen religious people in my life time, but she was a saint. How that tiny body of hers could withstand so much fasting and prayers, no one knew. She lived on so little food, it was a wonder she lived this long. Her fear for the non-kosher foods kept her away from most of it, and she lived mainly on the bread she baked herself and hot tea. She foretold her death that very day.

"Friday afternoon, she asked the girls to wash her body clean, as she knew that this was her last day on earth, and then she sat and prayed until it was time to light and bless her candles, and as she finished, she turned to the wall and was no more. At her funeral it became known how much charity she gave to the poor in the neighborhood, for when they came to the funeral, they cried bitterly for her. The street was packed with so many mourners, as if a rabbi had died. Now Ephraim is remarried, and the children ran from his house, they cannot see their father give his new wife a smile and when he says a kind word to her, they feel as if it's an insult to their mother. Two of the married girls took in to their house one boy and the youngest girl, but the youngest boy, well, he is really not a boy anymore, he is about twenty-two years old, does not want to live anywhere else, except here, with us."

"He begged me to take him in even if he had to sleep on the floor. I expect him tonight and do not know what to tell him." She looked at Avraham, her eyes questioning him.

"It seems to me that you should be glad to offer him your home," he told her, feeling that she wanted his approval.

In the evening while they were at their supper, there was a knock on the door, and before anyone answered it, it opened and a young man dressed in a blue serge suit walked in.

"Simon, come in, come in, we talked about you today. Meet my family and sit down and join us with supper." Mirele showed her joy with having her cousin with them, while he came close to the table, smiling broadly at them, and stretched out a hand to Avraham and bid him, "*Shalom aleichem.*" Avraham's face creased into smiles, and he returned an "*Aleichem shalom.*"

The children "took" to their American cousin immediately. They were drawn to his broad smile and warm personality. But Chaya sat looking at him with a puzzling expression, then thought, It is almost a half a century, but I could swear it was him. His crop of black curly hair that makes him look taller than he is, his laughing eyes and bright smile with the dimples playing around his mouth when he talks. He looks so much like my departed Simon, he makes me feel as if he had risen from the dead, and forgetting herself, she added, murmuring, "Like an apple cut in half, the likeness is that close." Rachel who sat near her wanted to know what she meant, but she only shook her head and stared at Simon.

Simon, why even his name was the same, and she was happy that he will be their houseguest.

26

Mirele's goal – II

THURSDAY MORNING, Simon was going to take the children to register in school so that they could begin their education at once. Simon had "doctor's hours," as Mirele called his work schedule. He did not have to go to the store where he worked as a luggage salesman before noon, as he worked until 11 p.m. at night.

Mirele pulled out a large carton from underneath the bed and took from it new dresses, pants, socks, and shirts for the boys and girls. The children stood around her with wonder in their eyes, watching her as she handed them out and telling them to put them on. The girls looked at each other and with little cries of joy slipped their dresses on quickly and ran to the mirror. The boys dressed in their new clothes looked lost, but without knowing it, were pleased that they too had new clothes.

"Come here, Avraham, look I guessed their sizes, well not all their sizes, Raphael's knee pants are a little too long and Isaiah's are a little too wide, but don't worry, they will soon grow into them." She looked around and found that she was talking to herself, and went to the front room to look for Avraham and found him in his prayer shawl and phylacteries standing in silent prayer. Knowing that she could not interrupt him now, she asked Simon to wait a while because she wanted their father to see them all dressed up before they go.

Through all the noise of the tenement—a mixture of utensils, and mothers screaming at children, and babies crying—was also a call to the telephone in the candy store, for someone of the Poil house.

Simon ran down, and was back within a few minutes, saying that he was unable to take the children to school because his boss was taken sick and he must run now to open the store. Mirele's children stood around looking crestfallen and Mirele cried, "Don't stand around feeling so woeful, the sky did not fall to the ground yet. I will take you myself, just wait until I get into my better clothes, we must make a good impression for the principal there. I too am anxious to go, this will be the first time I will be inside a school." She dressed while she spoke to them, not to keep them waiting too long.

When they emerged from the tenement hallway, a stiff cold breeze was blowing from the East River, and they had to pull the coat collars against it. The air was dry and stiff and smelled of fresh cucumbers. Men and women on their way to work carried lunches in brown bags, some already showing grease coming through. Children spilled out of the houses in small and larger groups, all shouting for one reason or another, pulling the caps off their friends' heads and finding ways to make the girls shy away from their rough play. While the girls held their books tightly under their arms, the boys were not even conscious of theirs, and a good many landed into the gutter. Windows facing the street opened, dustmops were shaken over the heads of passersby and bedding was put out to be aired. Mothers were heard instructing their young to be careful at the street crossing, to hold their books tight in their arms, not to lose their handkerchiefs, and a stream of other injunctions went on until the children were out of their mothers' sight.

Mirele and her excited flock had to push their way to the school through a noisy babbling wall of children, then they were led by a monitor to the principal's office and told to sit and wait until the clerk will call them. They sat for quite a while, looking at the charts hanging from the white-painted walls, the plants that crowded each other on the windowsills, and the rigid school furniture. Miss Ryan, the clerk, came in and asked Mirele to sit near her desk, then asked her many questions, which she answered with some difficulty because she did not fully understand what was asked. Now and then the clerk repeated something and the children saw their mother turn red with the effort of answering. Soon they witnessed a struggle between the two, the clerk trying hard to convince their mother of something and she holding her ground with determination, just shaking her head in dissent.

Miss McFeenie, the school principal, on the way to her inner office, glanced at the two women and saw their agitation and stopped at the clerk's desk. "What is it, Miss Ryan?" she asked without looking at Mirele.

"Miss McFeenie, I am trying to induce this parent to change the names of her children from the Hebrew to the American, but she refuses."

Mirele felt Miss McFeenie's keen steel-blue cold eyes bore through hers, but she looked into them bravely.

"Mother, don't you want your children to be Americans?" she asked crisply.

"Yes, I want them to be Americans, but you see, my husband just came with them two days ago, and he would not understand, and I want him to like everything in this country, don't you see?" she pleaded with her. "Please let them be with the names they brought from home."

The cold blue eyes, although still piercingly on Mirele, began to soften and soon give way. With a nod of her head to Miss Ryan, she walked into her own office.

Mirele felt her victory, but was not happy with it. Sure, she won the round, and Avraham will not be able to be critical of America, but will the children lose by it? While the clerk was busy with the enrollment sheets, Mirele's mind dwelled on the harm that the children may suffer holding on to their own names. She remembered that she heard her Jewish neighbors calling their children, Ike, Mike, Irene, Sammy, and Rosie, and didn't her own brother Schmuel change his to Sam? And didn't he change all his children's names too, for American names? American, yes, that's what Miss McFeenie meant, the children become American beginning with their names. She touched the clerk's hand who looked up questioningly, and said to her, "Forgive me, I was thinking it over, what Miss McFeenie said to me, and please may I ask you, maybe if you just changed their last name, it would make them Americans too?" she looked at her pleadingly.

"Well, I already changed the last name, from 'Poil' to 'Pearl,' because

I felt that it would sound better, and people will be able to pronounce it without difficulty," she told her with confidence.

"What, you changed our name without asking me about it first? Maybe I don't like to change from ours to another name?" she asked in anger.

"But you just told me that you want your children to be Americans, didn't you? And you even asked me right now to change your last name. Look, lady, you must make up your mind, I can't spend the whole day with you, I have other people waiting for me."

Mirele saw how mad she became, and felt that she better leave it as it is, for who knows, if she bothered her much longer, she might take it out on the children later, and remembered that she still carries around her fears of the Russian schools for the Jewish students.

"This is America, and I feel sure that what you did is best for my children, and I want to thank you very much," and she raised herself from the chair, all the while looking at the puzzled face of the clerk.

She turned to her children and with a happy smile said to them, "Now you are all Americans, not by your first names, but by your second, but it really makes no difference, just so nobody is hurt by it." The children were not sure that they understood her, but as long as she looked happy, they were too. "Mama, what is our last name now?" Rachel asked.

"That lady at the desk changed it from Poil to Pearl," she pronounced it with the "r" rolling in her mouth, "and it means *perl*, like those that a woman wears around her neck," she explained to them.

"That's America for you, at home our name meant in Russian *workman*, and here in this country it is a precious jewel." Rachel laughed with gaiety.*

---

* The family name in Kamenets-Podolski was Poil, which does not mean *workman* in any of the local languages. It is not possible to know what was meant here.

27

Mirele's goal – III

FRIDAY AFTERNOON FOUND BOTH Mirele AND her mother tidying up the kitchen of the many pots and pans they cooked and baked in all morning, but the good smells still hung in the air so heavy one could almost touch them. Nay, not hung, clung and battling would be more like it. And a battle it was! The sweet butter cakes had ganged up with the fresh-baked challahs that stood seven braids high and were sprinkled with poppy seeds, baked to a golden crust against the large platter of gefilte fish with a round of carrot on each portion giving off its spicy bouquet that found itself in alliance with the roasted duck and meat that boasted its piquant garlicky repute quite strongly. And one must not forget the golden chicken soup that cooked slowly on a low fire, with soup greens and soft dill to give it a heavenly flavor. But all in all, the battle for supremacy for the outstanding emanation got lost, because they became mixed up in each other in the battle and pervaded the house, then forced themselves through the smallest cracks in the door and soon joined the cooking aromas of the neighbors up and down the halls, wherever the Sabbath meals were in preparations.

Mirele glanced at the clock and looked worried. Twenty minutes past three and the children were not home from school yet. But she did not say anything and waited, not wanting to worry her mother who looked so contented as she went about her work. She knew well the satisfaction her mother drew from seeing so much food in the house and had to urge her time and again to use more of the ingredients in the cooking and baking, and begged her not to worry, that there was more where this came from.

"I feel as if I were a squanderer, God forgive me, I did not see so much food in one kitchen since I came in unexpectedly to Nahama's kitchen back home. But you know, my daughter, that it is easier to get used to plenty than to poverty," she laughed.

Three-thirty and Mirele opened the door to listen for her children and she heard steps coming up, but they were slow and of one person.

She walked out into the hallway and peered over the stairwell and saw Avraham coming up holding onto the banister and breathing very hard. "Why are you standing out here in the hall?" he asked her.

"I thought I heard the children, I wonder why they are not home yet."

They went into the house, but before they closed the door, they heard Rachel's voice, and she ran out to meet them and saw that Isaiah was not with them.

"Mama," Rachel began crying, but Adah told her mother that they waited at the place they had agreed to meet, and he did not show up, then added soothingly, "Anyhow he can't get lost, he has his card with his name and address hanging around his neck, so if he will not find his way, he will ask someone to direct him. Anyhow, we could not wait there any longer, we had to bring Raphael home, he needs to go to the toilet."

Instead of going into the toilet in the hallway, he began to cry. "What is wrong with you?" Rachel shouted at him, but he ran away from her and ran into the house, throwing his coat down and slipped to the floor sobbing.

Avraham bent over him and tried to find the reason for his misery, but did not succeed. "Tell me, tell your mother, does anything hurt you? I thought you said that you had to go to the toilet, why don't you go?"

Mirele petted his head, his shoulders, his hands, and then came in contact with something wet, and at once understood his unhappiness. "You wanted to go to the toilet in school, didn't you? But you didn't know how to tell your teacher, you poor soul, but don't worry, someday you will speak English better than her. Wait, I will get you dry pants." She kissed his head, went to look at the clock and, leaving him to change, pulled on her coat and left the house.

Once outside, she did not know where to turn, but walked to the school, finding the building and yard empty of children that she could get information from. She went to a candy store, and from there called Simon, spilling her fears into the telephone, and begged him to come home and find her child.

"You go home, and I will leave right now and search for him, and Mirele, don't worry, such bargains you can find plenty in America, and if anyone stole him, they will soon bring him back." A little cheered, she went back to the house.

Simon decided to go to the police station nearest their home, and as he mounted its steps, his eyes strayed to a window that faced onto the sidewalk, almost on the street level—and lo and behold, there was Isaiah, sitting on a desk, wearing a policemen's hat, reading a Jewish newspaper to some of the officers that stood around him! He jumped up the stairs two at a time and inside informed the sergeant that the boy downstairs was his lost cousin.

"Oh, yeah, how do I know he is your cousin?" the officer wanted to know.

"Well, he can tell you, can't he?"

"He can, hey? No one can make head or tail of what he is jabbering about, but go down, the men down there will know soon enough."

And they did, for as soon as Isaiah saw Simon, he shouted with great excitement, "Simon, you got lost too?"

"No smart guy, I didn't get lost too. I had to leave my work to go out to look for you. Why didn't you ask someone to show you how to get to the house if you couldn't find your way?"

"How could I ask someone to show me where I live when I didn't know where I live myself?" he answered, his black eyes danced with mirth.

"What became of the card I told you to wear, that carried your name and address? I do not see it on you."

"Oh, that card? I threw it away, I didn't want anyone to know that I am a greenhorn, looking like a cow with a bell around her neck, and you know what Simon? As soon as I threw it away, I right away felt like an American, just like you," he said it with an earnest mien.

"All right, we better go home now, your mother is at her wits' end and I think your father would like to remind you that you are still a greenhorn with a strap over your behind. Come along."

The policemen stood by and listened to their conversation and watched Isaiah's animated face and black eyes dancing, and smiled, then took the hat off him and gave him the three bagels that they offered him before.

When they walked out, the March snow was quickly descending, and the Jews in the community were already on the way to the synagogue to usher in Sabbath.

Simon hurried along, pulling the boy along with him, anxious to set all at home at ease.

28

Avraham the scribe is here

T HE FAMILY WENT TO THE SABBATH services in the Kamenetzer shul on Attorney Street. It was quite a distance from their home, and on the way Mirele, walking between her husband and mother, told them how the landslayt, those men and women who came from their hometown, built it with their own hard-earned money.

"It took a long time until we saw it finished. The monies came from many, many heads of families, but in small amounts, because of slack shop seasons, and because they had to have money with which to send for their families. Of course, we had some help from some of our townspeople who gave generously because they had it, but they are so rich now that they moved all the way up to the Bronx, and of course cannot ride on the Sabbath, so they do not even show their faces into the synagogue they helped to build."

They reached the house of prayer before the services began and found themselves surrounded by friends that Avraham and Chaya had not seen for many years.

Word got around that "Avraham the scribe is here," and more and more worshippers came to shake his hand and bid him welcome, and Mirele stood away to a side, her heart thumping with a great happiness. She looked on as her husband, mother, and children were greeted with the warmth and felicity accorded long-lost friends. The children were asked many questions, while they were kissed and petted. She invited everyone that she spoke to, begging them to come later in the day to their home where they will be able to really be together and will have a chance to make Avraham feel at home in America.

A heavy hand sounded on the lectern calling the congregation to their seats, and the women left for the curtained balcony. Avraham looked around from his seat between his two sons and found friendly eyes upon him, smiled back at them, feeling some of his resistance to America slipping.

Early in the afternoon friends and *landslayt* filled the house to over-flowing, bringing much talk about their families and asking questions about those they knew "back home." As they came, so were they seated around the table in the front room, upon which stood bottles of wine, cakes of many forms and taste, as well as fruit. When all the space around the table was occupied, the latecomers stood around those that were seated, and soon the room was so crowded, that it was hard to breathe in it. The women remained in the kitchen and the children got underfoot no matter where they found themselves. The house was thick with noise, everyone was talking and no one could hear what was being said. Everybody was eager to tell his story, ask his question, but no one succeeded because the tumult was too great.

"Listen," Chaya made herself heard, "listen to the men in there, and if you ask them, they tell you that we women talk too much."

Kolmin-Dodya's wife Gittel sat near the table at which Chaya stood slicing oranges for the children, and laughingly answered her, "Well why should we deny that women talk more than men? We do, and there are many reasons for it. But right now, they really have a lot to catch up with, and I do not think that the day will be long enough for them. They are trying to build a bridge between Kamenets-Podolski and New York. They can't forget the old world and cannot yet feel at home in the new. Let them talk, they will find themselves."

Chaya nodded her head with understanding and smilingly said, "I do not have to have a bridge; where there is bread for me, that's where my world is. I lived to see so many of my dear ones through this door today that I am drunk with happiness. Just imagine, when did

I dream of seeing my daughter Hannah's daughter Hovilla, or Sima and Velvl, and you and your Kolmin-Dodya, and all those *landslayt*? Still a human being sins; with all this gladness, I push the day so that in the evening I should be able to see my Schmuel and his family, may God forgive a sinful mother."

The evening brought more people, those that lived far and had to travel, but had to wait for the first star to appear in the heavens before they could board a vehicle to transport them from their homes. The very last to come was Schmuel and his family because they had to travel all the way from Brownsville with the train. Tears and joy filled the house as they all entwined one another in their arms.

Chaya wanted to pull her son into a quiet corner, she wanted to ask him so many questions, but every room was full of people, and she just had to be satisfied with looking at him and his family, and kissing them again and hugging them again! She barely recognized the older children and the younger ones she never saw before, because they were born in America.

Mirele sat at Avraham's side, but did not take part in the conversations around her. She just looked on, listening to what was being said or questioned while she watched the animated faces of her guests. When Avraham lost the thread of something someone had said, he turned to her, and she would just smile at him sympathetically as if to say, "It will soon be over, and I will explain." Many times she caught a fleeting glance from him, a warm, caring glance, and she blushed like a young girl. She felt as pretty inside of her as his glance told her she did, outside.

She wore a lace-trimmed black dress, with balloon-shaped sleeves that were tight at the wrists, and the high lace collar held up by whale bone gave her comely face the look of a flower. Her hand went up to her wig often; she still felt guilty about the wig, because it was not the full type she used to wear, but a partial. If only Avraham had said something to her about it, or had asked her why she did not wear the full one, then she could tell him of the head-burnings she suffered and that the doctor told her to discard the wig altogether and that she could not bring herself to do it, even though the partial sat on the very spot that burned.

At last the house began to empty of their well-wishers, and the house once more returned to its occupants.

Beds were opened and the children sank into them with groans of relief. Chaya, Bena, and Rachel were busy cleaning up, while Mirele and Avraham still sat in the front room and drank tea, letting the din in their ears dissipate.

"It was a good day for us was it not?" Mirele ventured.

"Yes, it was a good day, but I wish there was less talk and more to hear. I know that with so many people in the house, it's hard to have a heart-to-heart talk, but I cannot put together the little bits of conversation that drifted across the room," he told her with a smile.

"Well, it won't be so long now and you will meet these families one at a time and then you will learn so much more from them that you want to know, and you will then understand them better."

She got up from the table and wheeled out their bed from behind the door, and began to slip its cover off. Avraham's eyes followed her every motion with a puzzled frown which she noticed, and suddenly a wall sprang up between them. She slowed her movements and he began to recite prayers.

"Mother, do you still need the light in the kitchen?" Bena asked, then added, "We want to go to sleep, and I already put the boys into Simon's bed, and the light seems to disturb Isaiah."

"Turn it out, I do not need it." Mirele sounded dull. Inside the front room the air was thick with unspoken words between the husband and wife.

Avraham wondered why his wife was so affectionate when others were around them, and as soon as they were alone, she drew within herself, and looked almost afraid of him. Why? She called him to come to her, and looked to be happy with him, but only when others were around them! He undressed and laid down beside her, and felt her move away from him, slowly, but he felt it. He moved closer to her, and again she shrank away from him.

"Mirele what is wrong with you?" he whispered to her, and not getting an answer, put his arm around her waist and drew her to him, but she remained stiff and remote. He took his arm off her and tried to go to sleep, then heard her sighing, and again turned to her, this time without touching her.

"Mirele, this is the fifth night that I sleep with you, I am your husband not a stranger, why do you keep yourself away from me? We cannot go on like this, we are still young people. I longed for you all the years you were away from me, and now you make a stranger of me. If there is some reason for it, I want to know?"

She sat up, and in the dark, peered into his face, and said, "Yes, there is a reason, but I want you to treat it with understanding," and she bent closer to him and whispered, "Avraham I do not want another child."

He was silent a moment and then answered, "That's not for us to decide, such things are in the hands of God."

A long silence, then she spoke again, "In America, the women don't have children every year if they don't want them. There are ways to prevent pregnancies."

"Mirele, you know as well as I do that people of our faith, those that live and follow in God's ways, do not waste their seed, or is that new to you?" he questioned her.

"I know that, but I have to go to the shop and work, and I will not be able to do so when I carry a child. I refuse to do like many of the young Italian immigrant mothers do. I will not sit in the shop big with child until I give birth to it and then keep it with me in the shop all day so that I can nurse it. No, that I will not do even if you call it sinful!" and another sigh escaped her.

Avraham laid back on his pillow, one arm under his head and just emitted a "sooo. . . ."

Another sigh escaped her and she sank into her pillow with a heavy heart, feeling that his argument was within their moral principles and as a pious Jew had every right to fight for them, but what about herself? How can she go on having children and working?

Both in the same bed, both drawn to each other, and both had their reasons to build a wall between themselves.

❦

Chaya was happy the day long, but most of all she enjoyed the mornings when she heard through the kitchen windows the activities of the tenement at daybreak: the babies awoke, and called attention to themselves one way or another, some gurgled with joy, others crankily protested their wet nightclothes and still others just prattled, trying out the human language. Then suddenly, without warning, alarm clocks that stood silent for the last twenty-four hours, not able to contain themselves any longer, burst with fury, one after another, and brought the adults out of their beds. Mothers were shouting at school children, hurrying them to their tasks, and their husbands to work. Then it became quiet for a while. The mothers are eating their breakfasts, Chaya thought, while she herself sat at the table and chewed with her toothless gums a white roll which she washed down with hot tea.

Gradually, singing voices wafted through the courtyard, voices of the same mothers while they attended to their chores. The songs were varied but all on the same theme, of the immigrants; but of all, the outstanding was "Di Grine Kuzine,"* which they never seemed to tire of. Many a time was heard a woman's voice, who sang to her baby over and over again, "Di mame hat a kleyn meydl."†

Chaya had learned from her next-door neighbor Mrs. Richman that that mother was slightly "moved," because she had been engaged more than ten years to a boy she had met on the boat coming over. She worked in a factory to support him while he was studying to become a doctor, and he deserted her when she became pregnant with his child. She was in an institution for the mentally sick, for two months, and when she came back to the shop to work, the foreman there, who always liked and admired her, asked her to marry him, and she, feeling his understanding and sympathy and in need of someone to lean on in her condition, accepted his proposal and they married. Now they have this little girl, and his wish for a child of his own she was now carrying under her heart.

---

* Yiddish for "The greenhorn cousin."
† Yiddish for "The mother has a little girl."

Chaya felt at home with the stories of the tenement, they were full of the pathos she had known all her life, although she now counts her blessings like a Catholic counts her beads. She lived to see her grandchildren eat to the fullest, eat—and leave food on their plates! Most of all she liked the times when they came for their lunch, and noisily told each other how they got on in their work in school, their enthusiasm was so great they forgot to eat, and she had to stand over them and remind them to finish their meal because it was getting late. God forgive them, they became satiated soon and left so much on their plates it was sinful! Yes, she felt that she had much to be grateful for, and talked to herself, Dear God, I am thankful for what you are helping my children and grandchildren with, but there is one more thing that needs your help in mending, and that you can see for yourself. Mirele is not well, she thinks that I cannot see it, but I can, for her color and swollen eye sockets in the mornings coupled with her slow movements show it. And why has she left her husband's bed and is now sleeping with Bena! No that does not portend of happiness.

Avraham did not go to the Kamenetzer *shul* on the weekdays because of the distance, but attended a little house of prayer at the end of the block, where he met mostly older men. When he asked them where the younger men were worshipping, they looked at each other and one laughingly said, "That's a greenhorn for you, what do you mean where? Don't you know that in America a man owes his first loyalty to his boss! The first thing in the morning he runs to the shop, and if he gets a holiday off, then he comes to the synagogue."

Another worshiper asked him, "Mister, where you come from did all the Jews go to the synagogue every day?"

A man well into his years stood near him and smiled as if at a child, then said very sadly, "I see that you are not long in this country, or you would not have asked for our young men here. You will find out soon enough that today's youngsters become great philosophers, socialists, and such big thinkers that they think out of their lives, and the praying is left to us old Believers."

Avraham did not know how to answer all the bitterness of the men and just went on with his prayers. One day he decided to find his way to his kin Kolmin-Dodya's house and as he walked along on Clinton Street to find the number, he saw on each corner of the street young boys and girls selling shopping bags, and smaller items that they carried in a little basket over their arms. He became attracted to some of their brashness, for as soon as someone came near one to buy something, many crowded in, and called their wares and prices loudly, trying to outsell each other. When he came within two blocks of the number he was seeking, he came face to face with a girl of about twelve, and in surprise shouted out, "Yentl," then saw that she too held a little reed basket with wares such as hairpins, safety pins, handkerchiefs, and other articles.

"What, what are you doing here with this?" he stammered.

"Uncle Avraham," she said shyly, "are you looking for our house? I will show you where it is, just wait here a minute, until I will give my basket to one of my brothers." And she ran across the street and left it with one of the boys there.

"Tell me why do you and your brothers stand on the corners and sell these things?" he asked her. "Well Uncle, we all peddle something, except Donya, she is too grown up for that, and besides she makes more money in the shop. Did you see my other two brothers on the corner before this?"

When they came to the house, she told him to walk up to the top floor and look for 5D, that that was their flat. When he knocked on the door, Gittel opened it, and was full of smiles when she saw her guest. "Kolmin-Dodya," she called into the front room, "we have a guest, look who found his way to us!" and she led Avraham to her husband, who was stretched out on a black leather couch, his long legs sticking past its length, apparently just awakened from his sleep.

"Avraham? I see that you are already getting acquainted with New York streets, that's good, and I am glad that you decided to pay us a visit already.

"Come, sit down, and how about you Gittel, make some hot tea for all of us?" The two men sat close to each other and smiled their happiness at seeing each other.

"So now we are in America, Kolmin-Dodya, do you like it here? And how about your family, do they feel at home here?" Avraham probed.

"Well, what should I tell you first, my dear kin? After all, we are not here very long yet, barely two years, and you can see for yourself, we live in a nice house, wear nice clothes, and certainly eat more than to the full," he told him with a satisfied smile.

"That's good, but then why do you let your children stand on the street corners and peddle goods?" he asked pointedly.

"You see my friend, America is a land of opportunity; it is true that the streets are not paved with gold, but if one uses enough stamina, he digs until he finds some. My children do what they want with their lives, and with my encouragement."

"Our oldest son Moishe, now fifteen years old, wants to become a doctor so he works hard and studies well, sitting late into the night with his books. Between his school hours and homework at night, he peddles out there in the street, so that he can attain his goal later on. Now, my Chayim has big ideas too, he wants to become a lawyer, so he too works toward the future, both with his studying and peddling. My youngest son Daniel, well he is still too young to make up his mind, one day he says he wants to be a ship's captain, the next a street cleaner. With him there is plenty of time to wait, but just the same, he wants to peddle and put away the money for later when he decides to do with it what he wants to."

"But with our Yentl we have many arguments, she wants to become a nurse, and Gittel and I tell her that a girl does not need a profession, she needs a husband and children, so she cries and tells us that this is not Kamenets-Podolski, that here in America, women become what they want to, marriage or no marriage. You know what? I like her for her strength!"

"And when do your children have time for the study of Torah?" Avraham asked coldly, "and at what do you make a living?"

"I do here what I did at home, I teach Hebrew to youngsters, and also sell wine for the holidays, to the very families from where I draw the pupils. Thank God, we get along very well, and as for the worry you seem to have about the children not having time to study the Torah, Avraham, you know that my children had a deep and strict education, they studied the Talmud, Rosha, and Gemara, at an age when other children begin their A-B-C's."

"Now they have grown, and have other studies, but they will never forget what they learned before. Then you must remember that they are with me, and while they are in my house, they will never forget what they absorbed in their younger years," Kolmin-Dodya almost pleaded for understanding.

Gittel came in with a tray on which the tea and cut cake was on and said, rightly, "Avraham, don't let him talk you out of a hot cup of tea, don't pay any attention to him, or he will talk your head off before you go home."

The tea was hot, so there was time to sit a long time over it, and many questions turned in Avraham's mind, yet he did not give word to his thoughts, because he felt that he did not yet find his bearings among the people around him. Something strange that he could not understand made them all seem so different, so intent on something he did not grasp. After Kolmin-Dodya gave him addresses of some *landslayt* who lived in his community, Avraham went to visit them, and found among them many children that were in their advanced Hebrew studies, and he was engaged to further their education. Within a few days he was able to record ten boys and two girls and started his rounds to their homes after public school hours. The homes were far from each other and he had to do much fast walking to fit in all the children into what few hours that were left from school.

It was in these homes that he found an answer to some of his confusion. In these homes he saw how his former countrymen lived in America, he saw that with the exception of very few, they left God to Himself on weekdays, and only on Saturdays and holidays did they remember to worship Him. And he was to teach their children to become "good Jews." He could not help seeing the squalor they lived in and hear their worries about the short seasons in the shops. Women sat all day over machines in their kitchens, working on bundles of aprons, underwear, and children's clothes. Fathers did not see their young children for many days because they left home before sunup and came back home when they were asleep. The "breadwinners" all carried a haunted look between their eyes; true some of the poverty was relieved by groaning phonographs, fake cut-glass punch bowls that were hung around with fake cut-glass cups by S-shaped hooks, gotten with soap coupons, and fancy gas mantles that brightened the kitchen, but nevertheless, the poverty stunk in the homes. He could not help making the comparison between the old country and the new, asking why people ran away from one wretchedness to another. Mirele saw him brood a great deal and tried to draw him out, but he would only shake his head and say nothing.

Mirele Poil

Original artwork: Adrienne Ottenberg

29

The reach for help – I

SUNDAY MORNING AVRAHAM sent ISAIAH DOWN to the candy store for a newspaper, and in short time the boy came running back panting with exhaustion and with great excitement, bellowed, "I told you that I heard fire engines screaming yesterday, but you didn't believe me, now look for yourself."

He unfolded the Jewish *Forverts*,* its front page framed in a wide black border, and its headlines big and screaming about a fire that killed more than a hundred people. Avraham read in haste of the Triangle Shirtwaist factory that had its doors locked against the workers when the fire broke out, so that they were trapped in the inferno. The estimate of the victims was close to two hundred with many fighting for their lives in hospitals.

Chaya and the children stood around him and listening, their faces wet with tears, as he read about young girls falling out of windows like human torches, while more perished behind the locked doors out of which they could not escape.

"Thank God, Mirele and Bena are at work and don't know about it," Chaya broke in.

Avraham asked her if she thought that this kind of news could be kept from anyone and as he read on, the door opened, very quietly Mirele followed by Bena entered the house.

---

* *Forverts* (Forward) was a mass-circulation national daily Yiddish-language socialist newspaper founded in 1897.

Avraham looked up and exclaimed, "Look, Mama and Bena are back," his voice was gentle but triumphant. "I see that you already know of the terrible tragedy that befell many families. So many young girls, children, who did not have time to live yet, and fathers and mothers of children that become orphaned!" Mirele broke down and cried bitterly, while Chaya and the children too gave way to tears again.

Only Avraham stood, reading on, his heart madly pounding and his mouth becoming dry. He read on to the bitter end and then wanted to console his family, but had too much anger in him, which tied his tongue. In America, such a big and progressive land, he thought, can be found people that put so little value on human life, that they keep them locked up for fear that someone may steal a waist or piece of material! Almost two hundred people lost their lives, leaving so many families betrayed, why, it's even worse than the pogroms we lived through at home. At no time did we lose so many people in a half-dozen pogroms!

Mirele's voice came through his thoughts and he heard her say in a resolute voice, "When people came to us from the union and wanted to tell us how we protect ourselves from the greed of our bosses, we did not want to listen to them. Had that factory been under union contract, these beasts that live only on what they profit from the workers could not have had a system of locking their doors so that they could search the workers one by one as they went home, leaving only one door open to hundreds of men and women."

Bena's head was lowered, she did not understand how a union shop could be of use to the workers, how it would benefit them, but as she listened to her mother's words, their own shop with its fire hazards rose up in her mind, she saw the tall walls of bolts of woolens in the narrow dark hallway and the locked windows that no one could open and the wooden staircase from the ground floor to the top, now sunken in the middle of each step from the beat of thousands of feet. Dry, ready to become a pyre that would feed on many lives. That picture stood out in stark reality to her, and she began to pay closer attention to her mother's voice catching her last words, ". . . and should someone ask me to join a union, I will gladly do so now."

So that the public could pay their last respects to the victims of

The March 26 *Forverts*, the day after the 1911 Triangle Shirtwaist Company fire. The headline reads: "The Morgue Is Full of Our Victims!"

The front page of the March 28 *New York Call*, daily newspaper of the Socialist Party.

Members of the International Ladies' Garment Workers' Union and United
Hebrew Trades gather to march in memorial procession, April 1911 ,5.

Part of crowd of 400,000 viewing the memorial cortege leading the march up
5th Avenue.

the fire, the Needle Trades Union arranged a mass funeral in which tens of thousands of women and children dressed in black marched through the streets silently, but with clenched fists and tear-stained faces. When they came within view of the smoke-blackened building that became the crematorium for so many lives, they gave vent to their anguish. Heartbreaking sobs and cries of revenge filled the air. Women, hysterical and pulling hair from their heads, and men shot fists into the air and in hoarse voices shouted for retaliation to the absent bosses.

Mirele walked in the procession between her mother and Bena, both fearing her near collapse, but she surprised them with a show of stamina that they did not know she possessed. When they passed the shop they worked in, she said to Bena, in a decisive tone, "We must do something, we must not let the bosses do with us as they please, we must not stand by hoping they become benevolent and treat us like human beings. We must do something, we must teach them some way or another. As long as they make money from our labor, they themselves will never learn that we are human. May this fire be on their conscience as long as the bones of the victims last."

Chaya wondered at her daughter, not believing that she was cursing, for she always criticized her for it. And Bena wondered where she kept the reservoir of strength she was now tapping, for she felt that her mother was determined to put her words into action.

And it turned out so, for instead of going to work the next morning, Mirele found her way into the office of the Needle Trades Union and asked to see a union organizer. She was sent to a small cubicle off a long hallway, and there found a tall young man with intense eyes and intense manner; his name was Charlie.

"Yes?" he asked, looking up from his desk.

"I really don't know how to go about what I came for now that I am here," she put her hand up to her hair, adjusted her wig, while he stared at her, wondering what she did come for. After a while she stilled her confusion and began to talk.

"The tragedy of the Triangle Waist factory must have opened the eyes of many workers as it opened mine. I expected to see this office bursting with them demanding the union into their shop and give them some protection, but I see it's very quiet in the office."

"Don't be discouraged, little by little they will come to us, or we to them, and they will join up. Supposing we begin with one worker at the present moment. What can I do for you?"

"I do not rest since the fire, my mind is made up to do something before it is too late, I feel that the bosses will annihilate us unless we stay them somehow. What can we do in our shop?"

"One worry you should dismiss from your mind, your boss, or any other boss cannot destroy you completely. They need you, without your labor they could not exist. They make gain from every breath you draw, but they suffer many contradictions, and among the worse, their refusal to preserve the very people that make profit. The catastrophe in the Triangle Shirtwaist shop fire could not have happened, had it been under union contract. In 1909, just two years back, we tried to organize the shop, but when the bosses learned of it, they locked the workers out, causing a strike that lasted many weeks. When starving families could hold out no longer they went back to work. Then the exploitation became sharper and the speedup that they instituted became so unbearable that the older workers could not keep up and were fired and replaced by young girls. There were still attempts to organize, but the fire was the culmination of an unprotected shop. The workers who were worth so much to the bosses as profit, were worthless as human beings, and this is what the workers will come to recognize soon enough, and come to their senses."

They both remained quiet awhile as the organizer lit a cigarette and, blowing the smoke through his nose, made a movement as if to get down to the business at hand.

"Supposing you tell me how many workers there are in your shop, and who your boss is. I also want to know how many of the workers I can depend on to form a nucleus, those that will work from within the shop. We must have the willingness of at least half if we are to succeed," he explained to her.

She bit her upper lip in agitation, she was able to give him some information of how big the shop was, who the bosses were, and where they were located, but the workers she knew little of, that she could tell him. She had never taken time to speak to them about shop conditions, nor had anyone spoken to her about them. Yet something took shape in her mind as she thought of the hard-driven workers, of the women big with child that sat over their work in fear of raising their heads, the little babies in the straw wash baskets inhaling the spittle of the coughing workers, and the fathers of children whom they hardly ever saw.

Why should it be hard to organize them? But with whom should she begin? She looked hopeful one minute, crestfallen the next, until Charlie, who sat watching her, remarked, "Do you want to ask me any questions."

"Many of them," she answered, "but I am an ignorant woman and don't know where to begin. I thought that when I came to you, told you that you should try to organize the shop, that that would be all I have to do, and you will do the rest. Now I see that it means so much more, and I really do not know what to do or whom to turn for help in the shop. I am sorry I bothered you, let me go back and get to know my coworkers better, maybe they will be able to do something, yes?"

"Yes, that will be good, but I must tell you that you are far from being ignorant, or you would not have taken the first step in the shop. When you get to know a few workers that we can rely on, come back to me and I will start working with you."

She left with mixed feelings, she did not accomplish anything, and lost a half day's work, but on the other hand, she learned some things she did not know before, and hoped with this knowledge to someday lay a foundation to a future for the workers in her shop.

She began her campaign for a core of workers with Bena, but soon found out that her daughter was going to give passive help, and that she only went along because she wanted to please her. While Bena was convinced that a union would be good for them, she expected someone else to do the work to organize them; still she could not let her mother do all the work, and half-heartedly went along.

It was the end of March, the spring season in the shop was almost at an end. The workers were dividing the little of the work that was still there, some coming in half days, others only a few hours. On paydays all the "hands" came in, even those that had no work that day, and stood waiting around for their depleted pay envelopes until the bookkeeper was ready with them. Mirele would get close to them then and watch their worried faces and understand their struggle, with so little money. She spoke to them of her own hard existence, and they respected and believed her, and many poured their bitterness out to her, telling her what the "slack season" meant to their families. For the first time since she began to work in the shop, she got to know her shopmates as friends and experienced a happiness that she had never tasted before and helped her on to find a better life for them.

The month of April found the shop closed to all the workers, with the exception of the pattern and sample makers who were busy with new styles for the winter coats. A notice on the outside door informed whoever came to it that they reopen May 15 to begin the winter season. Mirele had been busy in the meantime and gathered around her ten women and eight men and had a meeting at the union headquarters where Charlie the organizer explained in great detail the work they were faced with convincing the rest of the workers to go out on strike when it is called.

"If you want to be recognized as human beings, given the considerations and wages for your hard work, then you must use the 'self help' method, which simply means that everyone must do his and her share." As he spoke, he looked into the faces of the men and women and felt that Mirele had judged well with whom to work. They looked like workers who were determined to go along with his plans.

When he finished speaking, he lit a cigarette, and passed the box around to the men, while asking for questions. No one raised a hand, but Mirele noticed Carla, the finisher who sat alongside of her in the shop, turn as if ready to leave and asked her, "What is it? Carla, why are you leaving so soon! Wait, maybe there is something more we need to know."

She took her hand, felt it clammy and shaking. "Is there something the matter with you, do you feel sick?" she asked her.

"No, nothing is the matter with me, I just want to go away from here," she said quietly, but everyone in the room turned toward her, and the room became silent like a tomb and she began to weep.

Bena turned on her mother, "See, and you think that everyone sees it your way." Mirele put her arms around the weeping young woman, and tried to still her, all the while asking softly to her, "Carla, what makes you cry so? Tell me, and if you need to be explained something, we will, just tell me."

She petted her head, sweeping her black, glistening hair off her forehead and looked into her swollen eyes.

"Tell you what? That I have troubles that no one can help me with? I cannot do what you want me to. I am the only one in the family that can work. My husband became crippled when he fell off a scaffold a year ago and can't go back to work. What can I do without the few dollars that I earn?" She looked at Mirele for understanding, while she heard the others in the room utter different opinions.

"You are not the only one that has to worry about a family, look around you, men who have larger families than you, men who must bring families from the old country, and women who have either sick husbands or no husbands, and have to feed their children. I brought my family across from Russia, thank God, but now I have to provide food and shelter for them. Do you think that I am not fearful of going out on strike? But just because we have such responsibilities, we must do everything we know how to better our future for ourselves and our dear ones. Who else will do it for us, the Morgans or the Rockefellers?"

Bena's anger subsided as she listened to her mother, and her wonder grew at the same time. "All of a sudden she speaks English like a Yankee," she said to herself.

Carla was silent with an inner struggle, she gathered her pocketbook and coat while everyone looked on. Then she made a step toward the door, but quickly turned back and put her things back on a chair.

"I must tell you that something else is troubling me, I am with child again, the third in the two years I am married. When I gave birth to my other two babies, my Church was a big help to me. I was given coal and wood to keep the house warm, and I was given food to keep us alive. They brought me clothes for the children and now if I should go against them, we will lose that to fall back on. The priest thinks it's a sin to go on strike."

Her eyes turned to Mirele for understanding, and she, in turn, looked to Charlie for an answer, not knowing what to say to Carla.

"So I should go to my rabbi and ask him if he approves my joining union maybe?" Morris the operator yelled. "Sure, he would tell me not to fight for a piece of bread for my children, but crawl to my boss on my knees instead. If I listened to him, I would now have a full house of children that I can't feed, instead of the two."

"You, freethinker, keep quiet, we can do with less of your philosophy here," a worker shouted in his direction.

"Yes, he is here with lessons how to drive the One Above to consumption already," another one added.

Charlie saw that the storm that should be brewing against their boss took a turn toward each other, and he rapped the table for some order.

"Do not forget the plans that we formulated here that you want to be carried out, then go home and rest while you may, for soon we will have to swing into action."

But Morris the freethinker was still full of anger and he shot out like a bolt, "Sure, your priest is not against your keeping your little bambinos in the shop all day growing in the filth of the floor and sucking you dry for want of food."

"That's enough, we do not want any arguments from anyone here, go on home, and don't forget to come back next Tuesday," the organizer reminded them in an authoritative manner.

30

The reach for help – II

A LL TOLD LEFKOWITZ AND SCHWARTZ employed eighty men and women and, had anyone asked them, they would have told you that all of them, every one of the workers, loved them like fathers. But when they got wind that their employees were girding for a struggle to gain some benefits for a better living, they swung into action ready to starve and, if need, to kill them. They looked and found among workers some that they were able to "buy" with money and promises to turn into stool pigeons to bring back information from the union and strike leaders.

At the head of this group was Rosa the prostitute, the only woman among them. She would attend all the meetings with the strikers and shout the loudest for justice from the bosses, would stay on the picket lines the longest. When one worker wanted to relieve her, she gave up her place with a show of regret.

Bena grumbled to her mother a great deal about Rosa's show of loyalty to the strike. "Why do you trust her, since when do you think that she can wash herself of her dishonest and treacherous nature. I cannot believe that such can change overnight."

"What would you have us do with her, deny her a chance to become decent? She works along with us, and that's what we want of her, nothing more." Mirele answered her with some uneasiness, promising her daughter to keep a strict watch on Rosa.

The winter season was fast approaching. It was nearing the end of June when samples and stock for the salesmen on the road should be piling up, but now the two partners would look into the empty shop and groan.

"What are we to do, what are we to do? The season will come and go and leave us in the soup. The salesmen are on my neck, they stamp and champ at the bit like racehorses before they go off. I have black days and white sleepless nights from them for the last few weeks. Can you suggest something we can do?"

Hyman Schwartz, the "outside" boss, the one that took care of the sales people and everything pertaining to business outside the factory, stood at the office window looking down at the pickets carrying signs and shouting loud enough for them to hear, "We want to have a union, we cannot live on starvation pay, we must have better working conditions!" He stood watching them from overhead, trying to see who led them, but because of the height, and because his anger boiled so strongly in him, his eyes were not able to function.

He turned his head and looked at his partner who seemed cool and comfortable in his swivel chair, and his anger knew no bounds. "I do not understand you, Sam. Don't it bother you at all?" he shouted.

"What makes you think that it don't bother me? What's the matter, I am richer than you? Just because I don't rave like a maniac, does not mean that I am not aware of our troubles. Calm down, Hyman, and just think, didn't we invest money in gangsters and stoolies, and even in a good lawyer? Do you think that it will go to waste? I don't, we must give them a little more time, that's all," Sam tried to assure his partner.

"We should give them a little more time, eh? When will we begin our line for the winter coats, in February? What I don't understand is how can those ungrateful dogs down there stay out of work so long! They have not drawn a penny since the spring season ended, and they know that the winter season is a long and profitable one for them." Hyman cracked his knuckles loudly.

"Now you see what I mean when I say that you get yourself into a tight knot because you don't think. Sure, how much longer can they hold out? Another day, another day, at most another week. Those paupers know that we can hold out longer than they can. Didn't Rosa tell us that some are ready to throw in the sponge? And a few fists from our hired men will convince others that it's better to work than to picket. Just sit tight, everything will work out alright."

In the homes of the strikers, misery reigned, anger was the mood of the adults in the homes, and children went to sleep hungry at night, crying that they had bellyaches. Rumors that scabs will take over their places, and that they may be housed in the factory, worried the hunger-weakened men and women, and they began to wonder if they did not do a bad thing by letting themselves be drawn into the strike.

No one had any "honey to lick" in Mirele's house either. Their only income was the few dollars that Avraham earned and that was not enough to cover the food in the household. As if that was not bad enough, Mirele had to go to the doctor often and buy medicines too. Simon, who could never hold on to his money more than a few days after he received his pay check, now pushed most of it into Chaya's hand to buy necessities with it. Bena wanted to look for other work, but Mirele begged her not to set an example for the rest of the workers, but stick it out to the end.

Rachel, always around her mother, was saddened by her unknown illness and worries and felt guilty because she was not helpful to her. She loved school like a pious man his worship, even though she was not learning very much. Together with Adah, she began in the second grade but she was unable to keep up with the class and just looked on with admiration when Adah and the other children, mostly immigrants like herself, knew how to answer the teacher's questions. Everything came hard to her; even when she thought she knew an answer, she turned to someone for confirmation. In the ten weeks that she attended, her teacher had learned that she was "good with the needle" and transferred her to the sewing class where she taught little girls how to sew French seams and make buttonholes by hand. This did not satisfy her, but it helped her with learning the language and gave her hope for next term to understand her teacher better.

She asked Adah and Isaiah to help her at home but they refused to take time with her, for they began reading books and discovered a new world to live in. They joined the library in the neighborhood and became its most appreciative members. Pennies they got from

Simon or a visiting relative went for Horatio Alger books gotten in second-hand stores, many with missing pages. How they loved the stories of the poor and unknown people that became rich and great in this golden land!

One morning Mirele became sick and could not go to the picket line with Bena and remained in bed, making light of it.

"Mama, I think it would be a good idea if Rachel took out working papers and got a job for the summer. What do you think of it?" Bena asked.

Mirele shook her head, then answered, "I thought of it myself, but I can't ask her to begin to work again, I just can't bring myself to it."

"But I mean only for the summer, and in the fall she can go back to school again," Bena argued, and her mother now shook her head in agreement.

Rosa stood in the dark shop her head bent forward and cried, knowing well that to her bosses her tears meant nothing.

"That's all I heard from you since the beginning, money and money. What do you do with it, eat it? So far you brought us so little information, we have nothing to work with. So you got a little beat up by the man; he is new, and didn't know you, so he made a mistake, so what? He took you for one of the strikers on the dark staircase. Now you want me to give you money for a doctor and a dentist! What will you ask for later, a mansion? You want the doctors to make you over again? Get the hell out of here, don't bother me, I have enough troubles without you," Sam shouted, then bit off the tip of his cigar and spat it out of his mouth, hitting her chin with it.

With a fast movement she ran the palm of her hand over it, wiping its pinge* while a treacherous smile lit up her eyes. "You call this a little beat up? That bastard knocked out two of my teeth and my back is almost broken. I hurt so badly I can't sit nor stand. You must give me at least 20 dollars, I must go to the dentist and doctor for help. And

---

* A wedge-shaped depression in the earth; used here to describe a cleft in the chin.

what do you mean that I did not bring you enough information? I gave you more than the others did, or did you want me to manufacture some for you that was not so? I'll tell you what, give me 50 dollars now, and I'll be able to pay my back rent for the room and take care of everything else so that I can work with a clear head."

Steps were heard in the corridor and both picked up their heads and listened, then heard the voice talking to the guard, and recognized it as Sam's partner Hyman, the excited partner.

"That's what we hired you for, so that you should beat up our own people? Fool, go stand in the doorway again, and make sure that you look good before you lay a fist on the next person," and he walked in with heavy footfalls. "So, I see that he made a swell job on you, Rosa, but the devil will not take you; sit down we must discuss our next move. Sam, you make me nervous standing and jingling the change in your pocket. All right, I did what we decided on, I hired enough 'hands' to fill two shops now," and he stopped, having caught his partner's wink, at once remembering that he was laying himself bare in Rosa's presence.

"Let us talk of the meeting they will hold at the union next Thursday night, that is if they can go hungry and remain living until then. Rosa you must find out just at what time they intend to start, and how long you think they will be at it, and above all just who the leaders are. I don't mean from the union, I mean from this very shop. With the union gang we will settle differently and in good time," Hyman Schwartz ended.

In a voice that sounded full with resolution, Rosa demanded 50 dollars, and right now!

Without a word, Sam Lefkowitz pulled the money out of his pocket and was about to give it to her when his partner Hyman roared, "An abscess under her arm you should give her. What do we need to stuff her so full of money for? We have all our plans in shape and our orders will go out in time, next week this factory will be humming with work." Again he caught a wink from his partner but the anger that was boiling him spilled over and he continued shouting, "She is a bloodsucker like the rest of them, for the lousy bits of information she wants us to bathe her in gold, to hell with her."

Now the calm Mr. Lefkowitz reduced the money he was holding

to half and put it into Rosa's hand and showed her toward the door. "Now look, Hyman, you should not get so excited that you let the words splatter out of your mouth without caution. I have to meet my Adela and take her to supper and then to a show, and I do not want to sit here and spoil my mood for the evening. After all it's Saturday night and we are entitled to a little fun, no?" he joshed. "So let's go on with our business. You say you have arranged for the scabs to come up to the shop Thursday night while they are at the meeting, and you already ordered canned food and the cots; that's good, so why did you have to call me to come here, and Rosa too? It's too bad the slugger made such a job on her, after all she is on our side, isn't she?"

But little did they know that Rosa had already left their side; she left in anger and was now lying in her bed, weeping with pain. The doctor had left her some white little pills which she swallowed with great difficulty, but so far felt no relief from them. Not being able to get a dentist Saturday night, she wondered if she will still be alive Monday to visit one. Again she helped herself to some of the pills and toward morning fell into a troubled sleep that gave her little rest. She moaned and then heard herself laugh out loud, so loud that momentarily it brought her out of her sleep and brought her into full consciousness of her pain again. She sank back into a deep sleep that lasted until the early morning hours and in the morning tried to get out of her bed, and screamed in agony, bringing her landlady to the room.

"What is it Rosa," she asked, but seeing her misery quickly sent her boy to fetch the doctor.

Again he came, and left her more little white pills, and told her to get out of bed with the sagging spring and mattress and lay on the floor instead. The woman brought her an old quilt, soiled and smelling of bedbugs, and spread it out for her near the bed, then together with her boy helped the screaming Rosa down onto it. There she lay all day Sunday, now and then taking a little cold tea to wet her dry, aching mouth, feeling as if she was asphyxiated, dreaming, and drifting in suspended animation, now peaceful, now in misery. All sorts of thoughts sprouted from parts of her brain, and mingled them into a knot that tried to choke her. Her childhood carrying a mask of an old hag on a stick stood laughing at her, while her sisters and brothers were slamming doors in her face. Her mother appeared wearing her Sabbath clothes with the old bracelet that came down from great-grandmother, coughing, coughing, until Rosa woke again and it brought her out of lethargy to feel the pain again.

She reached for the box of pills and took a double dose, washed down with the cold tea, and lay staring up at the ceiling and wondered what time of day it was, then thought that it really made no difference, it was all the same. She drifted to a cloud again, the pain cushioned by it, and she felt good, just lying on the cloud of time, swinging as she did when she was a little girl and her father took her to the park on 7th Street, where he would swing her so high it would knock the breath out of her, but she would shout down to him, "Higher, Papa, higher," as she tried to do now, but her papa was not around.

What became of him, she wondered? Why did he leave me so high in the swing and is not to be seen down there? While she peered from her height, she saw many men come out of the ground, their heads appeared, then their chests, all wearing white shirts with colorful neckties, and when the rest of them emerged, they were naked from the waist down to their bare feet.

She stopped the swing and was about to get off and woke up with a feeling of being in great haste. She had to get some place before it was too late! But where to? She was puzzled and again drifted off to hear her mother's coughing coming from somewhere, and she went to look for her, and when she thought she found her it turned out to be Mirele instead, standing in front of her with her sweet smile and the look of a *rabbanit*.

Rosa was disappointed to see her instead of her mother, to whom she had to tell something of importance in a hurry, yes, that was it, she had to tell her about it before it was too late, and now where did she go?

"Mama, Mama, I must tell you, you must know before it is too late. Why is Mirele standing there instead of you? Tell her to go away."

With the last complaint, she woke up in a cold sweat, finding herself weak and spent. She looked toward the window and saw the gray wall stare back at her, and was surprised that the day did not end yet, but she soon heard her landlady hurrying her boy off to school, and she knew that she had slept through the night and it was Monday morning. What was it about today that she must hurry to do? Her mind began to recall some of her fantasies, at first a snatch here and there, then she remembered seeing her mother, or was it Mirele? She could not recall who it really was, they were so much alike. Little by little her mind became lucid and she panicked. "My God, I better get up and go see someone before it is too late," rang like an echo in her mind.

She had difficulty rising from the floor; she held on to the iron frame of the bed and pulled herself to her feet. She stood awhile trying to adjust to her new position, then took a few steps and found that she was able to walk. Quickly she slipped on her clothes and not stopping to comb her hair, left the house to walk fifteen blocks to the union office because she was afraid to be pushed by people in the streetcar.

When she came to Charlie's office, she found him at the desk talking to someone on the telephone, and he motioned her to a chair; then he saw her face and broke off with the other party, promising to call back later.

"My God, Rosa, what in the world happened to your face? How did it get so black and blue? Here sit down, you look sick."

He shoved a chair under her and tried to sit her into it and was shocked to hear a scream of agony from her.

"What did I do to you, how did I hurt you!" he wanted to know, watching her face. She opened her mouth to talk and he saw her lacerated lips and mouth with the missing teeth where the gums were still bloody.

"What is it Rosa, why are you so badly hurt; did the bosses' thugs attack you because you are working to win the strike with us?"

"Charlie, you sit down, I can't, and I must tell you something fast, before it gets too late for it," and she went on to tell him about the bosses' plans to staff the shop with scabs while they will be at the meeting Thursday night in the union hall. She spoke with difficulty, her lips hardly moving, but her eyes were lit up with happy excitement that hid the ugliness of her face. When she stopped speaking, Charlie said, "That I know, but how did you find out about it, and you still did not tell me how you got so beaten up?"

"What, you knew about it?" her voice was full of bitterness and frustration.

"Yes, I do, but why do you sound so disappointed, do you think that we in the union are asleep and aren't you glad that we knew?"

"Oh, Mama, Mama, I should have shriveled up in your womb," she lamented, forgetting her torn mouth and sobbing out her story of collusion with the bosses to him.

"And to think that I was paying off those bastards by coming to you with this information!" She held her head in her hands and moaned.

"Don't feel so sad, we knew right along that you were in their pay, and we know of a few others that are still with them, bringing every bit of information they can get to them. But that's not going to help you right now, you must get medical help. Here is some money, go to a doctor and then to a dentist, and when you get mended, come back, we need you."

She left him without saying good-bye because his compassionate words locked in her throat.

31

The reach for help - III

O F THE EIGHT WORKERS THAT MR. Lefkowitz bought to spy on the workers, Morris the freethinker, as the workers in the shop called him, was closest to his heart. Morris knew how to tell a joke that could even embarrass a Cossack, and in the next breath sing a hymn that could melt a stone with its sweetness, and reminded Mr. Lefkowitz of his boyhood days in Vilna, where his father was known to be the most pious Jew in his community.

Mr. Schwartz, on the other hand, used to boil with anger at his partner, shouting that he kept the freethinker too long in the office, and that he was wasting his time for the money they paid him. But the calm Sam Lefkowitz only laughed and tried to convince his partner that he was cultivating the young man's abilities and trustworthiness with an eye to the future.

"Don't you understand what I am trying to do, Hymie? I am building him up to be our man, so much so, that he will see everything our way and will be of much use to us later on, when the strike is broken. Don't think that the scabs will make a picnic for us here. How long do you think we can keep so many men and women locked up in the factory day and night and eating out of cans? It's true that we must do it, but a picnic I don't expect it to be. So, what am I doing with Morris, I am breaking him in to do the work that it will be hard for us to do. Right now, he already brought me a list of operators, finishers, and pressers that will be ready to come in Thursday night, while the wise guy pickets will be having a meeting. We will be able to use him for many emergencies that I am sure will arise, so don't go around with your blood boiling, feeling as if I was selling you out."

This did not make Hyman Schwartz any happier; he had no trust in anyone, from his partner down to the scabs he paid his good money to. His head was full of fears of the time that was running out from his schedule, and no matter what came up, the question always arose whether the season will be lost. He paced the floor, his hands playing with the change in his pockets, his face bloated and almost blue.

"You know Sam? I have a heavy feeling in my heart, I feel that it won't work out. We will let up here an army of workers that we never saw or heard of before, never found out if they could work the machines or not, and they will not only kill our season, but ruin our machines as well as our materials. I know that this is not the time to talk like this, but my heart feels heavy."

"See, what did I just tell you, I know that *alter kaker*s* like you are not fit to do hard thinking. It will take a young mind like Morris's to work those things out. He worked at the machines, he worked on samples, and he has a way with people and knows what we want of him. Leave those worries you carry around with you to him, and he will take care of everything."

Hyman Schwartz smiled brightly at his partner.

But long the "inside" partner, the calm Mr. Lefkowitz did not smile, for a tragic doom befell him and his partner. On the night when the scabs were to be brought in, Mr. Lefkowitz invited his partner to his house for supper, along with his wife. He kept the conversation away from the shop, "not to worry the women" he told Hyman, but really not to excite his turbulent associate. But once the women left them to their card game, he saw Schwartz's cards shake in his hands and how unsteadily he handled his overworked cigar. "So, everything is in order already, no, Hyman?" he said to still his anxiety.

"No, Sam, everything is not in order, not yet," came the answer.

"So why are you so upset tonight, because we are already at the end of our troubles?" Sam countered with some derision.

---

* Yiddish for over-the-hill old-timers.

"All right, so you asked for it, so I will tell you. You are an inside man, you, are not responsible for the salesmen and our buyers and I am. I am scared that we will not have anything to offer them if the shop is full of scabs. I am scared that they will do something to the styles that will ruin us for good. I am scared. Do something!"

"Now you talk like that? Now you remind yourself to be scared of the scabs after we paid out so much money to round them up and buy cots and canned food for them, and left so much time behind us? Now when they are probably already sitting up in the factory, you remind yourself to think whether it is good for us to use scab labor or not! Now you come with your funny ideas; forget it Hyman, go ahead and play your hand, it's done, and I am sure that with Morris around them, they will produce as good a garment as the regular workers would."

While they battled with their wits in the large living room hung with expensive curtains and drapes and lit by electric lamps that threw soft shade on their table, Morris the freethinker was leading the workers up the stairs to the factory, past the armed thugs who were hired to protect them if troubles arise.

Not all the lights in the shop were on, and although there were some seventy men and women at the machines and tables, it was quiet. So quiet that the "strong men" looked at each other in confusion and were glad when Morris paid them off and discharged them, locking the doors of the hallway behind them.

"*Mazel tov*, we are back," he stood up on a table to address the strikers. "Now we must understand what we are to do until the morning and in the morning. It is almost eleven o'clock and we are all tired I am sure, so as soon as we get through talking, let the women go to sleep on the cots that I placed on the east wall, and the men on the wall opposite. I am sure that it will not feel the comfort of home on them, but at least we'll have a night's rest."

He stopped talking and looked around. "Is anyone hungry?" he asked, and as no one raised a hand, he went on with their plans. "Good, we do have a load of canned goods here, but if no one is hungry, we will give it back to our bosses in the morning, showing them that honest workers don't want a handout."

He waited for a question, then proceeded, "I expect that in the morning when our bosses come in bright and early to begin the season with the scab labor and find you, here, the sky will fall down on their heads, so you must keep yourself well-disciplined no matter what they do or say. Let us elect a committee of three to do the talking for the shop. Before you get to your beds, elect the committee who will represent you, one presser, one operator, and one finisher. I will give you a few minutes to think, then we will go on."

He lit a cigarette and turned away from them for a while. When he turned back, he found only one presser standing near him. "Well, where are two more to join him?" he asked.

An operator stood up and told him that their section chose him, Morris. He laughed and accepted, and still asked for one more, from the finishers' section, but no one volunteered and, after a while, Carla raised her hand, and told Morris that the only one that should represent them should be Mirele, who was home sick Bena had told them. Then she added maybe she will be better tomorrow and come to work.

Morris said, "I wish with all my heart that she should be here with us, but I know that she won't. I visited with her yesterday, and she told me that she was not fit for work for a while yet. Take another 2 or 3 minutes and find someone else."

There was much talk among the women, each finding a reason why she could not serve, and at last Carla came up to Morris, and told him that she was told by many in the section that it would make Mirele very happy when she will find out that she accepted to be in the committee, and Morris and Bena agreed.

The chosen workers held a short meeting together with Morris in a corner of the shop, while the rest of the workers settled down for the night. The Catholic women of the finishers' section knelt at their beds in prayers and the pious Jews at theirs chanted the Kriat Shema.* Soon, only a small, single light remained burning, and all were asleep.

The morning brought both bosses early into the shop and were struck as if by a thunderbolt when they saw their old crew of workers sitting in their own former places! They raved and ranted, calling

---

* Hebrew for the bedtime prayer.

Morris names that were not fit for the ears of decent people. One threatened to call the police, while the other to jump from the window, but neither one carried their threat, for the shock was so great that they could not think straight.

Mr. Schwartz repeated over and over again something about losing time, all the while wringing his hands, pulling his hair, and saying, "Now we are in for it, no time left for the season. You with your friend Morris sewed it up for me, but good! I refuse to talk to that committee, they are not my friends, they are yours, your sweet-singing friend that turned renegade is in it too. You talk to that bunch of paupers, not me."

In the end, the committee of three convinced them that for their good, they should call Charlie at the union, and have him come and give them more information. By the time Charlie came, the two bosses were so infuriated at each other that, to spite each other, they gave way, and settled for a union contract, of course giving Charlie and the committee a bad time all along the line. They fought every clause in the contract, but fought against an iron wall, and fell cursing at each other and at the same time signing the papers.

The only clause Charlie let them run wild with and win was the one stipulating that they must rehire every one of the workers who were striking against them. At that, the raging Mr. Schwartz screamed hysterically, loud enough to be heard in the factory, "Go ahead and tear up the lousy contract, I do not care, I will not have that stinking betrayer in my shop, I should have to go begging for a living! Morris must go, you hear, he must go!"

And Charlie let him win; he needed Morris in the union office, he proved himself to be a fine organizer.

Once again the machines were heard to whirr and the steam in the pressers' irons to whistle their soft *shhhhhh*, and above all the singing of workers at machines and tables.

The factory was pervaded with holiday spirit, the work flying fast, as if it is more valuable now. Herschel the loudmouthed factory foreman was now subdued. Charlie warned him that the workers will not stand for his former way of driving them as if they were dogs. It was no easy task for him to keep his tongue in bondage all day and wait until the

evening to rattle the windows in his house with the bellowing of his
chest that he hoarded all day long.

All the workers were now back on their jobs, except Morris the
freethinker, Mirele, who was still sick in bed, and Rosa the prostitute,
now in Bellevue Hospital, sinking slowly into death.

Bena brought all the shop news to her mother, and Mirele felt good
to hear that Carla found her way and lost her fears of joining the other
workers in their struggles for a better life and was elected shop steward.
But what made her very unhappy was that she could not see Rosa. She
instructed Bena that her shop mates, men and women, should not fail
to be with her as often as they will be permitted.

When Mirele complained to Doctor Feldman about her lack of
strength, he gave her some medicines from a drawer and told her
grumblingly that she had no business to come to the office, but she
should go directly to Mt. Sinai Hospital instead of home, as there was
not much more he was able to do for her. Her illness needed many
tests for diagnoses, and only in a hospital could they be done.

"Why don't you do what I tell you? Go to the hospital through the
clinic, they will take good care of you." And as she began to look in
her purse for his fee, he raised the palm of his hand against it, "I don't
want your money, I have enough to live on without your fee, but do
what I tell you before it is too late." He turned his back on her and
called for the next patient.

She walked back to the house telling herself that he was mistaken
that she was not as sick as he makes her out to be; anyhow, if he could
not tell her what was wrong with her, how could he know that she was
that sick? She decided not to go to doctors anymore, and go to work,
there, in the shop, busy with something to do, and being able to earn
some money, she will forget herself, and get well.

When she reached the house and began to climb the stairs, she felt
them run away from her one minute, and the next threatening to pile
on top of her! She put her hand on the bannister and stood in confusion,

drops of sweat pouring off her. Children ran past her chasing each other and found her in the way and shoved her to one side, causing her to fall down two steps and landing in a sitting position on the hallway floor. More children ran in, Raphael among them, and when he saw his mother on the floor with her hands covering her eyes, he screamed so loud that neighbors opened their doors and ran to see what befell him.

They found Mirele trying to pacify her boy, all the while trying to raise herself from the floor, but she felt like a block of cement and a wave of fear swept her face. Two women went to her aid, and with difficulty brought her to the apartment, with Raphael crying all the way.

"Stop that infernal noise, you crybaby," a woman scolded him, but he only cried louder, until his grandmother opened the door and he saw her put his mother to bed. Mirele's illness caused a lot of worry in the home, the doctor came again, and again told her to go to the hospital, but this time with anger, and left without his fee, telling Avraham not to call him anymore, he will not come.

The family looked to her approval before they began to prepare her to go, but she gave none, only shaking her head and said with a little smile playing around her lips, "Don't let him scare you, he probably does not know what is the matter with me, so he wants me to go to a hospital, why doesn't he send me to another doctor? He is probably afraid that the other man will know, and show himself to be the better doctor of the two. Don't worry in a few days I will feel fine and I beg of you not to pressure me to do otherwise."

Feeling a wave of faintness again, she stopped talking awhile, then continued, "As a matter of fact, I intend to go back to the shop tomorrow, then you will see how wrong he was," and she wet her lips in determination as Bena had seen her do so many times before when she had to undertake some things that were too difficult for her.

"Look, Mama, Papa is earning some money, and now I am back at work again and earning more than before, and Rachel can continue to work so that we really don't need your income, we can manage without you going to the shop," Bena begged her.

"Don't talk to me about Rachel leaving school, I will not hear of it, she needs the schooling more than the younger ones do," she said with bitterness.

Avraham made the mistake of trying to console her that schooling was a hard thing for Rachel, that she would not learn there anyhow, but only received a bitter look from her while she shook her head. "My poor child, she is the sacrificial lamb of the family. She cannot learn because she was dulled with work at the machine when she was still so young," and she sighed.

She went back to the shop, and to save her the effort of walking the four flights of stairs when she came home, they found an apartment on Stanton Street on a first landing. After settling in the four rooms which were light and large, they were driven out of it by the bedbugs that ate their bodies at night and the roaches that ate their food all day.

When they moved to Suffolk Street, they had to get out of there too because facing their kitchen windows in a narrow shaft lived a little bewigged Jewish woman who ran a whorehouse. Her girls ran around naked all day and night and in the evenings made such barbarous noises it was impossible to sleep.

In desperation Mirele found an apartment on East 5th Street, on the fifth floor with the consolation that in the summertime when the heat in the flat gets unbearable, they will have the roof so near them to sleep on, and so overcame the family's objections.

The summer passed, the younger children went back to school, while happy-go-lucky Rachel made peace with her lot and continued at her job. She went from one shop to another, as the season ended in them. To her it made no difference what work she was at, just so she was able to bring her wages home to her mother at the end of the week.

Simon followed the family around from one dwelling to another, for more reasons than because he liked to be with them. He fell in love with the quiet unfeigned Bena, whose comely face and girlish figure drew her to him. He saw her struggle with the family and it hurt him, but he stood at a distance because he was not in a position to marry her. The status he held as the top salesman in a luggage store brought him enough to live on, but not to take on the responsibility of a marriage and family.

Bena was aware of his feelings for her, for love needs no definite nudge to establish its meaning, but at first was unhappy with it. But for the time that she was tutored by Aaron Bronstein she was in love with him and lived with the hope that someday he would come to feel that way himself, and tell her so.

But Mirele, who saw her time and emotions going to waste, discouraged the young man from coming to give her lessons and so stifled her daughter's feeling for him, that is, perhaps outwardly, but for many months she brought him back to her in her dreams. Even when the dreams subsided somewhat, she still carried on her warm feeling of his hand on hers. Even now when she became aware of Simon's love for her, she felt that her love for Aaron was not completely smothered.

In this new home large and bright, Mirele invited the ladies' auxiliary of the Kamenetzer Society to meet every last Thursday of the month. There they took up such important matters as funds for hungry orphans in their hometown of Kamenets, funds for a burial ground to be raised at the annual masquerade ball, as well as money to be put away for the poor for the Passover holidays to provide them with matzoh.*

Mirele begged her husband to join the society of *landslayt*, but he refused, saying that he was not sure if he wants to remain in America.

The meeting of the ladies' auxiliary brightened the household. Chaya worked two days in advance to clean it, and baked her most delicious cakes, then saw to it that the youngsters kept at a distance from the table laden with sweets while she herself sat beaming at all the women she had known a lifetime. Yes, she would say to herself, in Kamenets-Podolski they were women too, but only to raise children and worry about their poverty. But here, they come together to plan, to discuss and argue about their work just like men do. America, what a country!

To Avraham those meetings were a bore, they were like a thorn in his flesh, for each time, another one of the women would latch on to him and ask him to join the society, and each time he had to find another excuse to turn her down. Toward the end of the winter, when the last meeting was held, one of the women sat down near him and

---

* Hebrew for the unleavened bread to be blessed and eaten at Passover, to remind the faithful of their hasty forced departure from Egypt in biblical times.

talked so long and with so much compulsion that he felt his gorge rise and he walked away from her in anger and stayed in the cold front room until they all left. Then he came back and joined his wife and mother-in-law at the table. The room was thick with silence, and they all felt his anger, but tried not to call it out.

32

What stunts children's souls

T HE DOOR OPENED WITH A BANG and Simon walked
into the house bringing the smell of the outdoor with
him, and as was his wont, handed Chaya a package.
"They had a sale on sweet potatoes, so I bought some," and seeing
her look accusingly at him, laughed, his dimples playing in his cheeks.

"By you, every day is a sale for something else," she smiled back at
him.

Simon hung his coat on the hanger and sat down at the table and
sniffed the aroma of the sweets on the table.

"My, what a good smell, and on a mere Thursday night too!"

He looked around at the sullen faces at the table and wondered if
they were tired, then ventured forth.

"As long as it feels like a holiday here, I would like to talk to you about
something that may justify my feeling. Come in here, Bena, leave the
dishes for later, no one will steal them away from you."

His mood was counter to theirs, his eyes showed a merry twinkle
and his face a radiance full of gaiety. Bena came away from the kitchen
sink and sat down near him, wondering what brought him to such
humor, but soon blushed very red when he put his hand over her's
that was resting on the table.

"I wanted to ask you, Avraham and Mirele, if I may expect to marry

Bena in the near future, if she will have me," he announced.

Avraham raised himself from his seat and was about to leave the table but Simon urged him to sit down again and to tell if he has any objections, and if so, what they are.

"I have a good reason," he answered, and left the room.

Bena went through many mixed feelings. While she was not sure if she would want to marry Simon, she knew that lately she enjoyed his admiring glances and the remarks he made in the presence of her grandmother, that she is the kind of a girl he will marry when he is ready to settle down. Now that her father handled such a delicate matter without feeling, she felt sorry for Simon, and her hands reached out to him to show him sympathy, saying quietly, "He is in a bad mood as always when the ladies' auxiliary meets here," her eyes convinced him that, with her, he won his suit.

Avraham was not going to have Simon for his son-in-law, he was not going to give away his first daughter to an infidel of a man who sleeps to the last minute of the morning so that he will not have time to put his prayer shawl on and give himself over to worship.

The silly arguments that Mirele put up for his defense made no impression on Avraham; he knows that when one wants to live in the ways of God, a Jew lives, he finds time for His devotion. So what if he comes home late at night, couldn't he get up a half hour earlier than he does? But who can convince that young man, when he shows the stubbornness of a mule. He argued with Mirele, showing her how lazy and irresponsible a man he was.

"I know that you want to marry Bena off because you live in fear of her remaining an old maid, but is that a reason for wanting her to marry the Devil himself?"

Quarrels broke out between the two very often and the children became tense and tried to avoid the house as much as possible. After they were finished with the evening meal, the two boys ran down to the street as soon as their father finished with them at the religious texts and the two older girls went to visit friends and neighbors, but Adah stayed home and absorbed their quarrels like a sponge. She feared leaving the house for some reason she herself could not explain, but began coughing again as in the old days.

Something had gone bad with her world. Adah, who always liked the Saturdays when everyone except Simon was home from work and the house was clean and bright and smelled of the good cooking and baking her grandmother worked so hard over, and everyone had their best clothes on, saw nothing of the good in it now. Not even the leisure that was her father's wont on the Sabbath when he came back from the synagogue and with measured patience to all in the house, and later in the afternoon sat with the boys over the Torah. And this Saturday she was told to stay at home, because she would annoy the congregation with her insistent coughing.

Left to herself, she went through the flat and straightened up, then set the table for the midday meal. She brought into the dining room the plates and cutlery and stood over it a long time setting up everyone's place. She placed the little wine glass that her father made the benediction over near the *challah* that was covered with a white doily and stood in deep thought that seemed of one wish: peace between her parents. If only they would talk to each other as they did before, without sharp words that stuck into her like knives, if only they would smile to each other as before!

"When before?" she suddenly asked herself and she became confused. Yes, when before? And she found herself looking deep into her past of the thirteen years of her life and did not seem to remember her mother smiling very often. She tried to brush away the uneasiness that overtook her by reasoning that she was too young to remember much about her mother. She was a silly little girl when she came to America, so how could she remember? But she recalled the first few weeks when they came here, how her mother and father looked so happy and joked a great deal about the old country and the new. She felt whole then she had both, and saw them happy and she basked in that wholeness.

She picked up the little wine glass and warmed it in her hands, turning it, its design of cut glass making a faint impression in the palm of her hand. She set it down quickly when she heard voices in the hall outside the door and went to the kitchen to prepare the traditional

Sabbath entree of sliced-thin radish garnished with rendered chicken fat placed around the chopped eggs and onions.

Rachel's voice was heard above the others as they entered the house. She was telling her mother how her boss told the workers that if he catches anyone trying to unionize the shop, he will lock the whole shop out. Mirele laughed and told her not to let that scare her, that she could tell her shop mates about the victory they had in the shop of Schwartz and Lefkowitz, and Bena mimicked an immigrant who picketed with them and shouted, "Its must be a union."

While her father was making the benediction over the wine, the girls admired the table set, smiled at Adah approvingly, and then Bena and Rachel began to serve the food. While the meal was in progress and the two boys were laughing over something, both her father and mother said something to each other in undertones, and their faces showed a terrible anger and soon a quarrel broke out between the two, leaving the family in such a misery that no one finished the meal and one by one drifted away from the table, with the exception of Adah. She sat picking at her food, she stayed on as if waiting for them to make up soon and become friends again. She waited, and shut her ears to what they said to each other, hoping that soon they will stop but instead she heard her father say that he wants to divorce her mother and go back "home"!

That hit her so hard that she felt that her legs were dying under her. She tried to leave the table and felt as if she were walking on stilts, but forced her steps into the bedroom she shared with Bena. She stopped there, not knowing where to go, or what to do. She stood near the window, her hands turned into fists that were tight knots, listening to her pounding heart. How could she go on living if they get divorced? How could she live away from either one of them? A little devil playing in her jumbled mind reminded her that she had lived almost four years without her mother before, and she remained alive. She thought on that awhile, but found that she had reason to believe that she could not be without her now. Then, I was a little girl, I did not even know if I missed my mother and used to laugh at Rachel when she cried for her "beautiful Mama." But now is not then; now, I know that I want to be with her always. I did not seem to get my fill of her yet, perhaps because I did miss her and was too young to understand it, and now want so much of her, to make up for the time lost! And certainly I could not live without my father, how could I?

She stood tensed in every part of her body, her face flushed and her eyes held a burning sparkle that made them look almost mad. Suddenly the ground six stories below seemed to beckon to her, and in fear she backed away from the window. Where to go now! The boys were down in the street, the two girls sat with her grandmother in the front room but she did not want to join anyone. She went back to the window and again the hard cement pavement below, in the canyon-like depth, called to her, this time bathing her in a cold sweat. Fear and fascination took hold of her and she stood so until something, she knew not what, made her turn and run into the dining room where she found her parents still at the table, silent, but with agony in their faces.

"You hear? I will throw myself down from the window to the court below, I will, I will, you'll see, I will," she screamed and screamed until her father took her into his arms and tried to pacify her. "What kind of crazy talk is this?" he asked her, but she broke down and cried as if her heart would break. "You cannot leave me, neither one of you, I will not live without you. I cannot, you hear? I cannot, Papa, and you, Mama."

She coughed and cried until her mother put her into her bed and laid down with her until they both fell asleep.

Both Mirele and Avraham suffered a jolt from Adah's wretchedness; it brought home to them how much they hurt their children and silently vowed to restrain themselves in the future. But not only did they repress their show of anger toward each other but also the show of awareness as well, by cutting off their communication to the minimum, and that with downcast eyes. The home became a *genem**; it was crowded with animosity so that when a child turned to one parent it felt the resentment of the other, causing Bena and Rachel to hold with their mother and the younger ones with their father.

Chaya felt sympathetic toward Avraham's problems. She knew that he found himself out of place in this country, that wherever he

* Yiddish and Hebrew for Hell.

came in contact with friends and family he was very critical of them, and they of him. She saw the anguish between the two, and could not help in any way and said nothing, keeping her thoughts to herself. It was painful for her to hear Mirele's accusations of his blindness to the children's necessities, his concern for the next world while he was losing this one. Her biggest complaint was over his objections to Bena's marriage to Simon.

She kept arguing to herself, How blind can he be, can't he see how the girl likes him and he, her? Does he want her to fade into an old maid and sit in the shop for the rest of her life? Bena is no youngster anymore, and no great beauty either, and a big dowry he can't give her, why does he remain so stubborn? And what has he got against Simon? He comes from a religious home, he himself is an educated young man, both in the Torah and in the American schooling, and in time will make a good living for her and a family. What else does he want of him? So he sleeps late in the mornings, what else has he got to do? He comes home after midnight from work, so he rests and sleeps to make him ready for the next day's work, is that a crime? He wants him to be as pious as himself. Little does he know that the younger generation does not give itself to religion as the older people do.

Chaya tried to soften Mirele's anger, but only succeeded to turn it against herself. "I know that you do not agree with me, you always held with him, even in the younger days. You are more fond of him than of me, you think of him as a son."

The two older girls not understanding Adah's distress tried to draw her to their mother's side by deriding her for sitting on Saturday after-noons with the boys who "knew no better" and their father while they read and explained from the Tanakh.* Rachel would add a snicker and say, "Sure, why should she not sit with them, does she want to miss the candy and halvah he brings her and the boys."

Tears of anger glistened in her eyes and she would hold her fists tight but would not answer, and Rachel taunted her further, "Why should she love Mama more than Papa, does she give her 50 cents

---

* The 24 volumes of biblical Hebrew scripture, including the Torah, the Nevi'im, and the Ketuvim.

every week for piano lessons? No, but Papa does, and he does not care if we need the 50 cents in the house for bread."

"That's enough, when she gets older she will understand better," Bena said.

Besides the piano lessons the girl lost herself in the books. From both she derived escape to a good extent from the misery of the home.

Miss Hirsh, her piano teacher, held out great hopes for her young pupil and invited her to concerts where she became aware of the world of music. Miss Hirsh's old mother used to sit and watch Adah practice by the hours and then remind her that it was getting dark and that she better go home for supper.

The old woman admired the girl's enjoyment at the piano as she practiced her lessons over and over again. Knowing that Adah read a lot, she gave her books from her overcrowded bookcase that, she said, had been read by her daughter and are now wasting away in the dust on the shelves. Books by Alcott, Dumas, and Lester Cohen began to replace the Horatio Alger and Carter books, and led her to read the better works.

Her, as well as Isaiah, "being always buried in books" caused additional disturbance in the house. This time it was between the two children and their grandmother, who expected them to do many more chores for her as they grew older. But it seemed just the reverse; she had to do much prodding and scolding and cursing before she could move one or the other to do what she wanted of them. "You just wait, when your mother comes home from work, she will get to know everything that goes on here, just you wait!" But Chaya "forgot" to tell on them, and the next day, the same troubles went on as before.

In the evenings when Avraham came home, Isaiah's dreamy eyes would, as by magic, move from all the reading of the afternoon, and he showed his father a readiness to sit down with the Hebrew studies.

And Adah would find herself near her mother one minute, and the next, her father, as if trying to fuse them together. She watched her mother to see if she wanted anything, and in short time brought it with a smile, then she would cling to her father, asking all sorts of questions just to be near him. But she could bring no change between them, they seemed to be so charged with bitterness toward each other. On the pretext that she was going to the toilet out in the hallway, she would hide a book under a coat and sit on the hallway steps, those nearer the gas light that hung from the ceiling and read. All Adah's reading brought her little knowledge or understanding. What she profited from was the escape into the story, with its emotions that gave her a glimpse into other people's lives. She derived pleasure or sorrow from the characters but remained too unsophisticated to know what the author was pointing out to his readers. She was a little too simple for a fourteen year old and had no knowledge whatever about sex, and never asked anyone about it because it had not disturbed her yet, it was waiting for a time when life will point the way.

Sex, the instigator of life in the name of propagation, need, or love, had to have its way with the two young people drawn toward each other, living under the same roof and worked its charm on them to discover each other.

Adah awakened from her sleep one night, became aware of some strange actions in the bed beside her, and in her drowsy state believed that she was dreaming and began to drift off into sleep again, but a voice disturbed her, and she heard that it was Simon's and that he was whispering some endearing words to Bena, who kept saying, "Simon, be careful, Simon, be careful," over and over again. Now she knew that she was not dreaming, but she became mixed up with excitement and confusion laying with a pounding heart at the brink of knowledge, yet not able to understand.

Even after Simon left the bed and Bena fell asleep with heavy breathing, she had her eyes open wide with wonder and turmoil. In the morning she claimed a headache and was told to stay home from school. She sat at the kitchen table and watched her oldest sister's every move trying to find a trace of her last night's queer behavior but only saw the same gentleness. She went about helping prepare breakfast and the little packages with their luncheons. Her eyes could detect nothing unusual in Bena's face or actions and began to believe that after all, she probably dreamed of it. Just the same, something stirred in her, something that was both puzzling and not unpleasant, making her feel somewhat languid.

Avraham had been on the way to the toilet, out in the hall, when he passed Bena's bedroom and heard the two lovers, who were so engaged in their embrace that they did not hear him, and felt as if the house had fallen in on him! His fury knew no bounds, and very early in the morning, went into Mirele's bedroom and told Rachel to go out and shut the door behind her.

"What happened to you, that you disturb everyone in the house this early?" Mirele asked him. "It's not early for what I must tell you, it's perhaps too late."

"Whatever it is, leave it for later, when the children will be gone from the house. Don't start anything now, wait."

She got out of her bed and began to dress while he turned his back on her. She dressed slowly, understanding what may have happened and he witnessed. Then she went out to the kitchen and hurried the youngsters off to school and told the two older girls to go to work without her, that she will follow them later on.

When he came into the kitchen and found it free of the children, he let go of himself with such a rage that it was akin to madness, but she did not try to subdue him, though she had much to say to him.

Chaya sat hunched over the stove mortified and helpless, afraid to move or say anything or leave the two alone to themselves

After Avraham had spent himself, he walked into the dining room and put on his prayer shawl and phylacteries, and began his morning prayers, the hot tears running down into his beard. When he ended, he glanced at the clock and decided to pay a visit to a friend he made of a man that he got to know through Mirele.

Moyse-Dovid was known on the East Side as the Sage of Broadway. He lived together with his wife and daughter in a basement of a tenement, facing the street. His wife Toba was a short, stout pretty-looking woman who enriched their family by one child, a girl. The child grew up like a bloom, her freshness and vigor constantly with her, and they had named her Rayzilli. She was a brilliant student when she attended the public schools and then went on to the yeshiva, where she was the only girl student of her class, and there met Nahum. Now, at nineteen, she was betrothed to become his wife.

Moyse-Dovid's home carried the name "Castlegarten," so named by his wife Toba because the house of four tiny rooms that were divided by walls of raw boards was always full of strangers to this country. Whenever a family arrived and they had no home to go to, Moyse-Dovid's home was open to them until they were able to find a job for the man and a home for them to live in. Or if someone was turned out of their dwelling for not being able to pay their rent, they appealed to Moyse-Dovid and was taken care of.

Toba would go out with another woman to the tenement houses collecting money for an orphan or a family that lost its breadwinner, a white handkerchief spread in the palm of her hand, and come home with enough for their help, for they knew her well in the community and knew that she will use it to the best advantage. Toba was always cooking her meals in large pots, knowing well that someone will come in hungry to them, and she will need to feed them. She wheedled bones and lung and whatever pieces of ends the butcher could not sell, and made meals that were badly needed by those that lived with them.

Moyse-Dovid was a poor man, for how much can he earn selling wine to his poor *landslayt* for the Sabbath and holidays? Not only for material help would people come to him, but also men and women who had stress in their family lives, those who carried burdens about daughters who went wayward, others whose daughters remained spinsters, and sons who were disobedient, or had trouble with their spouse. They all came to him for the panacea, and he would give them attention, listening to every complaint and then tried to work out some solution to their troubles. "The sage said thus and so," became the hope of the troubled around him, and they felt fortunate that they were able to get his considerations.

Avraham came to this home and found his friend at the end of his breakfast, and received a warm welcome from him. In short time he began to unburden himself of his distress, as they sat close to each other at the table.

Avraham spoke to him of the "holiday Jews in America," that lived for what he termed "themselves," without need of a God to worship except on the holidays. He spoke of the families that he knew that are here now in this country, who were raising sons without any knowledge of their past history, as Jews, satisfied that they gave them a year's study to prepare them for their bar mitzvah day. With a sigh he then turned his conversation to his own family life and slowly pulled out the poverty of the union as husband and wife between Mirele and himself, and the relationship between his oldest child and Simon.

"What can I expect from the rest of my children raised in such a home and such a country?" A long silence hung in the room, both sitting with their own thoughts, until Moyse-Dovid broke in, "Perhaps you see things a little darker than they are, my esteemed friend, perhaps the picture of America is different than you find it. You know that not all Jews are the same, at 'home' either."

"No, that is true, not all the Jews remember that they are Jews, not even at home, but when I visit some of our people I know from there, I go away feeling sick, when I see what America did to them. You have met in my house a kin of Mirele's, he came with his wife Sima, his name is Velvl Licht, they are from Smotrich, you remember him now? Well, they came from this small town where he was a Hebrew teacher and made a living for his family like all Hebrew teachers do, a poor living, but an honorable one, and the people he came in contact with looked up to him with respect. Why they decided to come here, I still do not know, but they are here, with the two children, boys of twelve and eight.

"What do you think they are doing here in this country to make a living at? No, you could not guess if you had two heads on your shoulders, so I might as well tell you. Last week I decided to pay them a visit, and as you know that I am free with my time in the mid-mornings, I went then, and to my horror, found Velvl on his knees scrubbing the stairs of the tenement they live in. Yes, they became janitors to clean the hallways and cart garbage from the house so that they can live rent-free there! I wanted to run away, but he saw me, and got up and begged me to go with him into the house. I did, for I didn't want him to see how shocked I was at seeing this gentle soul in that position, but was further shocked when I entered the house with him and found his wife big with child, standing over a big boiler of wash that was steaming up the kitchen with its hard bubbling on the stove."

" 'Come inside here, in the front room, Sima turned the kitchen into Valley of Hell with the vapors. You see, Monday is wash day for her, and she has so much to wash from the boarders and ourselves that she spends the day over the tubs.' "

"I spent a miserable half an hour with him while he told me how hard they both worked to keep themselves alive, and got out of the house before I showed him my bitterness.

"And I must tell you of another family that ran away from home to the Golden Land. You heard of my wife's sister Hannah, well, her daughter Chava, an extremely clever and educated woman, came here with her husband because he was about to be drafted in the Czar's service, and what do you think they make a living from here? With him it's not too bad, because he became a worker in a factory where they manufacture trunks, but she took in a houseful of boarders and cooks and washes for them! A woman who was able to graduate with the highest honors in Nikolaev's antisemitic universities!"

"But what were they to do if they had to run away, so that he should not have to serve in the army?" Moyse-Dovid was glad to find a weak link in the chain of Avraham's grievances.

"That's it, that's my point. If those children came from poor homes, they could do nothing but run away, but both have rich parents who wanted to buy off the corrupt officials to free him, but the lure to America was so great in them that they refused to be kept at home, can you tell me why?"

"What can I say to you, my friend, that I do not agree with you? I can see the very same contradictions in our lives. I see that our people are so engrossed in the future of their children that they don't take the time to think of today. They saw the poverty in the homes of their parents, the hopelessness of their lives, and security for themselves and their children, and fled from it. Today they are here, and have their families to safeguard from the former bitterness, so they work hard, no matter at what, and live with the hope for a better future. And there is a better future here, no matter how hard they will work and no matter at what, they have the security they lacked at home.

"Another thing, Avraham, that you must understand, and that's change. It's the element that changes circumstances and along with it, people. You and I have already forgotten the times when our own parents were critical of our dress and conduct. It's a long time hence, but I remember my father say to me that I will never grow up in the ways of God, because I had the tailor make my coat a little shorter so that it does not drag in the mud. We cannot stop time's changes than we can stop our beards from turning white. And you know that not all changes are bad, for we can register many changes that are progress for mankind. We are now living in a great city, nay, I should say a whole world, for here we have every kind of nationality, religion, and culture, among the people who ran from their native lands to find some security for themselves and those they love. Among so many, some will make missteps while others will find the paths they seek and walk in them with pride and glory. Those that see only the bad will not find the good, and will be critical of everything around them all their lives."

He looked pointedly at Avraham, and continued, "Why do they stay on here? You are not the only one that misses the old way of life. Yet very few return to their hometowns. Why? Well, I think you will agree with me that we do it for our children's sake. Here they have all the opportunities to grow into well-educated men and women. Yes, it is true, with a great deal of hardship. But they who want to have the doors of day and night schools open to them, not as in Russia where even for the rich Jewish child, there is a quota against him. Another thing, how many parents at 'home' lost their children to America, never to see them again? The young people the world over do what young people must do. They take time in their own hands and push it with their curiosity and with will to make a better time to live in. This is change, the good part of change. We have to expect some of the old ways to drop by the wayside, while we old people hold on to our ways of life." He leaned back into the comfort of the chair and shook his head from side to side, adding, "It's hard, it's hard."

"I feel as if I will never get used to this kind of life, and I am thinking after my older boy will become bar mitzvah of going back. I am doing no one any good with my presence here, not my children and not my wife. Not materially and not emotionally. Well, I took away so much of your time, I better go now."

He rose from his chair and, looking at his friend, fondly said, "Forgive me for my bundle of troubles on your shoulders, I know how they weigh on you." And left the house.

The winter of 1913 was cold, the sky frowning with dark clouds most days, and the evenings bringing down cold, hard snow. Not only was it cold and desolate in the streets, but in many workers' homes as well, for a crisis in many trades turned away workers.

Afterword

In 1914, a couple of years after the union victory where she worked, Mirele died of pernicious anemia. She was 44 years old. Avraham died a year later of a heart attack at age 46. Chaya continued to take care of her family through the 1920s. She died in 1929 at age 79. Mirele's children grew up, married, and started families, whose descendants were inspired to do the work of getting Anna's unfinished memoir published.

Mirele and Avraham Poil, New York, c. 1910

Mirele's family

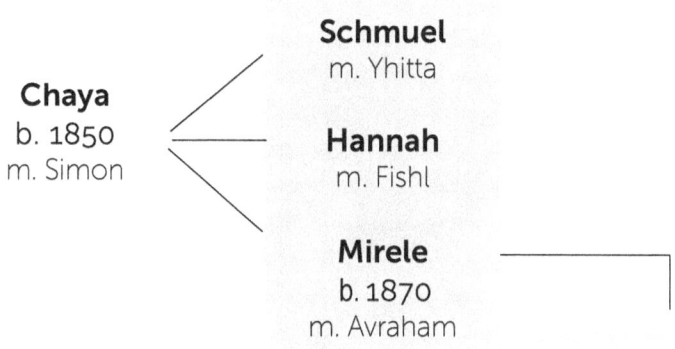

Chaya
b. 1850
m. Simon

Schmuel
m. Yhitta

Hannah
m. Fishl

Mirele
b. 1870
m. Avraham

Bena (Bessie)
b. 1889
m. Samuel

Rachel (Rose)
b. 1892
m. Alex

Adah (Anna)
b. 1900
m. Jack
m. Joseph

Isaiah (Irving)
b. 1902
m. Freida

Raphael (Ruby)
b. 1905
m. Rose

Anna Galstuck at a tenants' rights picket in Albany, New York, 1949.

About Anna Galstuck

As a young child, I was occasionally dropped off at my maternal grandparents' farm in Farmingdale, New Jersey.

To a kid from a small New York City apartment, and then a couple of city housing projects, everything about the visit was exotic. Grandpa Joe's car, when he picked us up at the bus station. The countryside, with its pine trees and fresh smell. And the farm, with the chicken coops and egg-processing area, the farm cats, and the house.

There was one room of the house that seemed like magic to me. It was called the breezeway and connected the garage to the house. This room had flagstone floors, wood-paneled walls, and an entire wall of windows, shaded with bamboo blinds. At one end of this room sat a large, glass-topped desk with a typewriter. This is where Anna wrote this memoir.

Under the glass were photos, articles, and other items that stimulated Anna's memory and thoughts about the world she was writing about. I remember only one of them, a photo of two Orthodox Jewish boys studying, their payes, or side curls, hanging along the sides of their faces.

"Grandma, who are these boys?" To my surprise she had a very negative response.

"These are Orthodox Jewish boys. Their parents make them study constantly. They never go out to play in the fresh air and are always pale like a peeled potato."

Well, that was a lot for me to absorb. What I was also taking in as I watched her typing away was the fact that Anna, unlike other grandma-aged people I knew, was a very modern woman. And at that time,

I didn't know the half of it.

Anna arrived in the United States in 1910, at the age of 10. She was a sickly child who had survived scarlet fever or rheumatic fever—the story varies with different relatives. This book is largely about the small city that she left in what is Ukraine today, a place steeped in the old ways, the drive by her mother Mirele to flee into the future, and the conditions Mirele found there.

Anna attended public schools on the Lower East Side through the eighth grade. Literate in three languages, she remained an avid reader her whole life and her bookshelf included the Yiddish editions of the works of Sholem Aleichem among others.

What was probably the most fascinating part of her life remains unrecorded and untold. How and why the young Anna became a communist and the political activities she became involved in remain a mystery. We do know that she grew into a young woman who worked in the garment industry, based on an early census. And we know from this memoir that her mother, like many garment workers, was so deeply affected by the 1911 Triangle Shirtwaist Fire that she became active in unionizing her shop, which must have had an effect on the young Anna.

We also know that Anna joined the Communist Party and was very active, at one point as organizer of a party branch in the Bronx borough of New York City.

While much of Anna's personal story remains a mystery, she was actually one of a whole generation of young Jews and other workers who responded to their times and conditions and the new Russian Revolution by wanting to fundamentally change society.

Her experience as a sickly child being taken in and nurtured by a Christian family probably influenced her approach to politics based on class, rather than religion or nationality.

Anna was also part of a whole generation of women who were becoming adults when women in the United States won the right to vote in 1920. My mother Marion, Anna's eldest child, told me that Anna shocked her first husband Jack by coming home one day with newly bobbed hair.

Anna met Jack on a streetcar, where he was a conductor. An early census report lists him as a violin teacher. He most likely did both. He went on to become a cutter in the garment industry. While Jack was a staunch unionist, he also had many backward ideas and attitudes. During the World War II years, he moved the family to Chattanooga, Tennessee, where he owned a grocery store. His wife and daughters witnessed him cheating the Black customers.

Although they subsequently moved back to New York, and Jack went back to work as a garment cutter, the differences in their values and natures contributed to a growing rift between them. When their younger daughter, my aunt Carol, announced in 1951 that she was going to marry a Black man, Jack had a dramatic, racist reaction, throwing 19-year-old Carol out of the house. When Anna explained to him that Carol was pregnant, he relented and said she could return.

Carol never went back home. This was the last straw for Anna, and now that both daughters were married and living their own lives, Anna divorced Jack in 1952, at a time when divorce, especially when initiated by a woman, was relatively rare.

According to Marion, Anna married Jack after she became pregnant, which could explain the union of these two very different people.

Anna met her second husband, Joseph Galstuck, at a Communist Party social club in New Jersey. They married soon after her divorce. Joseph was also a party member. A thinker and an activist with a gruff voice, Joseph had fled from Poland to the United States as a young man to avoid being drafted into the czar's army. He joined the Polish-language section of the Socialist Party and was part of the founding conference of the Communist Party in 1919.

At the time that I remember Anna working on her book, they ran a commercial chicken farm producing eggs. This was during the McCarthy period, when many Communist Party members refrained from public political activities and even destroyed their political libraries.

So many things that I remember about Anna and the farm began to resonate with particular clarity as I read this memoir from beginning to end. The constant instruction to "go play outside in the fresh air." Suddenly I understood this, coming from a woman who had been confined inside as a child with her siblings during much of the long winters because of a lack of warm clothes. She may also have been influenced by her childhood stay in the country, where the air was sweeter.

There was an art print that hung in her dining room that she referred to as Peshka's Farm. At the time, this was far outside my experience. Reading about the time she spent on Evdokiya's farm on the outskirts of Kamenets-Podolski, the healing respite it must have been for a sickly child living in urban poverty gives this modest reproduction new meaning.

Anna was also what would be known today as a neat freak, something that drove both her daughters crazy. Again, the conditions that she grew up in as a frail child probably had a lot to do with this.

Food, which was so scarce in Kamenets, was an important way that Anna showed her love for her family. My cousin David remembers always having fresh fruit at her place. My brother Mike loved her potato-nik. I relished the breakfasts, with fresh orange juice and eggs that were gathered that morning. My cousin Dajenya remembers the egg creams Anna made her with seltzer, milk, chocolate syrup, and the secret ingredient, strawberry jam, similar to the ingredient of love that opens this memoir.

Evenings at the New Jersey farm involved card games and discussions among the adults in the living room, often with my parents. Laughter and the sound of poker chips. I would lie in bed, listening, frustrated when the political discussions and dirty jokes switched over to Yiddish. I would occasionally appear asking for water and wanting to know what was so funny.

"It doesn't translate, go back to bed."

At some point during the 1960s, Anna had a falling out with Joe and went off to work as a companion to a wealthy disabled woman for a short time. She returned and they spent Joe's last years together.

During the mid 1970s I decided to get a job in industry so I could be a union activist. My grandmother instructed me, "If you go to work in a garment shop, I want you to promise me that you'll go to the bathroom when you need to. I saw too many young women ruin their kidneys trying to make piece rate." A partisan of the working class all her life, Anna took great interest in the activism of her grandchildren and was always looking forward to the future, right up until her death in 1980.

Anna, like Mirele, was both a product of her times and a citizen of the world in motion.

Diane Shur
Greensboro, North Carolina
July 2023

Glossary

Abdalah

The prayer at the end of the Sabbath and beginning of the working week.

afikoman

Hebrew for a piece of matzoh, or unleavened bread, that is hidden by the father during the Passover Seder; when the youngest son finds it afterward, a reward is exchanged for it.

alter kaker

Yiddish for over-the-hill old-timers.

chai

Pendants made up of the two-letter Hebrew word for life; worn since the late 19th century.

Cossacks

A people of the southern steppe of Ukraine and Russia known for horsemanship and military skills. In the mid 16th century Bohdan Chmielnicki, a Cossack nobleman and military leader, led a large-scale revolt against the Polish–Lithuanian Commonwealth by Cossacks and Ukrainian peasants. When they captured cities, Polish landowning nobles, Catholic priests, and most Jews were killed. In the course of the war, 700 Jewish communities were wiped out. In later years, different groups of Cossacks acted as an auxiliary military force for the Grand Duchy of Lithuania, the Polish–Lithuanian Commonwealth, and for two centuries, czarist Russia. In the time period of the memoir, Cossacks carried out numerous pogroms against Jewish communities in the Pale.

Day of Atonement

Yom Kippur, the holiest day in Judaism. Centered on atonement and repentance, the day's observances consist of fasting, accompanied by daylong prayer as well as confessions of sin.

"Di Grine Kuzine"

Yiddish for "The greenhorn cousin."

Di mame hat a kleyn meydl

Yiddish for "The mother has a little girl."

Dolina

Russian and Ukrainian for valley, canyon, or lowland.

erysipelas

An infection of the upper layers of the skin.

fleishigs **and** *milchigs*

Yiddish for flesh and milk; kosher dietary laws require two sets of pots and pans, one for meat and one for dairy products.

folvareki

Russian and Ukrainian for farmlands. In Kamenets-Podolski at the time of the memoir, there were outlying areas known as the Russki Folvareki and Polski Folvareki; both are now neighborhoods of the city.

Gehenna

Yiddish and Hebrew for Hell, the abode of the damned in the afterlife in Jewish and Christian theology. The metaphor comes from ancient Gehenna, a valley near Jerusalem where children were burned as sacrifices to the pagan god Moloch by some Israelites before the Babylonian Exile in the 6th century BC.

Gemara

The part of the Talmud comprising rabbinical analysis of, and commentary on, the Mishnah.

genem

Synonymous with Gehenna.

Haggadah

The Hebrew prayer book used at the Passover Seder.

Hasidism

Hasidic Judaism is an Orthodox spiritual revivalist movement that emerged in the Pale of Settlement in the 18th century. Followers drew heavily on the Jewish mystical tradition in seeking a direct experience of God through ecstatic prayer and other rituals conducted under the spiritual direction of a rabbi.

Isle of Tears
A well-known reference to Ellis Island, in New York Harbor, where millions of immigrants arrived and were processed in its heyday between 1892 and the First World War. Hundreds of thousands were deported, mainly for health or political reasons.

Kaddish
The Mourner's Prayer, said in honor of the deceased.

Kalmyk
A Mongol people residing chiefly in southwestern Russia. In the memoir, used in a racist manner by one person and used by Anna's family to indicate a newborn child did not "look Jewish."

kasha
Yiddish for cooked grain, typically boiled.

kheyder
Hebrew-language school for children prior to their coming of age, after which young men attend a yeshiva.

Kiddush
Hebrew prayer recited over a cup of wine immediately before the dinner starting the Sabbath.

kinehora
Yiddish for "May no evil eye set on her."

kopeks
The smallest unit of Russian currency.

kosher
Kosher foods are those that conform to Jewish dietary regulations, known as Kashrut.

kreplekh
Dumplings, filled with either cheese by the working classes or ground meat by the middle classes, usually served in soup.

Kriat Shema
Hebrew for the bedtime prayer.

landslayt
Yiddish for countrymen.

l'chaim
Hebrew for "To Life!"

lung fever
Pnemonia

Maariv
Hebrew for evening prayers.

malekh
Yiddish for angel.

matzoh
Hebrew for the unleavened bread to be blessed and eaten at Passover, to remind the faithful of their hasty forced departure from Egypt in biblical times.

mikvah
Hebrew for the flowing pool to be used, among other things, by women observing the laws of niddah (menstrual purity).

minyan
Hebrew for the customary gathering of at least ten men for daily prayers.

Mishnah
The Mishnah is the first major written collection of the Jewish oral tradition, also known as the Oral Torah.

New Plan
Neighborhood in Kamenets-Podolski where the Poil family lived for a time.

Passover
Jewish annual holiday commemorating the exodus of the Israelites from slavery in ancient Egypt.

phylacteries
See *tefillin*.

Queens of the Seder
Tongue in cheek and likely refers to the famous Yiddish-language number *A malke af peysekh* (A queen for Passover) in the musical comedy *Tants, gezang un vayn* (Dance, song, and wine), first performed in 1922 at the Thomashefsky Theater in New York by Aaron Lebedeff, who had emigrated to New York in 1920 and became an overnight sensation in the Yiddish theatre throughout the country. Tradition

accords the husband the status of king in the household, especially at Passover.

rabbanit
Hebrew for the wife of a rabbi.

Reb
A Hebrew and Yiddish honorific among Orthodox Jews meaning Mister.

Sabbath Brides
The author's use of Sabbath Brides is both tongue in cheek and likely a reference to *Lecha Dodi*, the Hebrew-language liturgical song dating from the 16th century recited every Friday at sundown in the synagogue to welcome the Sabbath. *Lecha Dodi* in turn interprets the ancient *Song of Songs*, the erotic poem found in the last section of the Tanakh in the Hebrew scripture. Both portray the maiden bride (the Sabbath) as representing the Jews and the lover is God.

samovar
Samovars, developed in the late 18th century in Russia, are large copper or brass urns with a metal pipe running vertically through the middle. To boil the water, the pipe is loaded with pine cones, charcoal, or wood chips which are set on fire. A small teapot is used to brew tea concentrate and is placed on top of the samovar to keep it heated. Tea is served by pouring tea concentrate into a cup and diluting it with boiled water from the urn.

scribe
A Jewish scholar who can transcribe holy scrolls, *tefillin*, and other religious writings.

Seder
Jewish ritual service and ceremonial dinner for Passover.

shadkhan
Yiddish for matchmaker.

Shalom aleichem
Hebrew for "Peace be upon you."

shamas
Hebrew for a caretaker or assistant in the synagogue who ensures things run smoothly.

Shavuot
Shavuot combines two major religious observances: the grain harvest

of the early summer and the giving of the Torah on Mount Sinai seven weeks after the exodus from Egypt.

shiva
Hebrew for the seven days' formal mourning period for the dead beginning immediately after a Jewish funeral.

shochet
Hebrew for the butcher who slaughters fowl and cattle following kosher ritual.

shul
Yiddish for synagogue, the Jewish house of prayer.

Simchat Torah
Jewish holiday celebrating the Torah.

tallis
Hebrew for the shawl worn by pious Jewish men usually during morning prayers.

Talmud
The generic term for the documents that comment and expand upon the Mishnah, the first work of rabbinic law, published around the year 200 AD.

Tanakh
The 24 volumes of biblical Hebrew scripture, including the Torah, the Nevi'im, and the Ketuvim.

tefillin
Hebrew for phylacteries, small leather boxes with Torah verses inside, that pious Jewish men strap to their arm and/or their brow before morning prayers.

Tisha B'Av
Tisha B'Av, the ninth day of the month of Av, is a major day of annual mourning in the Jewish calendar. It is the commemoration of the destruction of the First and Second Temples in Jerusalem.

Torah
The 5 books of Moses, the foundation of all Jewish religious instruction.

tschipik
A soft, shirred cap worn by some ultra-Orthodox Jewish women under their scarf or kerchief after their heads were shaved for marriage.

yeshiva
A place where Jews gather to study Torah and rabbinic traditions.

yichus
Yiddish for lineage, pedigree, family dignity, honor.

Zhyd
Russian and Ukrainian derogatory term for Jews; Yid.

Acknowledgments

Getting Anna's memoir from manuscript to published book took teamwork. Without Doug Cooper's work, feedback, and friendship, this book would not have been published. He did the heavy lifting of copyediting the manuscript, discussing edits with me over the course of a number of years, made useful suggestions and criticisms on the component parts of the book, and did much of the final proofreading.

Regular encouragement to keep going came from my sister Diane Shur, as well as advice and opinions. She also produced the wonderful artwork on the front and back covers and the biographical note on Anna.

Eva Braiman's design advice was essential in producing a professional and attractive book, inside and out. Jane Roland and Rich Ariza put in a good bit of time proofreading the formatted book.

A big thank you to friends and relatives who, on hearing about the memoir and its contents, regularly asked over the years for progress reports and expressed their anticipation of its publication.

Mike Shur
New York City
July 2023